39.95

The Hollow Core

The Hollow Core

Private Interests in National Policy Making

John P. Heinz
Edward O. Laumann
Robert L. Nelson
Robert H. Salisbury

Harvard University Press

Cambridge, Massachusetts

London, England   1993

Copyright © 1993 by the President and Fellows of Harvard College
All rights reserved
Printed in the United States of America
10 9 8 7 6 5 4 3 2 1

This book is printed on acid-free paper, and its binding materials have been chosen for strength and durability.

Library of Congress Cataloging-in-Publication Data
The hollow core : private interests in national policy making / John P.
  Heinz . . . [et al.].
      p.   cm.
  Includes bibliographical references and index.
  ISBN 0-674-40525-0
    1. Lobbying—United States. 2. Pressure groups—United States.
  3. Agriculture and state—United States—Decision making.
  4. Energy policy—United States—Decision making. 5. Medical
  policy—United States—Decision making. 6. Labor policy—United
  States—Decision making. I. Heinz, John P., 1936–
  JK1118.H55   1993
  324'.4'0973—dc20   92-27361
                                                                  CIP

Contents

Figures

Tables

Preface

Data are inconvenient. They interfere with one's theory. Time and again, in writing this book, we devised clever explanations of the nature of national policy making that would neatly encapsulate the process, only to find that important parts of the data did not fit. This is disheartening. Some of us vowed to forswear data collection in the future, opting instead to write heavily footnoted, synthetic essays that allow greater scope for imagination and creativity. For the present, however, we are stuck with our data, and we are therefore obliged to deal with them. This may be just as well. There is, after all, a case to be made for grit over elegance. By all accounts, Georges Carpentier's work was characterized by great elegance, while Jack Dempsey's, in contrast, was noted for its extreme reality orientation. We know how that one came out.

But perhaps we should begin somewhat closer to the beginning. On a pleasant June evening in 1980, five of us sat late over dinner in Madison, Wisconsin, and talked about some possible lines of research. We were in town for a meeting of the Law and Society Association, but, as so often happens at scholarly conventions, while our program participation reflected past work, our talk was of the future. Heinz and Laumann had just completed their investigation of the social structure of the Chicago bar, which was to be published under the title *Chicago Lawyers* (1982). Nelson's research on four large law firms was also under way and in due course would be published as *Partners with Power* (1988). Salisbury had written extensively on topics related to interest group politics, had most recently been investigating the role of congressional staff, and so had become familiar with Washington, D.C., as research terrain. Michael Powell, who was with us in the beginning but withdrew from the project upon taking a job in the department of sociology at the University of North Carolina, was then at work on his doctoral thesis, which became *From Patrician to Professional Elite* (1988).

We came from different, but complementary, disciplinary backgrounds. Heinz taught law but had also studied political science. Laumann was a sociologist. Nelson had a law degree and was soon to add a sociology doctorate. Salisbury was a political scientist. Salisbury and Heinz were old friends and had worked together several years earlier. The Chicago lawyers project had brought Heinz and Laumann together over an extended period of close colleagueship. Nelson and Powell had participated in that project, and Salisbury had kept in close touch with it. Thus it was that years of friendship, experience in working together, mutuality of interests, and complementarity of intellectual backgrounds prepared the way for the Madison conversation.

The starting point of the conversation was this: Now that Chicago lawyers have been dissected, wouldn't it be interesting to look at Washington, where by all accounts many lawyers are real movers and shakers who get the federal government to adjust public policy in behalf of private interests? Washington lawyers, in this parlance, were virtually synonymous with lobbyists, and this brought them squarely within the purview of students of interest groups and policy making. As our talk continued that evening and in subsequent meetings, the scope of the project grew. It soon became clear to us that, if we were to understand the role of Washington lawyers as lobbyists, we would also need to study nonlawyers engaged in similar tasks of interest representation. On the other hand, we would not be concerned with lawyers whose daily business involved divorce, real estate, criminal defense, and other such fields. This meant that we could not follow the Chicago study's strategy and draw our sample from the full roster of lawyers belonging to the D.C. bar. Moreover, we knew that while there were several available lists of individual lobbyists and of the organizations that hired them, the lists were acknowledged to be incomplete and skewed in one way or another.

We felt strongly that in establishing the boundaries of our investigation it was vitally important to attend to substantive public policy interests. Research on interest groups had displayed an alarming tendency to omit substantive interests from the research design, and we were determined not to do that. Laumann was already well along in a study, in collaboration with David Knoke, of interest organizations in two policy domains, health and energy. That study, which became *The Organizational State* (1987), served as a useful guide as to how to embed our research in domains of substantive policy.

Our choice of policy domains and the formulation of the interview instruments did not emerge quickly. With the generous support of the American Bar Foundation, we were able to make several trips to Washington to explore the research issues. We drew on the expertise of friends and of those to whom they directed us. This "soaking and poking" phase consumed more than a year and was wonderfully instructive. It enabled us to obtain a feel for the settings, to try out questions, and to pick brains. In due course, we talked with more than a hundred well-placed individuals. We do not pretend that this preliminary period enabled us to avoid all mistakes of omission or commission. It was, however, immensely valuable.

In the end, we constructed a research design that enabled us to undertake several levels of investigation simultaneously. The largest part of our study deals with individuals, the people who represent private interests before the federal government; we have a rich body of data on their social and political backgrounds, their career histories, and their present work. Each of them was the agent of some particular organization or set of organizations; we also have a considerable amount of information regarding these "interested" groups, including the nature of the positions they took, the identity of the organizations with whom they were allied or in conflict, and whether they won or lost on a set of specific policy disputes. A third level of analysis focuses on the policy domain. Our design enables us to compare four quite different policy areas and to assess the extent to which various patterns of behavior are domain specific. Finally, we have data on a set of government officials, identified by the interest group representatives as people with whom they often interact. These data permit us to assess, among other things, the degree to which the attitudes and behavior of the officials are driven by their organizational positions or by their principal areas of substantive policy involvement.

In virtually every respect, the study was a joint endeavor. All four of us participated in the preliminary fieldwork, the development of the research design, the construction of the instrument, the data analysis, and the writing. With respect to the authorship of specific chapters: Heinz was the principal author of chapters 1, 10, and 11 and coauthored chapters 3, 4, 7, and 12. He also contributed to several other chapters. Laumann was the principal author of chapter 7 and contributed to chapters 1, 3, 10, and 11. Nelson was the principal author of chapters 4, 5, 6, and 12, coauthored chapters 1 and 3, and contributed to chapters 7, 10, and 11. Salisbury was the principal author of chapters 2, 8, and 9, was a coauthor of chapter 1, and contributed to chapters 5, 10, and 12.

On the Title

The core of a policy-making structure might be hollow in any of a number of senses. The image could be taken to suggest that key Washington players are lacking in substance, or that nothing much of importance happens there. It might imply that the politicians and their supplicants make hollow promises or achieve only hollow victories. Or it could suggest that there is no there there. (The official Oakland interpretation, by the way, is that Gertrude Stein simply meant that the place had changed, so that it was no longer recognizable to her. In Oakland, apparently, only the topography has several levels.) To say that the political core is hollow might even imply that noise reverberates there, as in a bass drum or the bell of a tuba. Or it might mean that the networks of policy makers lack central actors who stand in the middle of the system and have the ability to shape winning coalitions. That is, the hollow core might be an image that is something like the opposite of the power elite. The meaning we had in mind is closest to this last. But we would not be quick to discount the validity of some of the other connotations.

Acknowledgments

A project of this size would not have been possible without the help of many persons and institutions. First in a long list is the American Bar Foundation. The ABF not only supplied the majority of the financial support for the project, with funds from the American Bar Endowment, but provided an ideal place to work and much valuable advice from a splendid assemblage of colleagues. The director of the Foundation at the time the project began, Spencer Kimball, deserves special thanks for his willingness to bet on a long shot.

Both financial support and professional colleagueship were also provided by the Center for Urban Affairs and Policy Research of Northwestern University. A portion of the work on the project was done in residence at the Center, and the support and advice of colleagues there were very helpful.

Financial support for the data analysis was provided by the National Science Foundation, through grant number SES-8320275. Both the money and the expression of confidence in our work were most welcome. The NSF grant was sought when the data had already been collected, and one of the reviewers for NSF was of the opinion that the data set was so large and complex that we would never be able to analyze it. Fortunately, the majority view was to the contrary, but on more than one occasion we had cause to remember that reviewer's wisdom.

Several generations of graduate students worked on this project, to one degree or another, and we are much in their debt. The list is so long that it would be inappropriate to reproduce it here, but we are nonetheless grateful to our research assistants for their indispensable contributions to this work.

Some of our associates and colleagues deserve special mention. Bernard McMullen and Susan Singer ran our Washington office and supervised the staff of interviewers there. Katherine Agar and Steve Heminger oversaw the telephone interviewing and the coding and cleaning of the data. In the early stages of the project, Marilyn Krogh and Andrew Shapiro executed an unusually elaborate sampling design, assisted in questionnaire construction, and undertook preliminary data analyses. The data presented many challenging problems, which were skillfully addressed over the years by several analysts: Peter Birkeland, Eric Fong, Paul Johnson, Won Kim, Michael McBurnett, Steven Neufeld, Paul Schnorr, and Jeff Sutter. Our principal data analyst during much of the life of the project was Tony Tam, now at Harvard University, and we are indebted to him for his many creative contributions. At the earliest and latest stages of the project, valuable assistance was provided by Robert Stout and James McDonough (in the preliminary fieldwork in Washington) and by David Shulman and Andrew Rosen (in the preparation of the manuscript). All of these people performed their duties with a high degree of skill and an even higher degree of good humor, and we are grateful for both.

Several colleagues at other universities and research institutions gave us helpful advice. We owe a special debt to Michael Powell, who was one of the partners in the project at the outset. Michael participated in some of the preliminary fieldwork in Washington, and he took part in our initial conversations regarding the design of the project. He made many important contributions to the work, and we continue to regret his decision to leave Chicago. Various pieces of the manuscript, in various versions, were read and criticized by Richard Abel, Ian Ayres, Robert Bell, Jonathan Casper, John Chubb, John Comaroff, Richard Danzig, John Donahue, Heinz Eulau, William Felstiner, Kermit Hall, Terence Halliday, Mark Hansen, Anne Heinz, Herbert Jacob, Christopher Jencks, Laura Kalman, John Kingdon, Peter Manikas, Peter Marsden, Andrew McFarland, Errol Meidinger, Thomas Merrill, Mark Peterson, Nelson Polsby, Susan Shapiro, Wesley Skogan, Rayman Solomon, John Sprague, Arthur Stinchcombe, David Van Zandt, and two anonymous readers recruited by the Harvard University Press. We profited greatly from their suggestions.

The figures in this book were prepared by Catherine Zaccarine with impressive skill. Several of the figures, especially the three-dimensional smallest space analyses, posed difficult problems of presentation. While some of those figures are necessarily complex, she succeeded in making them much clearer than they might otherwise have been.

The preparation of the manuscript was handled by several members of the ABF staff, but in largest measure that work was done by Lorrie Wessel. She worked with both speed and accuracy, and we appreciate her willingness to put up with four quixotic authors.

The editorial assistance provided by Harvard University Press far exceeded the usual standard in this business. Aida Donald and Elizabeth Suttell guided us thoughtfully in matters of both content and presentation, and Donna Bouvier edited the manuscript with such care and art that it was a pleasure to see how she transformed awkwardness into a semblance of grace.

Finally, the many lobbyists, lawyers, and government officials who consented to be interviewed—in the preliminary fieldwork and in the systematic samples—have our very real gratitude. Without them, of course, the project would not have been possible. If any of them should decide in the future to do a survey of academics, we would be happy to return the favor.

Prototypes of material included in some of the chapters were previously published in scholarly journals. Chapter 9 is a revision of our article "Who Works with Whom? Interest Group Alliances and Opposition," which appeared in the *American Political Science Review* (vol. 81, no. 4, December 1987, 1217–1234). An earlier version of chapter 10 appeared in the *Journal of Politics* ("Inner Circles or Hollow Cores? Elite Networks in National Policy Systems," vol. 52, no. 2, May 1990, 356–390), but additional material is included here. Portions of an article published in the *American Bar Foundation Research Journal* ("Private Representation in Washington: Surveying the Structure of Influence," vol. 1987, no. 1, Winter 1987, 141–200) have been incorporated into chapters 1, 3, and 4. Smaller portions of two articles are used in chapters 4 and 5: "Lawyers and the Structure of Influence in Washington," *Law and Society Review* (vol. 22, no. 2, 1988, 237–300); and "Who You Know versus What You Know: The Uses of Government Experience for Washington Lobbyists," *American Journal of Political Science* (vol. 33, no. 1, February 1989, 175–195). The last of these articles was co-authored by Paul Johnson, and that material is used with his permission. Chapters 2, 6, 7, 8, 11, and 12 are entirely new.

Part I

Introduction

Chapter 1

The Lawyer
and the Heavyweight

A Washington lawyer told us a story about the uncertainty of influence. In a sense, it is a story about the appearance and reality of power. The lawyer's client, an oil company, was seeking a revision in a federal regulation; the lawyer had worked for the agency with jurisdiction over the matter. Because he knew his way around in the agency, the lawyer was able to locate the key person, a relatively low-level bureaucrat who had been assigned the principal responsibility for evaluating the proposed revision. The lawyer had painstakingly supplied the official with information and arguments designed to make the case for the merits of the proposal, and the official appeared to be on the verge of recommending the change.

At that point, a new player intervened: another oil company that generally supported the lawyer's position, but that was apparently dissatisfied with the slow pace of progress on the matter. The second oil company concluded that what was needed was political muscle, so it decided to recruit a heavyweight. It did not have a Washington office and was not very familiar with Washington, but it knew the big names. It therefore secured the services of a highly visible former cabinet member and former holder of high elective office who had once aspired to the presidency.

The heavyweight made a few telephone calls, for which he reportedly charged his client a very handsome fee. But the effect of the calls was to alarm the bureaucrats who were handling the issue. The agency reaction, apparently, was something like this: "Watch out! If a heavyweight is involved, this proposed regulation must be a bigger deal than we had thought. We had better be careful and give this close scrutiny." Our informant believes that, as a direct result, action on the matter was delayed for some months.

Several lessons might be drawn from the story:

Influence is situation specific. In some circumstances, it may be counterproductive for a private representative to have a strong reputation for political influence.

Low visibility may be more advantageous than high visibility. A proposal may slip through if it is not given much attention, but have difficulty if it gets wider notice or a close look.

The merits may count more than clout. Reasoned advocacy will sometimes be more effective than will connections with politicians.

Newcomers would do well to take the advice of regulars. Insiders who know their way around in the agencies will usually obtain better results. Therefore, an interest group will want to have a continuing presence in Washington—either a Washington office or a regularly retained representative.

Interest groups, even those who share common objectives, may be clumsy and get in each other's way.

Above all, it is dangerous to assume that conventional notions of influence will accurately predict policy outcomes. Policy results are uncertain; hence, the success or failure of particular groups on specific issues is also uncertain.

Of course, these lessons tend to serve the interests of the lawyer who told the story. The lawyer is not a public figure, and he is not in the business of selling special access. Though he has experience in both the legislative and the executive branches of the federal government, he held middle-level positions rather than high office, and he does not have any significant power base of his own. He prefers to work quietly and methodically, and his principal stock in trade is substantive expertise and reasoned argument. No doubt these are important methods for influencing policy, but we would not wish to discount the possible value of clout. The lawyer's story, in sum, has some marked similarities to the fable about the tortoise and the hare. Still, it would often be unwise to bet against the hare.

Other stories, both in our interviews and in the daily newspapers, suggest contrary lessons. But the most fundamental message of the story of the lawyer and the heavyweight, and of much of our data, is that private interests confront pervasive uncertainty in national policy-making systems. From the perspective of the groups, the contemporary system of interest representation presents a central paradox: despite historically unparalleled levels of investment in attempts to shape national policy, the return on that investment is highly uncertain and often intangible. For many groups, including the most privileged and powerful corporate actors in this society, interest representation involves a game of running to stand still. Private interests have developed elaborate organizational structures in order to provide control over the processes through which they are represented, but the irony is that these efforts at control exacerbate problems of coordination and information exchange and may ultimately contribute to greater levels of uncertainty in policy systems generally.

We arrived at this argument not primarily through stories, but through the assessment of a substantial body of empirical data. Stories are often very evocative and of great heuristic value, but we make little direct use of them in this book. We have a greater taste for the general than for the specific. When we hear these stories, we find that we want to ask: "How often does this happen? How much of this sort of behavior is there?" Consider some of the issues raised by the story about the lawyer and the heavyweight. The lawyer had formerly been employed by the agency handling the matter. We have all heard about the "revolving door" between federal government employment and the Washington lobbying firms, but how common is it for lobbyists to have worked at the agencies that they now contact? If we examined all of the lobbying contacts with a particular agency, would we find that half of all contacts were by lobbyists who had once worked there? Three-quarters? A tenth? Would this differ from agency to agency? What is the usual career path for a Washington lobbyist? Do most of them have government experience, or do they go into lobbying firms straight out of college or law school, or work their way up the career ladder within the corporation or union that they represent?

The story also points out that the two clients chose to hire different types of representatives to work on the same matter. The heavyweight exemplifies the "influence peddler," and the lawyer exemplifies the "professional advocate." Both types no doubt exist, as do others, but how common are they? Are some types of representatives more likely to be used on one sort of issue or in one sort of institutional context, and other types to be used on other issues or in other contexts? The lawyer had worked for his client for some time, on a retainer, while the heavyweight was hired on a one-shot basis. How common is each of those arrangements? How many of the interest groups active on national policy issues maintain Washington offices or have regularly retained representatives? How numerous are the occasional players in Washington, who appear only infrequently on particular issues? Does any significant number of interest groups attempt to lobby the federal government without having Washington representatives? That is, do the folks from the Wichita office often choose to speak for themselves?

As you can see, we are inclined to want to count things. It is not that we are uncritical adherents to Lord Kelvin's dictum that "when you can measure what you are speaking about, and express it in numbers, you know something about it; but when you cannot measure it, when you cannot express it in numbers, your knowledge is of a meagre and unsatisfactory kind" (see Merton et al. 1984). It is just that we would like to have some view of the general contours of the landscape.

The story makes the point that influence is situation specific, but it does not define the types of situations or tell us which attributes or strategies are particularly suited to which situations. Does political party affiliation matter? That is, are Republican lobbyists preferred for contacts with Republican officeholders? Do some Washington representatives specialize in Congress, and others in the executive branch or in particular agencies within the executive branch? Do lawyers have any special advantages—either in access to the agencies, in skill at advocacy, or in reputation for honesty? How much does substantive expertise matter? Another Washington lawyer told us that he did not devote any time to reading trade journals or other such information sources. Instead, he seeks to locate a knowledgeable person to "drain" in order to get the information that he needs: "In an hour and a half with the right guy, I can find out all I need to know." Is this common? Where and how do Washington representatives get their information?

In the story, both of the clients are oil companies. Is this typical? What percentage of Washington lobbyists represents big business interests? How important are representatives of environmental or consumer interests? To what extent do relatively deprived groups—minorities, poor people, the homeless—even get on the playing field of national policy making?

More broadly, we want to explore two questions implicit in the story. The first involves influence: To what extent is the policy-making process driven by the demands of interest groups and their representatives? Would there have been any issue of regulation or its revision without the intervention of the oil companies? Are private group initiatives the principal sources of public policy, so that the system deserves Lowi's label, "interest group liberalism" (1969)? The second question pushes the issue back a step. What drives the expanded representational presence of private groups in Washington? Do they simply crave more benefits from the public trough? Are they primarily concerned to defend what they already have? Or are they unsure about what may happen politically to affect their interests, so that they establish themselves in Washington to keep watch and seek to reduce the uncertainty of their environment?

To address questions such as these, we have sought to develop a conception of the social structure of interest representation—that is, a conception of the nature of the links among individuals, organizations (both private and governmental), and policy systems. This approach allows us to assess the possible bases for the exercise of influence in policy making.

The Nature and Determinants of Influence

The nature of influence is a central concern in the study of political systems. In a complex, highly differentiated governmental system, who has the power to shape policy decisions? Who wins? Who loses? Indeed, do organized interests dominate the policy-making process to their own advantage, as has so often been alleged (Schattschneider 1960; Lowi 1969)? As important as these questions are, they have proven intractable as a subject of empirical study. The broad theoretical works (see, for example, Truman 1951) rely on the selective use of historical examples and are therefore criticized for failing to prove their generalizations. Case studies of particular communities (Dahl 1961), agencies (Selznick 1949), or governmental policies (Bauer, Pool, and Dexter 1963) cannot respond to Lowi's (1964) assertion that different types of policy proposals elicit characteristically different types of political behavior. If different communities, agencies, or policies were studied, Lowi suggests, we would find different sources and manifestations of power.

In a search for general propositions about the nature of influence, therefore, scholarly work has recently begun to move toward more systematic research that encompasses policy systems in which a range of private and governmental actors make decisions on a substantial set of proposals. An important precursor of our work is the research by Laumann and Knoke (1987). In their study of national energy and health policy from 1977 to 1980, they defined the concept of the policy domain as a system of mutually oriented organizational actors. Browne's research on agriculture policy (1988, 1990) is a similar attempt to canvass the activities of interest groups on a range of policy issues and events.

Another important line of analysis of interest group impact on public policy has followed a strategy of deductive reasoning from certain broadly plausible axioms regarding self-interested behavior. This is the so-called "public choice" tradition, and its exponents have included such distinguished scholars as Stigler (1971), Peltzman (1976), and Becker (1983). Most of these scholars are economists, and both their assumptions and their methods are characteristically those of that discipline. In general, they tend to begin with the assumption that public policy involves rent-seeking behavior (Tollison and McCormick 1981). That is, self-interested groups try to persuade governments to act (or to prevent action) in ways that will generate rents or subsidies for themselves. Influence is imputed to a group if we observe that the group has indeed received the benefit it sought. The intention of policy makers to benefit the group is inferred, and inferences are confirmed by looking, for example, at patterns of campaign contributions (Denzau and Munger 1986, inter alia). This approach to the study of group influence can be both elegant in its form and powerful in its analysis, but its assumptions usually remain untested.

Much of the literature about political influence focuses primarily on process. It seeks to identify the strategies and tactics through which influence is achieved. Do the actors maximize their influence in a particular context if they use propaganda, civil disobedience, violence, quiet persuasion, or PAC contributions? This book, however, is less concerned with process. Instead, we look for the structural attributes of influence. We seek to determine whether certain role positions are consistently more influential than others. Do certain types of organizations or individual actors enjoy positions in the structure of policy making that are more regularly in contact with the decision loci? Do they, in turn, more often get what they want from the policy process? In this respect, at least, we pose much the same sort of question as that asked by the classic works of ruling elites theory.

In *The Power Elite,* C. Wright Mills identified the elites that he believed to be particularly influential (1956, 288–289):

The inner core of the power elite consists, first, of those who interchange commanding roles at the top of one dominant institutional order with those in another . . . We refer to one man who moves in and between perhaps two circles—say the industrial and the military—and to another man who moves in the military and the political, and to a third who moves in the political as well as among opinion-makers. These in-between types most closely display our image of the power elite's structure and operation, even of behind-the-scenes operations. To the extent that there is any "invisible elite," these advisory and liaison types are its core . . . The inner core of the power elite also includes men of the higher legal and financial type from the great law factories and investment firms, who are almost professional go-betweens of economic, political and military affairs, and who thus act to unify the power elite. The corporation lawyer and the investment banker perform the functions of the "go-between" effectively and powerfully. By the nature of their work, they transcend the narrower milieu of any one industry, and accordingly are in a position to speak and act for the corporate world or at least sizable sectors of it.

In a graphic representation of the relationships among interest groups and their representatives, the mediators would of course occupy a central or "in-between" position, and structural images such as "inner core" or "inner circle" are therefore popular descriptive terms (see Useem 1984). These structural conceptions are firmly rooted in lines of social thought that proceed sometimes from Marx and sometimes from Robert Michels's "iron law of oligarchy" and Gaetano Mosca's "ruling class" (Michels 1959; Mosca 1939; see also Bottomore 1964). But while many theorists, both Marxists and pluralists, posit the existence of an inner circle of elites, few have attempted an empirical examination of the structure of elite policy networks.

Interest Groups and Their Representatives

"Washington representative" is a term that lobbyists now commonly use to refer to themselves. The meaning is somewhat broader than the technical denotation of the term "lobbyist,"[1] and it may sound more respectable. It partakes, perhaps, of association with "Representative in Congress" (a doubtful blessing).[2] Members of Congress and other public officials also function as advocates for interest groups, of course, but this book is only secondarily concerned with officials. It is primarily about private Washington representatives—persons who, usually for hire but sometimes as volunteers, represent the interests of others before the myriad agencies of the federal government.

There is little doubt that private representatives play a significant role in national policy making. Data on the numbers of interest groups and representatives present in Washington reveal an apparent explosion in their activity from the mid-1960s to the 1980s (Polsby 1981). The *National Law Journal* has estimated that in the decade from 1965 to 1975 there were about 3,000 to 4,000 lobbyists in Washington, about 10,000 to 15,000 by 1983, and about 15,000 to 20,000 by 1988 (Carter 1988). During the 1970s, scores of corporations and out-of-town law firms opened Washington offices, and Washington also became a leading headquarters city. In 1971, 19% of all national nonprofit associations had their headquarters in D.C.; ten years later that figure had increased to 29% (Salisbury 1984). There were as many as 80,000 association employees in Washington by 1983 (Taylor 1983), and more than 4,000 corporations retained Washington representatives. The 1984 edition of the *Washington Representatives* directory listed more than 10,000 individuals.

Despite widespread notice of the dramatic expansion in the legions of lawyers and lobbyists representing clients before the federal government and the recognition that this private establishment is an integral part of the exercise of governmental power, interest representation has only recently begun to attract major research investment. There have been seminal studies of the propensity of different kinds of interest groups to form and act collectively (Olson 1965; J. Wilson 1973; Moe 1980; Chubb 1983; Walker 1983), numerous case studies of particular organizations or legislative campaigns (for example, Fritschler 1983; Bauer, Pool, and Dexter 1963), and some systematic surveys of the activities that organizations pursue in their attempts to influence federal policy (Schlozman and Tierney 1986; Laumann and Knoke 1987). Much less work has been done on individual representatives.[3] Milbrath's study of lobbyists, which remains the *locus classicus* within the field, is based on interviews with a sample of 114 lobbyists on the registration lists (1963). Cherington and Gillen conducted unstructured interviews with business group representatives (1962), as did Hall (1969). More recently, Berry studied both organizations and individuals, but only among public interest groups (1977). Apart from Berry, there is little discussion of the relationship between the individual representative and the organization that he or she represents,[4] and the scholarly literature does not include a comprehensive, empirical analysis of private representation that spans a range of issues and organizations at both the individual and organizational levels of analysis. Although the interest group literature often recognizes the potential significance of representatives to the political behavior of organizations, it largely proceeds as though the units of action are the organizations themselves and treats the lobbying as if it were undertaken directly by the organization, with the individual representatives having no separate existence or autonomy.

The relative inattention to the influence of representatives in national policy making seems particularly odd given their theoretical importance. The increasing role of experts in American society generally, and in government in particular, has been a common theme among sociologists, political scientists, and historians (Bell 1976; Lane 1966; Wiebe 1967; Skowronek 1982). Moreover, the relationships between clients and experts have been a primary concern of the sociology of professions. Indeed, many of the current debates concerning the professions, particularly the legal profession, have centered on issues concerning the power of professionals in the decision-making processes of client organizations and, more broadly, in society (Heinz 1983; Freidson 1986; Halliday 1987; Nelson 1988). The interest group literature notes that the various actors within organizations—political entrepreneurs, leaders, members, staff, and so forth—play different roles in these decision-making processes, with different types of intraorganizational political resources and varying levels of intraorganizational influence (Salisbury 1969; Moe 1980; J. Wilson 1973).

The absence of a single professional identity complicates the analysis of representatives since it is necessary first to establish whether the conceptions and categories that have been used to discuss professionals apply to them. But the broader issue is the extent to which expertise confers power on representatives. To what extent do the representatives determine the goals and strategies of the client organizations? The training and credentials of lawyers and other professionals are one source of expertise, but former government officials, old Washington hands, and specialists in the rules and regulations governing an industry also possess expertise that may make them influential in policy making even if they lack formal professional training.

Government by Groups?

The interest group literature, on the whole, is remarkably unclear about the nature of the roles of government actors in the policy-making process—that is, about the nature of the relationships between private groups and public officials. Much of the literature virtually ignores the officials and appears to assume that, like billiard balls, they will go wherever the interest groups send them. Other pieces of the literature are more attentive to the public actors and recognize that they too have interests (for example, Skocpol 1985; Tullock 1965). Indeed, the concerns of officials may be as diverse and conflicting as those of private interest groups. Some writers, however, refer to "private groups" and "public groups" without recognizing any clear differences between the two.

Ambiguity about the role of government is reflected, for example, in Earl Latham's well-known essay, "The Group Basis of Politics." At one point it says (1952, 390):

> The legislature referees the group struggle, ratifies the victories of the successful coalitions, and records the terms of the surrenders, compromises, and conquests in the form of statutes . . . The legislative vote on any issue thus tends to represent the composition of strength, *i.e.,* the balance of power among the contending groups at the moment of voting. What may be called public policy is actually the equilibrium reached in the group struggle at any given moment.

This appears to be a statement of the most mechanistic view—the interest groups proceed along vectors of varying magnitude and direction, then they collide and produce a resultant vector, which determines the course taken by the government officials. But in the same essay (391), Latham also says:

> In these adjustments of group interest, the legislature does not play the part of inert cash register, ringing up the additions and withdrawals of strength; it is not a mindless balance pointing and marking the weight and distribution of power among the contending groups. Legislatures are groups also and show a sense of identity and consciousness of kind . . .

Thus, he manages to embrace both positions.

There are, in fact, several possible perspectives on the nature of the relationships among private and governmental interest groups. Five may be sketched:

1. *Pressure.* This is the mechanistic view. Government officials respond to pressure from private interest groups, and this pressure largely determines public policy outcomes. When the

demands of the interest groups conflict, the stronger (usually the wealthier) prevail.

2. *Bargaining.* In this view, interest groups within the government pursue their own program and jurisdictional objectives. They bargain with the private interests and among themselves, just as the private groups do.

3. *Aggregation.* This is a variant of the pressure perspective, but the government officials are not seen as passive. Although they do not pursue their own interests, they work to promote aggregation of private interests and to reduce conflict among the groups in order to create a greater degree of consensus on policy choices and thereby enhance their political position.

4. *Mediation.* A third party seeks to mediate the conflicts among the public and private groups, as both pursue their own policy goals. (This is a variant of the bargaining perspective, but it also has some kinship to aggregation.) Such third parties might include lawyers or other professionals, or even lobbyists not directly concerned in the particular controversy. The objective is a kind of negotiated consensus, or at least a reduction of conflict and an expanded acceptance of outcomes.

5. *Symbiosis.* The classic "iron triangle," in which private groups and their congressional and executive branch protectors pursue compatible and interdependent interests, is a strong example of a symbiotic relationship among interest groups and public officials. In this view, the line between public and private actors may be faint. They will occupy the same narrow policy network, or "niche," and each niche will be insulated against intrusion by other interests, legislators, or executive officials.

The pressure perspective presents a fairly simple picture. The groups know what they want and make their demands on officials accordingly, offering incentives or threatening disincentives in the event of noncooperation. Incentives often are in the form of material goods—campaign contributions, a job, or whatever—but may also consist of votes in the next election or some other form of political support. The officials, being ambitious for office or avaricious, succumb to the pressure and do what is asked. In general, group resources are thought to be the crucial determinant of group success, and the chief uncertainty arises from the problem of determining the relative value of some resources, such as money, as against others, such as deliverable votes. It seems fair to say that the prevailing mode of thinking about interest group politics has employed some version of the pressure model, and commonly there is a pejorative cast to the usage (for example, Green 1975). The implications are that, had it not been for the pressure, the policy in question would not have been enacted, and that in general the policy is injurious to the larger, more encompassing public interest.

The role of the interest representative in the pressure perspective is mainly that of agent, conveying the client organization's demands and reporting back on progress. The agent has relatively little autonomy to define the agenda or negotiate terms of trade. A lobbyist may search for clients to represent, but his or her expertise is presumed to be mainly tactical, not substantive. The content of the client's policy objectives has already been determined; the representative's job is to carry the message skillfully to the right people.

The bargaining perspective differs from the pressure perspective, first of all, in its denial that government officials are in a subordinate or reflexive position, characteristically waiting to hear the demands of powerful outside groups. Rather, it assumes that officials are autonomous actors, quite capable of making policy decisions whether or not any outside groups have expressed themselves. There are usually numerous officials involved in the decision process, and they may have diverse views. Each major issue entails a complex series of negotiations among the public and private participants as they search for the formulation that will attract a sufficiently large coalition to prevail. Bargaining is a process that occurs over time, and the key elements of the process are trade (or exchange) and compromise. Logrolling exchanges on pork-barrel projects are characteristic of this process.[5] An attractive feature of the bargaining perspective is its implicit assumption that no single interest group or any extant coalition of officials has the strength necessary to enact its policy preference without help. A further feature is that it accommodates a continuous process of goal adaptation by participants. Policy interests are not assumed to be fixed beforehand, though they may be in particular cases. Often, they are emergent, taking new shape and substance as a consequence of learning and persuasion, processes potentially affecting both interest groups and officials.

In the bargaining perspective, the private interest representative takes on a very different role, at least potentially, from that envisioned in the pressure perspective. The opportunity for creative formulation of arguments is far larger if representatives seek to strike the best possible bargain for their clients rather than act as instructed agents or messengers. Formulating persuasive arguments can entail a vast array of specific actions, from arcane research and highly technical exegesis to the crudest forms of bribery and force. Modes of expression can be similarly diverse, from the most orotund verbosity to the tersest communiqué. Representatives may often be uncertain about what arguments and strategies will be most successful, and one would therefore expect considerable trial and error, redundancy of effort, and general inefficiency.

When interest groups are in conflict, as they often are, some form of third party intervention may be required to enable a dominant coalition to take shape. In an essay on the politics of the Tennessee Valley Authority, Arthur Stinchcombe argued that government agencies sometimes have "the capacity . . . to serve as an aggregator of interests and a broker for bargaining out a common policy" (Stinchcombe 1975, 589–590). Charles Horsky, himself a noted Washington lawyer, assigned the broker or mediator role to his professional colleagues. Horsky contended that Washington lawyers stand between interest group clients, on the one hand, and government officials, on the other, transmitting and interpreting the demands of each and, in the process, helping to modify goals and dampen conflict (1952, 10–11). In Horsky's view, this mediating function contributes significantly to the building of a policy consensus broad enough not only to enact the policy but to implement it thereafter. The case study literature contains numerous examples of intergroup mediation by various kinds of political entrepreneurs, some of them lobbyists and some of them persons in official positions (see, for example, Masters, Eliot, and Salisbury 1964). Heclo suggests that substantive experts sometimes serve as mediators (1978). Most such accounts do not explicitly relate the mediating effort to professional role, as Horsky did, or to authority position, as Stinchcombe did, but simply take their coalition builders wherever they are to be found. At least some of the literature, however, recognizes the potential importance of private interest representatives as mediators or coalition builders who facilitate the bargaining in which interest groups and government officials work out mutually satisfactory policies.

If and when the respective pressures from private interests and government officials settle into an equilibrium—which usually requires a balance among the interest groups, the officials in the legislative branch, and the relevant agency personnel on the executive side—an iron triangle or subgovernment results, and the pressures are replaced by mutually beneficial symbioses. In order for such triangles or niches to remain in equilibrium, however, two related conditions must be present. Group conflict on the policy issues must be minimal, and, for that to be possible, the number of parties must be relatively small. Moving the locus of the decision to a larger arena (cf. Schattschneider 1960) or suffering the invasion of the niche by "outsiders" undermines the compatibility of policy views among participating groups.

We have no doubt that each of these five perspectives reflects a reality that exists to one extent or another in American national politics. Some politicians are perfectly happy behaving like billiard balls, some of the time. There may be many issues on which a public official does not perceive any particular personal stake, and he or she may then simply calculate the advantage of pleasing one set of interest groups rather than another in much the way that the simplest, most mechanistic version of the pressure perspective suggests. At other times, on proposals with different substance, the official may pursue his or her own deeply felt policy commitments or may seek to enhance the institutional position of his or her agency of government. And sometimes various sorts of parties will serve as mediators, aggregators, or brokers—and some elected and appointed officials will establish cozy, continuing relationships with particular sets of interest groups. No one of these perspectives captures a universal truth. The issue is: To what extent and with what frequency is each type of relationship among private interest groups and government officials found in national policy making? Where? When? In some kinds of agencies more than others? On some types of substantive policy proposals more than others?

In all but the last of these perspectives—the iron triangle or symbiotic view—policy outcomes may be highly variable and volatile, and thus unpredictable. In the pressure perspective, it can be problematic for government officials to calculate the relative advantage of adopting one policy position rather than another. It may be difficult to assess, for example, whether an interest group that claims to be able to deliver votes can actually do so. Thus, information costs will be high, and many politicians may therefore proceed to adopt positions without having full knowledge of the probable consequences or even without knowing all of their available options. In the bargaining, aggregation, and mediation perspectives, outcomes will also be uncertain because the decision processes will be similarly complex and fluid; it is difficult to predict which sorts of arguments will be persuasive or which sorts of threats will be credible and effective. In those perspectives, the coalitions among interest groups may be subject to realignment, the individual groups may modify their positions, and new parties may enter the negotiations as others exit. Only if the government officials and the private interests have a symbiotic relationship will the policy outcomes be consistently predictable. If all or most of the relevant public and private actors share the same interest (perhaps veterans benefits or tobacco price supports), there is little reason to expect any outcome other than the one desired by those groups. Therefore, if policy outcomes are observed to be unpredictable in most cases, that is reason to doubt that the decision-making processes are controlled by iron triangles.

The Research Design

The data analyzed in this book are drawn from interviews conducted in 1983–84 with samples of three distinct populations: (1) clients who employ Washington representatives; (2) government officials who deal with Washington representatives; and (3) Washington representatives themselves. To narrow the scope of the inquiry, we restricted our attention to four broad areas of policy, or "policy domains": agriculture, energy, health, and labor.[6] These four domains have distinctive features that might lead to differences in how policy is formulated and to related differences in the roles and effects of representatives.

They vary, first, in the constellation of interest groups. Agriculture and energy politics are organized around regionally segmented producer groups: milk, grains, cotton, tobacco, and so on in agriculture (Hadwiger and Browne 1978; Guither 1980; Heinz 1962); oil, natural gas, and coal in energy (Chubb 1983; Davis 1982). Health and labor, by contrast, are dominated by national organizations: the American Medical Association, the American Hospital Association, and the American Association of Retired Persons (Marmor 1970; Starr 1982; Laumann and Knoke 1987); and the AFL-CIO, the Chamber of Commerce, and the National Association of Manufacturers, for example (G. Wilson 1979; Greenstone 1969; Bok and Dunlop 1970).

Second, the level and form of conflict vary. Labor policy typically produces conflict between two broad groups, business and organized labor, and much of the contention has become institutionalized within the NLRB and various agencies of the Department of Labor. Health policy typically has involved disputes over the means of attaining widely shared goals, but has undergone considerable fragmentation in recent years as the interests of doctors, hospitals, insurance companies, medical schools, and drug and equipment manufacturers have diverged (Laumann and Knoke 1987). Energy and agriculture manifest more explicit conflicts among alternative producers and between consumers and producers.

Third, the institutional composition and general policies of the domains have exhibited very different patterns of change over the past two decades. Agriculture and labor have long maintained a relatively stable set of agencies and programs. Energy and health, by contrast, only more recently became the subject of cabinet-level departments and heightened government involvement.

Finally, lawyers and legal institutions play different roles in these domains. We expected agriculture and health to be less "lawyered," both in the sense that those domains have a larger share of direct bureaucratic negotiation and policy development and a smaller share of formal adjudicatory, licensing, and rulemaking procedures, and in the sense that farmers and doctors, respectively, might displace lawyers in policy-making positions.

Our selection of policy domains is skewed toward domestic policy issues. Agriculture, energy, and labor policy all involve issues of foreign trade and international relations, but these are not the primary focus within these domains. Because domestic policy controversies may be accessible to a broader range of interested parties than are matters of defense and foreign policy, our findings may not be generalizable to such fields. Within the context of domestic policy making, however, the four domains provide interesting similarities and differences.

In each of these domains, we pursued a sequential sampling design that identified the three sets of actors successively—the clients, then their representatives, and, finally, the government officials with whom the representatives dealt. That is, we initially sought to specify the organizations or individuals attempting to influence policy in a given domain. We then asked a sample of these potential clients to identify the representatives they employed or retained. In turn, we asked a sample of the representatives named to give the names and positions of "the five government officials or staff members you contact most often in the course of your work," and we drew the sample of government officials from the resulting list.

In the first stage, we devised a set of replicable procedures that allowed us to (1) identify the client organizations, (2) assess the level of policy-making activity by those organizations, and (3) sample organizations according to their level of activity. Because any one method of locating interested parties has a systematic bias toward identifying certain kinds of organizations and neglecting others, we combined nominations from several sources and thereby attempted to compile a comprehensive listing. Our first method was especially attentive to issues that attract mass media attention. We conducted a computerized search of newspapers and magazines published from January 1977 to June 1982, noting the number of stories mentioning each organization.[7] Second, we searched the abstracts of congressional hearings held during the Ninety-fifth through the Ninety-seventh Congresses, noting the organizations that testified. Less partisan and more specialized organizations were identified by this procedure.[8] Third, during the summer of 1982 we interviewed 20 to 23 government officials in each domain and asked them to name organizations that contacted them often and other organizations representative of those that contacted them episodically. Two criteria were used in selecting officials to be interviewed: (1) the position of the official and (2) his or her tenure. Finally, we compiled a list of organizations appearing under the industry headings related to each domain in *Washington Representatives* (1981), an annual publication that canvasses various public sources and surveys organizations in an effort to list interest groups represented before the federal government. If we had relied only on the listing produced by *Washington Representatives*, however, we would have underestimated the population of interested organizations by more than half in each domain.[9]

For each domain, we drew a random sample of 100 or more organizations, with each of the four sources contributing equally, but with each organization weighted by the number of mentions. Because the probability of selection increases with the number of mentions, our sampling procedure reflects the organizations' levels of activity in the domain. Laumann and Knoke (1987) found a high correlation between the likelihood that organizations would be seen as influential and the number of their mentions in newspaper stories, appearances in congressional hearings, and mentions by government officials. Hence, there is reason to treat the number of mentions in the various sources as a measure of perceived organizational influence. Thus, the sampling procedure generated a list of organizations that included the more active organizations disproportionately, but that also included less influential and less active organizations.

We then asked well-placed informants in the organizations to tell us the names and positions of their representatives. Telephone interviews were conducted in 1982 and 1983 with a minimum of 75 organizations in each domain, 316 organizations in all. The response rate was 75%. Only 8% of the organizations refused interviews, but another 12% could not be located, were located abroad, or had ceased to exist. The refusals did not follow a pattern and therefore do not appear to constitute a major source of bias. The client interviews generated more than 400 names of representatives in each policy domain, for a total 1,716 individuals. Representatives could appear on the lists as many times as they were mentioned; about 5% appeared in more than one domain. The samples were randomly selected from these lists, and we completed interviews with 184 to 206 representatives per domain, a total of 776. The response rate of the representatives was 78%. Of the sampled representatives, 10% declined interviews; the remainder of those not interviewed could not be scheduled for various reasons.[10]

We should emphasize that this is not a simple random sample. First, since both the representatives and the client organizations appeared on the nomination lists as many times as they were mentioned, the probability that they would be selected was proportional to their number of mentions. This was done so that the more active organizations and representatives would be more likely to appear in the samples. Second, we asked the organizational informants to name internal and external representatives separately, and allowed a maximum of four of each type. This approach is likely to have resulted in a slight oversampling of external representatives. Some 40% of the client organizations named the maximum number of internal representatives, and thus might have named more if allowed to do so, but only 23% named as many as four external representatives. To assess the extent to which these limits may have biased the composition of the sample, in the summer of 1987 we reinterviewed 51 of the client organizations that had originally reached the maximum of four names in one or both of the categories. The responses indicated that an unlimited solicitation of names might have elicited about 13 more organizational employees, but only 2 more external representatives. We conclude, therefore, that we have somewhat underenumerated the internal representatives.

The extent of the bias in the composition of the sample should not be exaggerated, however. For the 51 organizations included in our 1987 survey, the difference in the number of nominations would have been 191 versus 204 internal representatives and 123 versus 125 external representatives. These names would then have been included on the master list, which we subsequently sampled randomly. (For additional information on the 1987 survey, see Nelson and Heinz 1988.) For the most part, then, the samples should be representative of the organizations and individuals engaged in Washington representation, weighted by the level of their activity.

A sample of the government officials who are the targets of the representatives' lobbying activity was generated, as noted above, by questioning the representatives about their contacts. The officials named could and did include elected, appointed, and career positions. From the officials named by the representatives, we drew random samples of 101 to 108 names per domain and we completed interviews with 73 to 80 officials per domain, for an average response rate of 71%. The refusal rate was only 8%. The data gathered in the interviews with the government officials are discussed primarily in chapter 8.

The interviews with both types of respondents averaged more than an hour in length and included a considerable range and variety of measures. The several kinds of data require the use of several different analytic techniques, and they often address somewhat different theoretical issues. Moreover, the data can be viewed at three distinct levels of analysis: the individual representative, the interest organization, and the policy domain. Yet it is in the joint consideration of findings from all three levels of analysis that we get the best view of interest representation in the full context of policy making. Part II of the book, for example, examines the characteristics of individual representatives. But the employment relationships of the representatives, the career paths they follow to arrive at their positions, their political and social values, and the characteristics of their collegial networks are of interest to us not as elements of individual biography, but as measures of social structure. These characteristics of the representatives provide significant insights into how interest representation is organized, how it varies by policy domain, and how it is related to other dimensions of social and political life.

The Structure of Influence

The structural metaphor in the title of this book has both methodological and theoretical meaning. We seek to analyze the social structure of interest representation. We are therefore concerned not only with the formal institutions charged with making national policy, but with the broader set of social relationships in which they are embedded. To understand this context, we examine the representatives' career paths, beliefs, and networks of association. These structural characteristics reflect the mechanisms through which interest groups seek to influence policy making, and they may thus reveal the very bases of influence.

As our findings unfold, they display the extent to which national policy making is shaped by the distinctive structure of the interests that make up specific policy domains. The interest structure of any given domain is a product of the kinds of organizations that are concerned with that set of issues, the bases for conflict and accommodation among the groups, the types of policies that characterize the domain (for example, the mix of regulatory, distributive, and redistributive programs), and the nature and role of the government institutions that have jurisdiction in the domain. Theories of policy making that gloss over the unique character of politics in various domains can thus provide only an incomplete account of how national policy is made. But the interest structures of the domains share many organizing principles. Most prominent among these is the absence of a centrally positioned group of elites that is capable of coordinating or integrating disparate interest group demands. Our findings indicate that the structure of interest representation reflects and, quite probably, contributes to the uncertainty of the policy-making process. The story of the lawyer and the heavyweight, with its message about the precariousness of private attempts to influence government policy, may therefore prove to be a lesson that warrants systematic exploration.

APPENDIX: Operational Definitions of Policy Domains

Agriculture: Policies concerned with the production and distribution of food, natural fibers, and plants or animals produced in commercial quantities.

Energy: Policies concerned with the production, distribution, and consumption of fuels used for the generation of heat, light, or motive power, whether for ultimate consumption in industrial, commercial, institutional, or residential settings. The fuels include oil, natural gas, manufactured gas (propane), other petroleum by-products, alcohol, coal, electricity (whether generated by fossil fuel, nuclear fission, or water power), synthetic fuels, and stored solar energy.

Health: Policies concerned with the provision and distribution of medical (including dental) services, pharmaceuticals, and medical devices; prevention and containment of contagion or disease; and screening of food additives, drugs, and medical treatments or procedures for potential hazards. Specifically included within this domain are policies concerned with mental health; the regulation of doctors, nurses, dentists, medical technicians, hospital administrators, and other health care providers; the training and certification of such health care professionals and providers; the regulation of hospitals, clinics, and other institutions that provide medical services; the regulation of the manufacture and distribution of drugs and medical devices; the financing of providers of health care and the regulation of both public and private health insurance; and the special health problems of identifiable subgroups of the population, including veterans, American Indians, and the elderly.

Labor: Policies concerned with the direct relationship between employers and their employees, including the scope and processes of collective bargaining; the participation of labor in the management and control of enterprises; the regulation of all forms of collective action by labor and all forms of countervailing actions by employers; laws affecting the internal governance of unions; and the obligations of employers concerning the wages, safety, working conditions, pensions, and insurance of employees.

Chapter 2

The Policy Domains

What goals do interest groups pursue? What are they after? What motivates their investment in Washington representation? Though a fundamental objective of interest group activity is to affect public policy, this does not necessarily mean that every group action is single-mindedly devoted to gaining policy advantage. But the whole logic of the interest group tradition—and, indeed, of virtually any mode of political theory and analysis—rests on the assumption that political action is purposeful and that the purposes are ultimately served by the substantive policy decisions of governmental authorities.

It is at the intersection of public policy and the wants and values of private actors that we discover interests. What we call the interests of the groups are not simply valued conditions or goals, such as material riches, moral well-being, or symbolic satisfaction. It is only as these are affected, potentially or in fact, by public policy, by the actions of authoritative public officials, that the valued ends are transformed into political interests that can be sought or opposed by interest groups. In his classic analysis, Arthur Bentley (1908) preferred to regard interest and group as one for observational purposes; no group without its interest, no interest without its group. We agree with this view because it is indeed risky to anticipate whether or when an individual actor, organization, or group will come to believe that its values have been or may be affected by governmental action and may be advanced by entering the political arena. The only observables of political analysis are groups that have discovered how policy affects them. When we focus our attention on the political arena, all we see are groups with interests, and each gives substance and definition to the other.

This means that, in analyzing what interest groups do and with what effect, the very conception or definition of a group must be framed in terms of the public policy goals and objectives it seeks. If we are adequately to understand how groups function, it is necessary to study them in the context of policy. We cannot abstract groups from the substance of their interests without losing touch with what defines those groups.

The force of this conceptual point is felt very early in the process of designing research on interest groups. If interest groups are defined by their policy interests, then we must draw the sample of groups on the basis of their substantive concerns. This in turn requires us to have some conception of types of public policy that will allow us to determine the rosters of groups that are active in each type. The initial problem of identifying what we have come to call policy domains is not at all simple; but once that is done, the process of sampling is straightforward.

To highlight the importance to our analysis of the concept of the policy domain, let us consider alternative methods of generating rosters of interest groups. There is no definitive census, and none of the listings that have been compiled pretends to be complete or free of bias. The one "official" list, consisting of those organizations that register under the 1946 Registration of Lobbyists Act, is universally agreed to be inadequate, though Milbrath's (1963) sample was drawn from that list. One of its defects is that the policy concerns of the listed groups are spread across the entire range of federal activity so that any manageable sample is likely to contain only a few groups in any particular policy area and likely also to miss many of the core actors. Perhaps for this reason, Milbrath was unable to say much about the substantive policy concerns of his sample or to examine whether features of group activity varied according to the substantive interests involved. This latter point is clearly of central importance both to empirical analysis and to theory, and the design must allow it to be addressed.

Walker (1983) and Schlozman and Tierney (1986) undertook to gather data from a considerably larger sample of groups than Milbrath had done. Both utilized rosters compiled by private sources seeking to supply the Washington community with useful information about who is present there. These listings have become increasingly comprehensive during the past decade or so and are useful for many purposes. Nevertheless, because they try to cover the full range of public policy interests, a sample of manageable size is unlikely to include a sufficient number within any policy area to permit assessment of the impact of substance on group behavior. Moreover, the mix of organizations listed in the rosters differs from those derived from other sources; a larger proportion of business firms and trade associations appears on the lists used by Schlozman and Tierney and by Walker.

One method of developing a sample of interest groups active in Washington would focus on particular institutional arenas and list all the groups that come into contact with officials in each arena. In fact, the Registration of Lobbyists Act list does that, but it includes only groups seeking to lobby Congress. It does not include those contacting executive agencies or the courts but not Congress. It is possible to use the computerized Congressional Information Service (CIS) to secure a full list of groups testifying before congressional committees, and all those that file amicus curiae briefs with the Supreme Court or other courts are also readily obtained. None of these institution-specific listings, however, provides any control for policy substance, so the problem of sampling according to policy interests is not resolved by using these institution-centered lists alone. Indeed, as we noted in chapter 1, we did employ both institution-specific and comprehensive rosters of interest groups in constructing our sample. But we still needed to incorporate substantive policy interests into our design.

Over the years, several researchers have attempted to develop a typology of public policy that, while accommodating the rich variety of specific issues and interests, would allow the particulars to be aggregated sufficiently to be intellectually manageable and theoretically productive. One of the best known of these efforts is Lowi's tripartite distinction among distributive, regulatory, and redistributive policies (1964). There are numerous critiques and versions of the Lowi formulation (e.g., Salisbury 1968); and useful alternative typologies have appeared, such as Wilson's (1980), based on the configurations of group costs and benefits flowing from each policy action. For our purposes, however, the only thing that needs to be said of these typologies is that in order to draw from them a sample of particular substantive policy decisions it would first be necessary to classify each specific policy. Given the ambiguities of those typologies, such a task would be both burdensome and of uncertain analytic value.

Several students of Congress have sought to identify basic categories or dimensions of issues as they are manifested in the patterns of roll call votes. The method most commonly employed in this research analyzes member voting patterns with scale analysis; those vote clusters that satisfy the scalability criterion are deemed to be distinct dimensions or types of policy issues. Clausen (1973) reports finding five such dimensions: agricultural assistance, civil liberties, social welfare, international involvement, and government management. Sinclair (1977, 1978), looking at a somewhat different time period, found an essentially similar set of dimensions. Students of the Supreme Court have found a few reasonably well differentiated sets of policy issues involving economic regulation, civil liberties, and criminal procedure, but there has been considerable criticism among Supreme Court analysts both of this methodology and its alleged findings. Poole and Rosenthal (1991) have reported that over a period of several decades in Congress a single dimension of conflict, essentially between economic liberals and conservatives, dominated the system (see also Koford 1989). If that is true, it might make it unnecessary to search for multiple dimensions, and it would imply that American politics revolved much more fully around the issues of class conflict than most observers have concluded. In any case, one should note that both Clausen and Sinclair, before developing their issue scales, divided the roll calls into broad policy categories by means of "preliminary conceptual definitions of policy domains" (Clausen and Cheney 1970, 139). We are not told much about those conceptual definitions, but it would appear that if we are to frame our research in terms of substantive policy interests we must first devise some differentiating criteria rather than rely on behavioral data to sort themselves into categories that are both meaningful and manageable.

How, then, can we identify the groups whose activity is in some sense triggered by or based upon interests in a particular policy domain? In principle, we could select among many possible levels of aggregation, simply distinguishing foreign policy from domestic, for instance, or, toward the other end of the spectrum, differentiating food safety interests from drug safety concerns. In either case, we need criteria that will identify groups as active on a particular range of issues. Thus, having selected agriculture as one of our policy domains, we did not use the USDA or the Agriculture committees of the House and Senate to define the group universe, nor did we look at all of the groups that were active regarding a particular farm bill (cf. Browne 1988). Rather, we sought evidence of group activity in all controversies involving the "production and distribution of food, natural fibers, and plants or animals produced in commercial quantities" (see the appendix to chapter 1). Not everything within USDA jurisdiction is included; for example, nonfarm rural poverty and recreational aspects of the Forest Service are left out. Employing key terms from this definition, we could then identify from the New York Times Information Service, the Congressional Information Service, and the *Washington Representatives* directory the groups whose interests were engaged by these policy concerns. We also asked 20 to 23 government officials in each domain for nominations of active groups. We would expect to discover reasonably clear institutional configurations within what are, after all, substantially ordinary language definitions of our policy domains, but the important point is that we have generated our rosters of interest groups and, ultimately, of institutional targets by empirical means rather than as a matter of definition.

If, in the doing or the explication, this seems to have been more trouble than it was worth, we would emphasize that our major research objectives included estimating empirically the shape of interest group interaction and conflict within policy domains, determining whether there were significant differences among domains in group activation and strategy, and discovering the extent to which policy domains involved truly differentiated sets of participants or instead were linked by common ties to influential representatives. We wanted to be certain that the groups we examined had been chosen in a manner fully independent of our prior assumptions about which groups were important, what institutional targets mattered most, and whether certain notable actors served to link the elements of the interest group system.

The General Characteristics of the Domains: Participants and Political Context

To provide an orientation for the detailed analyses that follow, let us identify the principal groups active in the four domains, sketch the issue agendas and interest conflicts, and place these sketches in their institutional and partisan contexts.

The Participating Groups

The Washington interest group universe has grown substantially in recent years, and the result is an array of organizations that is vast in size and diverse in scope. We identified a total of 8,664 separate organizations that had displayed some level of activity on issues within the four policy domains between 1977 and 1982. To be sure, many of these were on the periphery, active only once or twice, or even short-lived as organizations. Fully three-fourths of all the organizations appeared only once in the four sources we drew upon. Only 127 organizations were sufficiently prominent to be named as many as ten times, and nearly half (57) of those were in the energy field. Another 284 were mentioned five or more times. Thus, the total universe of interest group action is very large, but relatively few groups appear with any regularity.

The categorization of interest groups, while in some degree inescapable, has not been given as much thoughtful attention in the literature as its importance to research warrants (cf. Wootton 1970). For years, scholars presumed that interest groups meant voluntary associations. Truman's (1951) magisterial work deals entirely with such organizations, and they are the focus of Mancur Olson (1965) and those who have followed his lead. Most of the abundant case studies of interest group activity also examine groups whose members choose, more or less freely, to support the group. Sorauf (1976) and Berry (1977) noted that a good many public interest groups had no members, thus presenting a rather anomalous situation in terms of democratic theory. Subsequently, the analysis of interested activity was explicitly extended to include organizations that had long been active in seeking to advance their interests but that were often omitted from the scrutiny of social scientists—business corporations, universities, state and local governments, church organizations, and other institutions that are not generally thought of as representing the policy concerns of their "members," whoever those might be (Salisbury 1984).

Another important dimension of the interest organization universe involves the timing and circumstances of group creation, or more properly of their entry into Washington policy making. Walker (1983) and others have called attention to the large number of citizens' groups that have come into existence since about 1960. The Nader organizations and Common Cause are the best known of this genre, but there are many others, pursuing very diverse objectives. Our data include a considerable number of such groups. The emergence of these non-self-interested organizations, sometimes referred to as externality/alternative groups (Hadwiger 1982), may tend to destabilize the policy-making process. Citizens' groups are not the only newcomers, however. A considerable number of business trade associations have been formed in the last two decades, and many new coalition groupings of organizations have appeared. While some of these are short-lived, particularly those that are formed to push for or against a specific policy proposal, many survive to become regular Washington participants. New firms of consultants and of lawyers have also appeared on the scene in significant numbers.

These newly organized interests might be thought of as belonging to two broad sets. One set is composed of groups whose members had some sort of policy interests in times past but until recent years were unable to overcome the free rider problem and other barriers to organization. Walker (1983) has shown that subsidies from foundations, the government itself, and other donors have been critical in bringing many of these groups into existence, and successful entrepreneurship on the part of Nader and others has also contributed. For some of these groups, the policy interest was clearly there and it needed only to be mobilized organizationally. In other instances, the interests themselves were perhaps quite inchoate until the entrepreneurs articulated them. In any case, these newly organized interests constitute one large set of additional participants in national group politics.

A second array of added interest group players may or may not be represented by new organizations, but their presence in Washington is new. Many of these are business corporations and other institutions. They have discovered that the vast scope of federal policies and programs affects them in distinctive ways. The firm can no longer be content with the efforts of its industrywide trade association, which may not be attentive to its individual needs. In some situations, this process of interest differentiation leads to the formation of new trade associations or less permanent structures of cooperation. More often, the firm establishes its own direct representation. There are, of course, limits to this. Many potential interests cannot afford the costs of individualized representation. Moreover, federal policy does not necessarily lead to an endless sequence of differentiating interests. The specifics vary from case to case and domain to domain, but most policies retain some degree of generic language and application so that individual claimants to funds or particular objects of regulation are affected as members of broader groups rather than as unique cases. It is the desire to be treated uniquely, however, that leads many interests to lobby for special tax code provisions or advantageous loans and contracts. Virtually unlimited interest differentiation is thus possible, but it is not inevitable.

Thus, the spectacular growth of interest group representation in Washington has been brought about in part by the newly organized and in part by the newly mobilized. The latter category includes many organizations, mainly business corporations, that have recently discovered how useful a Washington presence can be. It also includes organizations whose interests have come to be differentiated from others in the same industry or activity. Profit-making hospitals differ from nonprofit hospitals. Research universities have different needs and priorities from others in higher education. Soybean growers compete with both cotton and livestock interests for the cooking oil market. All these groups are significantly affected by federal programs, but their political interests differ. Hence, their desire for differentiated representation.

The Political Context

It should hardly need saying that interests are always pursued in some particular political context. There is a President with a party affiliation, programmatic priorities, and an array of staff and administrative subordinates who advance his purposes. There is a Congress with distinct partisan complexion, leadership cadres, and policy preferences, all of them with problematic relationships to those of the executive branch. There is the permanent bureaucracy, the higher reaches of which may have substantial impact in determining winners and losers among competing interests. And there are the courts, also varying across time in the balance of their policy leanings.

Our interviewing was conducted during the latter part of Ronald Reagan's first term as President, when his popularity was recovering rapidly from its low point a year earlier. Economic indicators were strong, though the federal budget deficit was rising. The primary policy targets of Reagan's first term in office—tax reduction, deregulation, and military buildup—had been attacked with vigor and some success. The reputation of the preceding Carter administration was, accordingly, at a low ebb.

Since the large majority of our respondents had been interest representatives during at least part of the Carter era, it was possible to recapture a reasonable portion of what they had done then and to probe their perceptions of differences between the Carter and Reagan years. Our survey instrument contained several questions designed to test how the business of representing private interests in Washington had been affected by the rather dramatic changes in the personnel, style, and policy agenda of the executive branch, and in several different ways we attempted also to capture some of the particulars of policy disputes that occurred between 1977 and 1982.

The Reagan administration was reputed to be vigorously assertive on behalf of a long list of major policy changes, while Carter was thought to have floundered ineffectually, unable to sort out program priorities. Ironically, most of the really dramatic issues during the period covered by our study occurred during the Carter years. Many of the Carter initiatives failed to win approval in Congress, to be sure, but in the four policy areas we examined there was more action then than during the Reagan years.

Each administration presented its proposal for renewing the broad program of agricultural price supports, and the proposals were roughly of equal impact. But it was Carter who imposed the embargo on grain shipments to the USSR, and none of the more specialized Reagan initiatives in agriculture drew as insistent a protest from interest groups as that. In the energy field, the Carter administration declared the existence of a national energy crisis, put together a broad package of proposals for energy conservation and alternative energy development, and created the Department of Energy. The Reagan commitment, by contrast, was to reduce government involvement in energy. After 1981, there were few proposals for new federal initiatives and a retreat from the urgent language of crisis.

This was largely true also in health policy. The Carter administration proposed some expansion of selected health care programs such as funding for HMOs, children's health assistance, and mental health centers. The Reagan administration, by contrast, backed certain proposals favored by business interests—such as extending the duration of drug patents, weakening the Delaney amendment's strict ban on carcinogens, and relaxing nursing home regulations. Both Carter and

Reagan confronted escalating health care costs, however, and both administrations supported proposals involving some degree of federal intervention to control them. Labor policy was a domain of major policy struggle during the Carter years, as organized labor tried to take advantage of the fact that the Democrats once again controlled both ends of Pennsylvania Avenue. Policies were advocated to shift the economic bargaining balance between unions and management, but most of these initiatives failed to pass. The Reagan forces, by contrast, made relatively few proposals for significant labor policy change, focusing instead on relaxing the enforcement of OSHA and EEOC requirements and placing members on the National Labor Relations Board who would be more sympathetic to management.

In the four policy domains covered by our study, there were no major changes during or just prior to the period of our interviews in the configurations of the relevant governmental institutions, but there had been some important restructuring a few years earlier and this had significantly affected opportunities for group access. During the 1970s, various reforms had weakened the impact of seniority in Congress, giving more authority and resources to subcommittees and subjecting the erstwhile barons of Congress, the committee chairs, to considerably more control from both the committee members and their respective parties. In the House of Representatives, the Speaker had been strengthened, and party solidarity became somewhat more readily achieved; but the Senate, controlled by the Republicans at the time of our interviews, remained highly decentralized. Also during the 1970s, member and committee staffs had grown so large as to permit every senator and many House members to function as a virtual "enterprise," eschewing policy specialization and taking an active role in several policy domains (Salisbury and Shepsle 1981). The principal effect of these developments was to expand substantially the number of points of consequential power within Congress, access to any of which might be of value to private interests. Yet no one of those points or even several together could guarantee success in accomplishing some positive policy result in so decentralized an institutional structure.

On the executive side, there was a rather different trend in institutional development. At least since the Nixon administration, though in some respects reaching back much farther than that, there had been a steady growth in the authority of the White House and the Executive Office of the President over the various elements of the administration.

Agency or departmental autonomy was increasingly circumscribed. Personnel appointments, legislative proposals, budget requests, spending management, and the promulgation of administrative rules and regulations had come more and more closely under the supervision of the Office of Management and Budget (OMB) to insure agreement with presidential priorities. For interest groups this meant that, while lobbying at the agency level was still necessary, it was less often decisive than it once had been, especially on major policy or spending questions.

The Carter administration had invested considerable effort in trying to reshape the institutional structure of the executive branch and to reorganize its personnel management system. The creation of the Departments of Energy and Education was a highly contested initiative that imparted more institutional focus to these policy domains and, at the same time, brought them more directly under the control of the president. The Senior Executive Service, created in 1978, was designed to increase the flexibility of bureaucratic performance, but it also gave the administration greater control over high-ranking executive personnel and hence over the substantive direction of policy implementation. The Reagan administration came into office promising to undo many Carter innovations, proposing (among other things) to disestablish the two newly created departments. Its strategy ultimately emphasized budgets and personnel appointments, however, and no substantial changes ensued in the organizational structures of the four policy domains. Budgets were reduced, at least in their rates of growth, and a careful effort was made to assure that appointees to administrative and regulatory positions fully shared the conservative policy views of the administration. These policies made the independent regulatory commissions so firm in their convictions that traditional forms of interest group lobbying might be expected to be less effective. By the end of Reagan's second term, however, there were abundant examples of ex parte intervention, some of which went beyond the bounds of legality, and it was clear that interest groups had not been deprived of their ability to affect executive branch action.

The interest group–government action systems involved in our study did not experience major destabilizing shocks from the external world during the period of our research. There was no headline-grabbing energy crisis; the only new energy issue attracting great public attention was nuclear safety following the Three Mile Island accident, and that evoked no new patterns of interest group activity (Baumgartner and Jones 1990). In the health domain, both funding of care and cost containment were essentially incremental problems growing ever larger and more insistent, but they did not change the basic structure of interests. The potentially explosive AIDS issue had not yet gained national attention. The basic farm program was renewed twice during the 1980s, and agriculture issues largely followed accustomed paths. There were good growing years and bad, and periodic distress over farmer debt, but these generated little actual policy change. The Reagan administration's preference for private sector solutions combined conveniently with the expectation that business interests would generally prosper under a "hands-off" labor policy, and the only really dramatic labor dispute was the successful Reagan administration opposition to and eventual defeat of PATCO, the air traffic controllers' union.

Thus, the period covered by our interviews saw fairly large differences in the rhetoric of policy proposals—Carter versus Reagan, Democrats versus Republicans—but much less contrast in policy results. In all four policy domains, there was a rough policy equilibrium. Important redirection did occur in some areas during the early Reagan years, but it was primarily in fiscal policy, especially the dramatic tax reduction of 1981 and the redirection of spending from social programs to national security. The effects of these shifts on the four domains were indirect. Funding levels were affected, of course, especially in health, but most of the groups whose interests were concentrated in our four domains continued to have some success. Moreover, these domains continued to experience growth in the number and variety of active interest organizations. Each of these policy areas was inhabited by large numbers of interests, and their relationships with government and with one another were structured in complex patterns, as we shall see.

The Agriculture Domain

In every advanced industrial polity, the question of what to do with and for farmers is troublesome.[1] The number of farmers steadily declines, but domestic markets are nonetheless unable to provide an economic return sufficient to satisfy the remaining farmers. Though farm interests seek government intervention in the markets, the programs are costly and the declining farm population makes it ever more difficult to secure the political support needed to maintain the expenditures. The United States shares with other nations many features of modern agricultural politics and, as an increasing share of U.S. farm production is sold abroad, these commonalities become of greater importance to an understanding of how the problems of agriculture are to be solved. Despite the numerous parallels of experience, however, each nation has gone through a unique set of historical circumstances that has generated the specifics of its politics.

In the decades following the Civil War, American agriculture began to be differentiated politically from the larger political economy. Cotton and tobacco had always been raised as cash crops, but in the postbellum years mechanization transformed the modes of production, processing, and distribution of wheat, feed grains, and livestock. Mechanization and the opening of large areas of the plains to agricultural pursuits had the effect of greatly increasing the degree of farmers' involvement with and dependence on banks, farm equipment manufacturers, railroads, and other parts of the business community. The primary thrust of farmer political action in this first phase was protest, expressed in part through voluntary associations like the Grange and the various forms of the Farmer's Alliance, culminating in the rhetorical enthusiasms of the Populist party in the 1890s.

Farm protest won some legislative victories and created a symbolic heritage to be drawn upon in song and story for the next century. Nevertheless, it had little impact on the power of business, and the political agenda, urging basic changes in the structures of power, yielded little of tangible value to farmers. In the early years of the twentieth century, the efforts to organize farmers shifted toward more narrowly focused purposes, emphasizing such matters as technical assistance through the Extension Service, improved marketing information, and regulation of some of the specialized institutional arenas where farmers did business, such as the stockyards. This shift to an agenda of self-interested policy concerns and away from broader social reform gave shape to the politics of agriculture from World War I until the New Deal. It was fueled organizationally by the rapid rise of the American Farm Bureau Federation (AFBF), which provided conscious and powerful constituency backing. Moreover, as Hansen (1987) has shown, members of Congress increasingly recognized that the issues of farm policy were recurrent. They would not go away, nor would the organized groups that articulated farmer concerns. If effectively cultivated, however, groups like the Farm Bureau could provide reelection support that was more dependable than party regularity could give. The result was that, given a large number of members of Congress with substantial farm constituencies, farm interests came to be well positioned to secure policy benefits regardless of which party controlled the institutions of government. Prior to 1933, this was still only a tendency; thus, Coolidge vetoed several major items of farm legislation with apparent political impunity. But many parts of the Department of Agriculture were working closely with farm groups, as were the key congressional committees, so that the elements of a classic iron triangle were in place by the time the New Deal arrived.

Farm policy was a major component of the New Deal array of domestic policy innovations. Structures of price support legislation were enacted, financed initially by a tax on processors and, after that was declared unconstitutional, supported from general revenue. Other programs provided assistance to farmers for soil conservation, rural electrification, and credit. The USDA greatly expanded its research efforts and other services, and there were attempts to provide a form of welfare to people who lived in the country but did not actually participate in commercial agriculture. This broadened conception of what an agenda for agriculture might include was resisted, ultimately successfully, by commercial farm interests led by the AFBF. By the end of World War II, the effective agenda had been restricted to programs providing price supports for the "basic" commodities, wheat, cotton, corn, rice, tobacco, and peanuts; a variety of income support programs for certain other commodities, notably milk; and an array of marketing agreements by which specialized producers, especially of fruit and vegetables, could regulate their own marketing efforts. The AFBF, much the largest farmer organization in size and the most effective in internal management of potential conflicts among commodity interests, exercised substantial hegemony in the group representation of political interests, working comfortably with congressional leaders of both parties and in close alliance with the USDA through a succession of Secretaries of Agriculture.

The 1948 presidential election marked the beginning of the breakdown of bipartisan consensus on farm policy. Truman's surprising victory was attributed in part to farm votes, responding to the alleged failure of the Republican Eightieth Congress to provide sufficient grain storage facilities. Whatever the reason for his triumph, Truman proceeded in 1949 to appoint Charles Brannan as his new Secretary of

Agriculture. Brannan came from the National Farmers Union (NFU), chief rival to the Farm Bureau, and his proposed plan for farm income support helped to polarize farm policy debate in the ensuing decade. Democrats, supported by the Farmers Union, lined up in favor of high, rigid support levels, while Republicans maintained their ties to the AFBF and sought lower and more flexible supports. Agricultural policy came to be the most starkly partisan issue domain in Congress and, as the conflict deepened, nonfarm allies came into play on both sides. Beginning in the mid-1950s, leaders of organized labor testified in favor of Farmers Union–Democratic farm policy positions, while the Republican–AFBF alliance was reinforced by support from the National Association of Manufacturers (NAM) and Chamber of Commerce. What had been a consensual policy domain, resting on the triangle of symbiotic support among a broad spectrum of farmers' organizations, members of Congress from agricultural constituencies, and the Department of Agriculture, had fractured. In its place was a policy domain characterized by heated debate couched in ideological and highly partisan terms, with policy outcomes largely dependent on election results rather than on the more complex processes of negotiation and bargaining.

By the end of the 1950s, it was beginning to be apparent that partisan conflict had made agricultural policy unstable. In part, this resulted from the steady shrinkage of farm constituencies. In 1926, 251 of the 435 House districts had more than 20% of their populations on farms, but by 1976 there were only 49 such districts, and in 1986 only one. Thus, farmers were less and less able to provide decisive margins of electoral success to members of Congress, much less to presidential aspirants. Alliances became more essential to farm interests, but were increasingly difficult to maintain. The Farm Bureau found itself in the role of general apologist for free enterprise, more often in the service of broad business interests than of farmers. It was widely regarded as keeping its membership up only through excellent programs of insurance and the like. Among Democrats, support for price support legislation by urban Congressmen after 1961 carried an explicit price tag: inclusion of food stamps for the poor.

A second element of the fragmentation process was reflected in the more insistent presence of commodity organizations. Some, like the National Milk Producers Federation, had been active for years, but many were either newly created, like the National Corn Growers Association, or more fully activated. In 1958 a group of nearly 40 commodity organizations banded together to frame price support legislation that would serve the disparate and often conflicting needs of the diverse interests, but despite some success in that year, the National Conference of Commodity Organizations could not hold together (Heinz 1962). Instead, individual commodity groups and combinations began to split off, looking for sufficient support to pass protective legislation for themselves but, when necessary, leaving other commodities to find their own allies. Many of these commodity groups had strong regional definition, and this was reflected in the efforts to build coalitions of support. Some of these quests for separate commodity status were successful, but after 1960 it could rarely be said that there was really much that resembled a farm bloc or general farm legislation.

The policy arena was further complicated by a substantial increase in the active participation of agribusiness interests. Some of these were trade associations, like the National Cotton Council, which included all the elements in the cotton industry from growers through ginners, co-ops, and manufacturers. Others, like the Grocery Manufacturers of America, contained no farmers but had substantial interests in the cost of farm products. Individual firms became active on farm legislation as well. Some, like Cargill or Archer-Daniels-Midland, were involved in processing; others, like Campbell's Soup or Holly Farms, were themselves producers; still others, like Coca-Cola or Pizza Hut, consumed large amounts of agricultural produce. All had a stake in farm policy, and they more and more actively sought to affect policy outcomes.

The political landscape of the 1960s was filled to overflowing with newly formed groups of many kinds pursuing a wide and diverse array of policy goals. Many of these groups fit with reasonable comfort under the general rubric of "citizens' groups" composed of individual persons for whom material self-interest was not the basis of participation or commitment. Among the many causes to which these citizens' groups devoted their energies in the years after 1960 were several involving agricultural policy (Hadwiger 1982; Browne 1988). Some groups were concerned about the environmental effects of commercial agriculture, some about the impact of food additives on consumers, some about the needs of the poor, and some about the quality of family life and values among those still clinging to rural ways. Some of these groups located their concerns in the external effects, whether intentional or not, of existing farm policy. Others

sought to exemplify and foster alternative models of farming in contrast to the technology-intensive commercial agriculture that had
come to dominate.

These citizens' groups had two main effects on the farm policy
domain. First, they greatly expanded the issue agenda of the domain,
introducing food safety and nutrition concerns, challenging the value
of agriculture science and technology, and emphasizing the importance of the environmental effects of agricultural methods. Second,
they provided a new structure of political conflict. We have noted
that in the 1950s a deep cleavage developed among agricultural interests that was partly partisan, partly organizational, and partly
(because the AFBF and NFU represented different crop groupings)
commodity based. By the 1960s, this rather simple fracture had broken further into numerous shifting coalitions and combinations of
commodity and agribusiness interests, with the general farm organizations and the political parties hard put to find viable coalition-building
formulas. The arrival on the scene of the citizens' groups soon led to
a hardening of some lines of conflict, pitting certain of the old players
(both farmers and nonfarmers) against the new ones. A heady brew
of abstract ideological and even religious commitment was sometimes
added to the mix. The rhetoric of the American Agriculture Movement in the late 1970s was reminiscent of the prairie socialism and
fiery populism of the latter nineteenth century.

The expansion of the issue agenda in the farm policy domain has
led many observers to talk about the "new politics of agriculture."
Consumer issues, resource conservation, water pollution, food safety,
nutrition, occupational safety, research direction, and unionization
of farm workers have come to occupy a place on the list of concerns
deliberated in this policy arena, which had once been the preserve of a
much narrower range of interests. In combination with the enormous
increase in the number and variety of participating groups, this has
produced a vastly more complex domain than during the "good old
days" of the self-interested triangles.

Accompanying these changes, and contributing to them in turn,
some important alterations were made during the 1970s in the institutional structures through which agriculture policy was formulated
and carried out. In Congress, the most important change was the
severe erosion of commodity interest constituencies and the parallel
rise to articulate status of agribusiness interests and the so-called
"externality" interests, concerned about the impact of farm policies

on other parts of the society. An early example was the emergence of urban demand for food stamps in exchange for votes for price supports. As this transformation took place, it was reflected in the composition and power of the agriculture committees. Urban representation came to be more than a symbolic gesture, and the committees themselves were brought more fully under the control of the entire House and Senate. It was symptomatic of the dynamic state of agricultural politics that when in 1975 the House Democratic Caucus set aside its reverence for seniority and ousted three committee chairs who had come to be notably out of step with the times, Agriculture chair W. R. (Bob) Poage of Texas was one of those deposed. Meanwhile, more and more Agriculture Committee members came from nonagricultural districts. It would be wrong to suppose that the agriculture committees or their subcommittees are now composed of members who are indifferent to farm policy issues, but the interests they speak for and the issues they emphasize go well beyond the old commodity combinations and organizations.

Similarly, in the executive branch the changing character of farm interests has been reflected in changes in the structure of the USDA. The establishment of the division of Food and Nutrition Services under an Assistant Secretary was an example of the growing importance of consumer interests, but the removal of food safety and inspection responsibility from this agency in 1981 and its transfer to another division of USDA reflected the Reagan resistance to those interests (Meier 1985).

One other change, this one in the fundamental processes of national policy making, significantly affected the agriculture policy domain, as it has most other areas of policy action. This is the congressional budget process, adopted in 1974, whereby Congress attempts each year to enact a comprehensive budget, establishing overall spending limits for each major functional area and stipulating the revenues that are to provide the income side of the federal ledger. Price support legislation is one of those "uncontrollable" items in the federal budget in the sense that, once legislation has set forth the standards of eligibility and levels of support, the actual expenditures that will be required in a given year depend primarily on such factors as the weather and international market conditions, not congressional decisions. Basic legislation in agriculture is enacted every three to five years so that there is relatively little flexibility on the most expensive items in the years in between. Even so, overall budgetary limits have a constraining effect on many other areas of farm policy, and when the aggregate costs of agricultural programs loom large as a fraction of total domestic spending—as they did during several years in the mid-1980s, for example—they become inviting targets to interests outside the agriculture domain who are looking for opportunities to save their own program budgets by cutting others.

This means that groups concerned about agricultural policy must expand the array of their institutional targets. Indeed, in recent years such groups have not only needed to be concerned about the congressional side of the budget process but also, insofar as they could reach them, about the key executive budget makers, including OMB and the White House. Yet this expansion of the issue agenda, the group universe, and the relevant institutional targets has had a rather paradoxical effect.

On the one hand, these changes have forced the larger interest groups to increase their staff and expand their contacts on every front, to do more of all that they used to do. As one senior lobbyist said, somewhat ruefully, "If we're not so visible to some people anymore, it's only because we can't restrict ourselves to the same old places any longer" (Browne and Wiggins 1978, 496). Thus, the hegemony of the Farm Bureau has been irretrievably undermined.

The other side of the paradox involves the scope of issue participation. In his comprehensive examination of farm interest groups, Browne (1988, 1990) concludes that many groups have adapted to agenda growth and group universe expansion by seeking out a narrow "issue niche." By focusing on a small piece of the issue space, they can maintain a tolerable level of policy influence. Only a small fraction of the 402 distinct issues he examined drew the attention of as many as five groups, and of all the groups that were seen to participate in the Washington farm policy arena only about one-fifth had multiple policy issue agendas of serious concern (1990). Browne reaches this result, however, by means of extreme disaggregation of the issues. He differentiates among each program provision or title of Acts of Congress and includes as separate issues a substantial number of USDA rulings that are very narrow in their scope. At a somewhat higher level of aggregation—roughly the level at which most public discussion appears to take place—the expanded group universe yields a considerable number of groups activated on almost every issue. The scope of group participation and extent of conflict is thus to a considerable degree an artifact of one's level of analysis, not an unambiguous fact.

The Energy Domain

Until the 1970s, there was no policy domain labeled "energy."[2] There were instead several distinct and largely separate combinations of interests and institutional components that would, under the pressures of OPEC, environmentalists, and inflation, come together in a rather loosely coupled array of relationships. The principal components that eventually constituted the energy domain were the producers, and in some cases also the processors and distributors, of the several kinds of fuel that are the sources of American industrial and residential energy. Although energy consumption in the United States rose at virtually an exponential rate throughout much of the twentieth century, the relative usage of the various fuels fluctuated with new discoveries, technologies, and cultural habits. Consequently, the interests involved in what came to be the energy policy domain were and are dynamic.

The dominant fuel in the early twentieth century for both industry and domestic use was coal, but by the 1920s the rapid growth of petroleum usage, not only for motor vehicles but also for home heating, had pushed coal into the status of a sick industry. Once improvements in pipeline technology made it feasible to transport natural gas over substantial distances, it too became an important energy source. Hydroelectric power was largely confined to particular areas of the country, but dramatic dam construction projects in the Tennessee Valley, the Northwest, and elsewhere were important national political symbols, and there were heated debates from the 1920s through the 1950s over whether waterpower should be developed by private or public authority. In the post–World War II era, the potential of nuclear power added yet another element, and the emerging concerns of environmentalists and ecologists over the deleterious effects and eventual exhaustion of fossil fuels brought solar, geothermal, and bio-mass energy sources into the picture.

Although the interests of fuel producers have provided the primary impetus for the policies and institutions of the energy domain, a considerable number of other policy concerns are linked to it. The issue of safety, for example, has long been a major concern in coal mining. Safety has rarely been as important in relation to oil or gas; but nuclear power, of course, also raises serious safety issues. Nuclear energy, however, is generally seen as a communitywide concern, and it has been danger to the community more than to nuclear plant workers that has spawned political action. Coal safety issues involve primarily the status and well-being of the workers, and indeed much of the history of coal politics is the history of labor union campaigns, strikes, and the United Mine Workers, especially during the forty years of John L. Lewis's union presidency. But labor union issues as such have played little role in any fuel politics other than coal.

Environmentalism, on the other hand, has come to be a dimension of every energy category. With respect to coal, one set of concerns is damage done to land and water by mining practices (especially strip mining), the extent to which such damage can be repaired, and who should bear the costs. Oil production raises the spectre of offshore spills and destruction of wildlife, as well as damage to wilderness areas in the course of exploration. Nuclear waste disposal raises such potential hazards to the environment as to be virtually intractable politically. And, of course, the very use of fossil fuels, in the eyes of some, damages everything from Greek and Roman antiquities to the ozone layer, causes global warming, and thus threatens civilization itself.

For several decades, a crucial conflict regarding hydroelectric power was whether the major production sites should be kept under government control or turned over to private developers, and in some parts of the country there was further dispute over how electricity should be distributed. The public-versus-private argument has also been part of the conflict over nuclear power production, ownership of oil and gas reserves, and the local marketing of electric power.

Government regulation is pervasive in the energy domain. Local public utilities have long been treated as natural monopolies subject to rate regulation, primarily by state government agencies. Interstate transmission of natural gas is regulated by the federal government, as is the price of gas at the wellhead. In recent years, moreover, there have been numerous efforts to control or moderate the prices charged for petroleum products, sometimes by utilizing various direct price control schemes, and sometimes by seeking to increase competition by breaking the huge oil firms into smaller units.

The major oil companies are the largest firms embroiled in the energy policy domain, and oil issues have tended to dominate the domain's politics. Oil prices are the biggest component of energy costs, and since the formation of OPEC in 1973 energy costs have played a major role in inflation. The United States imports well over one-third of its petroleum. Some American firms are involved in overseas production, so that both economic and national security interests are at stake in the many oil-related issues that arise in foreign relations. From John D. Rockefeller to J. R. Ewing, oil-based fortunes have been important cultural symbols of both wealth and greed. When inflation is high or oil company profits large, they have also been major targets of populist attack.

Despite the sometimes negative image of "Big Oil," however, its political strength, anchored in the producing areas of the Southwest, has been great. For several decades (from 1926, when the depletion allowance was enacted, until the 1970s, when oil policy was brought into more general debate) oil production interests received a bonanza in the form of exemption from taxable income of $27^{1}/_{2}$ percent of their revenue, and, in addition, they prospered mightily under the protective umbrella of state and federal production controls designed to prevent the price of oil from dropping below profitable levels. Oil has rarely been challenged by potentially competing fuel interests, and it has been powerful enough to brush aside most consumer groups, populist orators, and other occasional critics.

Those with interests in oil policy are no longer in such a favored position, however. Indeed, they are no longer always dominated by the big oil companies, nor are they necessarily in agreement concerning policy options. In the 1970s and early 1980s the energy issue agenda shifted away from fairly crude, self-serving policies (subsidies for oil, price control for natural gas, and rate regulation of electric utilities and atomic power) to a virtual kaleidoscope of proposals intended to moderate the inflationary effects of rising energy prices, to stimulate exploration and development of new energy supplies, and to improve the conservation of existing energy resources. In the mid-1970s, the dominant concern was controlling inflation. That led to price controls, the allocation by the government of supplies among competing energy users, and a general increase in the scope and weight of federal regulation, which had differential effects. Small oil refiners and distributors, especially those in the New England area where oil is heavily used for home heating, supported regulations that Big Oil and many business groups sought to have removed. Environmental and consumer groups were often divided on these issues, torn between the desire to keep prices down and the hope that higher fuel prices would stimulate conservation and turn the country toward greater use of renewable energy sources.

Despite the efforts of traditionally autonomous fuel interests to stay out of one another's way politically—the American Gas Association stayed neutral on oil price deregulation, for instance—the crises of the 1970s, the eventual packaging of several different fuel-specific program initiatives by President Carter, and finally the creation of the Department of Energy institutionalized continuing interaction among several previously separated interests. Policy impact no longer was containable within the old triangle subsystems. Chubb, in concluding his study of energy politics, puts the point well (1983, 255):

> Policy impacts may provide the final collective incentive that either awakes potential members to the size of common political stakes or makes those stakes worth defending through collective action. In this study recent energy policy was found to have catalyzed the formation of a number of important [consumer] groups . . . Moreover, many groups augmented their resources in response to energy policy. Without the stimulus of government-imposed costs, or the lure of program benefits, it is likely that many of the new groups would not have formed and many of the established groups would not have enlarged.
>
> Policy impacts determine organizational resources in an important way also by establishing common and opposing interests. Because public policies include specifications of cost-bearers, beneficiaries and other affected interests, they create classes of interests. The specifications sometimes reinforce established lines of consensus and conflict in society or the interest group arena. Oil price controls that redistribute income from producers to consumers, for example, reinforce a basic line of economic conflict and group opposition. Policies may also specify classes of interests that cross-cut established boundaries. The oil entitlements program, for example, caused a schism among large oil companies; refiners without substantial reserves of cheap domestic crude oil were required to buy entitlements from, and were thereby thrown into conflict with, companies dependent on expensive, foreign crude.

The differentiating effects of policies upon interests, to which Chubb refers, have led to a proliferation of distinct interest group actors participating in the energy domain. As in the agriculture field, the old peak associations—the American Petroleum Institute, the American Gas Association, the National Coal Association, and so on—often can no longer achieve the necessary harmony among their members and/or can no longer sufficiently fine-tune their policy advocacy to represent the particular interests of member firms or subgroups of corporate actors. The latter, therefore, operate on their own behalf. Of the four policy domains we examined, energy had the largest number of organizational players. Moreover, energy groups were actively interested in a larger fraction of the domain issues than were the groups in the other three policy domains.

This is an important statistic because, despite the efforts of the Carter administration to develop a comprehensive energy program embracing all the fuel types, and the Reagan administration's efforts to deregulate the production and distribution of energy (even to the point of dismantling the Department of Energy), the actual policy proposals in the domain continued overwhelmingly to be fuel specific. Seventeen of the twenty particular issue events we examined (and at least two-thirds of the larger list studied by Laumann and Knoke 1987) dealt with only one type of energy source: oil, natural gas, coal, nuclear power, or solar energy. Nevertheless, the organizations within each of those industry groupings, most of which still have direct concerns almost totally based on only one fuel type, are actively interested in issues involving other energy sources. The electric utilities are in a somewhat different position since most of them use several different types of fuel and can shift among them to capture cost differentials. It is not surprising that they would range fairly widely (though the utilities' primary political focus traditionally was the state regulatory commissions). But penetration by hitherto more modest and narrowly specialized energy interests into policy disputes that involve competition between or among fuel types is, in a sense, the primary consequence, from an interest group perspective, of the emergence of an energy policy domain.

The construction of a more or less bounded policy domain in energy rests quite heavily on the changes in governmental institutions that occurred during the 1970s. Not only was the Department of Energy established and jurisdiction over programs affecting several fuel types placed there; the old Federal Power Commission, which had controlled natural gas prices, was reconstituted as the Federal Energy Regulatory Commission, located within DOE. The Atomic Energy Commission was eliminated, and the Nuclear Regulatory Commission, the successor to the AEC, was far less insulated from competing fuel interests or from the increasingly vocal protests of groups concerned about nuclear safety.

There were institutional changes in Congress also. The Joint Committee on Atomic Energy—which, along with the AEC, had uncritically supported the atomic energy industry—was abolished. Jurisdiction over most energy issues was substantially fragmented among several committees and subcommittees. Amidst vigorous congressional competition for the expanding policy turf involved in energy-related programs, the barriers that had separated the fuel interests and allowed each to pursue its own agenda in its own forum largely gave way. The rapid expansion in Congressional staff enabled many more members to participate actively in the energy debates, while at the same time many of the old energy policy hands in Congress withdrew from the domain (Jones and Strahan 1985).

The Health Domain

The federal health policy domain has existed for a long time, but largely in embryo.[3] Some policy components, notably drug regulation and veterans' health benefits, have been in operation for many decades. Federal financing of health research was institutionalized as early as 1937 with the creation of the National Institutes of Health, and the Hill-Burton Act of 1946 provided substantial subsidies to assist in hospital construction throughout the country. Until fairly recently, however, the scope of federal health policy was so small as to attract little attention from interest groups or anyone else. As late as 1960, health expenditures as defined by the Statistical Abstract were only $756 million. By the 1980s, however, the amount expended in health-related programs had come to be so vast that trying to contain the growth of health care costs was a primary focus of policy debate.

Health programs were elevated to cabinet level with the creation in 1953 of the Department of Health, Education, and Welfare, but health was much the smallest component. In Congress, health issues were (and are) taken up in several different forums: health insurance is mainly considered in the tax-writing committees; health research and training in health subcommittees of the Commerce Committee in the House and the Labor and Human Resources Committee in the Senate; veterans' health care in the Veterans Committees; and so on. Such fragmentation of congressional authority has undoubtedly reduced the scope of interaction among health-related interest groups and may help to account for the relatively low level of conflict among the groups active in the health policy domain.

In 1980, the Department of Health, Education, and Welfare was revamped with the establishment of the Department of Education and the renaming of the remaining two components as the Department of Health and Human Services. The actual impact of this change on health interests was slight, however. Throughout the period of our research, there were no significant institutional alterations in the health policy domain, and health interest representatives reported relatively low levels of concern with issues of administrative structure.

By far the most prominent issue in the health domain is, and for forty years has been, health insurance. In the late 1940s, health insurance might have appeared to be the only policy question involving health. The predominance of this issue helped create the impression (not entirely illusory) that the American Medical Association (AMA), which led the campaign against national health insurance, was the hegemonic interest group on health policy. By the 1960s, however, when first Medicaid and then Medicare were enacted, the AMA no longer held unquestioned dominance. Hospital interests had split off, medical schools had their own agendas, private health care insurance interests had grown large, and the AMA itself was experiencing serious internal conflicts.

Since the 1960s, the health policy domain has continued to be characterized by great fragmentation of interests with no clearly dominant group or coalitions. These diverse groups do not exhibit great hostility toward each other, however. In contrast to the earlier period when the AMA was at its peak of influence, the contemporary period appears to be an "era of good feeling."

One factor contributing to the dampening of conflict is the presence of a large number of specialized medical and scientific organizations. More than half of the representatives active on health policy are employed by such associations. Many of them hold advanced degrees in medicine or science, and to a considerable extent they draw upon their scientific credentials in making their cases regarding policy issues. Though science has many deep conflicts, these are seldom expressed in terms of hostility between competing groups or interests. Competition for scarce resources might be implicit, but hematologists would not try to advance the cause of leukemia research by denigrating the scientific merit of investigations of brain function. The effect of such a large presence of research scientists and professionals in the health domain, then, is to reduce the extent to which policy debate is cast in terms of competing group interests. The implicit conflict inherent in the competition for federal funds remains unstated, and issues are framed instead in terms of scientific promise and the severity of the health problem under consideration.

Closely related to the focus on science and contributing also to the dampening of potential conflict is the disease-centered character of many key health domain interest groups. In the development of this domain, the role of entrepreneur-advocates of campaigns against specific diseases has often been crucial. Particular personalities have given critical impetus to expanded federal research support, and these efforts in turn have had great impact in structuring both the programmatic focus and the institutional framework of implementation of much health policy. "Disease-of-the-month" crusades were mounted to promote federally funded research programs and establish separate institutes at NIH. Each disease spawned its fund-raising/lobbying organization, to which were engrafted the scientific and research interests whose work would benefit. And as each major disease focus secured institutionalized autonomy, potential conflict in the broader health domain was minimized. The "disease interests"—cancer, heart, diabetes, and so on—did not usually compete directly with one another, but sought primarily to enlarge the pool of federal funding.

Issues of funding are therefore considerably more important in the health domain than in the other domains in our study. Both the interest representatives and the government officials active on health issues rated funding concerns of higher priority in their work than did their counterparts in other domains. Only in the health domain was funding rated more important than initiating legislation or rules. This focus on matters of money may help to account for the lesser degree of intradomain conflict, since competition for funds can be lessened by increasing the size of the pot and fungibility makes compromise easier. Very diverse interests can make common cause in behalf of increased appropriations for all of their respective programs.

Nonetheless, some group interests are not readily brought into mutual accommodation, and the health domain does contain contentious issues. Health insurance—traditionally the most controversial policy question—was not under consideration in any comprehensive form during the period of our research. Instead, the related issues of how to control the costs of medical practice and hospital care occupied the forefront. Hospital groups, medical practitioners, insurance companies, and assorted consumer groups, including organized labor, entered into varying patterns of coalition and opposition depending on the form in which the issue was presented. Carter administration proposals for hospital cost controls brought the AMA, the AHA, and the Federation of American Hospitals into concert. Reagan proposals to relax the planning regulations governing local medical performance produced a somewhat similar combination. Proposals on child health care and the regulation of long-term nursing care were greeted by different interest configurations, however, as were more narrowly drawn regulations governing various aspects of medical practice.

The health policy domain has a larger array of citizens' groups and of state and local government interests than any of the other three areas we studied. In part this reflects the energetic efforts of various groups of doctors and other scientists, some affiliated with Ralph Nader, as these reformers have tried to redefine the health policy agenda. It also reflects the increased impact of federal health policies on state and local governments, which bear administrative responsibility for many federally funded health programs and often, as well, must try to fill the gaps left by shrinking federal support. The health policy domain has also attracted the very active concern of labor unions, which have long played a major role in promoting expanded national health care programs. It is no mere happenstance that health and welfare are linked, however tenuously, within a single administrative structure, the Department of Health and Human Services. Policies in this domain are suffused with the symbols of concern for society's needy. They are designed and justified with reference to the have-nots, the stricken, and the unfortunate. There are many self-interested groups in this policy area, certainly, but the non-self-interested are represented more here than elsewhere.

A broad cleavage can be discerned between the health care providers' interests (such as doctors, hospitals, and local governments) and claimant interests (including veterans, senior citizens, unions, and sometimes the health insurance industry). Status ambiguity abounds, however. Providers want to be paid, so they too are claimants. Public hospitals want prompt Medicaid reimbursement, but they are also providers of care. Thus, alliances are uncertain and shifting. The centrality of funding issues has moderated the domain's conflict potential somewhat, but the question of cost containment often threatens to shatter the veneer of policy agreement.

The Labor Domain

The domain of labor policy differs in several ways from the other three.[4] Each of the others is largely confined to a single industry, a delimited set of economic interests plus whatever citizen groups might be especially concerned about the circumstances of that industry. To be sure, the agriculture, energy, and health domains all have quite broad economic scope, including in each case a number of interests that are clearly distinct from one another. In each, there is a broad demarcation separating the interests of producers and providers from those of consumers; but individual firms and organizations sometimes shift from producer to consumer status depending on the issue, and this may provide a basis for a realignment of interests. Each of those domains can be understood as a collection of subdomains, the interests of which are seldom aggregated in domainwide coalitions or compelled to confront one another along the fault line of some dominating issue cleavage. Policy goals in these domains thus tend to be narrow; conflicts are moderate in scope, though sometimes intense; and participating interests search for policy niches where their most important concerns can be quietly attended to with a minimum of fanfare and a maximum of sympathetic understanding.

The labor domain is different in almost all of these respects. First, labor policy is rarely industry specific, but involves broad sections of the economy. Some labor issues are confined to a single industry, however—mine safety now occupies a reasonably well institutionalized niche in which only a few groups participate. Similarly, labor-management relations in the rail and maritime industries are governed by specialized institutional agreements, and have been for many years. Such matters as the minimum wage level or pension regulation, however, affect vast numbers of workers and employers and are not easily disaggregated to enable niche politics to come into play.

Second, some of the most prominent issues in the labor domain directly involve the power structure of bargaining relationships between unions and management. Since the passage of the Wagner Act and the creation of the National Labor Relations Board (NLRB) in 1935, federal policy has set many of the terms and conditions that govern collective bargaining. Consequently, federal labor policy has much to do with how successful labor will be in organizing workers or winning larger contract benefits. By the same token, federal labor policy can have a significant impact on the labor costs that business firms incur. Proposals to alter the basic policy framework of labor-management relations involve fundamental questions about the economic power that the respective antagonists will possess. Thus the Taft-Hartley Act in 1947, the Landrum-Griffin Act in 1959, and the common situs picketing legislation proposed in 1976 and 1977 provoked conflicts that were passionate in their rhetoric and broad-ranging and intense in their group struggles. Not every union or company is affected equally by changing the collective bargaining process, of course, but the effects are generally broad enough on each side to assure that these issues, when they arise, will be argued at a high level of interest aggregation led by peak associations of labor and business. There are would-be (or once-were) peak associations in our other policy domains, but the policy issues in agriculture, energy, and health seldom involve such elemental matters of sectoral power and hence do not encourage domainwide aggregation of interests.

Third, the labor domain manifests ideological differences between contending parties. In every policy domain, there are sometimes ideological overtones to the disputes. In agriculture, the imagery of agrarian virtue and of a republic based on sturdy yeomen still abounds. In the health domain, medical care and research programs are suffused with an aura of startling medical breakthroughs and the prospect of curing almost everything that ails us. But these symbols do not have opponents. No one in American public life denounces farmers or opposes better health. The metaphorical dimension of political debate is one-sided. In labor policy discussions, by contrast, the emotion-laden vocabulary is not only prominent, it is employed on both sides of a well-defined line of conflict.

The term *labor* identifies not only a policy domain and one of the primary sets of antagonists; it also identifies an historic political movement that has occupied a central role in the theories and sometimes the practice of political, social, and economic change in modern industrial societies. For more than a century, the labor movement was the principal receptacle for the faith and devotion of politically conscious workers and intellectuals who sought to abate the evils of capitalism. Labor was thought to be the necessary instrument for the realization of socialism and the most promising vehicle of effective political or economic action to counteract the power of corporate business. In much the same way, the chief negative symbol used in rallying the forces of business and in appealing for support of free enterprise has been "big labor" and "union bosses."

The ideologically freighted character of the labor policy domain has a number of implications for our research. It reinforces the position of the aggregative peak organizations: the AFL-CIO on one side; the U.S. Chamber of Commerce, the National Association of Manufacturers (NAM), and the Business Roundtable on the other. It also reinforces the tendency of these groups (especially labor unions) to be active on virtually all the issues that arise within the labor domain and indeed to take positions and lobby well beyond the domain boundaries. The AFL-CIO needed seventy-nine pages to recount its issue positions and lobbying efforts in Congress during 1981 and 1982, and it required 35 votes in the House and 45 in the Senate to assess the two-year record of "key" votes of each member. Labor asserts itself on questions of food stamps, Medicare coverage, the Equal Rights Amendment, and many other issues, arguing that they affect in some way the condition of workers. Business peak associations take a somewhat narrower but still relatively broad range of issue positions, usually basing their arguments now on the impact of policy proposals on business costs and international competitiveness. Despite efforts during the Reagan years to expand the intellectual hegemony of free enterprise ideology, such broad-ranging arguments and counterarguments less often dominate debate or frame the ultimate choices in policy domains other than labor.

It is not surprising, in light of these considerations, that each principal in the bipolar structure of conflict over labor policy has a number of satellites—groups that, on particular issues, supplement the interest representation of the main players. The AFL-CIO is supported by its constituent unions. The Chamber of Commerce and NAM look to assorted trade associations and individual corporations. Rarely indeed will any of the satellites jump to the other side, though most are active on only a fraction of the total policy agenda addressed by the central actors.

Perhaps the most salient feature of American labor unions during the past thirty years has been their declining strength (Troy 1986). While never as strong as the unions in some European nations, U.S. unions had enrolled one-third of the nonfarm work force by the early 1950s. By the time of our study, this proportion had dropped below 20 percent, and by 1984 the labor movement had lost nearly one-fifth of its members in less than a decade. Erstwhile CIO unions, such as the Steel Workers, Auto Workers, and Machinists were the hardest hit, as heavy manufacturing industry employment, in which their strength was centered, moved to nonunion states and overseas.

Business associations, especially the Chamber of Commerce, suffered no comparable losses. Indeed, by the 1970s they had not only grown in numbers but in political sophistication and effectiveness (Vogel 1989). The number of business-sponsored PACs grew exponentially, far outpacing the growth of labor-sponsored PACs. The impact of this growth was moderated, especially following the Reagan victory in 1980, by a tendency for particular business PACs to disregard the urgings of conservative think tanks and Republican partisans and to support incumbent members of Congress (including Democrats), recognizing the reality that Congressional incumbents who sought reelection were almost always successful (Sorauf 1988). Individual business firms and many trade associations have appeared increasingly to give priority to the policy issues, usually defined quite narrowly, that were of greatest concern to their firm or industry.

Within the labor domain itself, the weakening position of the unions was to a modest extent counteracted by the growth of citizen groups, most of which took policy positions critical of corporate business practice. Issues involving racial and sex discrimination in employment and policy debates about urban and youth employment brought civil rights and civil liberties groups into the domain. In addition, the historic intellectual and political kinship linking labor to consumer advocates, welfare rights groups, and others seeking liberal social change helped shore up the movement's political position.

The structures of government dealing with labor domain issues have certain distinctive characteristics. One is that the courts are more heavily involved than they are in the other three domains. Litigation stemming from OSHA enforcement, pension complaints, and especially NLRB actions often bring labor domain interest representatives into court. A second feature of the labor domain's structure is similar to that in health; namely, there is no congressional committee devoted solely or even primarily to labor policy matters. On the Senate side, most labor issues are reviewed by the Labor and Human Resources Committee, which also deals with a variety of other concerns (including, in 1982–83, non-tax-related health policy). In the House, the main jurisdiction is exercised by the Education and Labor Committee and its labor subcommittees. Some labor questions, however, including most of those involving public employees, are taken up elsewhere. The broader agenda of the AFL-CIO, of course, also requires it to cultivate friendly access in many parts of each chamber's committee and leadership structure.

On the executive side, there is also an interesting difference between the labor domain and agriculture, energy, and health. The Department of Labor is, of course, the main administrative unit dealing with labor policy, and it has jurisdiction over such important matters as OSHA and other safety programs, and pension supervision. Many of the most contentious issues of labor policy do not go through the Department, however. The National Labor Relations Board and, to a much lesser extent, the Equal Employment Opportunity Commission are very important agencies of decision on labor matters. The other domains also have important independent agencies—such as the Food and Drug Administration or the Nuclear Regulatory Commission—but none of the others is as prominent in its domain's business as the NLRB is on labor policy, and conversely none of the other cabinet departments plays as small a role as the Department of Labor in domain policy making.

Conclusion

We have tried in this chapter to provide an orientation to the extraordinary variety of interest groups that participate in the four policy domains. We have emphasized the importance of placing these groups in the context of their substantive policy interests and of trying to discern the dynamics of group relationships within domains of policy making. In both agriculture and health, we find a pattern of progressive fragmentation of interests. Many of the groups in these domains have sought protected policy niches where their most salient concerns can be secured, without attempting to exercise wide-ranging influence. It has become increasingly more difficult to achieve such security, however, as a broader range of groups monitor and intervene in arenas of policy making that were formerly closed and as fiscal scarcity and the centralized budgetary authority of the OMB have combined to increase the level of scrutiny given to such arrangements.

The energy domain, only brought within definable boundaries during the latter 1970s, continues to be dominated largely by fuel-specific policy issues, but the multiple uncertainties surrounding energy issues (What will OPEC do? How will environmental pressures develop with regard to acid rain or oil spills? Will technology develop less expensive alternative fuels?) make it risky if not impossible for energy interests to seek safe policy niches. And the large differentials in the impact of policy on the diverse firms in the energy field—oil companies, chemical companies, pipelines, utilities, distributors, mining enterprises, auto manufacturers—often lead individual corporations to seek their own representation rather than rely on associations to speak for them.

Politics in the labor domain differs from the other three in several ways. This domain involves issues that cut across industry lines. It pits two sharply demarcated coalitions against each other, each led by peak associations with broad issue agendas expressed in substantially more heated ideological and partisan terms than are normally employed in the other domains. And it is the most litigious of our four domains, with significantly more court-related action by interest groups.

The contexts we have described in this chapter are composed of particular configurations of interest groups, institutional structures of government, and policy agendas. Although the data that form the basis of our analyses were gathered at a specific time, we tried wherever possible to capture a sense of the dynamics of domain development, and we are able to make some observations about patterns and processes of change in the structures of interest representation. Despite the impassioned political rhetoric of the early 1980s, which proclaimed that a profound redirection of national public policy was taking place, we found a considerable degree of equilibrium in our four policy areas, with growth in the number and variety of group participants but a good deal of stability in their relationships to one another and to the institutions of government. As subsequent chapters will show, issue agendas exhibit much continuity over time, and the shift from Jimmy Carter to Ronald Reagan, so important in its effects on fiscal policy and military spending, did not seem to bring fundamental alterations in the structure of interest group politics in the four domains we studied.

The interest organizations and the individuals who represent them in Washington tend, in the areas we studied, to be more or less permanent or at least long-lived participants in the policy process. This does not necessarily imply the existence of the oft-lamented iron triangles, however, or even of looser structures like issue networks. Our view, advanced very tentatively at this stage, is that the formidable array of groups at work in each policy domain neither dictates the content of the policy agenda nor decisively determines the outcomes of the policy process. Groups and their representatives are often influential, of course, but so are other actors, including government officials, academicians, and journalists. The broad impact of these interest configurations in a domain is primarily to limit the range and direction of feasible policy options. Bold new initiatives in labor policy cannot successfully be undertaken over the objection of either labor or management, and one coalition or the other is likely to object to anything daring. In health, energy, and agriculture, similarly, dramatic initiatives—comprehensive national health insurance, for example, or a sharp reduction in agricultural subsidies—run into formidable resistance. Incremental policy change and a focus on smaller fragments of the agenda are more likely to succeed. Despite election-centered rhetoric to the contrary, it is these smaller policy changes that are most often sought and accomplished.

We do not wish to suggest that policy change is rare. On the contrary, it goes on all the time through statutory revision, the promulgation of new rules and regulations, annual funding decisions, and so on. Interest groups affect many of these decisions, but they seldom control them, and it is rarely appropriate for the groups alone to be given either credit or blame for what government does or fails to do. For the most part, as we shall try to show, interested private organizations have relatively modest, highly circumscribed spheres of action. Only a broad and rather carelessly wielded brush would paint a picture of group domination. But there is much to be said about the particulars of how groups and their representatives operate, and what policy effects they achieve.

Chapter 3

Representatives
and Their Clients

Whether the representative or the client organization determines the strategy that is to be employed, the nature of the organization and its interests shapes and constrains the activities of the representative. Some clients have greater resources; some have less. Some, such as the environmental groups, have good access to the news media and substantial support from mass public opinion. Others—oil companies, perhaps, or thrift industry investors—have the support of influential government officials. The representative will make use of the differential advantages that are available.

The specific substantive contexts in which Washington representatives attempt to influence government policy also shape strategies. Actions taken on a bill concerning tobacco price supports, for example, may differ from those used on a proposal to restructure income tax rates. Different proposals call forth different politics. The substance of differing policy areas will, thus, motivate different interest groups, bring their particular political assets into play, and thereby create varying profiles of political activity.

Some client organizations pursue only narrow policy objectives, while others are active on a much broader front. Most business firms, for example, stick close to their particular business, but some labor unions attack a wide range of social issues. These agenda differences may, in turn, affect the number and kind of representatives that clients will choose to hire. Organizations active on only a limited agenda may use the home office staff for their irregular forays into Washington, while regular players maintain a Washington office or retain a Washington lobbying firm, or both. Whether the lobbyist hired is a lawyer, an old political hand, or a technical specialist depends on the nature of the matter at issue and the nature of the client's assets and needs. Thus, the characteristics of the representatives who are recruited for the work may indicate the extent to which particular kinds of skills and influence are valued in differing policy areas.

Bases of the Structure of Representation

There are three potential bases for the social organization of representation, each of which has implications for the influence of representatives. They are the knowledge-based model; the institutional model; and the organizational, or client-based, model.

Representation might be organized by substantive expertise. A detailed knowledge of tax law, for example, would no doubt be a valuable asset for a representative who is assigned to work on proposed revisions in the Internal Revenue Code. Thus, work might be allocated among representatives in accordance with doctrinal categories, ultimately resulting in the organization of representation according to the knowledge bases of the policy questions involved. Substantive expertise can develop in a number of ways, of course, such as through government experience or through a position in an organization that consistently confronts particular issues. Heclo, for example, argues that there are "issue networks" consisting of more or less stable cadres of substantive experts who flow in and out of government and private-sector organizations and maintain a dialogue about policy options (1978). In his view, it is from these networks of experts that a presidential administration must recruit for policy-making positions, with the result that any administration's policies will, to a certain extent, reflect the nature of the debates among substantive experts in the field. One could extend the analysis to private organizations, suggesting that interest organizations must depend on the same pool of substantive experts for representation in a given policy area, with the result that the goals and strategies of private interests also are affected by the policy discourse among a network of experts.

Perhaps the strongest variant of the model of knowledge-based representation is that in which expertise derives from training and experiences that are asserted to be unique to a professional group. The most pervasive professional group among representatives—and the one that has the most often asserted claim to autonomy and influence in processes of representation—is the legal profession. Charles Horsky argued that Washington lawyers are "an essential part of our present scheme of government" since they serve as "principal interpreter between government and private person, explaining to each the needs, desires and demands of the other" (1952, 10–11). Horsky's characterization of Washington lawyers was a version of the functionalist conception of the role of the professions in modern society, which was given its most influential expression in the work of Talcott Parsons (1954, 1962). Some political scientists have suggested that lobbying is itself a profession, with differentiated long-term career paths, a more or less standard set of practice routines, and a set of normative constraints that are widely acknowledged and generally adhered to (Eulau 1964; Zeigler and Baer 1969). The Horsky/Parsons model of the representative as an autonomous mediating influence has been questioned, however. Heinz and Laumann's study of Chicago lawyers (1982) and Nelson's study of corporate law firms (1988) argue that lawyers serving large corporate actors lack the autonomy from clients that is a necessary condition of the mediator role. Moreover, it is not clear whether the model of representatives as autonomous mediators applies to nonprofessionals, who are not schooled in professional ethics and may not possess the collectivity orientation that Parsons attributes to the professions. But other, nonprofessional experiences, such as government service or even participation in the Washington community, may supply such a broader social perspective to representatives. It is necessary, therefore, to examine the potential bases for the autonomy and influence of both professional and nonprofessional representatives.

A second basis for the organization of representation might be the differential access of representatives to particular offices or agencies within the federal government. If the fate of a proposed regulation were greatly dependent upon the actions of the chair of the Securities and Exchange Commission, for example, the services of a Washington representative who had served on the commission's staff or who was acquainted with the chair might well be preferred. Thus, the work of representatives might come to be organized by institutional target. The ability of private representatives to trade on their knowledge and contacts at an agency where they were previously employed gives Washington insiders a large stake in their relationships with the agencies. They may thus be as concerned to accommodate government officials as to satisfy their clients. Because Washington representatives are pulled toward both the client and the government, they may play one against the other and attempt to please both. The resulting mediative position of representatives might then be functionally akin to that postulated for lawyers by Horsky and Parsons, though it would not be motivated so much by a collectivity orientation or by adherence to professional norms as by political or economic advantage.

The third basis for the social organization of representation is the client organization itself, the structure being determined by the range of the concerns of particular clients. Exxon's lawyers, for example, might deal with investment tax credits, international trade policy, labor-management relations, occupational safety and health, pesticide regulation, the exploitation of government lands, and many other diverse issues. Thus, the allocation of work among representatives will reflect the range of interests of their client base. To the extent that the client organization has developed a specialized division of labor for representation, the work of a representative will reflect his or her position in the organization and the sorts of tasks, topics, and institutions to which he or she is assigned.

The three organizing principles tend to overlap. Expertise in the substance of oil and gas regulation is associated both with contacts at the Department of Energy and with employment by oil companies or other clients in that industry. Representatives who have one of these attributes are also likely to have the others, to one degree or another. But the difference in degree may be important.

The extent to which each of the three principles organizes the allocation of work may indicate the significance of each as a base for the power or influence of representatives. If it is the representatives' substantive knowledge or expertise that is of primary value to the consumers of their services (or even to the government officials with whom they deal, thus determining their success in those dealings), then we would expect the structure of representatives' work to reflect that fact. If their special access to government institutions is their principal stock in trade, then the structure should reflect that. Similarly, if they derive their influence from close association with powerful actors in a particular set of interest groups, the social structure of representation should display the importance of the client base. Thus, the value or weight attached to the three assets by purchasers of representatives' services and by government officials may be taken as a measure of the extent to which each is a base for the power of representatives. If the asset is important enough to serve as a source of influence, then the structure should reflect it.

Only the first two of these assets, expertise and access, might serve as a base for power in the sense of autonomy from the client. The third possible base of influence—close connection with the client—is antithetic to autonomy. Representatives may derive considerable influence with government officials from their positions as agents for powerful interests or may lose influence if the interest groups with which they are associated are notably weak; their established positions within the client networks may even give them influence in the clients' decision-making councils. But if the representatives' influence ultimately depends on their positions as agents of particular clients, then their autonomy must, at the least, be of a very different kind from that of the freestanding expert or the old Washington hand who has good friends in a cabinet-level department.

The Organization of Representation

Systematic variation in the types of organizations active in the four policy domains begins to indicate the structure of client demand for the services of Washington representatives (Table 3.1). Trade associations are the most prevalent sort of organization, but they are found much more often in the agriculture policy area than in the other domains. Agriculture trade associations include not only the

Table 3.1 Organization types active in four policy domains (percentages)

Type of organization	Agriculture	Energy	Health	Labor	Total
Business	20	54	15	8	24
Citizen issue group[a]	14	11	7	4	9
State and local govt.	3	5	6	1	4
Labor union	5	1	3	34	10
Minority group	3	—	14	11	7
Nonprofit	1	4	21	7	8
Professional	1	3	17	4	6
Trade association	51	22	16	26	29
Other	2	—	1	6	2
Total	100	100	100	101	99[b]
N	80	76	81	74	311

a. The term *citizen issue group* refers to an organization claiming to advance or defend the well-being of the public as a whole. These organizations include those concerned with environmental protection, abortion, political campaign reform, and so on.

b. Due to rounding, column percentages do not always add to 100%.

organizations of farmers or producers, but associations of processors and distributors, such as the Grocery Manufacturers of America. Individual corporations are included in the "business" category, which is the next most numerous class of clients. Again, there are substantial differences among the domains. Clients in the energy policy domain are especially likely to retain their identity as individual businesses. This tendency may be related to the scale of the units of production. Although grocery manufacturers, chemical companies that produce fertilizers, and other agribusiness concerns are often large corporations, many of the interest groups active in the agriculture domain are composed of producers that are much smaller and have fewer resources than the oil companies and public utilities that are the dominant players in the energy domain. The generally larger scale of the energy interests may permit them to act on their own.

As one might expect, the next most numerous category of clients, labor unions, is more often active on labor policy. Even in the labor domain, however, most of the clients are not unions. Similarly, nonprofit and professional organizations are more heavily represented in health policy than in the other domains, and minority group organizations are more active in the labor and health policy domains.

The organizations differ considerably in the extent to which they use internal and external representatives, and in the purposes for which they use the two types. Only a third of the organizations reported that they regularly retain law firms for policy representation; more than half reported that they never do. The organizations are much more likely to use trade associations regularly for advice and representation. But, again, almost half said that they never use such associations, nearly the same proportion that never use law firms. Almost two-thirds reported that, apart from their use of law firms, they never use outside consultants, lobbyists, or public relations personnel for representational work; little more than a fifth of the client organizations regularly turn to such outside representatives for assistance. Except for the several activities most clearly linked to lawyers' skills, particularly drafting legislation or regulations and litigating, the majority of organizations rely exclusively on their own employees to do the various representational tasks (Table 3.2). About a third of the organizations use a combination of inside and outside representatives to perform most tasks, which may suggest that the activities of the outside representatives are subject to review or direction by insiders. Only a small minority of organizations (well under 10%) rely

Table 3.2 The utilization of internal and external personnel in 316 organizations, by type of representational activity (percentage of organizations in each category)

Activity	Internal representatives	External representatives	Both	Neither
Congressional activities				
a. Testifying before congressional committees	60	6	29	5
b. Helping prepare congressional testimony (preparing and coordinating witnesses, etc.)	50	6	39	5
c. Developing or maintaining informal contacts with congressional committees	57	7	31	5
d. Drafting legislation (in whole or in part)	34	9	37	20
Executive branch and regulatory activities				
e. Testifying before executive agencies or independent commissions	52	7	29	13
f. Helping prepare testimony or comments for proceedings by executive agencies or independent commissions	40	6	40	13
g. Developing or maintaining informal contacts with executive agencies or independent commissions	54	5	34	8
h. Drafting regulations (in whole or in part)	35	9	33	23
Activities in court				
i. Planning or initiating litigation as a strategy for policy making	25	13	26	36
Organizational activities				
j. Keeping track of developments in federal government policies	55	6	38	1
k. Advising your organization on what issues are important or may become important to your organization	58	6	35	1
l. Participating in your organization's deliberations on what position to take on issues involving federal policies in this area	62	2	33	3
m. Serving as an officer or board member of other organizations active in this field	69	2	12	17
n. Otherwise developing or maintaining contacts with other organizations active in this field	66	2	31	1

exclusively on external representatives to perform most of the tasks (Table 3.2, column 2).

The lion's share of representational work appears to be done by employees of the interested organizations, sometimes in collaboration with outside representatives. Organizations that rely solely on external representatives are usually those that lack resources or that have highly delimited concerns requiring only part-time attention. Most organizations appear to engage in almost all of the activities (note the low percentages in the final column of Table 3.2) with the noteworthy exception of litigation for purposes of policy making. Nearly two-thirds of the organizations, however, report that they do use litigation as a policy instrument. The other two relatively unpopular activities (items d and h in Table 3.2) are also likely to require the services of lawyers. The cost of lawyers' services may restrict their use by some organizations.

In general, then, independent practitioners play a much smaller role in Washington representation than do full-time employees of the organizations represented. In the 1987 reinterviews of 51 client organizations, we asked the informants to estimate the percentage of their representation work that is performed by employees inside the organization versus that done by representatives located outside, whether in another interest group or in a freestanding law firm or consulting firm. The average percentage performed by employees of the organization was, we were told, 76%. We also asked whether this allocation of representational work had changed between the time of the original interview and the summer of 1987. More than 90% indicated that it had not.

From the viewpoint of both organization and representative, there is a major distinction between representatives who are employees or officers of the organization and external representatives who are retained for particular services. From the organization's perspective, the choice of representative involves a make-or-buy decision about how to spend organizational resources. The decision may depend on a variety of considerations, including cost, the volume of demand, the nature of skills required, and norms about organizational loyalty (Williamson 1975). For their part, representatives are confronted with the choice of making a commitment to a particular organization or establishing an independent practice in which their services are available to a range of clients. The latter arrangement is the traditional form for professional services, especially within the legal profession, and it is also the organizational form adopted by notable political consulting and public relations firms in Washington.

Although some scholars question the importance of the difference between independent and employed status in determining the degree of autonomy of professionals (Freidson 1986), in the context of Washington representation this difference may have significant implications. If a representative is an employee of an organization, the mediative stance of the representative implied in the professional model of representation may take on a different character than the relationship between an independent professional and a client. An employee within an organization often realizes a degree of independence from the control of organizational superiors, but the autonomy of the employed representative is probably of a different order than that of the professional who is a free agent or a member of a firm of free agents.[1]

Our findings are generally consistent with those of earlier studies. Two-thirds of Milbrath's sample of lobbyists in the 1950s were organizational employees (1963, 40), and Schlozman and Tierney's survey of interest organizations shows extensive use of both internal and external representatives (1986, 101). An inspection of the organizational positions held by our sample of representatives (Table 3.3) indicates that the proportion of representatives based in independent professional organizations—law firms and consulting firms—is quite modest in all four domains. Overall, about four-fifths of the representatives are employees of the client organizations. Organization executives account for the largest share.

External representatives may, of course, possess influence disproportionate to their numbers, perhaps because they devote a larger portion of their time to policy-making activity or have more connections with powerful officials than do other representatives. (We address that issue in chapter 4.) But the fact that most client organizations are directly involved in representation through their own officers implies that the organizations exercise close control over the objectives and strategies involved in representation. The active participation of the officers facilitates the monitoring of employee behavior.

Thus, organizational position and domain are strongly related, and the fact that they are is an important characteristic of the social organization of representation, but the relationship between these two dimensions makes our analytic tasks more difficult. Comparisons across domains entail latent comparisons among different types of

Table 3.3 Organizational position of representatives, by domain (percentages)

Organizational position	Agriculture	Energy	Health	Labor	Total
Executives					
Business	4	13	4	2	6
Nonprofit organizations	4	4	8	3	5
Trade associations	37	21	5	13	19
Unions	1	1	1	11	3
Professional associations	1	2	16	1	5
Citizen-govt. groups	5	3	13	6	7
Government affairs					
Business	2	14	3	1	5
Trade associations	12	7	1	8	7
Unions	3	1	1	11	4
Professional associations	0	1	12	1	3
Citizen-govt. groups	2	1	10	2	3
Internal lawyers	3	8	4	9	6
Research staff	8	11	6	14	10
External lawyers	15	14	11	16	14
Consultants	5	3	4	5	5
Total	102	104	99	103	101
N	192	184	206	194	776

Notes: Organizations were classified as follows. Businesses include all for-profit corporations and public utilities. Nonprofit organizations include universities, hospitals, research organizations, and humanitarian organizations such as the Red Cross and CARE. Trade associations include associations of business organizations as defined above and individuals engaged in business (such as farmers). Both single-industry and multi-industry organizations (such as the Chamber of Commerce) are included. Professional associations include associations of individual professionals (such as doctors, lawyers, and engineers), as well as associations of nonprofit organizations as defined above. The citizen-government category combines groups that advocate the interests of particular subpopulations (such as veterans, children, the elderly, minorities) or particular social and political issues (such as the environment, consumer rights, world population and hunger, drug abuse, abortion) with government interests (typically at the local or state level, such as the National Governors' Association). A small number of representatives working in political action committees (PACs) were sampled; these were classified according to the type of their parent organization.

Positions within organizations were classified as follows. The category "executives" includes organizationwide leadership positions, including chief executive officers, presidents, chairs, board members, and so forth. "Government affairs" includes such titles as government affairs officer, legislative director, D.C. office manager, public relations director, and D.C. representative. "Research staff" includes all other nonlegal positions inside organizations. A small number of individuals held two titles in the organization. They were classified by the highest ranked title, using the following ranking: (1) government affairs, (2) internal legal positions, (3) executive positions, and (4) other positions. Due to the small number of government affairs representatives in nonprofit organizations, these respondents were combined with the executives of nonprofit organizations.

Due to rounding, column percentages do not add to 100%.

* Chi-square $p < .01$.

organizations, and comparisons across organization positions entail latent comparisons among domains. Analyzing each domain separately, however, quadruples the number of analyses and drastically reduces the number of cases in certain categories. Therefore, we often break down the data by domain and organizational position separately, although rather more complicated relationships underlie the findings.

Representatives' Personal Characteristics

Washington representatives are overwhelmingly white and male (see Figure 3.1). It is possible that the paucity of women is due to the fact that less than a third of the representatives in the sample were under forty years of age, the age group containing the largest proportion of females. There are substantial differences among the policy domains in the numbers of women—the percentage in agriculture is little more than a third of that in the health domain (Table 3.4). This no doubt reflects the greater presence of women in the health professions than in agricultural management or agribusiness, and thus suggests the importance of industry experience and networks in the recruitment of representatives. In all types of organizations except citizen and government organizations, women are more heavily represented among government affairs officers than they are in the executive ranks (Table 3.4), probably reflecting the relative status exclusivity of the two position levels. Generally, it appears that the higher the status of the position or the greater the formal barriers to entry, the smaller the proportion of women.

The percentage of nonwhites is very small in all four of the domains. It is two to three times as great among representatives active on labor issues as it is in the other three domains, but even in the labor domain the percentage is only a little over 5%. Because there are fewer barriers to entry into Washington representative positions than to the practice of law, and because the presence of minorities might in itself be an asset in gathering political support, we expected nonwhites to be more numerous in the population of nonlawyer Washington representatives than they are in the bar. They are, but only a bit. The percentage of minorities among the nonlawyer representatives is 3.1%, while among the lawyers in our sample it is only 1.7%. The pattern of distribution of racial minorities is in some ways the opposite of the distribution of women (Table 3.4). The representation of minorities

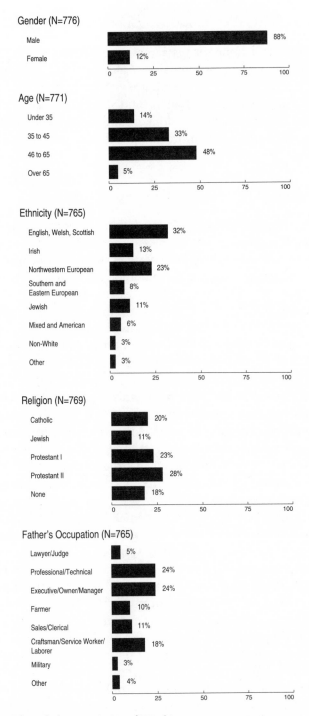

Figure 3.1 Selected characteristics of Washington representatives

City Size Origin (N=769)

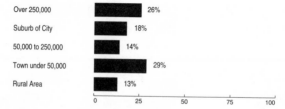

Over 250,000	26%
Suburb of City	18%
50,000 to 250,000	14%
Town under 50,000	29%
Rural Area	13%

Regional Origin (N=768)

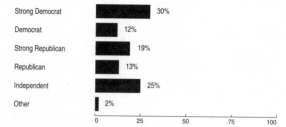

Northeast	45%
Midwest	21%
South	20%
West	12%
Foreign Country	2%

Political Party (N=767)

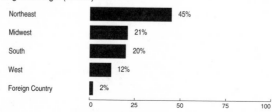

Strong Democrat	30%
Democrat	12%
Strong Republican	19%
Republican	13%
Independent	25%
Other	2%

1982 Income (N=722)

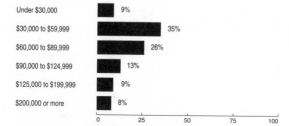

Under $30,000	9%
$30,000 to $59,999	35%
$60,000 to $89,999	26%
$90,000 to $124,999	13%
$125,000 to $199,999	9%
$200,000 or more	8%

D.C. Area Residence (N=776)

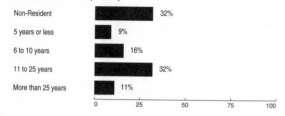

Non-Resident	32%
5 years or less	9%
6 to 10 years	16%
11 to 25 years	32%
More than 25 years	11%

Table 3.4 Social background characteristics, by domain and position (percentages)

	Women	Minorities	Jewish	Catholic	Type I Protestant	North-east origins	Southern or western origins	Metropolitan area origins	N
Domain									
Agriculture	7	2	4	12	31	19	44	28	192
Energy	10	2	7	20	26	29	42	41	184
Health	19	2	12	21	22	49	23	51	206
Labor	12	5	18	23	16	42	28	54	194
All domains	12	3	10	19	23	35	34	44	776
Organizational position									
Executives									
Business	7	2	5	16	30	30	37	37	43
Nonprofit organizations	6	9	11	11	26	50	23	46	35
Trade associations	5	1	3	17	24	17	42	33	144
Unions	4	8	12	24	0	37	33	33	25
Professional associations	13	3	13	16	26	50	21	39	38
Citizen-govt. organizations	29	6	8	25	19	35	23	35	52
Government affairs									
Business	17	3	3	23	29	37	34	37	35
Trade associations	24	0	4	22	37	17	54	24	54
Unions	17	10	20	30	13	47	27	50	30
Professional associations	26	0	30	11	15	59	22	67	27
Citizen-govt. organizations	19	0	7	22	26	59	26	56	27
Internal lawyers	13	2	19	21	15	32	28	53	47
Research staff	17	3	9	20	20	38	30	53	76
External lawyers	5	2	19	18	28	41	37	55	108
Consultants	6	3	11	14	23	35	32	54	35

is greatest in two of the executive categories where women are most underrepresented—the executives of unions and of nonprofit organizations. Like women, however, members of racial minority groups are seldom found in executive positions in trade associations. The presence of minorities is generally least where that of women is greatest—in the government affairs officer positions, especially in trade associations and professional associations. The distribution of blacks and other minorities across the various Washington representative roles does not, therefore, appear to correspond as closely to the status level of the position as does the distribution of women.

There are very large differences in the percentages of Jews among the representatives in the four domains. The percentages increase steadily as one moves from agriculture to energy to health to labor (Table 3.4). The percentage of Episcopalians, Presbyterians, and Congregationalists, called "Type I Protestants" in the table and intended to represent Protestants of higher socioeconomic status, is the mirror image of the percentage of Jews: The order in which the Jewish percentage increases is also the order in which the Type I Protestant percentage decreases. These differences no doubt reflect the composition of the client groups served by the representatives. Agriculture and energy contain higher proportions of businesses and trade associations, while health and labor contain more nonprofit organizations, professional associations, and unions. Business organizations have a marked tendency to recruit upper-status white Protestants, while other organizations recruit from more diverse social backgrounds. The mirror-image character of the distribution of Jews and Type I Protestants continues if one looks at organizational position. Jews are especially numerous among government affairs officers of professional associations and labor unions, while Type I Protestants are underrepresented in both of those categories. The opposite is true of the government affairs officers of trade associations, where high-status Protestants are numerous and Jews are few.

In three of the four policy domains, the proportion of Catholic representatives is constant, but the fourth domain, agriculture, has markedly fewer. This would again appear to reflect the composition of the constituency or clientele. Though the differences in the distribution of Catholic representatives across the organizational positions is less pronounced than is the case with Jews and Protestants, their percentages tend to be relatively low among the representatives of professional associations and nonprofit organizations and high among the representatives of unions and citizen or government organizations.

Overall, the characteristics of the representatives appear to reflect the nature of the clients they serve. This finding may suggest that the representatives are not drawn from a pool of free agents residing in Washington who possess special skills or special access to the councils of government and who are then selected to maximize such skills or access, but rather that the representatives are recruited from within the client constituencies themselves—that is, that the clients "grow their own." Alternatively, the clients may hire autonomous or semiautonomous Washington experts but select them to resemble themselves. Unless a resemblance to the client is thought to enhance the effectiveness of the representatives (perhaps because the government officials working in the policy area share the social attributes of both the clients and the representatives), however, clients would seem to select their representatives by criteria other than the maximization of skill or access. This may reflect the value placed on trust or confidence in the selection of Washington representatives. Clients may tend to choose representatives who have grown up in their own industry or organization, or who at least share their social characteristics, because they believe that such persons are more to be trusted than are autonomous experts. If the matters at issue are of great moment or consequence for the client's interests, perhaps involving the handling of confidential information and the sensitivities of important personalities, the client may prefer to entrust the matter to a representative who will intuitively understand, one who can be counted on, one with whom the client will feel comfortable—in short, one who thinks like, talks like, and looks like the client.

Patterns of regional variation in recruitment are also affected by whether the clients develop their own representatives. Systematic variation in the regional origins of the representatives may indicate that the clients recruit them through networks that are specific to the client groups. We found that far more of the representatives working on health and labor issues had resided in the Northeast during their high school years. Conversely, the agriculture and energy domains employ much higher percentages of representatives with southern and western origins (Table 3.4). Again, these patterns appear to reflect the clientele: agriculture and energy constituencies are more often located in the South and West (even allowing for the many agribusiness and food distribution interests that are active on agriculture issues, and the financiers and industrial consumers that concern themselves with energy policy). The medical establishment that is active on health issues is disproportionately concentrated in the Northeast; and the leaders of organized labor, as well as the management of large manufacturing concerns that employ a major share of union workers, come in large measure from the old industrial cities of the North and East. The highest percentages of representatives of Northeast origin are found among the government affairs officers of professional associations (mostly in the health domain) and of citizen or government organizations. If an eastern establishment is truly dominant in any of the four policy domains we studied, this is where its dominance appears to be greatest, at least in terms of numbers.

If we examine whether the representatives spent their high school years in a city with a population of at least 250,000 or in a suburb of such a city (Table 3.4, "Metropolitan Area Origins"), we again find substantial differences among the domains, differences that are closely associated with the patterns just discussed. More than half of the representatives active in the health and labor domains came from metropolitan areas, but little more than a quarter of those who work on agriculture issues did. Similarly, two-thirds of the government relations officers of professional associations were raised in cities or suburbs, while less than a quarter of their counterparts in trade associations were.

In sum, we find that these social background variables display strong patterns of differentiation that are clearly interpretable as the effects of selective recruitment by the varying client groups, with the clients appearing to exhibit a preference for representatives who resemble themselves. It is possible that the representatives rather than the clients do the selecting, but we doubt it. In any event, it is clear that if the representatives of the varying client groups come from a common pool, they are differentially recruited from that pool. The social background characteristics of the representatives are not independent of their organizational positions or of the kinds of work they do, but rather are associated with the characteristics of the clients they serve.

Representatives' Professional Characteristics

At the time of our study, some 60% of the Senate and 44% of the House members held law degrees (Congressional Quarterly 1983). Given the rapidly increasing number of lawyers in the District of

Columbia, we might expect lawyers to be the predominant group among private representatives. In fact, although lawyers are by far the largest professional group among the representatives, only a third hold law degrees. We lack solid longitudinal data for comparisons over time, but 43% of Milbrath's (1963) sample of registered lobbyists, interviewed in the late 1950s, were educated in law.[2] Of the representatives in our sample who were registered as lobbyists, 41% hold law degrees. Thus, the available evidence suggests that the proportion of lawyers actively involved in national policy making has stayed roughly the same since that time. Two-thirds of the representatives with law degrees work in law firms or serve as inside counsel; lawyers fill only 14% of the nonlaw positions. The proportion is somewhat higher among the government affairs staffs of citizen-government groups and among trade association executives, in part perhaps because of the sensitivity of trade association activity to the antitrust laws. This distribution of lawyers suggests that they usually become involved in policy making in their capacity as legal experts rather than in other occupational positions.

But is the role of lawyers in firms and on internal legal staffs limited to narrow questions of legal technique or doctrine? Or does it characteristically include broader participation in the development of clients' policy objectives? If lawyers are valued for their general wisdom or sound judgment, this quality might be equally valued in all four of the domains. But we find that the percentage of representatives who are lawyers is ten to fifteen points lower in the agriculture and health domains than it is in energy and labor. Formal legal procedures are relatively less important in agriculture and health, with the exception of some international trade issues, food and drug regulation, and the adjudicatory machinery established to settle claims concerning health care financing. As a result, there appears to be less demand in those fields for the special skills of lawyers. The energy and labor domains have substantially more lawyers. In energy, adversarial proceedings over pricing policies, the licensing of nuclear plants, and compliance with new environmental and conservation requirements have been important components of policy activity, and may have increased the prominence of the role lawyers play. In labor, lawyers have been key intermediaries in contests between labor and management in matters before the NLRB and in congressional battles over proposed changes in the law governing labor-management relationships. Moreover, industries subject to a variety of regulations concerning employment standards, occupational safety, and migrant labor retain lawyers to represent them in potentially adversarial relationships with government (Nelson and Heinz 1988, Table 6, 258–259).

Graduate education other than legal training is also common among the representatives. As a group, representatives are extremely well educated, some 91% having graduated from college and 74% having attended graduate or professional school. Advanced science or medical degrees are not uncommon among representatives working in the agriculture, energy, and health domains, the domains that are based in particular technologies; a sixth to a fifth of the representatives in these domains hold such degrees. Another third of the representatives hold advanced degrees in fields other than law, science, or medicine, but this category includes a broad range of degrees, from business to economics to the humanities and journalism, with no discernible concentration. Thus, though representatives are well educated, there is no single professional identity that most representatives share. Representatives come from a variety of disciplines and largely work in nonprofessional settings. Therefore, the high level of professional education among them does not necessarily imply a distinct or autonomous professional role. For many with professional training, commitment to the employer and to the client is probably much stronger and more immediately reinforced by organizational factors than is commitment to professional norms.

The standing of the various types of representatives might be measured by the price of their services, as well as by professional status. Washington representation is indeed lucrative. In 1982, the median income from the representatives' principal employment was $65,000 as compared to a national median household income of $20,171 (U.S. Bureau of the Census 1991, 449, table 722). Income varies by domain, from a low of $55,000 in labor to a high of $75,000 in energy, but these differences in earnings are overshadowed by the differences among the organizational position categories. The best-paid representatives are lawyers in law firms, whose median earnings were $137,000, more than twice the median of the sample as a whole. Next in rank are the business executives, at $112,000. Median earnings drop off substantially for other groups, ranging from $85,000 for the executives of trade associations to only $35,000 for the government affairs officers of citizen-government groups.

The income differences among positions are in part explained by age. The staffs of citizen-government groups, on average, are both the youngest and the least well paid. But age is not the principal determinant of income. In a multivariate analysis, it accounts for only 16% of the variance in income, substantially less than the 28% explained by organizational position. The principal explanation of the differences among organizations would appear to be differences in organizational resources. Representatives of business organizations, trade associations, and professional associations get substantially greater economic rewards than do representatives of nonprofit institutions, unions, or citizen-government groups.

One might expect Washington representatives to live in the Washington area, but we found that only about two-thirds of them do. Not surprisingly, fewer of the executives of businesses and nonprofit organizations live in the area; less than a third do. Other organizational employees, with the exception of government affairs personnel, are only slightly more likely to live in Washington than elsewhere. Even though more than 60% of the unions in our sample are headquartered in the D.C. area, only 40% of the representatives who are union executives reside there. This may indicate that unions prefer to use officials of their locals for some purposes, such as lobbying Congress.

The preeminent veterans of the Washington battles are the independent consultants and law-firm-based attorneys. More than three-quarters of both categories live in Washington. They have been there for an average of twenty years, which may help to explain the attention that the media gives these representatives. In the 1970s or before, it may have been appropriate to think of lawyers and consultants as the core of the Washington community. But there are clear signs of the erosion of their position. Our interviews indicate that many more lawyers work in the branch offices of out-of-town firms or even commute to Washington. A bare majority of the external lawyers work in firms that have their principal offices in Washington. Nearly a quarter live in other cities, mostly such major urban centers as New York, Chicago, and Los Angeles, and these lawyers reported that they spend an average of about two or three days a month in Washington. Moreover, the government affairs staffs of interest organizations, a newer set of arrivals in Washington, appear to have gained a larger share of the work. A great majority of them maintain a permanent Washington base. They have resided in Washington for twelve years on the average, four years less than the average of Washington-based representatives as a whole and eight years less than the external lawyers and consultants. This suggests that government affairs work is a faster-growing element of private representation; and, as we shall see, government affairs personnel are more deeply involved in policy activities than are other representatives.

For the four-fifths of the representatives who are organizational employees, the number of years at the current employer is a useful measure of the strength of the ties between representatives and organizations. If representatives circulated freely, working only brief stints with any one employer, that would suggest that organizational loyalty is not a particularly important feature of representation and that the demand for the skills of representatives is sufficient to assure them opportunities elsewhere. But representatives have usually spent more than a decade with their current employer. Executives tend to have especially long relationships with their organizations, as do the government affairs personnel of businesses and unions. The major exceptions to this pattern are the representatives of professional associations and citizen-government groups, and the government affairs representatives of trade associations. Even these categories have an average tenure of seven to ten years, however, in spite of the relative recency of the arrival of these organizations in Washington, the age of their representatives, and, for the citizen-government groups, higher levels of turnover resulting from relatively low pay. It is clear, therefore, that most representatives maintain stable employment relationships. The vast majority have devoted many years to their current employer and are likely to identify with, and indeed to have had a hand in developing, the policy positions of the organization.

Like their personal characteristics, then, the professional characteristics of the representatives suggest that they are unlikely to play autonomous roles. Though three-fourths of the representatives had some advanced education and thus might bring a professional orientation to their work, most have strong countervailing characteristics that enhance identification with the client or employing organization. Many representatives are based outside Washington at the headquarters of their organizations, and most have spent substantial portions of their careers working for their organizations.

Representatives' Political Characteristics

Partisan politics play a prominent part in some types of representation. Notable lobbyists and lawyers are often identified with a particular party or presidential administration, and the reputation for access to party leaders can be a lucrative commodity. But there are also risks in being identified as a partisan. The strong partisan may lose access to opponents in important policy-making positions and may appeal only to a narrow clientele. Whether representatives can avoid involvement in partisan politics depends in part on the configuration of the domains in which they participate. It is less likely that a representative will maintain political neutrality in an ideologically polarized domain, such as labor, than in a domain in which interest group coalitions are more fluid or in which there is no clear identification between particular interest groups and the national political parties. In some contexts, there is an informal norm that it is illegitimate for government officials to take account of the party affiliation of representatives, and in most contexts it is not done openly or explicitly. For example, rumors that the Department of the Interior under James Watt looked unfavorably on lawyers with Democratic party ties touched off a furor ("Don't come around here with any of your Democrat lawyers" was the reported statement; *New York Times,* Feb. 2, 1982, p. 10).

The political orientation and involvement of representatives is both theoretically and practically significant. To the extent that representatives influence the course of policy, it is important to know what political values motivate them. Their values may also indicate the degree of their autonomy from clients. Do representatives have values that differ from those of their clients, and do they thus seek to modify client demands? Or do they share the values of their clients? Chapter 6 addresses these questions. Here, we will merely note their party affiliations.

According to the folklore of Washington, more private representatives are Democrats than Republicans, perhaps because Democrats are more susceptible to Potomac fever—the malady that breeds a desire to work in the shadow of the federal government—and perhaps because Republican officeholders, who are far more likely than Democrats to have been recruited from business, have better opportunities outside of Washington after leaving the government. We found some support for this folk wisdom. A larger proportion of representatives identified themselves as Democrats (41%) than as Republicans (32%) or independents (24%). Among freestanding representatives (external lawyers and consultants), Democrats outnumber Republicans roughly two to one. But party affiliation also varies significantly by domain and organization position. In the health and labor domains,

Democrats outnumber Republicans two to one, but Republicans hold a substantial plurality among energy representatives and just exceed the number of Democrats in agriculture. These differences correspond to the types of organizations active in the domains. As one would expect, a large proportion of the representatives of businesses and trade associations are Republicans, while most labor union representatives are Democrats. Nonprofit organizations and professional associations are more balanced politically.

These political differences by domain and organization type, while hardly surprising, have important implications. They suggest that policies are made in differing ideological and political environments. Moreover, just as the social background characteristics of representatives mirror those of their clients, the political party affiliations of representatives reflect the clients' politics.

Most representatives claimed, however, that partisan political involvement is not significant for them. A majority said that party affiliation never affects their work, though this response varied significantly by domain and organizational position. Health is perceived as the least politicized domain, but this cannot be disentangled from the effect of organization type. Nonprofit organizations and professional associations have higher percentages reporting that party affiliation does not affect their work. In sharp contrast, representatives of unions are most identified with party politics—only a quarter of union executives said that party affiliation never affects their work—and most representatives of businesses and trade associations also acknowledged that party affiliation sometimes matters.

Participation in political fund-raising, which has become a prominent and much-watched element of national politics (Sorauf 1988), follows similar patterns. Half of the representatives had contributed to a political action committee, but PACs are a far more important form of fund-raising in energy and labor than in agriculture or health; and PAC contributions are very much a part of doing business in certain organizations (Clawson and Neustadtl 1989). More than three-quarters of the executives and government affairs officers of businesses and unions gave to PACs, as did a majority of the executives of professional associations. The only categories in which fewer than one-third of the representatives made PAC donations are the executives of nonprofit organizations and citizen-government groups, external lawyers, and consultants. As a matter of organizational style, nonprofit organizations such as universities and hospitals act through forms of representation other than PACs. Citizen groups are political organizations in their own right; instead of attempting to influence electoral politics through campaign contributions, their engagement in direct political activity usually consists of rating voting records and making endorsements.

Only a quarter of the representatives have held positions of party leadership, such as committee member or convention delegate, but more have participated in political campaigns. Union representatives and government affairs personnel have the highest incidence of leadership positions and of campaign involvement.

In sum, patterns of partisan activity reflect the political attributes and strategies of clients and the nature of the environments in which the clients are located. For the most part, therefore, representatives do not transcend the political divisions that exist among various interest groups; they reproduce them.

Conclusion

The policy domains are populated by very different sets of organizations, which retain lobbyists from a variety of professional and disciplinary backgrounds. The complexity of this world defies simple description and explanation. Yet, as the ensuing chapters demonstrate, many of the variables conform to coherent, interpretable structural patterns. The functionalist model of interest representation articulated by Parsons (1954) and Horsky (1952) saw representation as a process in which autonomous professionals, mostly lawyers, were key actors. The basis for professional power was expertise in government procedures, as well as in the complex subject matter of national policy. Because interest groups relied on their expertise, professional representatives were in a position to educate their clients to the systemic implications of various strategies and positions, and thus to engender a collective orientation. But Parsons and Horsky did not recognize (or, if things have changed since they wrote, did not foresee) the power and inclination of clients to exert control over representatives. It is clear from our preliminary analyses that independent professionals make up a relatively small portion of representatives, and that client organizations recruit representatives according to regional, ethnic, and political affinities. These findings suggest that the influence of representatives more often derives from their positions within client organizations than from substantive expertise or professional status. The representative who is closely identified with particular clients, and whose influence is derived from those clients, is less likely to act as an independent mediator in political decisions and, thus, less likely to occupy the core of the policy-making system.

Part II

The Washington Representatives

Chapter 4

The Organization of Work

The work of Washington representatives is highly varied: some are business executives who devote a major share of their time to organizational management, including personnel matters and budget decisions; some are government affairs officers for corporations, trade associations, or unions who devote almost all of their time to policy activities; others are lawyers who spend part of their time on conventional legal work; and some are doctors, scientists, or other sorts of substantive experts. Some do high-powered lobbying that is dramatic and visible; others pursue tasks that are more mundane, such as monitoring policy developments and compiling technical information, but that may have greater cumulative impact on policy outcomes. Some focus mainly on the "Hill"; others exploit close relationships with officials in the executive branch. But how common is each of these types of work? And which representatives do which parts of the work? Organizational titles are not a sufficient guide to their activities, especially when we compare very different sorts of organizations. The job of an executive in a professional association, for example, is very different from that of a business executive. To understand what Washington representatives do, therefore, it is necessary to look closely at the work of the several types of representatives.

We begin by analyzing three aspects of the work: general work activities, substantive specialization, and patterns of contact with government agencies. In general, and with some notable exceptions, we find that representatives do not focus attention on a specific area of public policy or a particular government institution. Instead, the work of representatives is defined primarily by the interests of client organizations—interests that characteristically require involvement in several policy areas before many agencies.

General Work Activities

We asked representatives how they allocated their time among five broad categories of work—federal policy activity, state policy activity, organizational activity, conventional law practice, and other activities (such as business ventures and research).[1] Table 4.1 presents the findings. As might be expected given the nature of the sample, the majority of time is spent on policy work. Most of this is at the national level (though a nontrivial fraction involves state policy). On average, and with substantial variation among organizational roles, interest representatives spend a surprisingly large portion of their time on the internal affairs of their organizations. It would be stretching things,

Table 4.1 Proportion of time spent on general work activities, by domain and position (percentages)

	Conventional law practice	Federal policy	State policy	Organizational duties	Other activities	N
Domain	*	**	*		**	
Agriculture	8	42	9	33	8	188
Energy	6	47	10	32	5	179
Health	7	38	11	35	9	206
Labor	11	40	7	33	8	193
All domains	8	42	9	33	7	766
Organizational position	**	**	**	**	**	
Executives						
Business	1	33	11	47	9	43
Nonprofit organizations	0.1	32	10	47	11	34
Trade associations	1	43	9	39	7	140
Unions	0.4	23	7	66	4	24
Professional associations	2	30	9	43	15	38
Citizen-govt. groups	4	28	19	44	6	50
Government affairs						
Business	0	57	9	31	2	35
Trade associations	0.3	56	9	28	7	54
Unions	0	60	6	29	5	30
Professional associations	1	54	6	34	5	27
Citizen-govt. groups	0.2	55	11	29	4	27
Internal lawyers	23	34	12	28	3	47
Research staff	0.8	42	10	36	11	75
External lawyers	42	39	5	10	4	108
Consultants	0.6	46	9	23	21	34

* F-statistic $p < .05$. ** $p < .01$.

perhaps, to suggest that this is a confirmation of Olson's (1965) conception of lobbying as a by-product of organizations' attempts to provide selective benefits to their members, but these data do emphasize the point that external representation and internal management are undertaken by the same people and therefore are closely tied together. It is interesting also that there is virtually no difference among the four policy domains in the amount of time spent on internal management. It appears to be a remarkably constant imperative of interest group operation.

Work activities vary considerably by organization position. Obviously, only the lawyers devote a substantial proportion of their time to law practice. Even they, however, spend a surprisingly small amount of time on conventional legal matters. To be sure, some of the policy work they do may include test case litigation and other efforts at changing policy through the law, but only 25% of the external lawyers and 20% of the internal lawyers deal with the federal courts "regularly," and only a minority of both categories reported that litigation to change policy was of "considerable" or "great" importance to their work. Representatives who hold law degrees but occupy executive or other staff positions spend an average of only 4% of their time on conventional law practice. Their work does not appear to be very different from that of nonlawyers.

The representatives most actively involved in policy work are government affairs officers and executives of trade associations, who generally occupy functionally equivalent roles. In most organizations, the executives are engaged primarily in running the organization. It is interesting to observe, however, that most of the employee roles entail substantial responsibilities for organizational maintenance. The principal exception is the external lawyers.

The patterns of time allocation indicate three distinct roles. The policy specialist is the most numerous category, consisting primarily of government affairs officers, executives of trade associations, internal staff, and external consultants. The central players in this category are government affairs officers and trade association executives. A second group consists of executives of corporations, union officers, and so on. It is sometimes necessary for the CEO to present formal testimony or otherwise speak for the organization if full legitimacy is to be accorded. The Business Roundtable has demonstrated that CEOs may influence Congress with their direct presence where less prestigious representation fails. Nevertheless, executives must also manage their organizations, and this limits their potential as interest representatives. The third group is the lawyers, both internal and external. They divide their time between conventional law practice and policy activity, but what is distinctive about them is the extent to which they focus their efforts on formally contested matters.

There is relatively little place in our data for the rainmakers and movers and shakers whose alleged exploits fill the Sunday supplements and energize reformers' zeal. We find that most of those who represent private interests in Washington attend to the specific needs of the organizations for which they work. Few are free agents. Among those who are, such as the external lawyers, much of what they do is of quite limited scope.

Substantive Specialization

In chapter 3, we commented on Heclo's (1978) suggestion that the policy-making processes of executive agencies are heavily influenced by "issue networks" that consist of policy experts who move back and forth between government jobs and positions in private organizations. We observed that it may be necessary for interest organizations to buy into such networks by recruiting substantive policy specialists. Alternatively, organizations may attempt to cultivate their own set of substantive experts by assigning particular fields to employees. However organizations go about acquiring substantive expertise, the work of representatives will reflect patterns of substantive specialization to the extent that such specialization is thought important to effective representation. In some domains, substantive issues may be sharply differentiated, permitting a high degree of specialization. Alternatively, there may be considerable overlap—as, for example, between energy and environmental issues.

To examine the degree of substantive specialization, we asked respondents who spent more than 5% of their time on federal policy to indicate how they allocated their time among a list of twenty general policy areas including, in addition to the four domains, such fields as civil rights, domestic economics, defense, and foreign affairs.[2] Respondents were also asked to indicate their allocation of time among a set of policy subfields within the domain.

Table 4.2 presents the basic findings. At first glance, representatives appear not to be highly specialized. They devote time to several broad policy areas, and although there are differences among the policy

Table 4.2 Patterns of substantive specialization, by domain and position

	No. of federal policy fields worked in	% Federal policy time on domain in which they were sampled	% of Domain subfields worked in	% Time in domain spent in principal subfield	N
Domain	**	**	**	**	
Agriculture	5.6	65	48	65	171
Energy	4.6	73	62	54	169
Health	4.7	77	61	55	175
Labor	5.9	59	52	56	165
All domains	5.2	69	56	58	680
Organizational Position	**	**	**	**	
Executives					
Business	4.8	64	60	57	35
Nonprofit organization	5.5	69	55	53	26
Trade associations	5.7	63	55	57	129
Unions	6.7	59	54	64	25
Professional associations	4.3	85	68	52	34
Citizen-govt. groups	5.9	70	54	55	39
Government affairs					
Business	5.3	68	63	47	35
Trade associations	5.7	60	56	60	53
Unions	9.8	50	61	44	29
Professional associations	3.4	91	77	47	25
Citizen-govt. groups	6.7	62	52	66	27
Internal lawyers	4.3	71	50	67	38
Research staff	5.1	71	60	55	66
External lawyers	3.2	73	41	68	95
Consultants	4.7	87	57	54	29

** F-statistic $p < .01$.

domains, none can be said to be narrowly focused. The differences among the domains appear to reflect variation in the scope of the interests of the organizations active in the domains. Thus, labor unions participate in a wide range of issues, as indicated by the fact that the government affairs officers of unions spend time in an average of almost ten policy areas. This reflects the long-standing philosophy of the AFL-CIO and many individual unions that it is their duty to represent workers on a broad range of economic and social issues (Bok and Dunlop 1970, 395–403). The representatives of two other categories of collective purpose organizations, citizen groups and trade associations, also devote time to a broader array of policy areas than does the sample as a whole. The range of their interests may reflect a greater diversity of internal constituencies. Peak business associations, such as the Chamber of Commerce or the National Association of Manufacturers, necessarily give attention to many policy areas. In contrast, the interest organizations with the most focused concerns are individual business corporations and professional associations. This pattern is consistent with reports from the literature on political action committees that such organizations take a more pragmatic view of politics, pursue policy goals of a more narrow, instrumental nature, and are less often caught up in symbolic or ideologically framed disputes (Sorauf 1988).

It is interesting to discover that external lawyers display relatively narrow sets of policy concerns. This finding runs counter to the image of Washington lawyers as policy-making generalists, available for hire on a wide range of issues. A few such mandarins of the bar may exist, but the modal pattern is for Washington lawyers to specialize in a relatively small number of substantive fields.

Although representatives typically spend some time in several fields, they do tend to concentrate on a particular substantive area. In order not to give too narrow a definition to policy categories, we combined some that were obviously close to one another[3] and found that more than two-thirds of total federal policy effort was in the domain for which the representative was interviewed. Given the fact that the sample was not explicitly drawn from substantive specialists and thus may include some representatives whose specialty lies outside the domain for which they were sampled, this finding would appear to indicate considerable specialization.

The proportion of time devoted to the domain varies by domain and organizational position. Representatives in labor and agriculture are somewhat less specialized than those in energy and health. Representatives of professional associations active in the health domain are extremely specialized; their government affairs officers allocate 91% of their time to that domain. Labor unions have broad policy agendas; accordingly, government affairs officers of unions spend only half of their federal policy time in the domain for which they were sampled. Consultants are among the most specialized; they devote an average of 87% of their policy time to the domain. Clearly, the expertise they bring to bear tends to be specific to the policy domain rather than to the process of policy formation. But the external lawyers, whose special credentials relate to the legal process, are also relatively specialized in substantive policy.

Each of the four domains we have chosen to examine in depth is a complex policy-making system embracing several relatively distinct subsystems of activity. Thus, for example, representatives may work on health cost issues and never get involved in medical research or food and drug regulation. On the basis of extensive preliminary investigation, we developed lists of subfields that covered the major specialties within each domain. A list was presented to the respondents, and they were asked to indicate how they spent their time.[4]

Just as representatives tend to specialize in a particular domain, they concentrate on one subfield within the domain. Of the time spent on the domain for which they were sampled, they spend an average of 58% on one subfield. Agriculture representatives are a bit more specialized, spending 65% of their time on their principal subfield. At the subfield level, the most specialized representatives are the external lawyers, who devote more than two-thirds of their time to their leading subfield. The least specialized are the government affairs representatives of unions. This essentially parallels our findings regarding domain specialization.

The average representative spends some time in more than half of the major substantive areas in the domain. The scope of coverage is somewhat broader in energy and health than in agriculture and labor. The differences are not very large, but the pattern is the opposite of that we found for work outside the domains, where agriculture and labor representatives had the broader range of involvement. This suggests that there is more internal differentiation among the interest configurations in agriculture and labor; there may be little interdependence between food safety and price supports, for instance, or job safety and pension issues. Professional associations, on the other hand, most of which are in health, are interested in only a very few broad policy domains, but they are concerned with a wide range of policies within their jurisdiction. The most specialized representatives, again, were the lawyers.

While these findings reflect some specialization by domain and by subfield within domain, the measures of concentration that we have used may overstate the degree of substantive specialization. The measures are based on allocations of time spent on federal policy and time in a domain. But the sample as a whole spends only 42% of its time on federal policy work (see Table 4.1). When time spent on the policy domain is weighted by the proportion of total time devoted to federal policy, we find that representatives, on average, spend barely more than a quarter of their time on the policy domain for which they were sampled and only 15% of their total time on their principal subfield.

The scope and intensity of time commitments to substantive fields do not appear to be determined by the nature of the fields themselves. One might expect some fields to involve more complex or technically demanding subjects, which would result in a greater proportion of experts in these fields, while fields requiring less investment in mastery of the subject matter would be populated more by generalists. Heinz and Laumann's analysis of time allocation by lawyers suggested such a pattern of specialization, though the pattern was also associated with the type of client served (1982, 43–48). On the whole, we did not find such a pattern. Rather, we found organizational position to be a stronger determinant of the time commitments of representatives. It appears that the allocation of work is driven by organizational variables more than by the technical demands of substantive areas. It may also be that the structure of work is mandated by the nature of the general objective: access to and influence upon government officials. Similarities in task profiles across both policy domains and organizational positions may result from the fact that all interest groups face essentially the same challenge. Said differently, the governmental structures may impose very similar imperatives regardless of the specifics of policy substance or interest group type.

Contacts with Government Agencies

To assess the degree to which representation is organized around government institutions, we examined patterns of contact between representatives and federal agencies. The received wisdom suggests that a significant proportion of Washington representatives specialize in particular government institutions—Congress, the White House, the Food and Drug Administration. The "revolving door," after all, posits an institutionally based model of representation in which representatives lobby their former employers. Other institutional theories of representation also suggest that representatives will concentrate on particular government targets—for example, the argument that much of the policy-making power in Washington is held by "iron triangles" composed of the executive agency charged with responsibility for specific policies, the congressional subcommittee with jurisdiction over these policies, and the interest groups directly affected.

To examine the relationships between representatives and government institutions, we presented the representatives with an extensive inventory of agencies involved in each domain (including congressional committees, independent commissions, executive agencies, the federal courts, the White House, and the majority and minority leadership in both houses of Congress) and asked them to indicate whether during the last year they had contacted each "occasionally," "several times," or "regularly." Table 4.3 presents some of the findings.

Representatives in the labor domain have regular contact with fewer government organizations than do those in the other three domains.[5] For the most part, this is because union executives reported a lower level of regular contacts and, of greater political interest, union government affairs officers maintain few regular contacts with executive branch (at the time, Reagan Administration) agencies. On the Hill, also, union people clearly prefer working with Democrats, reporting higher levels of contact with them in both the House and the Senate despite the fact that Republicans controlled the Senate at the time of the interviews. The percentage of union government affairs officers who maintained regular contact with the Senate and House Democratic leadership is more than three times as great as the percentage of other representatives; the percentage who maintain regular contact with the Republican leadership of the two bodies, however, is only about half of the average for the whole sample.

Frequency of contact with a given level of position—congressional leaders, say, or the executive department of primary concern to the domain—is remarkably constant across policy domains, a point to be explored more fully in chapter 7. As noted above, we would not have been surprised to find that representatives tended to specialize in either the legislative or the executive branch, depending perhaps on their personal background or the special needs of their client organizations. In fact, however, branch specialization does not characterize contact patterns. More than two-fifths of the representatives reported that they maintain *regular* contact with agencies in *both* the legislative and executive branches. Of the policy specialists, only the government affairs personnel of unions and the external consultants specialize in a particular branch. Again reflecting the antagonism between organized labor and the Reagan administration, a majority of the union government affairs representatives have regular contact

Table 4.3 Contacts with government organizations, by domain and position

	Mean no. of regular contacts with govt. orgs. in domain	% Who regularly contact					N
		No orgs.	Both legislative and executive branch orgs.	Only legislative branch orgs.	Only executive branch orgs.	Federal courts	
Domain						**	
Agriculture	5.5	22	49	9	18	3	192
Energy	5.3	25	44	11	18	5	184
Health	5.3	21	45	10	22	4	206
Labor	4.3	27	34	15	16	11	194
All domains	5.1	24	43*	11	19	6	776
Organizational position	**	**	**	**	**	**	
Executives							
Business	4.0	30	33	16	21	0	43
Nonprofit organizations	3.4	43	29	11	17	3	35
Trade associations	6.5	23	53	13	11	0	144
Unions	3.0	52	20	4	24	4	25
Professional associations	4.5	16	42	11	32	0	38
Citizen-govt. groups	5.0	23	44	8	25	8	52
Government affairs							
Business	6.1	26	49	20	6	0	35
Trade associations	7.3	9	65	19	7	0	54
Unions	5.9	10	37	53	0	0	30
Professional associations	8.7	4	70	11	15	4	27
Citizen-govt. groups	7.4	11	63	19	7	0	27
Internal lawyers	4.1	23	38	2	21	19	47
Research staff	3.2	41	32	1	26	3	76
External lawyers	3.6	20	35	5	23	26	108
Consultants	5.1	17	31	6	43	3	35

* F-statistic $p < .05$. ** $p < .01$.

only with legislative branch units; none works exclusively with executive branch units, and only 37% have any regular contact with executive units. By contrast, external consultants tend to work exclusively with executive agencies. More than two-fifths of the consultants, twice the proportion in the sample as a whole, deal regularly with executive agencies only. The consultant category includes a considerable number of representatives who focus on matters of administrative regulation and policy implementation. The executives of professional organizations also tend to concentrate their attention on the executive branch. It may be that health policy issues, which are the principal concern of the professional associations in our sample, are dealt with in larger measure by the executive branch agencies.

Lawyers again are a distinctive group. Not surprisingly, virtually the only representatives who contact the federal courts regularly are lawyers—but this is true of only a fifth to a quarter of both internal and external lawyers. Executive agencies are more important to lawyers than are congressional contacts: lawyer representatives are distinct from most other Washington representatives in their relatively low level of contacts with Congress and their relatively high level of contacts with courts and regulatory bodies. Even though lawyer representatives spend less time on conventional law practice than do other lawyers, traditional venues of the legal profession constitute the principal base for their participation in national policy making.

In examining specialization by branch of government, we may miss (or misinterpret) more subtle patterns of interrelationships between representatives and government agencies. A representative working narrowly in an "iron triangle" of relationships involving the client, a single congressional committee, and a particular executive agency is not distinguished in this analysis from representatives with a broad array of contacts. But fewer than a seventh of the respondents reported regular contact with only one government institution; only five respondents said that, over the past year, they had contacted just a single agency. Perhaps most surprising is the relative absence of the "Hill specialist," a figure celebrated in popular writing on the Washington lobbyist but elusive in systematic empirical work. Little more than a tenth of our sample specialize solely in legislative branch contacts. Milbrath found that his sample of lobbyists spent surprisingly little time "calling on members of Congress" and "chatting with people on the Hill." The modal category for each was 6 to 10% of their time (Milbrath 1963, 117). The prevalent pattern in Milbrath's findings and ours is that regular contacts are maintained by each representative with a cluster of agencies in both the legislative and executive branches. Whether contacts with government agencies are driven by client interests or by substantive expertise, only rarely are they confined to a single institutional location.

Task Differentiation

To examine the range of tasks performed by the different types of representatives, we presented respondents with a lengthy inventory of activities and asked them to indicate the importance of each in their work. Table 4.4 lists the eighteen items, the loading of each on four factors produced from a factor analysis of the items, and the percentage of respondents reporting each to be of "considerable" or "great" importance.[6]

The four factors are readily interpretable. The first appears to be a government relations dimension. All items that load highly on this factor concern interactions with the government, including formal interactions (for example, drafting legislation or providing written information to officials), informal contacts with officials, and monitoring of changes in public law. The second factor concerns relations with nongovernment groups, such as mobilizing grass-roots support and maintaining contacts with other groups, both allies and adversaries. Factor three concerns the preparation of public statements, such as testimony for official proceedings, speeches, comments for the press, and position papers. The final factor, litigation activity, is clearly distinct. Note, however, that item 5, "Drafting legislation or rules," also has a relatively high score on this factor, clearly indicating the affinity among those activities characteristically or exclusively performed by lawyers. Note also that, of the eighteen tasks, the two litigation items are rated of "great" or "considerable" importance to their work by the smallest percentages of the representatives. This finding adds more support to the hypothesis that, although there are some distinctly lawyerly tasks, they are relatively marginal to policy making.

To analyze the distribution of these task clusters across organizational positions, we report in Table 4.5 a breakdown of mean factor scores by position.[7] A clear pattern emerges. Government affairs personnel and trade association executives have the highest scores on both the government relations and interest group network functions.

Table 4.4 Importance ratings of representatives' tasks: factor pattern and percentage distribution

Variable number	Task description	Factor 1: government relations	Factor 2: interest group networks	Factor 3: public presentation	Factor 4: litigation	% Great or considerable importance
Government regulations						
1	Monitoring changes in rules, regulations, or laws	.70	.17	.04	.17	62
2	Providing written information to officials	.64	.11	.38	.10	52
3	Maintaining general relations with officials	.58	.50	.10	-.12	64
4	Maintaining informal, substantive contacts with officials	.55	.43	.20	-.05	62
5	Drafting legislation or rules	.47	.10	.37	.33	27
6	Alerting client organization about issues	.42	.29	.17	-.01	84
Interest group networks						
7	Mobilizing grass-roots support	.10	.61	.28	-.06	41
8	Maintaining contacts with allies	.43	.60	.14	-.03	50
9	Monitoring interest groups	.44	.51	.11	.12	29
10	Political fund-raising (PACs)	.09	.50	-.01	.02	19
11	Maintaining contacts with adversaries	.37	.46	.15	.14	18
12	Resolving conflicts within organization	.14	.35	.20	.19	23
Public presentation						
13	Testifying at official proceedings	.10	.15	.73	.16	27
14	Preparing official testimony	.41	.00	.71	.16	47
15	Commenting for press, publications, or speeches	.07	.31	.43	.05	44
16	Developing policy positions or strategies	.33	.24	.35	.03	83
Litigation						
17	Pursuing litigation aimed at changing policy	.05	.02	.10	.77	17
18	Working on and filing amicus briefs	.06	.03	.11	.66	5

Table 4.5   Representatives' scores on four factors of tasks, by organizational position and law position

Organizational position	Factor 1: government relations	Factor 2: interest group networks	Factor 3: public presentation	Factor 4: litigation	N
Government affairs[a]	.18	.38	.10	−.19	314
Executives	−.26	.01	−.03	−.11	188
Internal staff	−.22	−.40	.22	−.22	75
Internal lawyers	.12	−.34	−.07	.69	47
External lawyers	.04	−.59	−.22	.76	108
External consultants	−.01	−.33	−.38	−.44	34
All					765
p (F test)	≤ .001	≤ .001	≤ .001	≤ .001	
R^2	.049	.189	.030	.201	

Note: Factor scores are expressed as deviations from the sample mean, which has been set equal to 0 for each factor.

a. Includes trade association executives.

The two groups of practicing lawyers place second and third on the government relations factor, suggesting that they play an important role in cultivating relationships with government officials; but they have low scores on interest group networking. Executives score negatively on all but interest group networks, suggesting that although the primary job of executives is to manage their organizations, they are necessarily in frequent contact with other members of their own organization and with other groups within the same industry or constituency. Internal staff score highest on public presentation functions. The strongest pattern in the table, however, is seen in the scores of the legal positions on the litigation factor.

Lawyers' Specialization by Field

As we reported above, measures of the scope of lawyers' work indicate that they are more specialized, substantively and institutionally, than are other representatives. Since lawyers are so often portrayed as the prime rainmakers of the Washington interest group community, we want to identify the particular substantive areas that receive most of the lawyers' attention. To this end, we compared the allocation of lawyers' time to the time allocations of the rest of the sample.[8]

In agriculture, lawyers are overrepresented among specialists in foreign trade, commodities trading, and food safety, but underrepresented in food welfare, land use, and agricultural finance. In energy, they are overrepresented in the nuclear, oil, and coal subfields and absent from the alternative energy sources subfield. In health, lawyers are overrepresented in the food and drug area, a traditional specialty of Washington law firms, and they also tend to predominate in the regulation of both health care providers and the health professions. The largest group of lawyer specialists is in health care payment and insurance, a specialty that has expanded dramatically since the adoption of Medicare and Medicaid. Lawyers are not alone in this subfield, however; indeed, they make up only 20% of its specialists. There are no lawyers among the specialists in public health or manpower training. In labor, lawyers are predominant in labor relations, employment standards, and occupational safety, but are underrepresented in two subfields with major budgetary significance—jobs programs and social security—as well as in immigration. The area of private pensions, a growth field in labor law, contains a significant number of lawyer specialists, but they are complemented by substantial numbers of nonlawyers.

The common thread running through these findings is that lawyers predominate in fields where the primary institutional actors are courts or regulatory agencies. Foreign trade, commodities trading, food safety, nuclear energy, food and drug regulation, labor relations, employment standards, and occupational safety are largely controlled by specific regulatory bodies that follow, at least in part, formal adjudicatory procedures. The regulation of health care providers and of health care professions, two areas not usually associated with legal institutions, were under active consideration by the Federal Trade Commission during the period of our study. The subfields in which lawyers are underrepresented are those in which the principal activity takes place in Congress, such as jobs programs and social security, or in the policy-oriented units of executive branch agencies, such as the public health, manpower training, and alternative energy subfields.

These data also confirm the tendency of lawyers to specialize more narrowly than other representatives. Especially in agriculture and energy, lawyers are more likely than others to spend either a majority of their time in a given subfield or no time at all. Other representatives devote time to a larger array of subfields, monitoring the whole portfolio of their employer's interests. Since lawyers tend to concentrate on particular fields, they are often overrepresented among the specialists, but in most policy areas they are still relatively few in total number.

The source of lawyers' influence is thus neither their pervasiveness among representatives nor their control of the decision-making processes of interest groups. Rather, their influence stems from specialized credentials and knowledge concerning the operation of particular substantive regulations and institutional settings. The power of lawyers in policy making is therefore contingent on the strategic importance of the institutions and substantive areas in which they are active. Lawyers are key actors in policy decisions that utilize or create formal procedures, as in labor relations, employment standards, or nuclear licensing. Thus, the National Labor Relations Board is a body made up of lawyers that adjudicates claims of unfair labor practices. Effective representation before the NLRB requires a lawyer. Client organizations are likely to consult their own labor lawyers before making tactical decisions concerning labor practices, and proposals to change the labor laws are likely to involve the specialists who apply them. But in other major policy areas that are less concerned with formal procedures, such as legislation on jobs programs, lawyers do little.

This invites questions about the origins of the institutional structures that are controlled by lawyers. One could argue that it is the power of lawyers that leads to the development of the formalized procedures they dominate, not the reverse (see, for example, Abel 1989). But if lawyers are so powerful, why does their involvement vary so much by subject matter and institutional location? If proceduralization is the result of a conspiracy of lawyers, the conspiracy has certainly not been a universal success. Moreover, the history of the subdomains in which lawyers are more prevalent suggests that proceduralization is a response to other social forces. The original food and drug laws and their subsequent amendments were a result of muckraking exposés and prominent incidents of food or drug poisoning (Friedman 1985, 46–47). Similarly, the Wagner Act, which created the present institutional apparatus in labor relations, was a response to ongoing conflicts between organized labor and business and the failure of an earlier, simpler regulatory scheme (Irons 1982, 203–253). While lawyers no doubt played a prominent role in the development of the procedural structures and rules governing these fields, the demand for their services appears to have been independent of any manipulation by lawyers; and, as the recent wave of deregulation suggests, lawyers' procedures are not immune to shifts in demand.

Conclusion

Representatives' allocations of time and effort among general work activities, substantive specialties, contacts with government agencies, and representational tasks suggest that most representatives organize their work around the interests of the client organization, wherever those interests may take them. We found only weak patterns of specialization by substantive field or government institution. Moreover, according to several measures—including the amount of time devoted to policy work, the number of substantive areas covered, and the number of agencies contacted—it appears that the central actors in the interest representation system are the "policy experts," executives of trade associations and government affairs personnel. This is another indication that the structure of interest representation is client based. The largest group of private policy-making activists are not independent professionals, but representatives based inside, and presumably strongly identified with, client organizations.

Lawyers stand out as a distinctive subset. They are a notable exception to the general lack of substantive and agency specialization. Lawyers appear to be technical specialists within a system dominated by client-based generalists. In previous eras, client organizations may have relied on outside legal counsel to monitor the Washington scene and to devise a full range of strategies. Now those functions are performed by organizational insiders.

The dramatic growth in Washington law practice is evidence of the strength of demand for legal expertise. But our data make it clear that this demand is limited to a relatively narrow set of issues and functions. Lawyers are expert in the manipulation of formal rules, both substantive and procedural. Their competitive advantage increases with the level of formality of the decision-making process. But most of the policy decisions made in Washington are not dictated by preexisting rules, nor do they depend upon the interpretation of such rules. Rather, they are explicit choices made from available policy options; there is no pretense of determining winners and losers according to established legal rights. The formalities of procedural due process are much less the rule than are telephone calls, personal visits to members of Congress and other public officials, give-and-take negotiations with allies and adversaries, and close monitoring of the trade press.

In these latter activities, lawyers have no special advantage. Non-lawyer representatives who are experienced in the ways of the federal government are probably at least as skilled as lawyers in these procedures. Moreover, although many lawyers have considerable substantive expertise in the area of their specialization, they certainly have no monopoly on such substantive knowledge (and probably no comparative advantage). In the policy areas we studied, knowledge of medicine, agronomy, international trade, geological engineering, or mine safety is often useful, even necessary, to the representatives; we found many with these educational backgrounds. Whatever the claims of legal education, lawyers seem unlikely to match the substantive authority of representatives with M.D.'s, or Ph.D.'s in nuclear physics, who have spent their entire careers working in health care or atomic energy. As regulatory and other policy issues become more detailed and complex, effective representation requires substantive expertise, and that expertise must include command not only of the policy questions in all their technical specifics but of the position of the client organization itself and how it may be affected by alternative policy choices. Thus, the apparent preference for representatives who are substantive experts and organizational insiders reflects the decision-making requirements of both interest groups and government agencies.

Chapter 5

The Careers of Representatives

The careers of Washington representatives shape and are shaped by the social structure of representation. It is no wonder, then, that many of the conventional images of lobbying draw on accounts of representatives' careers. The revolving door hypothesis, for example, posits that the ranks of lobbyists are filled by people who have moved to the private sector from positions in government (Herring 1929; Deakin 1966). This is usually lamented. The revolving door is said to be an important mechanism for creating and maintaining "cozy triangles" of mutual support among congressional committees, executive agencies, and private interest groups; these symbiotic relationships, in turn, are held responsible for the size and intractability of the federal budget. A suggestion of scandal colors the hypothesis, which is often illustrated with accounts of lobbyists wining and dining their former colleagues.

A second hypothesis might be called the "good ol' boy" theory of representation. Its most familiar form is this: "It isn't what you know, but who you know." It asserts that lobbying success depends heavily upon cultivating officials, knowing them personally, and maintaining warm relations with them so that they will be disposed to respond favorably when they are asked to help the lobbyist's client. For example, when Ed Rollins, onetime White House political affairs director and manager of the 1984 Reagan-Bush campaign, described the credentials he hoped would enable him to attract clients to his new consulting firm, he said, "I know all the Cabinet officers, and I know all the under secretaries, and I know all the assistant secretaries" (Edsall 1985, 9).

Yet there is also evidence that "who you know" may be less important than "what you know." Milbrath reported that of the lobbyists he interviewed fewer than one in seven were willing to say that contacts were of "considerable" or "major" importance to them as lobbyists, and nearly half said "not at all" (1963, 62). Those respondents, however, showed a marked tendency to think that contacts might be more important for *other* lobbyists. Perhaps the "who you know" response was perceived as lacking in legitimacy. But Milbrath's lobbyists were emphatic in their insistence that knowledge of subject matter is the most important quality sought when lobbyists are recruited, and it seems a reasonable extension to suppose that this would be true on the job as well. A strong second choice was knowledge of the legal process. Thus, knowledge of process and substance were clearly preferred to possession of contacts. This finding may be elaborated into a cognitive or knowledge-based hypothesis of the sort we examined in chapter 3—that is, this is a complex, bureaucratized, and knowledge-based world, and the hearty talents of jolly old comrades-at-arms are therefore less important than are command of specialized information and technical skills. If the policy process is increasingly knowledge based, then what you know becomes vital; whether you are well liked or have the "right" social background characteristics is beside the point (cf. Miller 1949).

Despite the significance of these questions, there is little systematic research on the careers of representatives. There are anecdotes, stories, and case studies in considerable abundance (see Berry's review and sources cited therein [1984, ch. 6]), but these do not provide adequate data on the degree of movement between government positions and positions in interest organizations, the ways in which government experience is used by representatives, or the effect of social, political, and professional characteristics on the likelihood that individuals will enter government service or work for certain kinds of interest groups.

Career Histories

We asked respondents about the history of their careers with their current employers, in government jobs, and in positions at "other public or private organizations in which your work involved representation before state or federal government." With respect to each position, we collected data on the employing organization, the type of position held, substantive specialty, and the dates the job began and ended. This was not a complete career history. One-fifth of the sample had gaps in their careers—that is, periods of time in which they did not occupy positions that involved policy representation.

To analyze the welter of detailed career data, responses on job changes were recoded into seven "career state" categories: positions in state and local government, federal legal jobs, federal nonlegal jobs, positions in external law and consulting firms, government affairs positions (including trade association employees), organization executives and staff, and gaps.[1] Analyzing career states necessarily ignores some of the details of personal biographies. Nonetheless, these data allow us to track the most significant dimensions of career paths, including movements between government and private sector employment, between legal and nonlegal positions, and between executive or staff positions and government affairs positions.

Career States by Year

We begin by analyzing the distribution of career states held by respondents in preceding years. Examining the data in this fashion provides an overview of the timing of the career experiences of our sample. It also gives some insights into how the careers of representatives have changed over time. We lack a complete picture of the changes in these career patterns, however, because we interviewed representatives active in 1983 and do not know about the careers of representatives who left the system before then. Thus, these data may confound period effects (associated with a given time) with cohort effects (associated with particular age groups). Nonetheless, the patterns of change are both coherent and suggestive (see Figure 5.1, a diagram of the percentage of representatives occupying various career states from 1960 to 1983).

The proportion of representatives who had not yet entered one of the coded career states is shown by the line that begins at 75% in 1960 and steadily declines to zero in 1983. By that year, the entire sample has entered one of three current career states: external lawyers and consultants, government affairs and trade association officials, and organizational executives and staff. The "precareer" curve indicates that three-quarters of the respondents were not in any of the coded career states in 1960. By 1970, that proportion had declined to some 40%, but a quarter of the sample was still not in a coded career state as late as 1975. Thus, while there are many old hands

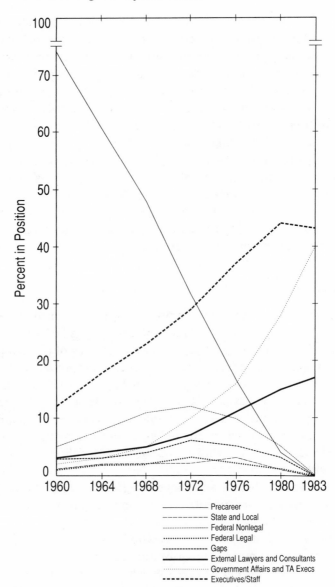

Figure 5.1 Career states by year (1960–1983)

among our group of representatives, they are outnumbered by more recent entrants to representation.

Figure 5.1 also suggests the significance of nonlaw positions in the federal government. State and local government jobs and federal legal positions, by contrast, both appear in the career histories of a relatively small number of representatives, at relatively constant levels. Those with specifically legal positions never exceed 3%. The proportion of the sample holding nonlegal federal positions, however, rises from about 5% in 1961 to 10% of the sample by 1965, peaks at 12% in 1974, and declines steadily thereafter.

Most representatives who possess government experience gained it between 1964 and 1974, the Johnson and Nixon years. This was a time of considerable expansion in the scope of both regulation and expenditure by the federal government. Whether measured in terms of pages in the federal register, bills introduced in Congress, or size of congressional staff, the federal establishment grew substantially during this period (see, for example, Ornstein, Mann, and Malbin 1987). In the view of many, this growth precipitated the expansion of interest representation, especially by business interests (Ferguson and Rogers 1986).

A third and related trend that is apparent in Figure 5.1 is the takeoff in the percentage of government affairs officers and trade association employees. The number of executive and staff positions also increases quite rapidly, but more steadily throughout the time period, starting at 12% in 1960, peaking in 1980 at 44% of the sample, and leveling off thereafter. External lawyers and consultants increase gradually from 3% in 1960 to 6% in 1972, and then more than double in the next ten years, reaching 17% of the sample in 1983. But by far the most dramatic change is recorded by government affairs personnel. Only 2% of the sample held such positions in 1960. By 1970, their share had grown to 7%, slightly higher than external law and consulting. This proportion then quadruples to 28% by 1980 and continues a rapid rise to reach 40% of the sample by 1983. This suggests that government affairs work emerged in the late seventies and early eighties as an organizationally distinct role. A portion of the growth may be attributable to relabeling existing executive or staff positions to identify government affairs responsibility more explicitly.[2] Even so, such a change indicates a new organizational recognition of the significance of government affairs. As interest organizations came to devote increasing amounts of resources to representation, they recruited both former government officials and organizational employees to work as government affairs specialists.

Career States by Age

To show how the careers of representatives unfold over the course of their lives, Figure 5.2 depicts the career states held by members of the

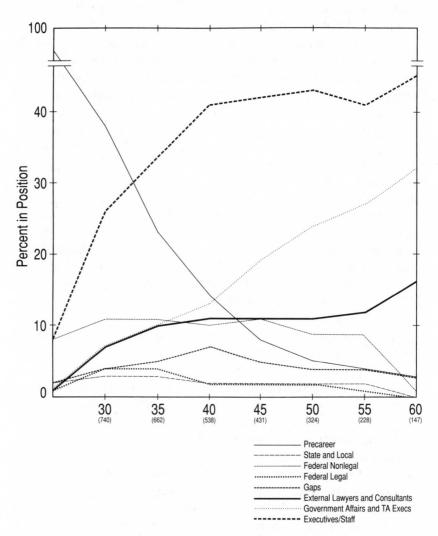

Figure 5.2   Career states by age (*N*'s in parentheses)

sample at different ages.[3] The number of cases declines with increasing age, reflecting the fact that a decreasing proportion of the sample had attained older age levels. The solid line representing the proportion of precareer respondents shows that 38% of the sample had not entered any of our categories by age 30. This proportion drops rapidly, however. Almost 90% of the sample had entered coded career states by age 40. For only a few is interest representation a truly late career choice—something a retired senator or long-time federal administrator might turn to later in life.

Positions in private organizations occupy most representatives at all of the career stages. After the age of 33, the largest share of the sample at any age is in executive and staff positions. This proportion grows very rapidly between the ages of 30 and 40, and then increases more gradually (and inconsistently, due to smaller numbers) at higher age levels. For the 30 to 40 age group, the curves for executive/staff positions and the precareer state are almost mirror images. This suggests that many individuals entered policy representation work by assuming such positions in private organizations. (Recall that all of these executive and staff positions must involve policy representation.) After the age of 40, the fastest-growing career state is the government affairs and trade association positions. The proportion of representatives in such work rises steadily, peaking at over 30% at age 60. The proportion in executive and staff positions outnumbers those in government affairs positions by roughly 3 to 1 at age 40, but by age 55 the ratio shrinks to roughly 1.5 to 1. Thus, the rapid growth in the government affairs positions that we observed in Figure 5.1 is not limited to younger representatives, but has impact on the careers of older members of the sample as well.

Of the three possible current career states, external lawyers and consultants exhibit the slowest rate of growth. The proportion of respondents in this category rises slightly from 7% at age 30 to just over 10% at age 36, where it hovers until age 55, and then rises again, reaching 16% at age 60. This pattern appears to reflect the relative longevity of law and consulting careers. Established lawyers and consultants thus make up a somewhat larger portion of the old hands involved in representation.

The percentage of the representatives who hold government positions remains remarkably constant across age levels. Many representatives enter government at a relatively early stage—in their late twenties and early thirties—and depart after two or three years.

Nonlaw federal positions peak at age 33, at some 13% of the sample overall (23% of those who had left the precareer state and entered policy work). Positions in state and local government and in federal legal jobs follow a similar pattern, albeit at a lower percentage of the sample. But Figure 5.2 shows that the probability of government employment remains roughly the same between the ages of 35 and 55. Whether this pattern will continue as the younger cohort ages is a matter for speculation.

The data reveal no single, definitive pattern in the careers of representatives as a function of age. But if age does not determine the course of representatives' careers, what does? To evaluate the possibilities, let us examine the nature of the transitions from one career state to the next.

The General Pattern of Career Transitions

If we can detect distinctive chains of career moves, we may be able to characterize the various paths that representatives follow, and we can then seek to explain why they follow one rather than another. But it is useful first to consider the full set of career transitions without regard to the sequence in which they occur since it is clear that most representatives experience relatively few changes in career state (see Table 5.1). Respondents with adequate career data, a total of 771, report a mean of 2.4 career states per individual. More than a quarter of the respondents (28%) report only one career state; another third (33%) report two career states; and another fifth (22%) report three career states. Less than a fifth of the respondents (17%) have four or more career states.

Many representatives spend their entire careers in one organization. Some 23% report employment in only one organization and no representative activity for other private organizations (such as for trade associations, which may be done concurrently with their employment). Another 10% began their career at their current employer, but worked elsewhere at some time. Many of the transitions reported in the table occur within the same organization. Of the 281 transitions that begin in executive/staff positions, 181 (64%) end in government affairs or trade association positions and, of these moves, 69% (125 of 181) take place within the organization that currently employs the representative. The reverse move—from government affairs into executive or staff positions—occurs less often, only 41 times in our

Table 5.1 Career transitions

Earlier position	Subsequent position							
	State and local government	Federal nonlegal	Federal legal	Gaps	External lawyers and consultants	Government affairs and trade assoc. execs.	Executives and staff	Total
Before career	65 (8%)	201 (26%)	73 (9%)	0 (0%)	54 (7%)	60 (8%)	318 (41%)	771 (100%)
State and local government	0 (0%)	15 (17%)	3 (3%)	22 (24%)	5 (6%)	10 (11%)	35 (39%)	90 (100%)
Federal nonlegal	10 (3%)	0 (0%)	12 (4%)	66 (22%)	40 (13%)	76 (25%)	98 (32%)	302 (100%)
Federal legal	0 (0%)	25 (23%)	0 (0%)	21 (19%)	34 (31%)	9 (8%)	20 (18%)	109 (100%)
Gaps	6 (4%)	24 (14%)	11 (6%)	0 (0%)	24 (14%)	31 (18%)	74 (44%)	170 (100%)
External lawyers and consultants	2 (4%)	8 (16%)	9 (18%)	8 (16%)	0 (0%)	7 (14%)	17 (33%)	51 (100%)
Government affairs and trade assoc. execs.	2 (3%)	7 (12%)	0 (0%)	7 (12%)	3 (5%)	0 (0%)	41 (68%)	60 (100%)
Executives and staff	5 (2%)	22 (8%)	1 (0.5%)	46 (16%)	26 (9%)	181 (64%)	0 (0%)	281 (100%)
Total	90 (5%)	302 (16%)	109 (6%)	170 (9%)	186 (10%)	374 (20%)	603 (33%)	1,834 (100%)

N of respondents = 771; N of transitions = 1,834. Row percentages may not add to 100% due to rounding.

sample. But again a substantial proportion (25 of 41, or 61%) take place within the representative's current organization.

Some 44% of the respondents begin their government policy careers in government employment, but representatives relatively seldom hold government jobs at later points in their careers. Roughly two-thirds of all government experience occurs at the beginning of a career. That is, for most of those who have worked on both sides of the representational relationship, public and private, it is the public service that occurs first. Of the 502 transitions into government positions, only 97 come from private representative positions or gaps.

Points of Entry and Points of Destination

After inspecting the full set of career transitions in sequence (state 1 to state 2, state 2 to state 3, and so on), we concluded that the nature of the paths could be summarized by presenting only the starting and current positions (Table 5.2). The table includes all of the starting positions (by definition, gaps can occur only after a career has begun), and all three of the possible current positions. By moving across the rows in the table, we see where people who start in various positions end up; moving down the columns, we see where people currently occupying certain positions began their careers.

Law or consulting firms currently employed some 18% of the sample, with the remainder roughly equally divided between government affairs/trade association positions and executive and staff positions. The three main entry points for representatives working in law or consulting firms are federal government service, in both law and nonlaw jobs, and direct entry into law or consulting firms. Not surprisingly, those who begin in federal legal positions are likely to end up in law firms (but only 55%), as are those who begin in law firms (70% of whom start and stay there). Although government service (state and local, federal legal, federal nonlegal) is an important entry point for persons employed in government affairs or as trade association executives, many organizations appear to grow their own. Some 15% begin their careers in such positions; another 37% move from other organizational executive or staff positions into government affairs work. The tendency of organizations to recruit internally is even more pronounced for executive and staff positions. A substantial majority (59%) of the representatives occupying executive or staff positions began their careers in that same category, while slightly

Table 5.2 Starting career position by current position

Starting position	Current position			
	External lawyers and consultants	Government affairs and trade assoc. execs.	Executives and staff	Total
State and local government	9	25	31	65
(row %)	(14%)	(39%)	(48%)	(100%)
(column %)	(7%)	(8%)	(10%)	(8%)
Federal nonlegal	33	100	68	201
(row %)	(16%)	(50%)	(34%)	(100%)
(column %)	(24%)	(32%)	(21%)	(26%)
Federal legal	40	14	19	73
(row %)	(55%)	(19%)	(26%)	(100%)
(column %)	(30%)	(5%)	(6%)	(10%)
External lawyers and consultants	38	11	5	54
(row %)	(70%)	(20%)	(9%)	(100%)
(column %)	(28%)	(4%)	(2%)	(7%)
Government affairs and trade assoc. execs.	2	48	10	60
(row %)	(3%)	(80%)	(17%)	(100%)
(column %)	(2%)	(15%)	(3%)	(8%)
Executives and staff	13	116	189	318
(row %)	(4%)	(37%)	(59%)	(100%)
(column %)	(10%)	(37%)	(59%)	(41%)
Total	135	314	332	771
%	(18%)	(41%)	(42%)	(100%)

Note: Row percentages may not add to 100% due to rounding.

more than one-third (37%) started in some kind of government work.

Government service is a frequent entry point for all types of positions, but there are distinctive routes to each kind of job in the system. Government law work tends to lead to law firm jobs; nonlegal federal positions tend to lead to government affairs work; representatives who begin in executive or staff positions are very likely to remain there or to move to government affairs positions in the same organization. Initial entry into a career state dramatically increases the odds that representatives will end in the same state (if, indeed, they ever leave).

The overall pattern of career paths underscores the organizationally differentiated character of the modern system of interest representation. Organizations attract and deploy individuals with particular portfolios of experience. This means, for example, client organizations will employ government affairs personnel with government service relevant to the policy needs of the client. Insofar as those needs are specific to the client, however, it may be more effective for the organization to recruit straight out of school and train the budding representative in-house. In that case, interest groups will be more likely to fill these positions from the ranks of organizational insiders than from those who begin in government work.

The Government Career

Earlier studies of interest representation found that previous government employment is a common, but far from necessary, experience for lobbyists. Lester Milbrath's pioneering study, based on a 1956 sample of 114 registered lobbyists, found that 50% had held positions with the federal government (1963, 68). In Berry's study of public interest group lobbyists in the early 1970s, 26% had come to their present jobs from positions with the government (1977, 90). In a four-state examination of state-level lobbyists, Zeigler and Baer reported that the proportion with previous federal government experience ranged from a low of 14% to a high of 33%, and roughly that many again had held state and local government jobs (1969, 51–52). These studies suggest that less than half the lobbying community can claim the advantages of prior government experience.

Schlozman and Tierney found that 86% of the organizations in their large survey of Washington-based interest groups had at least one professional with federal government experience (1986, 269). Schlozman and Tierney's analysis is at the organizational level, however, and does not address the individual actors. Organizations may find government experience attractive in a job candidate (cf. Berry 1977, 93), but it does not follow that such experience will invariably lead to personal riches in the K Street corridor. Though accounts of the careers of individual lobbyists often emphasize the importance of their government experience, these accounts do not establish that experience is a major factor in lobbying success. The biographies are sometimes instructive and quite sophisticated, but the persons and events they choose to describe may not be representative. In fact, we have only the most rudimentary knowledge about how much traffic or what kind of traffic moves through the revolving door. Nor do we know what kind of benefits such experience confers, or whether these benefits derive from contacts or substantive expertise.

The Descriptive Parameters

Our findings regarding the incidence of federal government experience among Washington lobbyists are not dramatically different from those previously reported in the literature. Some 55% of our respondents had held some kind of government position, but 9% had worked only at the state or local level, so the proportion with federal experience is slightly lower than Milbrath's figure. About 17% had worked on the Hill, and a considerably larger number (30%) had worked exclusively in other parts of the federal government. Surprisingly few (5%) had held positions in both the executive and the legislative branches before moving to the private sector, but many had held two or more jobs within one branch or the other. Nearly two-thirds of those with executive branch experience had held two or more jobs in that branch; the average length of service there was over eight years. A bit fewer than half of the Hill veterans had held two or more positions there; their mean length of service was slightly less than six years.

There are some real veterans, of course. Almost 20% of the lobbyists with Hill experience served there nine years or longer, and nearly 14% of the executive branch group had government careers of that duration. In general, however, the length of government service was rather brief. Table 5.3 displays the distribution of the number of years of federal government experience, years elapsed since government service, and years with the current organization. Almost a quarter of those with federal experience had only two years or less.

We would expect government experience to be a more important asset when it is fresh. Contacts with officials are useful only as long as the officials are in office, and we know that the turnover rate among officials, especially among top administrative appointees, is quite high (Heclo 1977). Similarly, the grasp of particular issues acquired during government service decays as issue details change, though the rapidity of this may well vary from one policy domain to another. Given these limitations, it is significant that the mean length of time *since* holding the most recent federal government position is

Table 5.3 Years of federal government experience, years since federal government position, and years with current organization

Years	%	N
Years federal experience		
1–2	24.5	79
3–4	25.0	81
5–8	25.0	81
9–14	13.0	42
15 or more	12.4	40
Total	99.9	323
Mean	6.9	
Median	5.0	
Years since federal job		
1–2	10.6	35
3–4	14.2	47
5–8	26.0	86
9–14	26.5	88
15 or more	22.7	75
Total	100.0	331
Mean	10.7	
Median	8.0	
Years with current organization		
1–2	6.2	48
3–4	14.8	114
5–8	27.0	208
9–14	22.4	173
15 or more	29.6	128
Total	100.0	771
Mean	11.9	
Median	9.0	

nearly eleven years. Half of our 1983–84 respondents had left the government by 1976. Only 17% held government jobs during the Reagan years.

In contrast to this relatively brief and dated federal government experience (most did not have even that), some 80% of the sample had been with their current employer for more than four years. Over half had been there nine years or more, and some 30% had spent fifteen or more years in the current organization. The mean length of service with the present employer was twelve years.

The timing and duration of the various career states put the representatives' government service in even better perspective (Table 5.4). Representatives enter government when they are about 30, younger on average than for other career states, and they leave a few years later, between the ages of 34 and 36 on average. Respondents enter the private sector at a later age, are much less likely to change career states, and typically hold those positions considerably longer than they hold government jobs. Table 5.4 confirms what we found in the career transitions data presented earlier: representatives who hold government positions do so early in their careers, typically as a first job; stay a relatively brief time; and then move into relatively stable and long-lasting employment with the organization they currently represent.

It may be, however, that within the larger group with federal government experience there is a subset of representatives who move back and forth between government and private representative positions (that is, who "revolve" rather than walk through the door once) and who thus warrant further scrutiny. We found 51 individuals, 8% of the total sample and less than a fifth of those with government experience, who moved between private representative positions and federal government jobs more than once. The conventional wisdom does not tell us how many times the door must open in order to be defined as revolving, but our data suggest that it does not open often.

Nor do many of these cases indicate the presence of a mechanism

Table 5.4   Type of career state by mean age of entry, percentage exit, mean age at exit, and mean duration

Type of career state	Mean age at entry	% Exit	Mean age at exit[a]	Mean duration (years)	N
State and local government	30.6	100	35.4	4.8	90
Federal nonlegal	30.2	100	36.2	6.0	302
Federal legal	29.7	100	33.7	4.0	109
Gaps	33.6	100	38.5	4.9	170
External lawyers and consultants	34.7	27.4	35.1	9.5	186
Government affairs and trade assoc. execs.	38.6	16.0	38.1	6.6	374
Executives and staff	33.9	44.9	40.6	10.0	603
All career states	34.0	57.8	37.0	7.5	1,834

a. Of those who exit.

through which private groups can gain privileged access to public officials. Only 23 of the 51 revolvers held government positions that dealt with matters affecting the organizations with whom they were employed before or after their government service. Moreover, of these 23 representatives, 10 came from public interest or advocacy groups or from political parties and related ideological groups, rather than from business, trade, labor, or professional organizations. The movement of public interest advocates or political ideologues into and out of government may well affect government decisions, but it represents a very different form of influence than the typical worry about the manipulation of government by narrowly self-interested parties.

Of the subset of "revolving" representatives, several (13) are lawyers who retained a particular legal specialty throughout their moves back and forth between government and private sector positions. Another 12 cases involve at most some kind of general credentialing, with little or no discernible link between the work done in the private sector and that done in the government. The remaining cases include one career path determined by personal patronage, when a representative followed a superior back and forth between private and public jobs; and only two "generalist heavyweights" who, having gained high public office early in their careers, continued to move in and out of government.

But suppose that, rather than focus on the representatives, we focus on the agencies and ask what proportion of representatives in frequent contact with an agency are former employees of the agency. Let us define "prior employment with an agency" broadly. Any experience in the House, for example, will constitute prior employment for representatives who contact any House committees or the Democratic or Republican leadership of the House. Similarly, employment in any subunit within a cabinet department will count as prior employment for representatives contacting any and all parts of that department; employment with a predecessor agency will also count as prior employment. Even if we use this broad definition of prior employment, we find that only a relatively small proportion of the regular contacts involve former agency employees.

If we examine a set of especially prominent government agencies (see Table 5.5), we find that the highest proportion of frequent contacts by former employees is only 18% (contacting the House in the energy domain). Among representatives contacting various Senate

Table 5.5 Representatives contacting agencies who previously were employed by the agency (percentages)

Place contacted	Agriculture	Energy	Health	Labor
Senate	11	13	8	13
House	14	18	16	14
White House/OMB	—	10	7	10
Cabinet depts.	11	5	13	12
Selected Agencies/Commissions				
Food and Drug Administration	10			
Environmental Protection Agency		6	14	
Federal Energy Regulatory Commission		7		
Health Care Financing Administration			1	
Pension Benefit Guaranty Corporation				3
National Labor Relations Board				16

Note: Contact is defined as "several times" or "regularly" within the last year.

bodies often, from 8% to 13% are former Senate employees. The proportions are somewhat lower for the White House and OMB and for the cabinet departments. One might expect that former employees would play a more prominent role in contacting specialized regulatory or adjudicatory agencies, such as the Food and Drug Administration, the Environmental Protection Agency, or the National Labor Relations Board. As the lower panel of Table 5.5 reveals, however, this is not the case.

Even though former employees are not numerically predominant in the contacting, they might be expected to be especially influential. While we do not possess specific measures of influence with particular agencies, we have compared former agency employees to the other representatives who frequently contact those agencies on various dimensions that are plausibly related to influence. In a series of comparisons of income levels, mean reported success on policy events, and number of especially prominent representatives known by the respondents,[4] we find there are few statistically significant differences between these two groups. Thus, former agency employees do not appear to possess characteristics that would indicate that they are more influential than other representatives who are in regular contact with the agencies.

Interest organizations, when asked to evaluate some fourteen possible reasons for hiring one kind of representative rather than another, ranked government experience below experience in the industry. Executive branch experience was more highly valued than a Hill background (but see the discussion below of how representatives themselves value the two types of background). Both forms of experience ranked well above contacts, party affiliation, or elite educational background, however. Having had a federal job was not irrelevant, but it was not seen by employers as a dominant criterion for selection of representatives.

We are not ready to declare that the revolving door presents no threat to equitable interest representation. Other policy domains, such as defense contracting, may present different problems. But our data suggest that the circulation of individuals between the private and public sectors is not a prominent or consequential feature of the system of interest representation. Representatives of private interests typically stay in their jobs for long periods of time and do not move in and out of government. Thus, our findings tend to support other studies that have failed to discover such links between specific government agencies and the organizations that they regulate (see Quirk 1981 on the FDA and Katzmann 1980 on the FTC). Since 1977, former government employees have been forbidden by law to contact their agencies for one or more years after leaving the government or on specific matters they had handled (18 U.S.C.A. §207, 1991). This legislation may have been effective in discouraging representation before previous employing agencies even after the legally mandated period.

The Uses of Government Experience: Who You Know versus What You Know

In our interviews, we asked the representatives: "As a Washington representative in [policy area] matters, have you found that your previous government experience has been significantly helpful?" If this was answered in the affirmative, we asked: "In which of the following ways has it been helpful? (1) I was familiar with the substantive issues. (2) I knew the right people in the administration. (3) I had good contacts on the Hill. (4) I knew how decisions were made in this area. (5) I was well acquainted with other Washington representatives in this area." Responses 1 and 4 indicate that government service contributes to "what you know," while responses 2, 3, and 5 indicate that it provides a "who you know" advantage.

The value of government experience in the practice of lobbying may, of course, depend on the nature of the experience, as well as on the present position and context of the respondent; but we will begin with an analysis of the overall effect of government experience, broken down into four categories: Congress; Executive; both of these; and "Other," which includes positions in state and local government, regional officials, consultants, judges or law clerks, and the like.[5]

If we examine the percentage of affirmative responses within each category of government experience (Table 5.6), three things are clear. First, government experience is not a homogeneous commodity. Those without experience in either Congress or the executive branch (the "Other" category) were more likely to say that government experience was not helpful in any way, and their assessments of each of the specific ways in which experience might be helpful were lower. Second, government experience in general was thought more likely to confer familiarity with issues and the decision-making process than to provide helpful contacts (though there are some notable exceptions). Finally, respondents with congressional experience, not surprisingly, were substantially more likely to say that their experience helped them make contacts in Congress; those with executive experience were not especially likely to think that they had acquired useful contacts in the administration.

Table 5.6 Representatives' perceptions of the helpfulness of government experience (percentages)

	Location of government experience				
	Congress only	Executive only	Mixed (Congress and exec.)	Other	Total
Experience was not helpful	5	14	2	25	13
Experience provided:					
Issue familiarity	72	72	76	62	70
Contacts in administration	48	53	64	29	48
Contacts in Congress	87	49	86	35	59
Knowledge of decision-making process	92	81	98	58	80
Contacts with representatives	55	51	61	29	47
N	88	174	42	79	383

Note: Percentages are calculated from those interest representatives who had job experience with the federal government. Some 49 respondents failed to complete some part of the question and are therefore missing from these calculations.

Most representatives with government experience (87%) found it helpful in their present work; 80% of those who found the experience helpful said that they had gained familiarity with the decision-making process, while 70% reported gaining familiarity with issues. Logistic regression models suggest that, with other variables held constant, congressional experience is more likely to provide an understanding of the policy process, and executive experience to provide issue background. (See Table 5.A1 in the appendix to this chapter.) The regression models also indicate that government experience in the agriculture, health, and labor domains provides substantial issue familiarity and better understanding of the decision-making process, but government experience has no effect in the energy domain. This underscores the extent to which the energy area had changed in both substance and process, so that past experience had relatively little present value.

We also found an interesting difference in the impact of government experience on familiarity with issues and understanding of process. Experience generally provides useful substantive expertise, and this effect is even greater when the respondent is presently employed by a firm in the same domain, but experience has no significant effect on an understanding of process. These findings tend to confirm the "what you know" hypothesis: issue-related experience does have a substantial effect on issue familiarity. Interest representatives assign less importance to the personal contacts gained in prior federal government experience than they do to the knowledge of substance and process.

The difference between executive branch and Hill experience becomes clearer if we examine job variety. A single position on the Hill is nearly as likely to provide useful contacts with the executive branch, Congress, and other representatives as is more than one position. Representatives who held multiple positions in the executive branch, however, were significantly more likely than those who had only one executive branch job to report having gained useful contacts of all three kinds. This probably indicates that executive branch jobs are generally more circumscribed, narrower in substantive scope and exposure to others, than are those on the Hill. Since the mean length of experience in the executive branch (8.4 years) is substantially greater than that at the other end of Pennsylvania Avenue (5.9 years), Hill experience clearly has the greater impact and requires a less varied job history in generating contacts that are useful to interest representatives. In general, the congressional milieu is more open, accessible, and permeable than the executive branch. In the latter, personnel do not often move from one agency or department to another, and becoming well connected in one office may open few doors elsewhere. On the Hill, by contrast, members sit on several committees and subcommittees, and staffers also tend to wear several hats, seriatim if not simultaneously. A given level of acquaintance within the legislative branch, therefore, is likely to be more diffuse and wide-ranging than it would be in the executive.

The extent to which the benefits of government experience decay over time can be assessed by examining the percentage of respondents with experience at different times who still find their experience to be helpful (Table 5.7). In this analysis, changes in presidential administration are used as dividing lines, and respondents are categorized according to their most recent government service. We might expect contacts to fade more rapidly than issue familiarity or process expertise because personnel probably change faster than does policy substance or procedure. We might also expect that issue familiarity would decay more noticeably than process knowledge. Issues change rather steadily, albeit marginally in most cases, while the main elements of the decision process shift less often and less smoothly.

Both of these hypotheses receive some support from the data in Table 5.7. Issue familiarity decays steadily. The farther back the government experience was, the less likely it is that value will be claimed. But process knowledge remains intact for fifteen years, back

Table 5.7 Decay in usefulness of government experience (percentages)

	Held last government job			
	1968 or earlier	1969–76	1977–80	1981–83
Government experience helpful on:				
Issues	54	68	77	81
Process	56	83	87	84
Executive branch contacts	26	53	53	52
Hill contacts	31	63	67	69
Contacts with representatives	36	50	50	58
Not useful	33	12	40	9
N	70	131	115	17
	(18%)	(35%)	(29%)	(17%)

to 1968. This is also true of contacts, especially those on the Hill and in the executive branch; little change is evident until the sudden and drastic drop for the cohort leaving government prior to the accession of Nixon in 1969. Apparently, there is both a generic decay process at work, primarily with respect to issue familiarity, and a threshold, or generational, effect. Those who left government more than fifteen years before our interviews were much less likely to regard their government experience as useful to them. The relevant world of politics and policy had changed far more for them than for the other cohorts. The leaving dates are only crude indicators of the aggregated experience acquired by a set of former government workers, of course, but they are the years of party change in the presidency and so might be expected to differentiate a meaningful set of experiences shared by those who left at more or less the same time. Still, only 1968 seems to mark a major change. That was a dramatic year in a turbulent time, to be sure, and the change from Democratic to Republican control brought a major turnover in personnel. But note that no comparable effect is observed following the other years of change in partisan control of the presidency.

To summarize our findings: lobbyists with congressional or executive experience are more likely to have found the experience useful than are lobbyists with other kinds of governmental experience. This holds for both who and what you know. But there are important differences in the impact of congressional and executive experience. Executive experience confers issue familiarity, while congressional experience confers an understanding of the policy process. It is easier to cultivate contacts in Congress than in the executive branch, but the contacts in both will often be limited to the branch where the representative worked.

Three points are of particular interest. One is that, although government experience is fairly common among the representatives of private interests, it is far from universal and, indeed, appears not to have increased much above the levels of two or three decades ago. Not only is there stability in the proportion of interest representatives with government experience, but the time elapsed since that experience suggests that the accounts of revolving door abuses, in which officials trade on their experience to their advantage and great profit, should be regarded as horror stories. After all, one of the reasons that horror stories frighten us is that they are contrary to our experience. Michael Deaver, the former Reagan White House aide convicted for improperly exploiting his previous position for private gain, is pretty clearly an ugly exception.

Although several years had elapsed since many of the interest representatives held government positions, most of them who had such experience found it valuable. Moreover, most reported that their experience was valuable both for the substantive knowledge gained and for the contacts made with significant players. When there was a difference in the value attached to these two types of assets, the substantive knowledge was more often deemed important. What you know outweighed who you know.

Finally, the evidence suggests that congressional experience conveys more value to those who become Washington representatives than does employment in the executive branch or with independent agencies. Broader substantive expertise is gained in Congress, and gained more quickly. The same is true of contacts. About half of those with exclusively congressional experience reported that they even acquired useful contacts within the executive branch. This effect could result from different levels of job placement in the two branches, with executive positions carrying, on average, less responsibility or opportunity for learning than those on the Hill. It is probably the case, however, that Congress is a less rigidly bureaucratized institution and that jobs there tend to have a broader range of responsibility.

The Professional Career:
Legal Education and Representatives' Careers

If the primary value of government experience lies in what representatives learn about the substance or process of policy making, we should also look at other kinds of career development that might give representatives similar expertise. Several theorists have commented on the increasing importance of the professions in processes of government (Lane 1966; Bell 1976; Wiebe 1967; Skowronek 1982; Halliday 1987). The legal profession has received by far the most attention in this respect, and it is the most numerous professional group in our sample.

The common view that lawyers play an especially powerful role in American politics rests in large part on observations about the relationship between the nature of legal careers and the nature of the political process. Eulau and Sprague (1964) advanced the thesis that the disproportionate involvement of lawyers in politics results from a convergence between legal and political careers. Not only are the contacts lawyers make in the course of their practice useful in politics, but many of the risks and costs inherent in seeking and holding political office are smaller for lawyers than for other occupational groups. Political exposure aids professional practice. Another theory suggests that legal education develops cognitive skills or role expectations that are well suited to law making. One of our law students asserted in the course of a class discussion, "It is as natural to find lawyers in legislatures as it is to find chefs in a kitchen. Chefs write recipes, and lawyers write laws. That's what they do."[6] Gold (1961) has made much the same argument. He suggested that, because lawyers are accustomed to procedurally oriented systems of decision making, they are better able to negotiate and compromise in the legislative process.

Although the literature focuses on the propensity of lawyers to hold public office rather than positions as private representatives, it has implications for the kinds of roles that we might expect lawyers to have in the system of private representation. It suggests two potentially overlapping career paths for representatives who hold law degrees: one in which legal education is important primarily as a general credential that opens the door to heightened levels of political involvement and government experience, but for which legal skills are not terribly important; and one in which the technical skills developed in law school are used in government positions or in positions with interest groups active in the policy-making process. The first path would lead to broad-ranging policy work of the sort that is performed by government affairs officers and trade association employees. The second path might lead to such positions as well, but would also lead to conventional law practice with law firms or as inside counsel.

We should therefore examine the effect of legal education on the amount of time that representatives devote to federal policy work. Time allocation is significantly and positively correlated with other measures of the scope and intensity of policy activity, including the number of government agencies contacted by the representative, the number of policy-making events in which he or she is interested, and the number of his or her acquaintances among a group of notable representatives (see chapter 10). For the sake of parsimony, in these analyses we have converted time spent on federal policy work into a dichotomous variable, distinguishing respondents who devote more than half of their time to federal policy from those who devote less.[7]

In addition to current organizational position, three variables that might lead to a high level of involvement in federal policy work are obtaining a law degree, working in the federal government, and being involved in electoral politics. The last of these, political involvement, is measured by whether the respondent had ever worked in a political campaign on more than a casual basis. We measure federal government experience by whether a representative had held a full-time, paid position in the federal government, excluding judicial clerkships and military service. Current organizational position is a four-category variable consisting of: (1) executives; (2) government affairs personnel and trade association employees; (3) internal staff; and (4) external representatives. Note that, although none of these positions is explicitly a law position, some 40% of the internal staff positions are held by internal legal counsel and 80% of the external representative positions are held by attorneys in law firms.[8] (The full array of the data concerning these relationships is presented in Table 5.A2 of the appendix to this chapter.)

To assess the relationships among the variables, we tested three sets of log-linear models (see Figure 5.3; Goodman 1972, 1973a, 1973b; Fienberg 1980). The first set of models examined the relationships between law degree, federal government experience, and political activity. The second analyzed the effects of law degree, federal government experience, and political activity on the allocation of individuals into different organizational positions. The third set of models tested the direct (that is, net or partial) effects of all four of

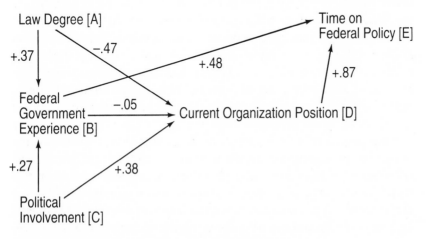

Figure 5.3 Determinants of time spent on federal policy work

the prior variables on time spent on federal policy.[9] The arrows in Figure 5.3 represent statistically significant direct effects among the lettered variables according to the three models selected at each stage.[10] The coefficients included in the figure represent the simple bivariate relationships between variables without controls for other variables.

We find that law-educated representatives are neither more nor less likely than others to have been actively involved in political campaigns. (Some 41% of representatives with law degrees have been active in political campaigns, compared to 43% of those without law degrees.) Contrary to what Eulau and Sprague (1964) found for state legislators, it appears that in the careers of private Washington representatives legal training and political activity are alternative, not convergent, routes to policy involvement. Legal education and political activity are both positively associated with federal government experience, which in turn has a direct and positive effect on policy participation. (The coefficient in Figure 5.3 is potentially misleading. Only after controlling law degree and political involvement does the effect of government experience on organizational position become significant.) But there is no evidence that legal training leads to political involvement and then to higher levels of policy activity.

All three of these variables—legal education, government experience, and political involvement—significantly affect the allocation of representatives to their current organizational positions. Dropping any of them results in models that have a poorer fit. But the most striking feature of the models is the explanatory power of organizational position on federal policy time. Models that include a term for the effect of organizational position on policy time (DE in Figure 5.3) fit the data well; models that do not contain this term fail to achieve a good fit. (Appendix tables 5.A3, 5.A4, and 5.A5 summarize the model selection results.) The only other variable that has a direct effect on federal policy time, net of the effect of organizational position, is federal government experience. Neither legal education nor political involvement has such a direct effect.

These patterns may be more readily grasped by examining the relationships among the organizational position categories and the other four variables we analyzed. Table 5.8 presents the data in this form. The largest concentration of lawyers is of course found among the external representatives, since the law firm attorneys are in that category. While almost two-thirds of the external representatives

Table 5.8 Organizational position, by law degree, political involvement, federal government experience, and time on federal policy (percentages)

Organizational position	Law degree**	Political involvement*	Federal experience	Spending +50% time on federal policy	N
Executives	16.2	37.4	38.2	19.8	184
Government affairs[a]	22.2	50.2	45.0	55.7	313
Internal staff	40.7	32.5	35.8	37.7	122
External representatives	78.9	39.7	64.8	34.8	140
All	34.0	42.3	45.5	40.2	759

a. Includes trade association executives.
* $p \leq .01$. ** $p \leq .001$.

possess federal government experience, only about a third devote a majority of their time to federal policy. In contrast, of the government affairs officers and trade association employees, a majority spend more than half of their time on federal policy making and half have been active politically. Hence, government affairs representatives are somewhat more likely than external lawyers to convert federal employment into active involvement in policy making. Note that this is true even though the external lawyers were selected through a process that identified only lawyers who were active in policy representation, not lawyers in general.

The nature of government experience also varies by organizational position. Some 62% of those government affairs officers and trade association employees who held federal government posts had held congressional positions, but only 34% of the external representatives with government experience had been employed in Congress. An analysis of the titles of government jobs held by representatives suggests that lawyers typically held positions as legal counsel of one type or another, while other representatives held posts that were more clearly political in nature or involved substantive policy making. Of the 158 government affairs officers and trade association executives who had held federal jobs, 118 (75%) held politically appointed jobs. While it is clear that different organizational positions are recruited from different types of government experience, it is also true that organizational position has an effect on policy involvement that is independent of recruitment patterns. For instance, even though a substantial percentage of executives had government experience, only a relatively small proportion of them devoted a majority of their time to federal policy, and this is true even though the sample was selected from those identified as active in policy representation. Thus, while the organizational functions performed by government affairs officers and trade association employees reinforce their involvement in policy making, the functions performed by those in other organizational positions reduce their participation in policy making.[11]

These findings underscore the observation that lawyers do not have a special calling for policy making. Legal education is primarily important in channeling individuals into federal government employment, typically in executive branch positions, which then leads to private law positions that include some federal policy work. The path that leads to the highest levels of policy activity starts not with law school but with political involvement, followed by federal employment (usually as congressional staff), and then by a position as a government affairs officer or trade association executive. Legal education may be a more generally accessible route to participation in policy making than is the route that depends on political involvement and congressional experience, but legal training appears to lead to a more limited form of participation based on technical knowledge and skills. The more political careers of government affairs and trade association personnel typically bring greater levels of involvement in policy work and quite possibly more influence over the course of policy deliberations than is possessed by most lawyer representatives.

Social and Political Background Characteristics as Determinants of Representatives' Careers

Several clear career patterns appear in these analyses of career transitions and of the uses of government experience and law credentials. Instructive as these analyses are, however, they leave out a potentially important dimension of the social biographies of representatives. Do the class, ethnic, religious, or political backgrounds of representatives affect the nature of their careers, including the kinds of interests they eventually represent?

Career development may be depicted as a process that begins with early social and political background characteristics (Figure 5.4). These shape political preferences, which in turn affect the intermediate career stages—education, political campaign activity, and govern-

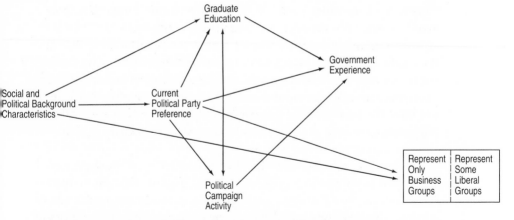

Figure 5.4 Hypothesized relationships among social and political background, political party, graduate education, political campaign activity, and type of clients represented

ment service. The combination of social characteristics, political preferences, and career events then leads representatives to particular types of clients, where we found them. We distinguish two broad types of destinations: (1) representatives who exclusively represent business or trade association interests, and (2) those who represent public interest groups and labor unions (in the figure, "liberal groups"). Dividing representatives in this fashion is admittedly crude. Various categories of business enterprise often disagree, of course, and liberal groups also part company on some issues. Yet, as later chapters demonstrate, this is a meaningful, if inexact, distinction in the system of interest representation, just as it is elsewhere in American politics. Business organizations are far more likely to see other businesses as their allies, while identifying liberal organizations as adversaries. (See chapter 9.) Moreover, there are significant ideological differences between business and nonbusiness representatives. (See chapter 6.)

The social and political backgrounds of representatives may affect careers in two salient respects. First, they shape the intensity and ideological direction of representatives' political preferences, and representatives may well seek positions that are compatible with their political attitudes. Members of traditionally liberal socioeconomic categories—Jews, minorities, and children of working-class parents—may be less likely to pursue careers as representatives of business organizations than are members of more conservative socioeconomic groups, such as Protestants from upper-class backgrounds. Individuals who are nonpartisan should be less likely to engage in political campaigning; if they enter government positions, they may be more likely to have followed the professional training route. Second, social background may also define the career opportunities that are open. Persons from less advantaged backgrounds may not have the opportunities for achieving advanced education or direct entry into positions with business organizations that are available to members of other social groups.

Government jobs may also be more accessible to or more preferred by people from certain social or political groups. Government jobs have long been an avenue of achievement for lower status social groups who were precluded from career opportunities in the private sector (see, for example, Auerbach 1976). Moreover, government jobs may be more desirable on ideological grounds for social groups who favor government intervention in society or who are negatively disposed toward certain business interests. Thus, social groups traditionally associated with the Democratic party—Jews, Catholics, minorities, the urban working class—might be more likely to have government experience. But more recently, conservative ideologues flocked to the Reagan banner in hope of reducing the role of government. Although many of this latter cohort subsequently moved "downtown" to work as lobbyists, few had yet done so at the time of our interviews.

Social and political background may thus have an effect on the nature of the clients served that is independent of its effect on the representatives' political preferences or graduate education. (See Figure 5.4.) But the direct links between type of clientele and the background and party preference of representatives run contrary to the observations of some of our informants in the preliminary fieldwork. These practitioners asserted that, with certain rare and notable exceptions, social background and political ideology are not important organizing dimensions of representation. Many of our own early impressions suggested that representation had become a highly rationalized process characterized by an extensive division of labor that was organized by task and substantive field rather than by personal characteristics such as class or belief. But research in other contexts had uncovered largely unacknowledged effects of ethnicity and religion on the structure of professional work (Heinz and Laumann 1982), and preliminary analyses of our quantitative data suggested that ethnicity and religion are important correlates of the organizational positions of Washington representatives.

Background Characteristics

To test the model of career development summarized in Figure 5.4, we employed a number of standard background variables that might influence political attitudes and career opportunities:

1. An ethnoreligious variable that divides the sample into five groups: Catholics; Jews; nonreligious; and two groups of Protestants—Type I Protestants, consisting of Congregationalists, Episcopalians, Quakers, and Presbyterians, and Type II Protestants, consisting of other Protestant churches. Type I Protestants are identified with the early waves of immigration into the United States and tend to occupy higher social status (see, for example, Baltzell 1958, 1964).

2. Social class, measured by father's occupation. We divided the sample into five groups: professional or technical occupations; owners, executives, and managers; farmers; sales and clerical occupations; and blue collar occupations.

3. Region of origin, measured by where respondents reported residing during the time they were in high school. States were grouped into four census-defined regional areas—Northeast, South, Midwest, and West.

4. Family political preference, as measured by questions about the political party preferences of the respondent's mother and father. Respondents were coded as coming from Democratic, Republican, or independent/mixed political backgrounds. Combinations of Democratic and Republican parents were coded "independent/mixed." Combinations of a Democratic or Republican parent with an independent were coded Democratic or Republican.

Political Party Preference

Ideally, a model of career development that seeks to examine the impact of political attitudes on career choices would include measures of those attitudes at various junctures in the careers. The only satisfactory measure we possess, however, deals with the respondents' current preferences. Based on questions about the direction and strength of party preferences in national politics, we coded the sample as Strong Democrats, Democrats, independents and others, Republicans, and Strong Republicans. Some of the multivariate analyses treated strength of party preference (strong or not) as a separate variable from party preference (Democrat, independent, Republican).

Intermediate Career Activities

The model includes two activities that can be of pivotal importance in shaping the careers of representatives: achieving an advanced degree and taking part in political campaigns. Graduate education is a prerequisite for a variety of positions involved in policy-making systems—lawyers, many kinds of technical experts, and the executives of certain organizations. Political involvement may be a requirement for entry into a position in government, which then creates career opportunities in private representation. Graduate education and political activity are "intermediate" career activities in the sense that they are stepping-stones for certain career transitions, and the respondents typically pursue them before embarking on the full-time positions analyzed in the career transitions data. Both variables were constructed as dichotomies—the presence or absence of a graduate degree beyond college, and work on an election campaign on more than a casual or short-term basis.

Government Experience

We divided the sample into those representatives who had no government experience, those who held positions only in state and local government, those who held congressional positions, and those who held other federal government jobs. Respondents with more than one type of government experience were placed in the "congressional" category if they had such experience and in the "other federal" category if they did not.

Current Employment and Clientele

The dependent variable in the analysis is the nature of the organizations that the respondents represent. Respondents are designated as business representatives if they are employed by or exclusively represent business organizations or trade associations. If the representatives are employed by or spend any time representing professional associations, nonprofit institutions (such as universities or hospitals), public interest groups, or unions, they are not coded as business representatives. Even with this stringent criterion, a majority of respondents (52%) qualify as business representatives. Respondents are designated representatives of liberal groups if they are employed by or spend some time representing labor unions or public interest groups (which include liberal national membership groups, associations of state and local officials, civil rights organizations, and special claimant groups such as the American Association of Retired Persons). While this definition is less stringent than that employed for business representatives, inspection of the time respondents devote to such client groups indicates that the vast majority of representatives in this category devote a significant portion of their time to liberal clients. Only 30% of the sample qualify as liberal representatives, however, even using this less exclusive definition.

Analysis and Findings

Most of the relationships among these variables can be summarized in simple cross-tabulations (see Tables 5.9 through 5.12), but to investigate more complicated patterns among the variables, and given the categorical nature of the data, we tested a series of log-linear models on various subsets of the variables. The results of these multivariate models are depicted in Figure 5.5. Arrows indicate the presence of significant relationships among variables, controlling for the effects of other variables within selected subtables of the entire set of variables. (Additional subtables and corresponding model selection results are reported in the statistical appendix to this chapter.)

Table 5.9 presents the relationships between ethnic and religious group membership and other social background and career characteristics. All of the bivariate relationships are statistically significant. As with the findings on professional occupations generally (see Heinz and Laumann 1982), a large portion of the sample as a whole (55%) comes from the two highest status social classes. Respondents with blue collar backgrounds are far more likely to be Catholics or nonidentifiers. Most respondents from farming backgrounds are Protestants. Jews attain advanced degrees at a higher rate than other groups. A majority of Jews, nonidentifiers, and Catholics come from the

Table 5.9 Ethnoreligious group, by father's occupation, graduate degree, region, family party preference, current party preference, business representation, and liberal representation (percentage distributions; N in parentheses)

	Catholic	Jewish	Type I Protestant	Type II Protestant	None/ Refused	Total
Father's occupation*						
Professional/technical	27	29	34	25	39	31
	(41)	(25)	(60)	(55)	(52)	(233)
Owner/manager	18	35	27	25	19	24
	(27)	(30)	(48)	(54)	(25)	(184)
Farmer	6	1	12	20	3	10
	(9)	(1)	(21)	(43)	(4)	(78)
Sales/clerical	12	18	11	10	10	11
	(18)	(15)	(19)	(22)	(13)	(87)
Blue collar	37	17	16	20	30	24
	(56)	(14)	(28)	(43)	(41)	(182)
Possess graduate degree*	63	79	60	60	70	65
	(95)	(67)	(106)	(131)	(98)	(497)
Region*						
Northeast	55	77	39	25	55	45
	(84)	(65)	(68)	(55)	(74)	(346)
Midwest	22	12	18	28	16	21
	(34)	(10)	(31)	(62)	(22)	(159)
South	10	8	27	31	12	21
	(15)	(7)	(47)	(68)	(16)	(159)
West/foreign	13	4	17	16	17	14
	(19)	(3)	(30)	(34)	(23)	(109)
Family party preference*						
Democrat	54	68	33	37	43	44
	(78)	(56)	(55)	(79)	(57)	(325)
Independent/mixed	19	24	22	28	24	24
	(27)	(20)	(37)	(60)	(32)	(176)
Republican	28	7	45	34	33	32
	(40)	(6)	(76)	(73)	(43)	(238)
Party preference*						
Strong Democrat	31	52	22	27	32	30
	(46)	(43)	(39)	(59)	(42)	(229)
Democrat	12	13	13	9	12	12
	(18)	(11)	(22)	(20)	(16)	(87)
Independent	24	25	23	23	36	26
	(35)	(21)	(41)	(49)	(47)	(193)
Republican	10	7	15	19	11	13
	(14)	(6)	(26)	(41)	(14)	(101)
Strong Republican	24	2	27	22	9	19
	(35)	(2)	(47)	(48)	(11)	(143)

Table 5.9 (continued)

	Catholic	Jewish	Type I Protes- tant	Type II Protes- tant	None/ Refused	Total
Employment by or exclusive representation of businesses or trade associations***	55 (83)	25 (21)	63 (113)	63 (137)	35 (49)	52 (403)
Employed by or representation of unions/public interest (liberal) groups***	32 (48)	48 (41)	19 (34)	23 (49)	39 (54)	30 (225)
Total	100 (152)	100 (85)	100 (179)	100 (219)	100 (141)	100 (776)

* Chi-square $p < .05$. ** $p < .01$. *** $p < .001$.

Northeast, as do a plurality of Type I Protestants, but a majority of Type II Protestants come from the Midwest and the South.

Ethnoreligious identity is strongly correlated with political characteristics. A majority of Jewish and Catholic representatives were raised in Democratic families, while for nonidentifiers and Type II Protestants there is a closer split between Democratic and Republican family backgrounds. Type I Protestants form the only clearly Republican bloc. The patterns for the current party preferences of the respondents are largely the same. Jews again have by far the clearest party identification, with a majority reporting that they are "strong Democrats." Although a plurality of Catholics report being Democrats, the proportion of Democrats is smaller than that among their parents, indicating a slight shift to Independent and Republican party preferences. Type I Protestants also show a slight shift from Republican family backgrounds toward a closer split between Republican and Democratic party preferences; Type II Protestants shift the other way, toward a preference for the Republican party.

Most striking in the table, however, is the powerful effect of ethnoreligious identity on business representation. Only a quarter of the representatives who are Jewish work exclusively for businesses or trade associations, but almost two-thirds of those with Protestant backgrounds do. The nonidentifiers also are less likely (35%) to serve exclusively as representatives of business, while a majority (55%) of Catholics are business representatives. The representation of liberal groups is the mirror image of this pattern. Nearly one-half of the

Table 5.10 Father's occupation, by graduate degree, region, family party preference, current party preference, business representation, and liberal representation (percentage distributions; N in parentheses)

	Professional/ technical	Owner/ manager	Farmer	Sales/ clerical	Blue collar	Total
Possesses graduate degree***	70	68	43	74	59	65
	(162)	(125)	(33)	(64)	(107)	(491)
Region* **						
Northeast	50	46	14	49	51	45
	(114)	(84)	(11)	(43)	(93)	(345)
Midwest	14	19	46	22	19	21
	(33)	(35)	(36)	(19)	(34)	(157)
South	19	22	27	15	19	20
	(43)	(41)	(21)	(13)	(34)	(151)
West/foreign	17	13	13	14	12	14
	(40)	(23)	(10)	(12)	(22)	(107)
Family party preference*						
Democrat	44	36	39	43	55	44
	(99)	(63)	(29)	(37)	(97)	(325)
Independent/mixed	23	24	32	16	24	24
	(52)	(42)	(24)	(14)	(42)	(174)
Republican	33	40	29	41	21	32
	(73)	(71)	(22)	(35)	(37)	(238)
Party preference						
Strong Democrat	33	29	33	21	33	31
	(75)	(52)	(25)	(18)	(59)	(229)
Democrat	15	10	12	14	9	12
	(34)	(17)	(9)	(12)	(15)	(87)
Independent	23	25	23	24	32	26
	(53)	(44)	(17)	(21)	(56)	(191)
Republican	12	16	12	17	11	13
	(27)	(28)	(9)	(15)	(20)	(99)
Strong Republican	18	21	20	24	15	19
	(41)	(37)	(15)	(21)	(27)	(141)
Employment by or exclusive	42	56	77	67	43	52
representation of businesses	(98)	(103)	(60)	(58)	(77)	(396)
or trade associations***						
Employed by or representation	35	24	15	21	39	30
of unions/public interest (liberal) groups***	(81)	(43)	(11)	(18)	(70)	(223)
Total	100	100	100	100	100	100
	(233)	(184)	(78)	(87)	(182)	(764)

Note: 12 cases were missing information on father's occupation.

* Chi-square $p < .05$. ** $p < .01$. *** $p < .001$.

Table 5.11 Party preference, by graduate degree, campaign activity, federal government experience, business representation, and liberal representation (percentage distributions; N in parentheses)

Party preference	Possess graduate degree***	Held campaign positions***	Government experience***				Employment by or exclusive representation of business/trade associations***	Employment by or representation of unions/public interest groups***	Total
			None	State/ local	Congress	Other federal[a]			
Strong Democrat	56 (129)	60 (137)	36 (82)	10 (22)	27 (62)	28 (63)	31 (72)	55 (123)	100 (229)
Democrat	5 (65)	4 (29)	40 (35)	13 (11)	17 (15)	30 (26)	44 (39)	31 (26)	100 (88)
Independent	72 (139)	29 (56)	47 (90)	7 (13)	12 (23)	35 (67)	48.2 (93)	26 (49)	100 (193)
Republican	71 (72)	35 (35)	56 (57)	4 (4)	6 (6)	33 (34)	73 (74)	12 (12)	100 (101)
Strong Republican	55 (79)	44 (63)	50 (72)	10 (14)	15 (22)	25 (35)	80 (115)	6 (9)	100 (143)
Total	64 (484)	43 (320)	45 (336)	9 (64)	17 (128)	30 (225)	52 (393)	29 (219)	100 (753)

Note: 23 cases were missing information on party preference.
a. Excludes military duty and judicial clerkships.
* Chi-square $p < .05$. ** $p < .01$. *** $p < .001$.

Table 5.12   Business representation and liberal representation, by party preference and federal government experience

Party preference	Government experience				
	None	State/local only	Congress	Other federal[a]	Total (N)
	% Employed by or exclusively representing businesses or trade associations				
Strong Democrat	18	27	50	32	31 (229)
Democrat	37	27	60	54	45 (87)
Independent	47	46	65	45	48 (192)
Republican	79	50	100	62	73 (101)
Strong Republican	79	79	73	89	80 (143)
Total (N)	51 (335)	44 (64)	60 (128)	52 (225)	52 (752)
	% Employed by or representing unions/public interest groups				
Strong Democrat	65	62	36	57	55 (225)
Democrat	32	55	29	20	31 (84)
Independent	25	46	17	25	26 (192)
Republican	11	25	0	15	12 (100)
Strong Republican	3	14	9	9	6 (141)
Total (N)	28 (332)	45 (63)	25 (127)	30 (220)	29 (742)

a. Excludes military duty and judicial clerkships.

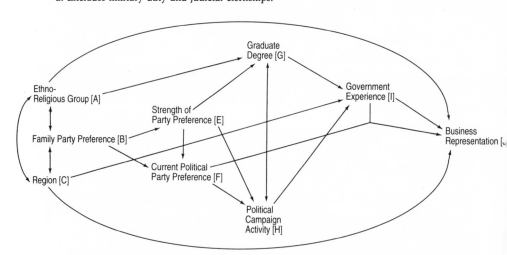

Figure 5.5   Variables influencing type of client represented (based on selected log-linear models)

Jewish representatives (48%) work for liberal groups, more than double the proportion among either Protestant group. The nonidentifiers are also more likely than the sample as a whole to represent liberal groups, while the Catholics are just about at the sample mean.

Although representatives may not be conscious of ethnoreligious identity, therefore, it clearly remains an important dimension of the social organization of representation. Moreover, the effect of ethnoreligious membership is not attributable to intervening variables (Figure 5.5). Controlling for the effects of advanced education and party preference, we still find a significant direct relationship between ethnoreligious identification and business representation. Whether this reflects self-selection or their exclusion from opportunities in business organizations, Jews and other non-Protestants are far less likely to serve as business representatives.

Father's occupation is strongly related to other social background variables and to the propensity of representatives to work for business clients, but it is not as powerful a determinant of either family or personal party preferences as is ethnoreligious identity. Children of the professional, managerial, and clerical categories are far more likely to attain an advanced degree than are the children of either farmers or blue collar workers (Table 5.10). All but farmers tend to cluster in the Northeast; farmers are concentrated in the Midwest and South. The top and bottom status groups—professionals and blue collar workers—are the most likely to come from Democratic family backgrounds. Only owners and managers are more likely to have a Republican family background than a Democratic one, but the relationship between father's occupation and the representative's own party preference is not statistically significant.

Like ethnoreligious identification, the effects of socioeconomic class on business or liberal representation are significant, and there are some interesting patterns in these relationships. Again, it is the children of the top and bottom status groups—professionals and blue collar workers—who are least likely to represent business interests exclusively and most likely to represent liberal groups. The children of farmers are most likely to be business representatives, followed by the sales/clerical and the owner/manager classes. These findings indicate that direct occupational inheritance has some effect on the careers of representatives. Part of the reason that the children of farmers are especially likely to represent trade associations is that many of them are farmers who participate in farm associations, and the children of blue collar workers are more than twice as likely as other representatives to hold positions in labor unions. To a less striking extent, the children of owners and managers and of professionals tend to carry their heritage into positions with business and professional organizations respectively. A high proportion of the sales/clerical category also work as business representatives, however, even though there is no clear nexus between clerical positions and particular organizational types. It may be that the sales/clerical category is a relatively nonideological group primarily motivated by considerations of upward mobility, and that children of sales and clerical workers therefore eschew positions with nonprofit organizations, unions, and citizen-government groups in favor of jobs in trade associations and law firms, which offer stable careers and economic rewards.

Because political party preference is more proximate to the career choice, we might expect this factor to have a direct effect on various aspects of career development, and it does. Party preference is significantly related to all of the remaining variables in the system (Table 5.11). Interestingly, strength of party identification rather than mere identification with Democrats or Republicans determines some relationships. Strong Democrats and strong Republicans achieve advanced degrees at a much lower rate than do representatives with more moderate political leanings; representatives who report that they are strong Democrats are far more likely than others to have held campaign positions, while strong Republicans rank second on that measure. These findings confirm our observation about the career paths of lawyers: there are two distinct routes to becoming a representative—one through political activity and one through advanced graduate training. Strong partisans are less likely to possess post-graduate education, but more likely to have been active in political campaigns.

Party preference also correlates with government experience in the predicted way. Democrats are more likely to have held government positions than either Independents or Republicans and are more likely to have worked in Congress. Moreover, party identification is strongly related to the probability of serving business or liberal clients. Strong Democrats are almost twice as likely to work for liberal groups as to act exclusively for business. Only a handful of Republicans represent liberal groups, while over three-quarters work exclusively for business groups. Like the ethnoreligious stratification, this pronounced tendency for members of different national parties to serve different clients goes unrecognized by most representatives. Some 52% of the respondents said that partisanship was not a factor in their work. Perhaps the reason that partisanship is invisible to so many representatives is that it is embedded in the very structure of organizational positions and representative roles.

The effect of social background on career development and on the probability that a representative will work exclusively for business interests occurs not only indirectly, through party preference, but directly as well (Figure 5.5). When we control for the representative's party preference, only the effect of family politics drops out (no doubt because the two are so highly correlated). Although region is not significantly related to party preference, it has other effects. About two-thirds of the respondents from Midwestern or Southern origins act solely for business clients, while barely one in five do any work for liberal groups. But 35% of the representatives with Northeastern or Western origins work for liberal groups. Among Democrats (including strong Democrats) only 35% represent business exclusively, but 53% of the Southern Democrats are business representatives.

Representatives with advanced degrees are more likely than others to have held government jobs (54% versus 39%) and, among those with government experience, an advanced degree makes one more than three times as likely (47% versus 14%) to have had a noncongressional job. Campaign experience raises the probability of having held a government position (from 50% to 64%) and increases the likelihood of holding a congressional position threefold (from 9% to 28%).

If we control for graduate education and campaign activity, the effect of party preference on government experience becomes insignificant, but government experience affects the probability that Democrats and independents will act as business representatives. (The intersecting lines between government experience and party preference in Figure 5.5 represent this interaction.) Government experience does not affect the clientele of Republicans, most of whom exclusively represent business groups no matter what government experience they have had (Table 5.12). The proportion representing businesses steadily increases for Democrats and independents, however, as they move from no experience to noncongressional federal experience to congressional experience.

The channeling effects of social and political background are all the more significant because representatives tend to continue to work for the same kinds of organizations throughout their careers, though nearly half of the sample indicated that they had previously represented other specific organizations. Table 5.13 analyzes how the previous employers compare with the kinds of organizations that currently employ the respondents. The table provides overwhelming evidence that representatives who change organizations tend to remain with the same kind of organization. Some 59% of the instances of prior representation appear along the main diagonal of Table 5.13, showing no change in type of employer. This stability or consistency is strongest for business and trade association representatives and for union representatives. Representatives working in law and consulting firms come from a more diverse set of employer relationships, although many more lawyers and consultants previously worked for business organizations than for public interest or nonprofit organizations. Representatives of nonprofit and professional associations report somewhat more inbreeding than those in law and consulting firms. The table underscores the fundamental divide between the representation of business and the representation of liberal groups. Representatives seldom cross this boundary. They are employed either by businesses/trade associations or by unions/public interest groups.

Table 5.13   Type of prior organizations represented, by type of current employer

Prior organization represented	Current employer				
	Law and consulting	Business and trade assoc.	Unions/public interest groups	Nonprofit and professional assoc.	Total
Law and consulting	33 (50.0%)	26 (17.9%)	2 (3.1%)	5 (7.6%)	
Business and trade assoc.	25 (37.9%)	111 (76.6%)	9 (13.8%)	18 (27.3%)	
Unions/public interest groups	13 (19.7%)	9 (6.2%)	47 (72.3%)	16 (27.3%)	
Nonprofit and professional assoc.	9 (13.6%)	16 (11.0%)	11 (16.9%)	39 (59.1%)	
Total prior types/ respondents	80/66 (121.2%)	162/145 (111.7%)	69/65 (106.1%)	78/66 (118.1%)	389/342 (113.7%)

Notes: Percentages in parentheses based on instances/respondents in type of current employer. Some individuals previously represented more than one organizational type.

Less than 5% of the reported changes are movements across these camps.

The inescapable lesson of these findings is that social background has a profound effect on the careers and current work of representatives. Ethnicity and social class mold political preferences and professional career choices, which in turn shape the kinds of government experience that representatives acquire and the types of clients that they represent. But in addition to these indirect effects, ethnicity and class also directly influence the likelihood that representatives will advocate the interests of business or liberal groups.

Conclusion

The careers of representatives present paradoxical images of the system of private representation. On the one hand, there is evidence that representation is structured by the substance of the work. Distinct career paths lead to organizationally differentiated work roles: organizations recruit from within for the representatives who occupy executive and staff positions; government affairs officers and trade association executives are recruited from political positions in government; lawyers are recruited from government law jobs or directly out of law school. For each of these positions, there is a strong correspondence between career experience and the knowledge requirements of the jobs. Our analysis of the uses of government experience indicates that what you know tends to be more important than who you know. The major qualification of that general rule—that contacts are more important to the work of representatives who had congressional experience—also is consistent with a functional interpretation. Congress operates less formally than do executive branch agencies and depends more upon interpersonal connections. Contrary to conventional wisdom, we detected only minor evidence of a revolving door between the interest groups and the government agencies that regulate them.

On the other hand, we found that this organizationally differentiated system of work and careers is embedded within and heavily shaped by ethnicity, class, and political party. The representatives of business interests are far more likely to have fathers who were owners or managers, to be Protestant, to have midwestern or southern origins, and to identify with the Republican party. The representatives of liberal groups are far more likely to come from the professional or working classes, to be Jewish, from the Northeast, and Democrats.

Why did our informants dismiss the significance of social background in the system of representation, and why did a majority of the respondents claim that party affiliation never affects their work? As Bourdieu (1977) suggests for social systems generally, the influence of status, class, and party can be invisible because it is the very fabric out of which policy systems and their constituent organizations are constructed. It may be that client organizations do not perceive these effects because they operate mainly to guide the behavior of the individual representatives. In a world in which social and political background so pervasively structures career choices, it may not be necessary for interest organizations to take social or political characteristics into account in recruiting representatives. These characteristics will be embodied in job applicants who are homogeneous by self-selection. We cannot determine, however, whether the channeling of individuals by ethnicity, class, and politics occurs through individual choice or organizational policy. But the consequences of such a social structure seem clear. Our findings imply that, beneath the surface tensions among interest groups over current policy debates, deeper conflicts reflect fundamental ideological differences arising from status-class alignments in American society.

APPENDIX: Additional Statistical Models and Model Selection Results

Logistic Regression Models of What You Know

Table 5.A1 contains the results of logistic regression models for issue familiarity and process understanding discussed in the section of chapter 5 on the uses of government experience. (For a full elaboration see Salisbury et al. 1989.)

Data and Model Selection Results Pertaining to Relationships Shown in Figure 5.3

Table 5.A2 contains the data that make up the system of variables that is analyzed in the section of chapter 5 on the relationship between legal education and representatives' careers. Tables 5.A3 to 5.A5

Table 5.A1 Logistic regression models: what you know

Variable	Issue familiarity		Process understanding	
	Model A *b*	Model B *b*	Model A *b*	Model B *b*
Intercept	0.42	−0.33	0.4	−1.43**
Long-run effect of govt. experience in (dummy vars.):				
Congress	0.85	0.71	3.3*	3.7*
Executive	1.80*	1.99*	2.45*	2.9*
Both	−0.16	−0.15	0.72	0.28
Delay (−1/length):				
Congress	1.03	1.5**	2.53*	3.1*
Executive	1.93*	3.3*	1.82*	2.4*
Other	0.004	−0.13	−0.73	−1.28
Decay (yrs. service):				
Congress	−0.001	0.03	−0.059	−0.047
Executive	−0.073*	−0.075*	−0.080*	−0.08*
Other	−0.002	−0.015	−0.033	−0.047*
Govt. experience in domains (dummy vars.):				
Agriculture		1.61*		2.12*
Energy		0.69		−0.07
Health		1.44*		0.92
Labor		1.33*		1.79*
Present domain:				
Energy		−0.06		0.80
Health		−0.44		0.64
Labor		0.53		0.50
Govt. experience in present domain (dummy)		1.24*		−0.13
Present position:				
CEO		0.01		0.28
Head of trade assn.		−0.10		0.75
Govt. affairs		0.24		0.90
Lawyer		−0.85**		0.12
Percentage of time in fed. policy		−0.12		−0.21
Percentage of time in own domain activity		0.11		0.40*
N	386	384	386	384
−2LLR	29.6	119	32.16	109.4
df	9	23	9	23
p <	.01	.01	.01	.01
Correctly predicted	70.2%	76.3%	82.6%	85.2%

* $p < .05$ according to $t = b/\text{S.E.}$ ** $p < .10$.

Table 5.A2   Percentage of representatives spending more than half their time on federal policy work, by organizational position, government experience, political experience, and law degree (N in parentheses)

Organizational position	Political experience with a law degree		No political experience with a law degree		Political experience with no law degree		No political experience or law degree		Total
	Govt. experience		Govt. experience		Govt. experience		Govt. experience		
	Yes	No	Yes	No	Yes	No	Yes	No	
Executives	42.9	33.3	50.0	14.3	24.0	13.8	30.3	10.3	20.4
	(7)	(9)	(8)	(7)	(25)	(29)	(33)	(68)	(186)
Government affairs[a]	68.4	60.0	68.4	47.1	73.1	43.6	51.4	47.0	55.8
	(19)	(15)	(19)	(17)	(67)	(55)	(35)	(83)	(310)
Internal staff	40.0	25.0	57.1	26.1	50.0	26.3	52.9	35.7	37.7
	(5)	(8)	(14)	(23)	(8)	(19)	(17)	(28)	(122)
External representatives	28.1	30.8	37.2	32.0	50.0	60.0	45.5	33.3	35.5
	(32)	(13)	(43)	(25)	(6)	(5)	(11)	(6)	(141)
Total	42.9	40.0	48.8	31.9	58.5	33.3	43.8	31.4	40.4
	(63)	(45)	(84)	(72)	(106)	(108)	(96)	(185)	(759)

a. Includes trade association executives.

Table 5.A3   Chi-square values for some models pertaining to relationships among law degree (A), federal government experience (B), and political involvement (C)

Model	Likelihood ratio chi-square	Degrees of freedom	Probability value
[AB][BC][AC]	2.32	1	.127
[AB][BC][a]	3.45	2	.178
[BC][A]	20.02	3	.000
[AB][C]	13.76	3	.003

a. Denotes the model selected.

Table 5.A4   Chi-square values for some models pertaining to relationships among law degree (A), federal government experience (B), political involvement (C), and organizational position (D)

Model	Likelihood ratio chi-square	Degrees of freedom	Probability value
[ABC][AD][BD][CD][a]	14.31	12	.282
[ABC][BD][CD]	177.81	15	.000
[ABC][AD][CD]	31.18	15	.008
[ABC][AD][BD]	28.08	15	.021

a. Denotes the model selected.

Table 5.A5   Chi-square values for some models pertaining to relationships among law degree (A), federal government experience (B), political involvement (C), organizational position (D), and time spent on federal policy work (E)

Model	Likelihood ratio chi-square	Degrees of freedom	Probability value
[ABCD][BE][CE][DE]	20.29	26	.725
[ABCD][AE][BE][DE]	20.31	26	.777
[ABCD][BE][DE][a]	20.58	27	.806
[ABCD][DE]	42.76	28	.037
[ABCD][BE]	87.15	30	.000

a. Denotes the model selected.

report chi-square values for some models pertaining to these relationships.

Model Selection Procedures Pertaining to Relationships Shown in Figure 5.5

The following describes the model selection procedures employed to construct Figure 5.5. Because of the number of variables and categories included in the system of variables, it was necessary to analyze subsets of relationships in sequence. In some models, variables were recoded to reduce the number of categories and provide more stable results. The overall logic of the analysis was first to investigate the relationships among variables moving from the left to the right in Figure 5.5. If there was no zero-order relationship between two variables, we did not test for higher order effects between the variables. After establishing models for subsets of variables, we then tested the relationships between the ultimate variable of interest—business representation—and other variables. In this phase we moved from right to left in Figure 5.5, beginning with models incorporating variables that were more proximate to business representation and then progressively including less proximate variables while controlling for other significant variables.

Letters in the following explanation are those assigned variables shown in Figure 5.5.

1. *Social and political background characteristics.* We originally employed four background variables—those shown in Figure 5.5 and father's occupation [D]. The four social and political background variables were strongly interrelated (see Tables 5.9 and 5.10). A model based on all three-variable interactions, [ABC][ABD][BCD], achieved only a marginal degree of fit (LR chi-square = 32.1, DF = 24, p = .124). Thus, the full four-effects model, [ABCD], is needed to explain the relationships among these variables.

   Given the number of categories in the ethnoreligious and father's occupation variables, it was statistically difficult to employ both variables in more elaborate models. Forced to choose, we opted for using ethnoreligious group because it had stronger relationships with the other variables in the system than did father's occupation. In the later stages of model selection results, therefore, we do not include father's occupation.

2. *Strength of party preference and party preference.* The variables are strongly related to each other at the zero order (chi-square p < .0001). 73% of Democrats, 59% of Republicans, and 0% of independents are strongly identified politically. (Independents were not asked the question on strength of identification.) Strength of party preference is significantly associated with family party preference (B), but with none of the other background variables (A, C, or D). 54% of the representatives from Democratic families, 47% from Republican families, and 43% from parents who were independents or who had conflicting party affiliations strongly identified with one of the national parties. Thus, the model [BE] is adequate to express the relationships with this set of variables.

Party preference is significantly related to all prior variables except region of origin (C). (See Tables 5.9 and 5.10.) For the four-variable subtable consisting of variables A, B, C, and F, acceptable fit was achieved for the model [AB][AF][BF] (LR chi-square = 13.53, DF = 16, p. = 634). Dropping either the AF or the BF terms produced models that did not fit the subtable.

3. *Graduate degree and political campaign activity.* The variables were significantly related at the zero order (chi-square p = .0004). Of representatives with no advanced degree, 51% had been active in a political campaign, compared to 37% of those with advanced degrees. The relationship between party preference and graduate degree drops out when we control for strength of party preference, however. The model [EF][EG]—which includes no direct effect of party preference on graduate degree—attains good fit (LR chi-square = .354, DF = 4, p = .986). Ethnoreligious group has a zero-order association with graduate degree, which remains significant after controlling for party preference. Thus, the model that explains the relationship between ethnoreligious group, party preference, and graduate degree is [AF][AG][FG] (LR chi-square = 5.77, DF = 8, p = .672). Dropping the AG term leads to a statistically significant drop in chi-square.

Political campaign involvement is not significantly associated with ethnoreligious group, family politics, region, or father's occupation, but it is strongly associated with both party preference and strength of party preference. (See Table 5.11.) Models dropping any of the two variable effects on campaign activity— [EH][FH][GH]—do not fit the data.

4. *Government experience.* For purposes of testing log-linear models, the government experience variable was recoded into a three-category variable: those with no government experience, those with state and local experience and noncongressional experience, and those with congressional experience. None of the social background variables as they were recoded for this analysis was significantly associated with government experience. The model selected from among the remaining prior variables was: [EFGH][FI][GI][HI] (LR chi-square = 24.7, DF = 38, p = .953). Note that eliminating the term for the direct effect of strength of party preference, [EI], did not affect the fit of this model. Dropping any other terms resulted in a poor fit with the subtable.

5. *Business representation.* Government experience (as recoded) is related to business representation at a marginal level of significance (chi-square p = .13). Nonetheless, we included government experience in models testing the effects of party, graduate degree, and campaign activity on business representation. Terms for the direct relationships of business representation with graduate degree and campaign activity, respectively, can be dropped without impairing the fit of simpler models in which these variables affect propensity for business representation through their effects on type of government experience ([GI][IJ], LR chi-square = 3.45, DF = 3, p = .328; [HI][IJ], LR chi-square = .29, DF = 3, p = .962). A different pattern held for party preference. Dropping the direct effect of party on business representation [FJ] resulted in a weak fitting model (LR chi-square = 6.13, DF = 4, p = .19). The model [FIJ], which includes the interaction between government experience and party preference, is necessary to explain the subtable more satisfactorily.

The last set of tests examined the direct links between background variables and business representation controlling, one at a time, the government experience and party preference variables. Ethnoreligious group, region, and father's occupation each had a significant direct effect on the dependent variable, while controlling the other variables. Perhaps not surprisingly, family politics did not have a significant direct effect on business representation after controlling for current party preference. (The addition of the [BJ] term to a model based on [BF][FJ] increased the chi-square by 3.5, with change in DF of 2, for a probability of .21 that the change was significant.) This is an instance where a more proximate measure overwhelms the direct effect of a less proximate but related measure.

Chapter 6

Ideology,
Colleague Networks,
and Professional Autonomy

Most private Washington representatives probably see themselves as advancing their clients' interests rather than their own, but the representatives' own political views and the character of the networks in which they discuss policy matters may have important effects on their perceptions of issues and of policy options. Yet we know relatively little about representatives' political values. Are representatives a "liberal establishment" that endorses the expansion of government programs in spite of the conservative philosophies of recent presidential administrations? Or, given their privileged positions (in terms of education, income, and community standing), are they more conservative than most Americans? Despite differences in social background, clientele, and party affiliation, do representatives share a basic philosophy of government, or are they polarized into groups with fundamentally antagonistic views of social and political issues?

Representatives may seek out clients with policy views similar to their own. Or they may approach employment opportunities as "hired guns," or simply identify with the interests of the organizations that nurture them. The social and political connections among representatives might facilitate discussion and compromise among contending groups, or more isolated sets of networks could work to insulate opposing groups from each other and thereby reduce the prospects for accommodation. The networks that representatives form with respect to policy matters may thus serve either to ameliorate the effects of ideological differences or to make political conflicts more intense.

The political values and the role orientations of "professionals" among the representatives, especially lawyers, are of particular interest. Two ideals that are hallmarks of the professions are that they serve the public interest and that they exercise autonomous decision-making authority in their work. If a substantial segment of representatives embodies these ideals, conflicts that arise from ideological and pragmatic differences among interest groups might to some degree be dampened.

Social and Political Values

We gave the respondents a set of statements concerning social and political issues and asked them to indicate whether they strongly agreed, agreed, were undecided, disagreed, or strongly disagreed with the statements. In Tables 6.1 and 6.2, the items are grouped by broad subject matter. When presented to the respondents, however, the items were mixed together and not placed in categories.

Value preferences vary significantly by organization and political party. The general pattern is clear: employees of businesses take the most conservative positions, followed closely by trade association employees and more distantly by the employees of nonprofit organizations. As a group, outside lawyers and consultants occupy the middle ground. Employees of professional associations embrace more liberal positions than do lawyers and consultants on many, but not all, issues. Employees of citizen and government groups and of labor unions anchor the liberal end of the values spectrum. The responses are even more orderly with respect to political party. For all but one item, the categories of party affiliation correspond perfectly to the percentage agreeing, with strong Democrats taking the most liberal positions, followed in rank by Democrats, Independents, Republicans, and strong Republicans. The overall findings establish beyond question the existence of a clear ideological structure among representatives, with sharp divisions corresponding to the organizations they work for and their party identification.

A solid majority of the respondents prefer vigorous competition to federal government regulation on behalf of consumers. This position is most strongly held by business and trade association representatives, but attracts close to majority support from all categories except union and citizen-government representatives. The latter appear politically isolated on this issue and suspicious of competition as a means of consumer protection. But consumer groups and organized labor part company on import restrictions, which are perceived as imposing

Table 6.1 Agreement (strongly agree and agree) with social and political values items, by employing organization (percentages)

Item	Business	Trade assoc.	Non-profit	Profes-sional assoc.	Citizen-govt. groups	Labor unions	Law firms	Consulting firms	Over-all	N	Sig. Level
Federalism/free market											
a. The protection of consumer interests is best insured by a vigorous competition among sellers rather than by federal government regulation on behalf of consumers.	86	72	63	49	24	22	55	52	56	725	.0000
b. In general, the U.S. should impose greater restrictions on imports of goods from abroad.	23	23	21	16	20	85	22	28	27	726	.0000
c. To cope effectively with the problems facing our society, what is needed is a general strengthening and reliance on local government institutions, rather than the federal government, in finding solutions to these problems.	66	70	50	40	40	17	39	32	50	715	.0000
Inequality											
d. One of the most important roles of government is to help those who cannot help themselves, such as the poor, the disadvantaged, and the unemployed.	77	72	77	87	94	94	85	79	82	727	.0004

										N	
e.	Economic profits are by and large justly distributed in the U.S. today.	75	55	65	38	23	8	42	43	45	726	.0000
f.	All Americans should have equal access to quality medical care regardless of ability to pay.	60	69	68	83	86	97	75	93	76	725	.0000
g.	Affirmative action programs have excessively restricted freedom to hire and promote the best qualified individuals.	59	63	46	50	25	19	56	59	50	724	.0000
h.	Differences in income among occupations should be reduced.	8	10	23	22	38	52	17	21	21	720	.0000
	Corporate vs. labor power											
i.	There is too much power concentrated in the hands of a few large companies for the good of the country.	14	29	33	38	58	91	41	48	41	727	.0000
j.	The gains that labor unions make for their members help make the country more prosperous.	26	25	42	32	48	96	44	54	40	726	.0000
k.	Labor unions have become too big for the good of the country.	52	59	42	46	27	9	37	29	42	725	.0000

Table 6.1 (continued)

Item	Business	Trade assoc.	Non-profit	Profes-sional assoc.	Citizen-govt. groups	Labor unions	Law firms	Consulting firms	Over-all	N	Sig. Level
Regulation of fund-raising/ representation											
l. Severe sanctions should be imposed on persons in your line of work who fail to dis-close the continuing illegal activities of their clients.	75	75	78	72	73	87	44	48	70	670	.0000
m. Fund-raisers who generate income for political causes have become too influential in Washington policy making.	48	44	63	57	71	66	59	48	55	728	.0003
n. There should be a strict limit on the total amount of money that can be spent for or by a candidate in his or her campaign for public office.	59	63	63	72	80	88	70	12	68	729	.0013
Economic liberalism scale	2.48	2.67	2.91	3.18	3.67	4.35	3.06	3.34	3.08	705	.0000

higher costs on consumers while improving the employment prospects of some workers. Union representatives are thus alone in their strong endorsement of greater restrictions on imports. Despite the union support, import restrictions do not enjoy majority support from any political subgroup, not even strong Democrats.

Respondents from businesses and trade associations support strengthening local government institutions rather than the federal government, while only a minority of representatives from most other types of organizations agree with the proposition. But this question splits the sample more evenly than the free market questions. Thus, while the sample quite broadly supports reliance on competition in economic matters, only the business groups are likely to believe that local government can take the place of federal programs.

There is general agreement that government must play a role in providing for the basic needs of the disadvantaged, however. More than four-fifths of the respondents agree with the statement that government must "help those who cannot help themselves"; and more than three-quarters believe that all Americans should have equal access to quality medical care regardless of ability to pay. But the sample rejects more radically redistributive policies. Only one respondent in five agrees with the proposition that differences in income among occupations should be reduced; union representatives are the only category in which a majority supports that view.

Respondents are again more evenly divided, however, on questions concerning the justice of the prevailing distribution of economic profits and the disadvantages of affirmative action programs. A majority of the representatives of businesses, trade associations, and nonprofit organizations support the view that economic profits are by and large justly distributed in the United States today. No other organizational category contains a majority of favorable opinion on the proposition, although a substantial minority of respondents from professional associations, law firms, and consulting firms also agree. Fewer than one in ten of the union representatives endorse this view. There is widespread concern that affirmative action programs have excessively restricted freedom to hire and promote the best qualified individuals. The proposition attracts majority agreement from all but the representatives of nonprofit organizations, citizen-government groups, and unions. The inequality items thus indicate that representatives as a whole have a moderately liberal ideology. With the exception of the business representatives, they perceive patterns of

Table 6.2 Agreement (strongly agree and agree) with social and political values items, by party affiliation (percentages)

Item	Strong Democrat	Democrat	Ind.-Other	Republican	Strong Republican	Overall	N	Sig. level
Federalism/free market								
a. The protection of consumer interests is best insured by a vigorous competition among sellers rather than by federal government regulation on behalf of consumers.	30	43	63	78	85	56	710	.0000
b. In general, the U.S. should impose greater restrictions on imports of goods from abroad.	36	27	25	25	17	27	711	.0035
c. To cope effectively with the problems facing our society, what is needed is a general strengthening and reliance on local government institutions, rather than the federal government, in finding solutions to these problems.	21	45	54	70	83	50	701	.0000
Inequality								
d. One of the most important roles of government is to help those who cannot help themselves, such as the poor, the disadvantaged, and the unemployed.	94	84	78	80	64	82	712	.0000
e. Economic profits are by and large justly distributed in the U.S. today.	23	37	48	66	73	45	712	.0000
f. All Americans should have equal access to quality medical care regardless of ability to pay.	90	78	75	63	62	76	710	.0000

g. Affirmative action programs have excessively restricted freedom to hire and promote the best qualified individuals.	23	46	58	63	73	50	709	.0000
h. Differences in income among occupations should be reduced.	40	21	16	6	7	21	706	.0000
Corporate vs. labor power								
i. There is too much power concentrated in the hands of a few large companies for the good of the country.	71	42	38	16	13	41	712	.0000
j. The gains that labor unions make for their members help make the country more prosperous.	67	51	29	25	16	40	711	.0000
k. Labor unions have become too big for the good of the country.	18	39	47	56	67	42	711	.0000
Regulation of fund-raising/representation								
l. Severe sanctions should be imposed on persons in your line of work who fail to disclose the continuing illegal activities of their clients.	74	70	68	69	66	70	661	.2291
m. Fund-raisers who generate income for political causes have become too influential in Washington policy making.	67	55	63	40	36	55	715	.0000
n. There should be a strict limit on the total amount of money that can be spent for or by a candidate in his or her campaign for public office.	82	74	70	57	48	68	714	.0000
Economic liberalism scale	3.84	3.22	2.93	2.58	2.32	3.08	705	.0000

economic inequality; they favor specific human services programs, such as for medical care and unemployment; but they oppose broadly redistributive policies and worry that affirmative action may unduly limit meritocratic personnel policies.

Three items in the survey dealt with the power of corporations and labor unions. As expected, few of the business representatives thought that there is too much power concentrated in the hands of a few large companies for the good of the country, while most union representatives thought that there was. Similarly, almost all the union representatives, but only a quarter of the business and trade association representatives, thought that the gains that labor unions make for their members help make the country more prosperous. The union representatives, again not surprisingly, also had sharply different reactions than business and trade association respondents to the statement "Labor unions have become too big for the good of the country."

Most other representatives, however, were modestly sanguine about both large corporations and organized labor. Although a majority of citizen-government representatives view large corporations as having too much power, only a third to a half of the respondents in the remaining organizational categories hold this view. Washington representatives, in fact, appear to be substantially less concerned about concentrations of corporate power than are national cross-sectional samples. The proportion agreeing with the proposition in national surveys increased steadily from 53% in 1959 to a high of 79% in 1979. In 1983, the year our survey was administered, the proportion was 75% (Lipset and Schneider 1987, 30). The overall proportion in our sample, 41%, is very low by comparison, but this is not surprising. The majority of the representatives work exclusively for business organizations. Even nonbusiness representatives have usually spent their careers in large organizations of one kind or another, be they government agencies, universities, professional associations, or foundations. The specter of corporate power, or perhaps of power in general, may appear less threatening to them because they have been immersed in organizational milieus and are therefore less suspicious of them, or because they have a sense that countervailing sources of organizational power balance the power held by private corporations.

The pattern holds in the attitudes about organized labor. Although the specific questions we used with respect to unions have not been administered to national samples, organized labor has received high confidence ratings from only a little more than a quarter of the respondents in national opinion surveys (Lipset and Schneider 1987, 200–201). Among nonbusiness and nonlabor representatives, between 32% and 54% see the gains labor unions win for members as benefiting the country economically, while between 27% and 46% see unions as too big for the good of the country. The central tendency of our respondents thus appears to be somewhat more favorably disposed toward organized labor than is the American public at large, but the organized business community remains dubious. In general, and in contrast to other samples that express hostility to the private institutional power of both labor and business (see, for example, Heinz and Laumann 1982), representatives as a group are relatively comfortable with the power wielded by these organizations. There is a strong partisan dimension at work, however, and in subsequent analyses we examine the extent to which the observed differences result from personal opinions rather than client positions.

The last three items explore attitudes about issues of more immediate interest to representatives. A strong majority take the view that representatives who fail to disclose the continuing illegal activities of their clients should be severely sanctioned. Indeed, this is the only item that does not produce significant differences by political party. Independent lawyers and consultants exhibit stronger support for confidentiality, however. The deviation on the part of lawyers presumably reflects their sensitivity to questions of attorney-client privilege; the legal profession's ethical rules allow for such disclosures only under certain circumstances. External consultants are a more heterogeneous group, but they too tend to disagree with a strict disclosure principle.

The two items concerning political fund-raising divide the sample by both organizational and partisan characteristics. A majority of respondents agree that political fund-raisers have become too influential in Washington policy making. The only organizational categories in which less than a majority agree are business and trade association representatives and external consultants. Democrats and Independents strongly support the proposition, but only 40% of Republicans and 36% of strong Republicans agree. There is stronger overall agreement on limits on campaign spending, but there are similar differences by organization type and political party. A bare majority of business representatives and less than a majority of strong

Republicans favor such limits. Among representatives of citizen-government groups, labor unions, and strong Democrats, 80% or more endorse spending limits. This pattern corresponds to traditional partisan alignments on such issues. Republicans in Congress and elsewhere have opposed measures to curb the use of their superior financial resources, while Democrats tend to favor such limits.

Viewed as a whole, the responses reveal a consistently structured set of divergent opinions about the problems that face American society and the sorts of institutional responses that might best address them. Representatives of business groups, on the one hand, and representatives of public interest groups and labor unions, on the other, hold clearly opposed visions of the proper role of government in economic markets, of the nature of inequality and whether and how it should be addressed by government, and of the power of corporations and labor unions. Representatives of nonprofit organizations and professional associations, lawyers in firms, and external consultants take positions between the ideological lines drawn by business and liberal groups.

Thus, it is possible to talk about "the" ideology of Washington representatives in only the most general terms. As a whole, representatives are political moderates: they favor a balance of competition and government regulation; they support government social programs that address particular ills, but not programs that would fundamentally redistribute economic rewards; and they are not opposed to the power wielded either by large corporations or by labor unions. What is most apparent in their social and political attitudes, however, is not similarity but difference—difference structured by organizational base and, even more sharply, by corresponding political party affiliation. And because the four policy domains contain different sets of organizational actors and varying proportions of Democrats and Republicans, each represents a distinct ideological climate. Agriculture and energy are ideologically conservative. Health is more liberal. Labor is deeply split.

The Determinants of Economic Liberalism

To what extent are ideological differences among representatives the product of personal background, career selection, or current work activities? Do individuals seek out ideologically congenial work environments? Were they partisans before becoming interest representatives, or do they adjust their political views to suit the job? To consider these questions, we turn to a multivariate analysis.

The ideological variation within the sample can be effectively summarized by combining eight questions into a scale of economic liberalism. The items are scored from a value of 1, indicating strong agreement with the conservative position, to 5, indicating strong agreement with the liberal position.[1] Mean economic liberalism scores by organization type and political party identification are shown in the bottom line of Tables 6.1 and 6.2.

The patterns conform to those we observed on the individual items. Business and trade association representatives are significantly more conservative than the sample as a whole, while citizen-government and especially union representatives are at the liberal end of the scale. Nonprofit and professional organizations and representatives based in law firms and consulting firms occupy intermediate positions. Political party identification is highly correlated with scale values; strong Democrats register the highest mean, followed at consistently lower levels by Democrats, Independents, Republicans, and strong Republicans.

The economic liberalism of representatives might be affected by early political and social background, by career experiences prior to the current job, and by the current work context. We already know from our career analysis (chapter 5) that the three sets of variables are related. Early political and social background strongly affects the type of clients and employers that the representatives serve. Similarly, prior experience in politics is likely to lead to specialization in policy work. It is plausible, therefore, that the ideological divisions among organization types might primarily reflect the social context in which client organizations operate. That is, for example, the political conservatism of business representatives might reflect the fact that businesses are embedded in particular social networks, resulting in the recruitment of individuals with particular social characteristics, who coincidentally have conservative political values. In this account, political ideology as such would not be an important independent factor in organizational recruitment; once the social and political background variables were controlled, the type of organization involved would account for little additional variance in the economic liberalism scores. The divisions in political values might still be considerable and could well exacerbate conflict among the groups, but the level of conflict would presumably be even greater if organizations were to recruit or mold their representatives on ideological grounds. The essential hypothesis, then, is that the political values of individuals are pragmatic, reflecting their backgrounds and experience but nudged toward moderation by the exigencies of group politics.

With this hypothesis in mind, we did a regression analysis of the effects on economic liberalism of social background characteristics; educational, political, and governmental career experience variables; and the type of organization represented. The background variables employed were religion, father's socioeconomic status, region of origin, and parents' political orientation. The career experience variables consisted of measures indicating whether the respondent had held a position in a political campaign; possessed an advanced degree; or had congressional experience, experience in another branch of the federal government, or experience in state or local government. Organization type was measured by a series of variables indicating whether the representatives were employed by unions, businesses, citizen-government groups, professional associations, or trade associations; were external lawyers and consultants who devoted all of their time to business and trade association clients; or were other external lawyers and consultants who did not exclusively represent business interests.

Table 6.3 reports the regression results in four equations. Equation 1 contains the full set of independent variables. Equations 2, 3, and 4 each contain all but one set of independent variables. These procedures allow us to assess the unique contribution of the three sets of variables. Entering all variables simultaneously (equation 1) explains a substantial portion of the variance in the liberalism scale, 43.6%. The model indicates that representatives with Jewish backgrounds are significantly more liberal than other religious groups, but that otherwise religion is not significant. None of the variables measuring father's socioeconomic status has a statistically significant effect. Region of origin variables are also insignificant. Political background, however, does make some difference. Representatives from families identified with the Democratic party are significantly more liberal than those from Republican and Independent families or families where the parents differed in their party orientations. Taking an active role in political campaigns produces a statistically significant negative effect on liberalism. When other variables are controlled for, however, campaign activity appears to be associated with conventional political participation and relatively moderate political attitudes. Government experience is also inconsistent in its impact. Work in state or local government or with the executive branch displays no effect, but there is a considerable positive liberal effect when the experience took place in Congress.

Contrary to the hypothesis that ideological differences primarily reflect social background or career experience, the type of organization that the representative currently serves has by far the most consistent and powerful effect on liberalism. Employment by a labor union increases liberalism scores by a substantial 1.3 (or about 45%) over the reference category of nonprofit employment. Citizen-government group representatives and lawyers and consultants who do not exclusively represent business or trade association clients also are significantly above the reference category mean. Employees of business corporations, by contrast, are well below that mean. Trade association employees are also relatively conservative. Lawyers and consultants who exclusively represent business are more conservative than their colleagues in more diversified practice, but fall just below the reference category. Finally, professional association employees have liberalism scores that are just above the reference group.

The power of current organization type as a predictor of economic liberalism is very clearly demonstrated in equations 2 to 4. When all social background variables are dropped (equation 2), the effects of other variables are largely unchanged. Possessing an advanced degree and employment by a trade association achieve conventional significance levels. But the total variance explained drops by only 3.4%, meaning that only 3.4% of the variance in economic liberalism is uniquely attributable to social background variables. A similar pattern holds in equation 3. When the career experience variables are dropped, the variance explained declines by a mere 2.2%. Dropping organizational employment variables from the analysis, however, as in equation 4, produces a dramatic change. The variance explained drops from 43.6% to 15.8%, indicating that 27.8% of the variance in economic liberalism under equation one can be uniquely attributed to the type of organization that respondents currently represent.

The strong effect of the current organization variable is best accounted for by the hypothesis that recruitment into organizational roles is based on ideological selection. It is impossible to tell from our data whether this occurs by self-selection (that is, individual representatives pursue ideologically congenial environments), by organizational selection (client organizations choose ideologically

Table 6.3 Economic liberalism regressed on social background, career, and current employment variables

	Equation 1		Equation 2		Equation 3		Equation 4	
	b	s.e.	b	s.e.	b	s.e.	b	s.e.
Background variables								
Religion								
Jewish	.38***	.10	—	—	.41***	.10	.59***	.12
Nonidentifying	.09	.09	—	—	.11	.09	.23*	.11
Type I Protestant	-.04	.08	—	—	-.002	.08	-.13	.10
Type II Protestant	.003	.08	—	—	.01	.08	-.01	.10
Father's occupation								
Professional/technical	.02	.10	—	—	.03	.10	.19	.12
Sales/clerical	-.01	.11	—	—	-.008	.11	-.005	.14
Owner/manager	-.007	.10	—	—	-.006	.10	.06	.12
Blue collar	-.006	.10	—	—	-.01	.10	.19	.12
Region of origin								
Northeast	-.05	.08	—	—	-.03	.08	-.01	.10
Midwest	-.10	.09	—	—	-.08	.09	-.15	.11
South	-.06	.09	—	—	-.06	.09	-.20	.11
Parents' political orientation								
Republican	-.09	.07	—	—	-.11	.07	-.19*	.09
Democratic	.13*	.07	—	—	.13	.07	.21**	.08

	b	SE	b	SE	b	SE	b	SE
Career variables								
Campaign positions	-.16**	.06	-.16**	.06	—	—	-.20**	.07
Advanced degree	.10	.06	.12*	.06	—	—	-.02	.07
Congressional experience	.17*	.08	.20**	.08	—	—	.14	.09
Other federal experience	.04	.06	.06	.06	—	—	.06	.08
State/local experience	-.09	.10	-.08	.10	—	—	.01	.12
Current employment variables								
Labor union	1.33***	.14	1.42***	.14	1.37***	.14	—	—
Business	-.38**	.13	-.43***	.13	-.36**	.12	—	—
Citizen-govt.	.74***	.13	.77***	.13	.75***	.13	—	—
Professional/nonprofit	.19	.13	.24	.13	.23	.13	—	—
Trade association	-.21	.12	-.27*	.12	-.16	.12	—	—
Business lawyer/consultants	-.01	.13	-.06	.13	.06	.13	—	—
Other lawyer/consultants	.39**	.14	.48***	.14	.42**	.14	—	—
Intercept	3.06		3.05		2.84		3.23	
R square	.436		.402		.414		.158	
F	20.81		38.55		24.20		7.12	

Note: The reference categories are: for religion, Catholic; for father's occupation, other; for region, West; for parents' political orientation, independent and mixed; for current employment, nonprofit organizations. All the career variables are dichotomous; the reference category for each is absence of the attribute.

* $p < .05$. ** $p < .01$. *** $p < .001$.

compatible representatives), or by some combination of the two. Socialization within the organization, however, seems to play only a limited part in producing ideological differentiation among organizations. We saw in the previous chapter that the number of years spent with an organization has no significant effect on liberalism within a given organizational type. That is, those who have worked many years for liberal or conservative organizations are not ideologically distinct from their colleagues who have spent fewer years in the same or similar organizations.

The import of these findings is that ideological differences among interest group representatives are not merely latent attributes of the system. Recruitment patterns reinforce political differences associated with the social and political backgrounds of representatives. The system of interest representation may, in this sense, add to the conflictual character of the policy-making process. Before developing this inference further, however, we should consider more evidence concerning the relationship between ideology and the social organization of representation.

Colleague Networks

Another view of the ideological structure of representation may be obtained by examining the character of the networks in which representatives most frequently discuss social and political issues. Do they talk mostly to colleagues from their own organization, or to members of the same political party or the same class, ethnic, or religious group? How did they meet? Answers to these questions may shed additional light on the principles that underlie representation, particularly on the relative significance of client organizations, government institutions, and substantive fields.

If the discussion networks include individuals with varying social characteristics and political values, they may function as a mechanism for the exchange of ideas among competing interest groups and may promote broader and more moderate conceptions of appropriate policy directions. If, on the other hand, the members of the networks have homogeneous organizational, political, and social characteristics, the networks may reinforce conflictual policy-making perspectives.

General Patterns

We told respondents that we were interested in assessing "the relations of different segments of the Washington community to each other." We then asked each to "think of the three persons with whom you are most likely to discuss your work."[2] The prologue may have directed the respondents' thoughts toward relationships with other Washington representatives, but the specific request was phrased more broadly to encompass all colleagues with whom the respondents talk about their work—whether the colleague was involved in representation or not. We then asked a variety of questions about the colleagues and the respondents' relationships with them.[3]

In presenting our findings, we concentrate on the portion of the sample that is based in Washington. Given the complexity of the items and the time required to administer them, these questions were dropped from telephone interviews. This is an unfortunate gap in our data.[4] We have colleague data on only about a third of the respondents based outside Washington, but these respondents appear to have significantly different networks than do the Washington residents. A larger proportion of nonresidents (and the colleagues they list) represent businesses and nonprofit organizations, and are Republicans or Independents. They see their colleagues less frequently than do the Washington-based representatives, and their colleagues are less likely to be in contact with each other. Given these fragmentary indications, it would have been valuable to have more data with which to test these differences.

Data from the resident portion of our sample suggest that Washington networks are active and densely connected. These respondents named a total of 1,361 colleagues, and report meeting them two to three times a week on the average. Almost half (46%) of the respondents indicate that all three of their named colleagues discuss work with each other; another third (36%) said that two of the three do. Only 12% are in networks in which their colleagues have no direct contact among themselves.

Collegial relationships are also of relatively long duration, but few are lifelong associations. Washington-based representatives report having known these colleagues for 9 years on the average. Given the mean age of our sample, 48, this means that most representatives developed their existing networks in their mid- to late thirties.

The duration of the relationships reflects work histories. After controlling for age, we found that representatives employed by business organizations, professional and nonprofit organizations, and citizen-government groups had known their colleagues for a shorter time than the sample mean, while those working for unions and law firms had longer-than-average relationships. The differences reflect the career patterns characteristic of these organizations, as well as the history of the organizations' involvement in Washington representation. As reported in chapter 3, representatives of citizen-government groups are relatively young and poorly paid and, not surprisingly, have worked for their employers for a relatively short time. Consequently, their networks were developed more recently. Representatives of business and professional associations have stable organizational careers, but many business firms and professional associations are themselves newcomers to direct Washington representation, and their networks are therefore relatively new as well. The opposite is true of unions and law firms. Most unions and many law firms are longtime Washington players. Moreover, their employees have typically spent most of their careers in the employing organization. Thus, the collegial networks in which these representatives are embedded are older and more established.[5]

How Colleagues First Became Acquainted

The origins of networks may indicate their character. Collegial relationships that begin in politics are likely to reflect or sustain the continuing salience of party affiliation and political ideology, while networks defined by "old school ties" suggest the priority of status and class. Networks produced by the work context suggest that the patterns of communication primarily revolve around instrumental concerns and organizational demands.

Our data make clear that there are two primary sources of collegial ties: work context, and politics and government (which we cannot disentangle because they were given as a single response category). A third of the colleagues listed by the Washington-based respondents became acquainted with them initially through employment in the same private organization, another 9% met them in the course of work, and 5% were sought out by the respondent because of the colleague's professional reputation. Although there is some ambiguity as to whether the latter two categories refer only to *private* representation, it appears that nearly half of the collegial ties originated with nongovernmental work activities. About a quarter of the Washington-based respondents indicated that they had met their colleagues through working in politics or government. Some 36% of the colleagues selected by respondents with congressional experience met in this fashion, compared to 29% and 27%, respectively, of colleagues selected by respondents with noncongressional federal experience and state or local government experience. Only 15% of the colleagues chosen by respondents with no government experience met in a political or governmental context. More detailed crosstabulations of government experience by involvement in electoral campaigns reveal that both political and governmental experience are significant sources of collegial ties. Roughly a third of the ties originating in politics or government were reported by respondents with political experience but no government experience, another third came from those with government experience but no political experience, and the final third came from respondents who had both kinds of experience.

There is a striking absence of collegial ties originating through social connections. Some 8% of colleagues were introduced by mutual friends, another handful (0.5%) through relatives, and 1% through attending the same school. The third largest response, given for 17% of the colleagues, was that they were introduced by colleagues. This category represents the self-reproducing component of Washington networks—the breeding of new collegial ties from established collegial networks.

Judging from the origins of collegial ties, the principal axis around which Washington networks revolve is the work context. A majority of collegial relationships begin in work for the same organization, be it private or governmental. Some other kinds of connections, made through colleagues or by professional reputation, are also work related. Connections made through friendship networks or attendance at the same school constitute only a small portion of the total set of collegial relationships.

It is of course in the workplace context that policy priorities are set, strategies are formulated, and a division of representational labor is determined. But if the work organization also effectively selects the reference group with whom representatives discuss policy issues, it exercises a kind of influence on representatives that is both more pervasive and less visible than formal organizational authority. The impact of the work organization on the formation of collegial ties would be less consequential if representatives moved readily from one type of organization to another. Indeed, the maintenance of collegial ties that were formed in a different organization might serve to enhance diversity. As noted in the preceding chapter, however, representatives seldom change from one type of private organization to another.

Colleague Choice

To assess the tendency of representatives to develop networks that are homogeneous in their organizational, political, and social characteristics, we examined the propensity of representatives to choose colleagues who are similar to themselves (Tables 6.4 through 6.7).

The tendency to select colleagues in the same organization (Table 6.4) is quite constant across different types of organizations. Representatives in nonprofit organizations, citizen-government groups, and

Table 6.4 Organization type of respondents and colleagues (D.C.-based respondents only)

Organization type	Percentage of respondents (N = 460)	Percentage of colleagues (N = 1,355)	Index of self-selection[a]		Index of inbreeding bias[b]	
			Same org.	Org. type	Same org.	Org. type
Business	9	13	36	59	−4	53
Nonprofit	3	4	33	56	−10	55
Trade assoc.	33	23	38	54	−2	40
Unions	9	8	42	71	5	69
Prof. assoc.	11	6	39	50	0.3	46
Citizen-govt.	15	26	32	79	−11	72
Law firm	16	16	53	60	23	52
Consultant	5	5	25	35	−23	32
Other	NA	0.4%	NA	NA	NA	NA
Overall	100	100	39	60	0	52

a. Self-selection within the same organization is computed from the number of pairs in which both respondent and colleague are from the same organization divided by the total number of respondent-colleague pairs in a row. Self-selection within organization type is computed from the number of pairs in which respondent and colleague work in the same type of organization divided by the total number of respondent-colleague pairs in the row.

b. Inbreeding bias equals (self-selection − percentage of colleagues)/(1 − percentage of colleagues).

The inbreeding bias measure was developed by Fararo and Sunshine (1964, 73) to divide self-selection into that which is based on chance alone and that which reflects more than chance. See also Heinz and Laumann (1982, 215, 223–231).

Table 6.5 Political party of respondents and colleagues (D.C.-based respondents only)

Political party	% of respondents (N = 455)	% of colleagues (N = 1,347)	Index of self-selection[a]	Index of inbreeding bias[b]
Republican	31	26	41	21
Democrat	46	42	59	28
Independent/other	23	8	12	5
Unidentified	0.7	25	NA	NA
Overall	100	100	43	21

a. The index of self-selection is computed from the number of pairs in which both respondent and colleague have the same party affiliation divided by the total number of respondent-colleague pairs in the row.

b. See note to Table 6.4.

Table 6.6 Ethnicity of respondents and colleagues (D.C.-based respondents only)

Ethnicity	% of respondents (N = 457)	% of colleagues (N = 1,331)	Index of self-selection[a]	Index of inbreeding bias[b]
Nonwhite	4	3	26	24
Irish	15	11	16	6
Jewish	13	11	19	9
England/Scotland/Wales	31	14	17	4
NW Europe	22	8	14	6
SE Europe	8	7	6	1
American/mixed	5	2	3	1
Other	3	3	44	−4
Unidentified	NA	42.5	NA	NA
Overall	100	100	16	6

a. See note to Table 6.5, substituting "ethnicity" for "party."

b. See note to Table 6.4.

consulting firms are somewhat less likely to make intra-organizational choices, perhaps in part due to the relatively small representational staffs in such organizations. The low rate of self-selection by consultants suggests that outside connections are particularly important for them, either as a source of clients or for representational functions. Even consultants, however, select a quarter of their colleagues from the organization that employs them. Representatives based in law firms, who choose more than half of their colleagues from within

Table 6.7   Religion of respondents and colleagues (D.C.-based respondents only)

Religion	% of respondents ($N = 455$)	% of colleagues ($N = 1,348$)	Index of self-selection[a]	Index of inbreeding bias[b]
Jewish	13	11	13	9
Nonidentifying	17	6	14	9
Catholic	20	16	24	10
Type I Protestant	23	5	10	4
Type II Protestant	27	13	27	11
Unidentified	NA	44	NA	NA
Overall	100	100	18	9

a. See note to Table 6.5, substituting "religion" for "party."
b. See note to Table 6.4.

their firms, exhibit the highest levels of self-selection. But among our limited sample of nonresidents, the proportion of choices from within the same organization is 60%, indicating that organizational inbreeding is even stronger and colleague choice more circumscribed outside Washington. Residence in Washington apparently gives representatives somewhat more access to networks outside the work organization.

Colleague choice within the same organization is a special case of the more general phenomenon of choosing colleagues from the same class or type of organization. Of the colleague choices by Washington-based representatives, 6 in 10 are made within the same organizational category. But there are interesting differences among organizations in these patterns. Inbreeding tendencies are strongest in the two most liberal types of organizations, unions and citizen-government groups. Their representatives select more than 70% of their colleagues from the same type of organization. A comparison of columns 3 and 4 in Table 6.4 shows that many of these ties are with representatives who work for other organizations, but categorically similar ones. Moreover, the citizen-government group representatives identify an exceptionally large number of outside colleagues. Most, though not all, of these are political liberals, as we have seen. Thus, we find that liberal representatives operate through large, politically homogeneous networks, which span numerous organizations. The proclivity of liberal groups to rely on inter-organizational coalitions has been noted in the literature (see, for example, Bok and Dunlop 1969; Berry 1977).

Business and trade association representatives also tend to select colleagues from similar organizations, but a larger proportion of these ties are contained within one organization. While the networks of liberal interest group representatives approximate a generalized community, networks of business and trade association representatives derive more directly from the client organizations that employ them.

Representatives also tend to select colleagues who share the same political party affiliation, but inbreeding tendencies vary significantly by party (Table 6.5). Democrats make up the largest proportion of colleagues (42%), followed by Republicans (26%), and independents (8%). The percentages for all three categories are lower than those reported for respondents because the party affiliations of one quarter of the colleagues were unknown.[6] Rather than exclude the unidentified colleagues from our analyses, which would have the effect of increasing measures of inbreeding, we have taken the more conservative approach. Despite this, we find modest levels of inbreeding by political party. Democrats are far more likely than other representatives to select colleagues of a similar political persuasion: Democrats self-select at a 59% rate, compared to 41% by Republicans and only 12% by independents. Democrats also have the highest scores on inbreeding bias (which controls for the proportion of Democrats in the colleague set). The inbreeding measure reveals that Republicans also show a tendency to select Republican colleagues, though theirs is somewhat lower than the bias of the Democrats.

Many Republican representatives cannot avoid working with Democrats because of the Democratic control of Congress. Moreover, in the early 1970s, when Washington representation began to expand rapidly, Democrats substantially outnumbered Republicans in the pool of former government officials and policy experts from which many representatives were recruited. Many business groups therefore adopted a pragmatic approach to representation; but liberal organizations, such as unions and citizen-government groups, pursue a political agenda that places greater weight on ideological goals. Lacking the economic resources of the business groups, they recruit representatives who have strong ideological commitments, thus trying to compensate in passion for their lack of size and budget.

Independents stand in stark contrast to other representatives. They show almost no tendency for self-selection. Being an independent simply does not create an associational affinity in the Washington context.

There is relatively little self-selection among representatives by ethnicity and religion (Tables 6.6 and 6.7). The only category with a significant degree of inbreeding is the nonwhites. Only 3% of the colleagues as a whole are nonwhites, but they constitute a quarter of the colleagues of the nonwhite respondents. This finding suggests that the few nonwhites among Washington representatives tend to work on a limited range of issues. Other groups self-select at rates that are only slightly higher than would be expected by chance alone. Religious inbreeding is also low. Type II Protestants have the highest inbreeding bias; they self-select at twice the percentage of their group among the colleagues. But even this modest tendency must be discounted because of the large number of colleagues whose religion is unidentified. If we used the proportion among respondents as the estimate of the distribution of the varying religious groups in the population, the inbreeding score of Type II Protestants would be zero.

The amount of missing data in Tables 6.6 and 6.7 leaves us unconvinced about the true nature of inbreeding by ethnicity and religion. But one of the more interesting aspects of these tables is the pattern of missing data. If we consider the differences between columns one and two of the tables—the percentages of respondents and of colleagues—we see that the smallest differences are for the traditionally lower status racial, ethnic, and religious groups: nonwhites, Irish, Jews, Southeastern Europeans, Catholics. Thus, it is probable that respondents failed to identify the ethnic and religious characteristics of disproportionate numbers of Northern Europeans and Protestants. There are no significant differences among respondents' own ethnic or religious backgrounds in the proportion of colleagues whose ethnicity and religion they are able to identify. Therefore, it is not the case that particular groups are more or less likely to report the ethnic or religious identities of their colleagues. Though minorities and ethnic groups often possess tangible marks of group membership, this is not unique to lower status groups. Respondents therefore seem to be unable or unwilling to attribute significance to the markers of membership in traditionally higher status groups. In sum, we believe that respondents who had colleagues with high status social characteristics were less willing to acknowledge those characteristics.[7]

Our findings demonstrate that organizational factors play a more consistent and pervasive role in structuring the networks of representatives than do party affiliation, ethnicity, and religion. This is no great surprise. The work organization is necessarily proximate to exchange about policy issues, while the other dimensions are not. We cannot conclude, however, that party, ethnicity, and religion are unimportant in these networks. As chapters 3 and 5 documented, the contexts in which representatives work are significantly correlated with their political, class, religious, and ethnic characteristics. Representatives may conceive of their professional world as free of such tendencies because these affinities seldom are explicitly recognized as bases of the relationships. But these "invisible" factors may influence choices about the organizations that the representatives work for and the colleagues they choose.

The variation in inbreeding tendencies by organization type is less intuitively obvious. Ironically, the organizations that show the greatest inbreeding bias are the most liberal politically. In the next set of analyses, this pattern becomes even more clear.

Diversity within Sets of Colleagues

Instead of focusing on individual respondent-colleague pairs, one can conceive of the respondent's set of colleague choices as the unit of analysis and then examine the degree to which the colleague set is diverse or homogeneous. We also pursued this approach. For each respondent, we created indices of homogeneity that measure the degree to which the colleagues share organization type, party affiliation, ethnicity, and religion.[8]

We again found evidence that organizational variables play the most significant role. For Washington-based respondents, 52% of the colleague set pairs work for the same type of organization, compared to 29% that share a political party identification, 27% that have the same ethnicity, and 20% that have the same religion.

We also found significant differences in the diversity of colleague sets by organization type and party affiliation. Representatives of predominantly liberal organizations—citizen-government groups and labor unions—are embedded in the most homogeneous networks. Citizen-government representatives score 72% on homogeneity of organizational type; union representatives score 62%. The representatives with the least homogeneous organizational ties are those working in consulting firms and professional associations (scores of 37% and 40%, respectively). Representatives of businesses, trade associations, and nonprofit organizations also fall below the mean (scores of 49%, 47%, and 49%), while law firm lawyers are at the mean.

Unions and citizen-government groups also have the highest level of partisan homogeneity. Of the set pairs reported by union representatives, 43% share the same political party identification, followed by 34% for citizen-government group representatives. The networks reported by respondents in nonprofit organizations, businesses, and trade associations are the least homogeneous politically. They score 22%, 23%, and 25%, respectively. Consultants, law firm–based attorneys, and representatives from professional associations cluster around the sample mean, with scores from 29% to 32%.

Democrats, wherever they work, have more politically homogeneous networks than do Republicans and independents. Strong Democrats and Democrats register scores of 34% and 41%, respectively, compared to values of 28%, 21%, and 20% for independents, Republicans, and Strong Republicans. This is generally consistent with the inbreeding tendencies observed earlier.

A breakdown of the party affiliations of each respondent's set of colleagues by the party and employer of the respondent brings these patterns into better focus (Table 6.8). The most common type of colleague set (reported by 32% of respondents) is one consisting of a combination of Democrats and Republicans, but interparty network ties are more common for Republicans (42% mixed) and independents (33% mixed) than for Democrats (25% mixed). Similarly, business, trade association, nonprofit, law firm, and consulting firm contexts are characterized by above average proportions of mixed colleague sets, while cross-party ties are relatively rare among the liberal organizations. Only 13% of labor union representatives and 20% of citizen-government representatives report sets containing members from both major parties.

The findings are thus similar to those produced by analyses of inbreeding and of homogeneity: business groups and their representatives maintain a more heterogeneous set of relationships than do liberal groups. The detail provided by Table 6.8 alerts us that we should not overinterpret the result, however. Business and trade association representatives seldom choose exclusively from Republican ranks, but a large proportion of them are embedded in networks of Republicans and independents (32% for business, 22% for trade associations). Democrats are very seldom in exclusive control of the representational activities of business organizations. Most labor union representatives (58%) are embedded in exclusively Democratic colleague sets, however, and another significant segment (27%) are in sets that contain Democrats and independents, but no Republicans.[9]

Table 6.8 Party affiliation(s) of colleague set, by respondent's party affiliation and type of employer (percentages) (D.C.-based respondents only)

Party affiliation(s) of colleague set	Respondent's political party			Respondent's employing organization								
	Republicans	Democrats	Independents/other	Business	Trade assoc.	Non-profit org.	Professional assoc.	Union	Citizen-govt. group	Law firm	Consulting firm	Total
All Republican	9	1	4	5	10	0	2	0	3	0	0	4
All Democrat	3	30	9	2	9	0	10	58	24	21	13	17
All refused/don't know	11	7	15	10	10	7	12	0	12	14	4	10
Republicans and Independents	26	9	19	32	22	29	14	2	6	15	13	16
Democrats and Independents	9	27	14	12	11	21	29	27	29	15	21	18
Democrats and Republicans	42	25	33	39	38	43	29	13	20	36	46	32
Other	0	1	7	0	1	0	4	5	6	0	4	2
Total	100	100	100	100	100	100	100	100	100	100	100	100
(N)	(139)	(210)	(108)	(41)	(151)	(14)	(49)	(40)	(66)	(73)	(24)	(458)

Professional Autonomy and Client Relationships

Not only are the social and political values of representatives strongly associated with the types of organizations they represent, but the very nature of the collegial networks in which policy is discussed is determined by the type of organization in which the representative works. Earlier chapters sounded a similar theme. Most representatives are employees rather than freestanding professionals (chapter 3). Moreover, in the division of representational labor, those who have the largest roles in policy matters are the organizational employees (chapter 4).

These structural patterns appear to be inconsistent with the view that representatives are highly autonomous in their work activities and are thus able to play a mediating role between private interests and the government (Parsons 1954; Horsky 1952). But we have not yet analyzed that proposition directly. It is time to take a closer look at the issue of autonomy, with particular emphasis on the largest professional group in our sample, lawyers.

The two categories of practicing lawyers in our sample—internal or "house" counsel and law firm attorneys—look like political moderates. On the economic liberalism scale, both types of lawyers fall close to the sample mean (3.07 for law firm attorneys and 3.15 for internal counsel versus 3.08 for the sample overall), even though Democrats substantially outnumber Republicans (47% to 32% among internal counsel, and 47% to 25% among external lawyers). Lawyers as a group are more liberal than the officers and employees of businesses and trade associations, but not as liberal as the representatives of unions and citizen-government groups. This might seem to support the Horsky-Parsons thesis that lawyers act as mediators, for it would appear that the predisposition of lawyer representatives is to moderate the political claims of their employers and client organizations.

Lumping lawyers together in this way, however, disguises important differences among them. If we divide the lawyers into groups according to the types of clients or employers they serve, we then find that the social values of the lawyers closely match those of their clients. Lawyers who devote all of their time to business and trade association clients score 2.76 on the economic liberalism scale, making them more conservative than all but the business and trade association representatives themselves. Those spending some time representing professional associations and nonprofit institutions score

3.08; those representing citizen-government groups score 3.74; and those devoting some time to representing unions score 4.14, which means that they are more liberal than all but the union representatives themselves. Thus, lawyers typically are more like their clients than they are like other lawyers who serve different clients. Given this ideological congruity between lawyer and client, it appears less likely that lawyers will conform to the Horsky-Parsons ideal by interpreting the dictates of law or the public interest differently than their clients. Other research on corporate lawyers suggests that even when lawyers are significantly more liberal on general social values than their business clients, the lawyers strongly identify with client interests on the particular issues that arise in their fields of practice (Nelson 1985).

Two measures of work autonomy provide more direct evidence concerning representatives' freedom of action. According to much of the literature, the essential question regarding the power of professional occupations is the degree to which they control their work (Johnson 1972; Freidson 1986; Abbott 1988). Respondents were therefore asked to locate themselves with respect to two opposite statements: "Strategies that I pursue are largely of my own design and execution" and "I work closely with others to design and execute a strategy for representation."

Of the sample as a whole, 30% associate themselves with the statement indicating individual control over work; 49% place themselves close to the opposite pole; and the remainder, 21%, indicate a middle position (Table 6.9). Internal lawyers are only slightly more likely than the average to report control over their work. The two groups of external representatives—law firm attorneys and independent consultants—report having the greatest degree of control over work strategies, but even the external lawyers are not much different from the government affairs officers of citizen-government organizations and research staff employees.

These findings may in part reflect professional ideology. Control over one's work is a principal element of professionalism, and lawyers and consultants may be eager to project a professional image. But the data already reported concerning the work of different categories of representatives may also shed light on these responses. Law firm attorneys and external consultants are more specialized than other representatives in both tasks and substantive fields. It is not surprising, therefore, that these technical experts perceive that they control the execution of their work. Within their areas of expertise, external

Table 6.9   Measures of autonomy, by organizational position

Organizational position	% reporting control over work strategies (N)	% refusing assignments against personal values (N)
Executives		
Business	33 (40)	35 (40)
Nonprofit organizations	21 (33)	27 (33)
Trade associations	17 (133)	21 (130)
Unions	22 (23)	40 (20)
Professional associations	24 (38)	32 (38)
Citizen-govt. groups	27 (49)	28 (50)
Government affairs		
Business	18 (34)	21 (33)
Trade associations	23 (52)	17 (52)
Unions	17 (30)	17 (29)
Professional associations	26 (27)	19 (26)
Citizen-govt. groups	41 (27)	35 (26)
Internal lawyers	34 (47)	14 (44)
Research staff	41 (71)	20 (74)
External lawyers	43 (106)	60 (100)
Consultants	53 (34)	62 (34)
Total	30 (744)	31 (729)
Chi-square p	≤ .001	≤ .001

representatives may enjoy considerable autonomy, but it may only be the autonomy to make tactical decisions within a highly circumscribed decision-making environment. The officers and employees of interest organizations, in contrast, as members of the decision-making core of the organizations, participate in a broader range of policy deliberations within a wider frame of reference. In the division of representational labor, the objectives that organizations seek to advance are determined by the "less autonomous" officers and employees, while many tactical decisions are made by the "more autonomous" external representatives. By shaping organizational goals, the employees who have less autonomy probably have considerably greater impact on the direction of policy making than do the external representatives.

A second piece of evidence relevant to autonomy concerns the propensity of different types of representatives to refuse assignments that are contrary to their personal values, an action that has substantial theoretical significance. The model of the representative-as-mediator suggests that representatives will perceive and confront moral conflicts, and it also suggests that representatives may then refuse to perform objectionable assignments. Representatives were asked, "Have you ever had occasion to refuse a potential client or work assignment, not because of a formal conflict of interest, but because of your personal values?" Only 31% of the sample overall had ever refused work on this basis (Table 6.9). Since only 14% of internal counsel report such an instance, identification as a lawyer, in itself, does not appear to enhance autonomy. Law firm attorneys and external consultants, however, are twice as likely as the sample as a whole to have refused assignments. These percentages are much higher than the levels of refusal that Nelson (1985) found among lawyers in four large Chicago law firms, where only 16% of the lawyers overall and only 22% of partners had ever declined work for personal reasons.

These findings must be interpreted cautiously. The measure used is not without its ambiguities. For example, the extent to which morally problematic work is presented to the various types of representatives, thus creating opportunities for refusal, is unknown.[10] Moreover, the question did not instruct the respondents to report only their experience in their current positions, which may create some errors in attributing responses to particular organizational positions.[11] Nonetheless, the findings are persuasive enough to merit discussion. Whether the representative is employed by the client organization or is external to it makes a significant difference in the likelihood that assignments will be rejected. External lawyers and consultants may be approached by a wide range of client groups, some of whom lack knowledge about which representatives do work that is politically or even tactically congruent with the group's interests. This lack of information may cause the clients to make inappropriate choices of representatives, which then become cases of refused assignments. The potential for such error is minimized in the employer-employee relationship, where there is presumably a shared understanding about the ideological and tactical content of the work involved.

The much higher rate of refusals by lawyers in Washington than in Chicago also may be explained by differences between the two sorts of practice and by self-selection of the practitioners. Lawyers who choose to do policy work in Washington may have a higher degree of political awareness or stronger political commitments than their counterparts in Chicago. Thus, Washington lawyers might well be more sensitive to ideological issues or to the political stance of their clients, while Chicago lawyers in traditional corporate practice might be relatively uninterested in and unconcerned with such matters. The substance of the work demands made upon the two groups of lawyers may also be greatly different. Our Washington sample was, after all, designed to select persons engaged in national policy issues. The lawyers in the large Chicago firms studied by Nelson (1985, 1988) worked on the usual range of legal problems of corporate clients. It is probable, therefore, that the Washington lawyers were far more often presented with work requests that posed ideological or political issues in ways that might give rise to questions of conscience.

An analysis of the reasons given for refusing assignments supports this interpretation. We coded the reasons into broad categories and separated the responses of lawyers from those of other representatives.[12] The most numerous category of responses attributed the refusals to disagreements on substantive policy issues. If we add to these the more ambiguous category "difference of political philosophy," which implies that the refusal was based on the substantive position that the representative was asked to take, about half of the reported refusals turn on disagreements over substantive issues. Although Washington lawyers no doubt confront work assignments that involve personal political choices far more often than is the case for corporate lawyers elsewhere, a greater proportion of the refusals by the nonlawyers than by the lawyers in our sample is attributed to differences over substantive issues. Only a quarter of the refusals by lawyers and a fifth of the refusals by nonlawyers were based on ethical concerns or lack of trust in the client. Nelson, by contrast, found that half of the less numerous refusals in Chicago law firms were based on ethical reasons (1985, 534).

Thus, these more direct measures tend to support the inference we drew from analyses of the structure of employment relationships and work. Few Washington representatives have a substantial degree of autonomy. The major exceptions are external lawyers and consultants, but these more autonomous representatives probably have less overall impact on the policy-making system. We noted in chapters 3 and 4 that external representatives are less likely to participate in decisions on the choice of policy objectives, and that trends in the social organization of Washington representation may be undermining the institutional basis for their autonomy. As a greater proportion of Washington law practice is absorbed by the branch offices of out-of-town firms, as competition among law firms intensifies, and as corporations internalize representation in their own government affairs departments, even external representatives may become more reluctant to decline work that they find morally ambiguous.

Conclusion

Just as clients are the dominant force shaping the work and careers of representatives, so do they organize the representatives' ideologies. Representatives serving different types of clients have fundamentally different preferences on political and social issues. They are embedded in networks that insure that most policy discussion is confined within particular organizations or within the same type of organization. Relatively few representatives characterize themselves as having control over the work strategies they pursue. And most representatives rarely decline assignments due to conflicts with their personal values. The two categories of respondents that appear by these measures to have more professional autonomy—external lawyers and consultants—play the most specialized roles in the system. Of all types of representatives, they are least likely to participate in the decision-making processes of interest organizations.

It appears, therefore, that the social structure of representation serves to reproduce ideological conflict rather than to transcend or modify it. If representation were organized for the most part by the substance of policy debates or by the dictates of government institutions, policy making might primarily reflect substantive rationality or institutionally legitimated procedures. But a system of representation in which the work, careers, and ideologies of representatives are all organized around clients is more likely to produce a process that is determined by the strategies and resources of the interest groups.

Part III

Targets
of Representation

Chapter 7

Contact with Government Institutions

Contacts between public officials and representatives of private interests may be very casual or they may be highly stylized. Either party may initiate them. The motivation can be merely information, or it can be influence. Many contacts are private, but others are fully public, as in testimony before a congressional committee. The content of the communication sometimes consists solely of factual information, reasoned arguments, or a simple statement of interest group concerns and needs, or it may include an offer of a campaign contribution or a promise of electoral support.

We can derive some important clues to the nature of interest representation by examining the pattern of these contacts. Do private representatives tend to specialize in a narrow range of government agencies, focusing primarily on only a few officials, or do they spread their contacts more broadly? Are the targeting patterns substantially the same in all four policy domains, or do they have unique, domain-specific characteristics? Do lobbyists devote most of their efforts to officials at the top of the government hierarchies (who presumably have greater potential impact on public policy), or do they concentrate instead on cultivating more accessible officials? Similarities and differences in the contacting patterns of different types of interests may reveal implicit affinities among the groups or particular strategic choices.

The representatives were asked whether in the last year they had contacted a long list of relevant targets regularly, several times, occasionally, or not at all. The lists varied in both length and substance from domain to domain, but they shared several key targets, such as the White House and the congressional leadership of both parties. Other targets, such as the principal congressional committees, were comparable across domains.

We found that the typical representative manages to see from 16 to 20 government targets at least once over the course of the year—roughly a third of the total number of possible government targets (see Table 7.1). But each representative is in regular contact with less than 10% of the possible government targets, on the average—only about 4 or 5 targets per representative.

As we noted in chapter 4, the labor domain representatives tend to be somewhat more specialized than those in the other domains (see Table 4.3). More of them were involved with the courts on a regular basis, and they were also more likely to focus exclusively on Congress (this was especially true of the representatives of unions). Outside of the labor domain, lobbyists tend not to specialize in a particular governmental unit or even in one branch to the exclusion of another. Lawyer lobbyists, however, are more likely to concentrate on the courts; about a quarter of them contact the judicial branch regularly. But even the lawyers spend most of their time communicating with other parts of the federal structure. They cultivate connections at both ends of Pennsylvania Avenue, and they work with several subunits in each branch.

If we look at the frequency of contacts with targets that are comparable across all four policy domains (Table 7.2), several points are immediately apparent. First, and most impressive, there is substantial consistency in the rates of regular contact in the four domains. There

Table 7.1   Contact frequencies and selected other characteristics of individual representatives in the agriculture, energy, health, and labor policy domains

	Agriculture	Energy	Health	Labor
Mean number of government targets contacted per respondent				
Occasionally	8.5	8.4	7.9	6.6
Several times	6.8	6.6	6.7	5.1
Regularly	5.5	5.3	5.3	4.3
Total (= any contact)	20.1	20.3	20.1	16.0
Number of possible government targets[a]	74	66	62	56
Number of representatives in each domain	192	184	206	194

a. This total includes government organizations named by respondents under "other, please specify" in addition to organizations listed in the response booklet.

Table 7.2 Representatives having regular contact with particular government targets, by domain (percentages)

	Agriculture	Energy	Health	Labor
House of Representatives				
Democratic leadership	21	12	15	19
Republican leadership	14	14	12	10
Primary committee	39	31	21	26
Secondary committee	—	15	19	—
Senate				
Democratic leadership	14	13	12	17
Republican leadership	16	16	13	12
Primary committee	41	35	26	30
Secondary committee	—	18	20	18
Executive				
White House	6	12	4	10
OMB	6	8	6	8
Office of secretary, primary department	26	19	14	13

is little variation, for example, in the rates of contact with the Senate congressional leadership or with the OMB across the domains. But the energy and labor lobbyists appear to have greater access to the White House than do those in agriculture and health. Most of the difference is due to partisanship. Republican representatives of businesses active on energy and labor issues were those who were more likely to go to the White House. Another domain difference of substantial size is that the office of the Secretary of the Department of Agriculture attracts much more traffic than do the secretariats of the Departments of Labor or Health and Human Services. This differential probably reflects the comparative significance of the department leadership in shaping policy in the domain. In the same way, the House Democratic leadership appears to have greater importance in the agriculture policy domain than it does on energy issues.

But the frequency of contact with a government target is clearly determined by more than institutional power. Accessibility is also involved. We would surely not conclude that, because only 6% to 8% of the lobbyists were in regular contact with the White House or the OMB, those offices are therefore only about half as important as the congressional leadership. In general, Congress is more porous, more readily penetrated by outside interests, than the executive branch. It is intended to be so. And line administration agencies are, of course, more accessible than the office of the president. These appear to be systematic tendencies in the frequency with which lobbyists turn to particular government targets. Since these are cross-sectional data, however, we cannot determine whether these tendencies are stable or, instead, merely the current position in a longer trend. But the similarities among the domains suggest that our findings are not entirely episodic or random.

The Structure of Contacts

Contacts, of course, are selectively concentrated according to the particular policy concerns of the representatives' employers or clients. A representative working for the National Association of Wheat Growers will be especially attentive to officials responsible for wheat price supports and international grain trading policy, while a representative from the National Forest Products Association will attend to government agencies responsible for public lands policy, water quality, and so on. Subsets of government targets might thus be characterized as being located near each other in the policy system to the degree that they share overlapping constituencies of private representatives. In a map of the policy space, government targets that do not elicit the concern of overlapping constituencies would be found at greater distances from one another. For example, policy pertaining to managing the national forests may have no implications (at least for the moment) for the concerns of sugar beet growers. The lack of a need to coordinate these highly disparate and specialized policies is signaled by the absence of representatives jointly targeting the relevant government institutions. On the other hand, if an agency attracts the attention of a large and heterogeneous constituency of representatives, that agency may perform higher-order coordinating functions, resolving conflicts among inconsistent or incompatible policy initiatives.

In the following analyses, therefore, we use the degree of overlap in the constituencies of all possible pairs of government agencies to estimate the relative proximity of the agencies in terms of their mutual policy relevance. Two general principles govern the spatial locations of government targets in a national policy domain: center/periphery and interest differentiation (see Laumann and Pappi 1976, 138–143, for a related discussion of local community decision-making structures; Laumann and Knoke 1987, 226–248, for national policy domains).

The center/periphery principle is a type of order that occurs in many social networks, such as friendship ties and authority relations. Some government actors receive many contacts because they possess broad mandates, covering a wide range of policy concerns. Other targets have more specialized and limited mandates that attract a narrower range of parties. Thus, this principle asserts that the center of the policy space will be dominated by organizations possessing broad governmental authority, such as the White House staff, the Office of Management and Budget (OMB), the Office of the Secretary of cabinet departments, and the Senate and House leadership. Peripherally located targets, in contrast, will have constituencies that are smaller in size and more homogeneous in the interests represented.

The interest-differentiation principle organizes the spatial locations of government targets into sectors sharing a common focus. Thus, government targets located in the same sector of the periphery have overlapping constituencies, composed of a relatively narrow range of representatives sharing specialized policy concerns.

Together, the center/periphery and the interest differentiation principles suggest a model like that in Figure 7.1. The concentric rings represent degrees of centrality; the cross-cutting pie-shaped wedges delimit distinct interest subsectors. Positions are represented by letters, here subsuming two or more individual organizations. Thus, position A occupies the center of the space, at a minimum average distance from all the other positions. The government targets occupying A presumably invest a portion of their interest portfolios in every subsector. Moving away from the center, we encounter the more peripheral positions located in specialized interest sectors. Any position (such as F) that lies in close proximity to others (such as E and B) will share some interests with these neighbors and will have a greater degree of constituency overlap with them than with more differentiated and more remote positions (such as I). We would thus expect targets in position F to interact more with others in its subsector, to participate less often with those in adjacent sectors, and to avoid involvement with those in positions lying farthest away.

To measure the constituency overlap of two government targets, we explored several alternative measures that differ in their sensitivity to the size of the targets' constituencies. Since we found very similar results, we will present only the analyses based on Yule's Q. In the

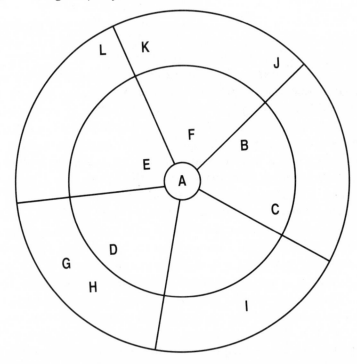

Figure 7.1 Hypothetical model of a government target space organized by center/periphery and issue differentiation principles

real world of policy making, size of constituency may be an important factor. For example, targets with large and diverse constituencies may be overloaded with conflicting messages and demands, while targets with small and homogeneous constituencies may not.

In these analyses, representatives are included in the constituency of a government target if they report contact with it several times or regularly. Representatives with only occasional contact are excluded because such contact is presumably of less relevance to the representatives' interests, and including it would result in randomness, or "noise." On the other hand, analyzing only regular contact would suppress some of the dynamics of the system.

A positive Yule's Q indicates that representatives interested in government target X are also interested in target Z, and vice versa; a negative Yule's Q suggests that representatives active in target X's constituency are likely to avoid contact with target Z; and, finally, a Q of zero indicates that the overlap between the constituencies of X and Z is random (see Table 7.3).[1] Since all of the government targets analyzed here have some responsibility for national policy in a particular domain, one would expect a positive bias in the Qs. In fact, all four domains show strongly positive biases in the value of Q, suggesting that the need for policy coordination across government targets is substantial, at least from the vantage point of active private parties who do the rounds of government targets. Remember that, if the Qs were close to zero or were negative, it would indicate that the government targets were relatively freestanding and autonomous, with limited need to coordinate their decisions—that is, the government targets would lack mutual interdependence.

The means for agriculture, health, and labor are strikingly alike, falling within a narrow range of .40 to .44 in mean Q, while energy appears to have a somewhat higher mean and a notably lower rate of negative values, suggesting that the target agencies in the other three domains are more specialized or independent than are those in the energy domain. This may reflect the more unsettled character of the energy domain. During the early 1980s, a wide range of government agencies competed in initiating new policy measures and dismantling those begun in the Carter administration, and interested parties lacked clear guidance on the division of policy responsibilities (see chapter 2; and Laumann and Knoke 1987, chapters 2 and 4). Major governmental and private actors vied in formulating policies addressing rapidly rising oil prices, and environmentalists challenged nuclear energy initiatives in the wake of the Three Mile Island accident and expressed concerns about protecting the environment from the ravages of acid rain, strip mining, and other industry-generated threats.

The patterning of negative Qs can be used as an indicator of

Table 7.3 Summary measure of constituency overlap of governmental targets for each policy domain (Yule's Q)

Domain	Mean	Number of pairwise comparisons	Number of negative values	% negative values
Agriculture	0.44	1,722	54	3.2
Energy	0.55	1,482	25	1.7
Health	0.44	1,406	48	3.4
Labor	0.40	930	66	7.1

the emergence of subdomains with specialized, autonomous policy responsibilities. An example of this may be found in the health domain: governmental agencies responsible for biomedical research attract constituencies (notably representatives from professional research organizations) that are not active in other government venues (Laumann and Knoke 1987, chapters 2 and 4). Particularly noteworthy is the high rate of negative values in the labor domain, which has been a highly institutionalized domain for a long time, with well-developed subdomains that manage specialized policy concerns such as pensions and occupational safety.

Constructing a Model of the Government Target Space

To reveal the structure of the proximities among the government targets, we use the technique known as smallest space analysis (Guttman 1968; Lingoes 1973; McFarland and Brown 1973; Kruskal and Wish 1978). This technique depicts the relationships among items or cases (the target agencies, here) by representing the items graphically as points in a Euclidean space. The axes or dimensions of the space are not important in themselves and may not have substantive meaning, but vectors within the space that are substantively interpretable may sometimes be discerned. What is important is the structure of the relationships among the several pairs of points.

The proximities of the agencies in these analyses are measured by the extent of overlap among the representatives that contact them.[2] Agencies that are contacted by many of the same representatives will be located close together, and agencies that share few constituents will be far apart. Agencies that are contacted by widely varying constituencies will therefore be placed where the constituencies overlap, which will usually be near the center of the space. Broadly speaking, the configurations of points in the smallest space solutions follow the center/periphery and interest differentiation principles of organization.

Let us examine the center/periphery structure. Table 7.4 presents the correlations between selected features of the constituencies for various government targets and a measure of the targets' distances from the center of the space. In all four domains, the number of representatives in the targets' constituencies is negatively correlated with the distances—that is, the agencies with larger constituencies

Table 7.4 Correlations of selected constituency characteristics with the centrality of government institutions, by domain

	Agriculture	Energy	Health	Labor
Size of constituency	−.71**	−.37*	−.55*	−.46**
% Republican	.05	.01	.23	−.37*
% economic liberals	−.28	.47**	.05	.23
% reporting stable coalitions	−.13	.42*	.00	.03
% reporting high conflict	.37**	−.10	−.10	.44*
% representing unions	NA	NA	NA	.07
% representing citizen interest groups	.04	−.14	.65**	.35*
% representing business or trade assoc.	−.47**	−.66*	.11	−.57**
% in top position in organization	.34*	−.42*	.37*	−.10

Note: The centrality of a government target is measured by the Euclidean distance of the target from the centroid of the smallest space solution.
* $p > .05$. ** $p > .001$.

tend to be more central. Since larger constituencies are usually more heterogeneously recruited, this finding generally supports the notion that centrally located targets have a more heterogeneous clientele. Note that the relationship between centrality and target popularity is weakest in the energy domain, although it is still statistically significant.

Table 7.4 also includes correlations of the centrality of the targets with a number of other attributes of the targets' constituencies. These differ across the four policy domains in ways that suggest that the nature of the decision making is determined by the characteristics of the substantive policy under consideration. Only in the labor and energy domains is the centrality of the agencies associated with either a partisan or an ideologically distinct clientele. The more centrally located targets in the labor domain attract disproportionate contacts from Republicans, presumably reflecting the importance of ideology to the Reagan administration appointees. Similarly, the central targets in the energy domain have constituents with significantly conservative economic views, while peripherally located targets tend to attract constituents who hold more liberal views.

In the energy domain, the percentage of the agencies' constituents reporting that their work is characterized by stable coalitions is significantly higher for agencies that are located farther from the center of the space. Thus, the politics of the more peripheral energy agencies appears to be more stable, while the center of the structure is characterized by a greater degree of coalitional instability. In the agriculture domain, however, the tendency is in the opposite direction. Similarly, the constituents of agencies located near the periphery in the agriculture and labor domains are significantly more likely to report that their work is characterized by a high degree of conflict, while the tendency is in the opposite direction in both the energy and the health domains. Thus, agriculture and labor appear to be characterized by relatively consensual politics in the central agencies, with a greater degree of conflict in the more peripheral agencies. In energy, the opposite is the case: the central agencies tend to be relatively conflictual and unstable politically. In health, there is no clear pattern, suggesting a more diffuse, undifferentiated political structure. We should keep these differences in mind and continue to seek explanations for the variance in the patterns.

The last four rows of the table characterize the organizational composition of the more central agencies. In the labor domain, unions appear to be equally active across the whole system. (In the agriculture, energy, and health domains, there are too few union representatives to permit assessment of their contacts.) In two domains, health and labor, citizen interest groups tend to be relegated to peripherally located agencies. At the opposite extreme, in three of the four domains the businesses and trade associations target the more central agencies, which have the broadest policy-making mandates. Health is again the exception, perhaps because fewer businesses and trade associations are active in this domain. The domains also differ in the patterns of participation by top executives. CEO's are overrepresented in the constituencies of centrally located targets in the energy domain, but deal with the more peripheral targets in health and agriculture. As we have already noted (chapter 3), business corporations tend to play an active and direct role in the energy domain rather than delegate the work to trade associations, and businesses are more likely than other types of organizations to use their CEO's for lobbying purposes. In the agriculture and health domains, by contrast, a larger share of the representational work is undertaken by trade and professional associations.

Thus, agencies with heterogeneous clients usually occupy the central, or core, regions. These central agencies may perform a mediating role or an entrepreneurial role, either of which would generate contact with a diverse set of representatives. Core agencies might therefore be expected to absorb political disagreement, serve as generalists coordinating a considerable scope of the policies considered, and exercise broad discretionary power. The periphery of the space, in contrast, would be populated by agencies with specialized roles and narrow mandates. The representatives contacting peripheral agencies would then tend to be homogeneous in the substance and scope of their policy concerns.

These core/periphery and regionalization principles give some indication of what to expect, but are too general to provide much analytic power. Accordingly, we next suggest several models of the policy space that reflect alternative conceptions of the state's organization of decision-making authority.

Models of Structure

The process of political decision making assumes a particular shape as streams of interested parties, authoritative decision makers, and decision events come into recurrent juxtaposition, subject to particular historical and social constraints and inducements to action. We should therefore attend to these factors in our description and explanation of the structure of the policy domains. In each domain, certain key actors exercise higher-level oversight and give policy guidance that has broad impact. These actors include the congressional leadership; the budget, finance and appropriations committees of both houses of Congress; the White House; the Office of Management and the Budget; and the respective Secretaries of cabinet departments. The constitutional separation of powers between the executive and legislative branches divides these actors into two broad institutional groupings. The third branch, the judiciary, performs primarily adjudicatory and review functions and is subject to highly restrictive access rules, such as the concept of legal "standing." We may therefore expect judicial targets to be in the periphery, reflecting the relatively small and specialized constituencies involved in contested matters. The independent regulatory agencies may also be expected to recruit specialized and well-bounded constituencies. In the spatial representations of the policy domains presented below, the locations of these agencies will provide important clues to the politics of the domain.

Consider, for example, several possible models of how the high-level congressional and executive agencies might be distributed in a policy domain. One model, interpenetration, suggests that the high-level congressional and executive agencies will be intermixed in central locations of the policy space in order to manage the political fallout of the recurrent controversies in more fluid and politically dissensual domains. By fluidity, we mean that the boundaries of such domains are ill defined and are subject to negotiation by interested parties vying for control. In these domains, it is not just the substantive policies that are in contention, but, more fundamentally, the definition of who may participate in the determination of policies. We might expect the energy domain to resemble this interpenetration model most closely. A cabinet-level Department of Energy was created only during the Carter administration; and the producers of traditional fuels, who had lost ground because of environmental and safety concerns, mounted a major effort in the Reagan administration to undo the damage to their position. Thus, high-level actors might be expected to dominate the core region of the policy space.

A second model, one that has a long history and that we have described earlier (see chapter 1), is the iron triangle. This model predicts that legislative and executive agencies that share a common substantive concern will occupy a distinct region of the space along with the interested parties that contact them, and that these public and private groups will jointly coordinate consensually developed policy initiatives. These iron triangles should only arise in settled, politically well-defined domains, since coordination of institutionally autonomous agencies is their distinguishing feature. In an unsettled or fluid domain, or one in which persistent partisanship plays a prominent role, it would be difficult to sustain such coordination for any substantial period of time. The agriculture domain probably most nearly approximates the iron triangle model, since it has enjoyed a long-standing consensus about the overarching policy framework within which the well-being of farmers is to be achieved. Because a high-level settlement has been established for some time, it may not be necessary for the peak government agencies, such as the White House and the OMB, to be present in the central region of the space in order to negotiate the terms of relative peace.

A third model is polarization. A polarized situation exists where well-defined and stable groupings of interested parties are in recurrent and predictable opposition on a range of policy initiatives rooted in partisan differences. In such a domain, we would expect congressional Republicans to be aligned with executive branch Republicans in opposition to congressional Democrats. The polarization model differs from the interpenetration and iron triangle models in that it predicts that agencies recruit their constituents primarily from their partisan supporters, while the other two predict either that high-level agencies will contend for control in a common, centrally located region of the space (interpenetration), or that the key agencies will be scattered around the periphery in niches that have narrow policy concerns (iron triangles). The labor domain may best approximate the polarization model. It is the most ideologically differentiated domain, dominated by the overriding cleavage between labor and management.

A fourth model might be called the appropriation model. In this model, the principal debate is over how government money should be allocated and who should participate in the allocation decisions. This most nearly describes the situation in the health domain, where the principal concern is the overall cost of health care as a share of the total budget. We would thus expect the core region of the health domain to be occupied by governmental agencies concerned with finance and the overall budget, while the periphery would be occupied by more specialized interests. To a large extent, then, the substantive executive agencies would be peripherally located, and the congressional appropriation committees and the OMB would be centrally located.

The smallest space analyses presented in this chapter depict the proximities among authoritative government targets in the four domains. We have adopted several conventions in presentation. First, government targets are numbered in order of increasing Euclidean distance from the centroid of the solution, so that the lowest number indicates the most centrally located and the highest number the most peripherally located target. This allows the reader to find the core and peripheral agencies rather easily. These numbers cannot be directly compared across policy domains, however, because they reflect the relationships among the agencies within each domain rather than points along a common metric or scale. Some policy domains have relatively empty cores, with most of the action being relegated to peripheral locations, while others have more heavily populated cores. Second, we use five symbols to designate an agency's institutional context: congressional, cabinet department, other executive, judicial, or independent. This allows us to apprehend the overall configuration of the agencies and to consider whether a particular model best describes a specific domain.

Energy: Policy in Development

During the 1970s and early 1980s, oil companies lost some of their dominance over matters pertaining to oil exploration, development, and sale, while groups interested in the environment, safety, and alternative fuels gained ground. In addition to the expansion in the number of groups with an effective voice on energy policy, however, there was a growing complexity in the government's efforts to manage energy issues. More than eighty congressional subcommittees claimed jurisdiction over all or part of the domain (Laumann and Knoke 1987, 100 n. 9). Democrats and Republicans contended bitterly on issues concerning deregulation and the environment. President Reagan advocated the relaxation of pollution controls and other energy-related regulations, but the administration did not succeed in changing existing law. The administration was able to relax enforcement actions, however, which raised the ire of congressional Democrats and environmental groups. The policies of Secretary of the Interior James Watt concerning coal leasing, offshore drilling, grazing rights, water rights, mineral rights, and timber contracts also enraged the opposition. These conflicts mobilized the interests of a large number of organizations and engaged the attention of high-level government officials, who were pulled to the center of the space in order to manage the political consequences.

Figure 7.2 depicts the proximities of the government targets in the energy domain. This structure approximates the interpenetration model. Among the most centrally located actors are the standing committees of the Senate (under Republican control in 1983)— Energy and Natural Resources, and Environment and Public Works—as well as the White House and the Office of Management and Budget (OMB). The specialized regulatory and land management agencies and the courts are more peripherally located. The Senate Energy and Natural Resources Committee may have been placed in the core of the space by its hearings on the nomination of William P. Clark to replace Watt as Secretary of the Interior, a highly politicized decision that involved a heterogeneous array of groups. But agencies concerned with alternative fuels and with resource use are also in the core, as are the congressional leadership and the White House. Clearly, the debates about the future direction of energy policy were broad ranging.

The left side of the space is composed almost entirely of congres-

1 Senate: Energy and Natural Resources Committee	15 House: Appropriations Committee	27 Dept Energy: Office of Energy Research
2 House: Subcom–Energy Research and Production	16 House: Budget Committee	28 Environmental Protection Agency
3 Senate: Environment and Public Works Committee	17 Senate: Budget Committee	29 Senate: Finance Committee
4 White House	18 House: Subcom–Health and Environment	30 Dept Interior: Office of Secretary
5 House: Subcom–Energy Development and Applications	19 House: Democratic Leadership	31 Dept Energy: Federal Energy Regulatory Commission
6 House: Subcom–Energy and Environment	20 Dept Energy: Office of Secretary	32 Dept Energy: Asst. Secretary, Nuclear Energy
7 Office of Management and Budget	21 House: Interior and Insular Affairs Committee	33 House: Subcom–Commerce, Transportation and Tourism
8 House: Subcom–Water and Power Resources	22 Senate: Democratic Leadership	34 Dept Energy: Office of Policy, Planning, and Analysis
9 House: Subcom–Energy Conservation and Power	23 House: Science and Technology Committee	35 Dept Energy: Asst. Secretary, Environmental Protection
10 House: Subcom–Fossil and Synthetic Fuels	24 Dept Energy: Asst. Secretary, Conservation and	36 Dept Interior: Bureau of Land Management
11 Dept Energy: Asst. Secretary, Fossil Energy	Renewable Energy	37 Nuclear Regulatory Commission
12 House: Subcom–Energy and Water	25 House: Energy and Commerce Committee	38 Dept Energy: Economic Regulatory Administration
13 House: Republican Leadership	26 House: Subcom–Mines and Mining	39 U.S. Court of Appeals
14 Senate: Republican Leadership		

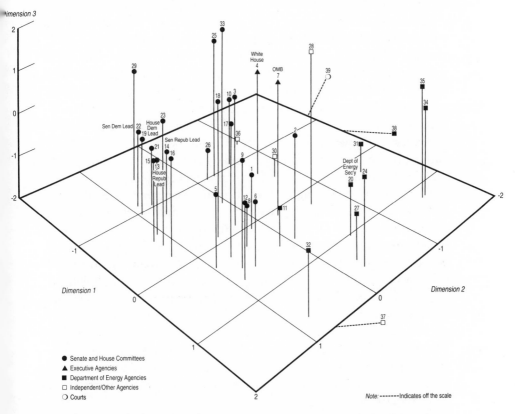

Figure 7.2 Proximities of government targets in the energy domain, based on contact by representatives (three-dimensional smallest space analysis; stress = .17; R^2 = .82)

sional actors, while the right side is dominated by executive agencies. The higher-level actors are scattered throughout the central region of the policy space. The relative isolation of the Department of Energy cluster on the right side of the space (points 20, 24, 27, 31, 32, 34 and 35) suggests that representatives active there had a narrow range of interests and were less involved in the broad issues that were debated in the core of the space.

Agriculture: Established Niches

In the early 1980s, the chronic surplus of American agricultural commodities was aggravated, in part because of the embargo on wheat sales to the Soviet Union, and the farm recession led to a rapid increase in subsidy payments. In 1981, the federal government spent $4 billion in farm aid; by 1983 that amount had jumped to $19 billion. But a drought in the Midwest in 1983 reduced grain yields substantially. Farmers participating in the payment-in-kind (PIK) program then realized great gains since they were entitled to receive allocations of government supplies of commodities, but nonparticipating grain farmers and livestock and dairy farmers who had to buy grain in the market were hard hit by the reduced yields.

The analysis of the agriculture domain displayed in Figure 7.3 shows that agencies dealing with the prices and markets for farm commodities are on the far left side of the space, while those responsible for food safety and land use are on the far right. The center is occupied by the Agriculture Secretary and the main congressional committees. Unlike the energy domain, where there is a well-defined division between the congressional and the executive agencies, the agriculture domain has the two juxtaposed within particular regions of the space. This suggests that the agriculture domain more closely resembles the iron triangle model. Agriculture representatives apparently organize their routine contacts in a substantive way, without much regard to the institutional distinction between congressional and executive targets.

There are some well-defined clusters in Figure 7.3. At the right of the space, in the rear margin, we find several agencies that deal with land management issues (points 26, 33, 36, 37, 38, 40, and 41). The concerns of these agencies include forests, water resources, public lands, parks, and environmental issues. Also on the right edge of the space, but toward the front, we find a loose cluster of agencies dealing with food safety and nutrition issues (28, 32, 35, and 42). The White House and the OMB are located between these two clusters, which suggests that the top leadership of the executive branch is more

Dept Agric: Office of Secretary
Senate: Agriculture, Nutrition and Forestry Committee
House: Agriculture Committee
House: Budget Committee
House: Democratic Leadership
Farm Credit Administration
Senate: Budget Committee
House: Republican Leadership
Senate: Republican Leadership
Dept Agric: International Affairs and Commodity
Programs
House: Subcom–Dept. Operations, Research and
Foreign Agriculture
Office of Management and Budget
Senate: Democratic Leadership

14 Dept Agric: Agricultural Cooperative Service
15 White House
16 Dept Agric: Agricultural Marketing Service
17 Dept Agric: Foreign Agricultural Service
18 Dept Agric: Farmers Home Administration
19 House: Subcom–Livestock, Dairy and Poultry
20 Dept Agric: Agricultural Stabilization and Conservation Service
21 Dept Agric: Federal Grain Inspection Service
22 House: Subcom–Conservation, Credit and Rural Development
23 Dept Agric: Federal Crop Insurance Corporation
24 Dept Agric: Commodity Credit Corporation
25 House: Subcom–Domestic Marketing, Consumer Relations
    and Nutrition
26 House: Subcom–Forests, Family Farms and Energy
27 U.S. International Trade Commission

28 Dept Agric: Animal and Plant Health Inspection Service
29 Commodity Futures Trading Commission
30 House: Subcom–Wheat, Soybeans, and Feed Grains
31 House: Subcom–Cotton, Rice and Sugar
32 Dept Agric: Food and Nutrition Service
33 Senate: Environment and Public Works Committee
34 Dept Agric: Soil Conservation Service
35 Dept HHS: Food and Drug Administration
36 House: Subcom–Water and Power Resources
37 Senate: Energy and Natural Resources Committee
38 House: Subcom–Public Lands
39 Agency for International Development
40 Dept Interior: Bureau of Land Management
41 Dept Interior: Office of Secretary
42 Dept Agric: Food Safety and Quality Service

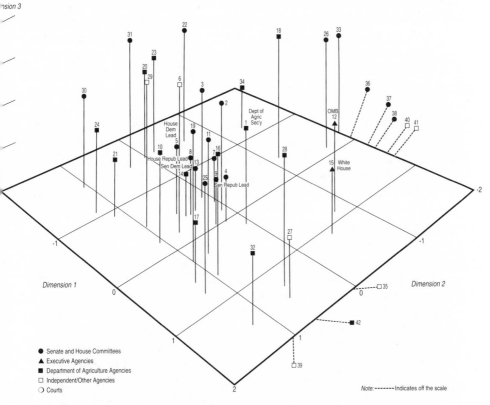

Figure 7.3 Proximities of government targets in the agriculture domain, based on contact by representatives (three-dimensional smallest space analysis; stress = .17; R^2 = .80)

involved in the concerns of these clusters than in the remainder of the agriculture domain.

The prices and markets cluster forms the outer edge of the left side of the space. Agencies concerned with price-support policies attract representatives who have relatively little involvement in food safety or land management issues. The Secretary of Agriculture and the congressional leadership mediate between the price/market and non-market regions of the space.

The agencies concerned with international agriculture issues form a ring around the congressional leadership, and this ring crosscuts the other clusters. For example, the Agency for International Development (point 39) and the International Trade Commission (27) are in the same region as the food safety and nutrition agencies. Representatives contacting agencies in the international ring therefore probably tend to contact other agencies as well. But the distance between the food safety and land management clusters, on one hand, and the congressional leadership cluster, on the other, suggests that the former tend to be relatively autonomous from congressional oversight.

Notice that specialized agencies surround the central actors. This probably means that agriculture policy is demand driven: agencies specializing in policies of concern to particular geographic regions vie for advantages conferred by Congress. But the less central location of the White House and the OMB suggests that those agencies were not initiating or mediating agriculture issues generally. Instead, the issues appear to arise from the demand of the representatives in a bottom-up fashion, with Congress acting as a coordinating broker.

Health: Appropriation Politics

Policy in the health domain has been oriented primarily toward cost containment. This focus has coincided with the emergence of third-party payers, such as Blue Cross, as well as with the dissatisfaction of large employers and other organizations faced with rapidly increasing outlays for health insurance benefits. Since the implications of these financial issues tend to be national in scope rather than regional, the emphasis in the health domain on both public and private expenditures is of a different character than in the agriculture and energy domains. Health issues are usually not systematically associated with a particular region of the country, as is often the case in agriculture and energy. Moreover, health representatives are more likely to possess a knowledge advantage over congressional officials than are representatives in the agriculture and energy domains. A senator from an agricultural state may often possess a considerable degree of knowledge about agriculture policies, production, markets, and the whole range of issues related to agriculture, and a member of Congress from the Southwest may know a great deal about oil exploration, production, and distribution, but few members of Congress have specialized knowledge in medicine or health-related matters. Even the bureaucrats in the Department of Health and Human Services may have great difficulty in keeping abreast of the rapid medical and technological advances in the field.

Thus, government officials are often unable to assess the severity of need for attention to any one disease or medical condition, since each tends to be defined as a crisis. This produces a "disease of the month" phenomenon in which a specific ailment is briefly given concentrated attention. Lacking the ability to make more substantive choices in the health domain, government officials turn their attention to budgetary and financial issues, and its appropriations power therefore places Congress in the core of the space.

Figure 7.4 indicates the relative proximities of the government targets in the health domain. The congressional committees are all concentrated in the center of the space, surrounded by the executive agencies. The first thirteen institutions in order of proximity to the centroid of the space belong to Congress. The fact that the congressional and executive agencies are so clearly bounded indicates specialized (nonoverlapping) constituencies. Furthermore, the data clearly show that targets cluster on an institutional rather than a substantive basis. For instance, the Senate and House Veterans' Committees are closely aligned with other congressional committees rather than with the Veterans' Administration, indicating a degree of institutional specialization that is not found in the agriculture and energy domains.

The Veterans' Committees are located at the top of the congressional cluster, while the bottom contains committees with broader jurisdiction, including the House Ways and Means Committee and the Senate Finance Committee. Notably absent from the core are the Health and Human Services Secretary, the White House, the OMB, and other agencies of the executive branch.

The top periphery of the space contains a cluster of biomedical research organizations: the National Institutes of Health (31); the National Academy of Sciences (29); the Alcohol, Drug Abuse, and Mental Health Administration (32); and the Centers for Disease Control (33). This biomedical cluster stands out from the other targets in several ways. The mean level of issue conflict reported by representatives who contact agencies in the biomedical cluster is substantially above average. Moreover, representatives contacting the biomedical

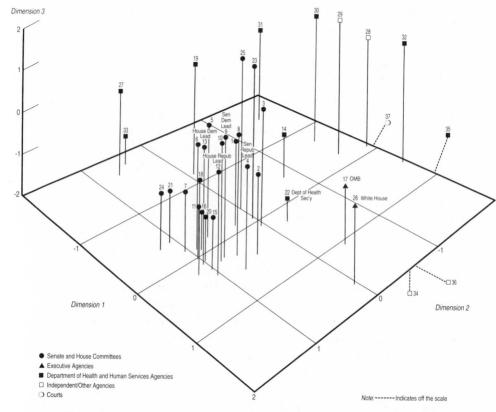

1 Senate: Subcom–Labor, HHS, Education
2 Senate: Labor and Human Resources Committee
3 House: Subcom–Hospitals and Health Care
4 Senate: Republican Leadership
5 House: Subcom–Labor, HHS, Education
6 House: Budget Committee
7 House: Ways and Means Committee
8 Senate: Appropriations Committee
9 Senate: Democratic Leadership
10 House: Appropriations Committee
11 House: Subcom–Health
12 House: Republican Leadership
13 House: Democratic Leadership

14 Dept HHS: Office of Health Research, Statistics and
   Technology
15 Senate: Finance Committee
16 House: Subcom–Health and Environment
17 Office of Management and Budget
18 Senate: Budget Committee
19 Dept HHS: Health Resources and Services Administration
20 House: Energy and Commerce Committee
21 Senate: Subcom–Health
22 Dept HHS: Office of Secretary
23 Senate: Veterans' Affairs Committee
24 Senate: Subcom–Social Security and Income Maintainance
25 House: Veterans' Affairs Committee

26 White House
27 Dept HHS: Social Security Administration
28 National Academy of Science
29 Veterans Administration
30 Dept HHS: National Institutes of Health
31 Dept HHS: Alcohol, Drug Abuse and Mental Health
   Administration
32 Dept HHS: Centers for Disease Control
33 Dept HHS: Health Care Financing Administration
34 Federal Trade Commission
35 Dept HHS: Food and Drug Administration
36 Environmental Protection Agency
37 U.S. District Court

Figure 7.4 Proximities of government targets in the health domain, based on contact by representatives (three-dimensional smallest space analysis; stress = .17; R^2 = .85)

cluster report more stable coalitions of interest groups than do those contacting other agencies. The biomedical cluster thus appears to be a clearly identifiable niche that attracts repeat players who have strong alignments.

We would have expected the OMB to be located closer to the center of the space, given the domain's emphasis on issues of finance and budget. Perhaps the White House and the OMB are relatively peripheral here because of their inaccessibility. This is the case in all of the domains except energy, where the large energy producing and distribution companies appear to enjoy better access to these top levels of the executive branch. The most striking feature of the findings in the health domain is that *all* of the congressional institutions are located in a common region of the space, surrounded by the executive agencies and independent commissions. We do not observe regional niches of the sort that are produced by the interest groups associated with particular agricultural commodities or fuel types. Indeed, even one of the issue areas that is sometimes cited as an example of an iron triangle, veterans issues, does not span the gulf between the congressional and the executive branches; and the ring of biomedical agencies does not include any congressional committees. Thus, the health domain is the clearest example of congressional centrality.

Labor: Stable, Bipolar Opposition

Although the conflict between labor and management is often highly charged, the labor domain exhibits considerable stability and predictability. But what is the structure of relationships among the agencies that is produced in this context of recurrent conflict?

During the Carter administration, when Democrats controlled both the House and the Senate as well as the executive branch, unions attempted to push through a controversial bill concerning common situs picketing. The attempt failed, but it infuriated and mobilized management groups. The patterns of contact analyzed here reflect the situation during the Reagan administration, in the aftermath of that struggle, a period during which the Democrats controlled only the House of Representatives.

As was true in the health domain, there is a clear separation between the Congress and other government units. At the lower left of Figure 7.5, we find all of the congressional targets. The Secretary of Labor, the White House, and the OMB are located above the congressional cluster. The Secretary is closest to the center of the space. As in the agriculture domain, the cabinet department appears to play a more central role in the representative contact structure than does the White House or the OMB. The more specialized executive agencies, independent commissions, and the courts occupy the extreme upper region and right periphery of the space.

1 Dept Labor: Office of Secretary	12 Dept HHS: National Institute for Occupational Safety	21 Office of Management and Budget
2 House: Education and Labor Committee	and Health	22 Senate: Appropriations Committee
3 Senate: Judiciary Committee	13 Occupational Safety and Health Review Commission	23 Senate: Finance Committee
4 Senate: Labor and Human Resources Committee	14 House: Budget Committee	24 Dept HHS: Social Security Administration
5 Dept Labor: Employment Standards Administration	15 Senate: Budget Committee	25 Commission on Civil Rights
6 House: Judiciary Committee	16 House: Democratic Leadership	26 Pension Benefit Guaranty Corporation
7 Senate: Republican Leadership	17 Senate: Democratic Leadership	27 National Labor Relations Board
8 House: Republican Leadership	18 House: Ways and Means Committee	28 Equal Employment Opportunity Commission
9 House: Subcom–Labor, HHS, Education	19 Dept Labor: Labor–Management Services Administration	29 Federal Labor Relations Authority
10 White House	20 Dept Labor: Occupational Safety and Health	30 U.S. Court of Appeals
11 Senate: Subcom–Labor, HHS, Education	Administration	31 U.S. District Court

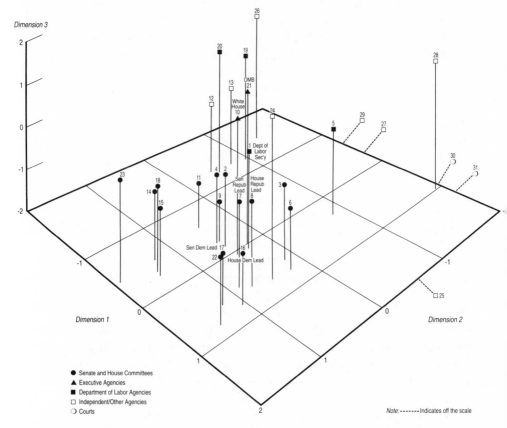

Figure 7.5 Proximities of government targets in the labor domain, based on contact by representatives (three-dimensional smallest space analysis; stress = .14; R^2 = .88)

Among the congressional committees, there is a distinct cluster of appropriations and finance committees (points 23, 18, 15, and 14) on the far left side of the space. This grouping is not produced by partisan alignments, since the Senate committees were controlled by Republicans and the House committees by Democrats, but partisanship does play an important role in differentiating among other targets. In the center of the figure, we see successive layers of partisan players. At the bottom is the Democratic congressional leadership, next above is the Republican congressional leadership, followed by the Labor Secretary, with the White House and the OMB on top. If we examine the percentage of Democrats among representatives contacting these targets, we find systematic, predictable differences. Democrats are less likely to contact executive branch agencies, the Republican leadership, Department of Labor agencies, or Republican-controlled Senate committees than they are to contact House commit-tees and the Democratic leadership.

Like the congressional finance cluster, several executive agencies and commissions are arrayed in identifiable groupings. At the top middle of the space, we find three agencies concerned with occupa-tional safety (points 12, 13, and 20). Adjudicatory bodies—including the NLRB (27), the Equal Employment Opportunity Commission (28), and the federal courts (30, 31)—ring the right border of the figure. But the Pension Benefit Guaranty Corporation (26), the Social Security Administration (24), and the Employment Standards Admin-istration (5) each occupy relatively isolated regions of the space, reflecting the specialized profile of the representatives who contact them.

Note that we do not find conflict-absorbing agencies at the center. Rather, the claimant groups appear to contact government agencies that are sympathetic to their views. A significant portion of the con-flicts among these groups are pushed to the periphery, where they are adjudicated by specialized boards and the courts.

Conclusion

The most striking characteristic of these findings is their lack of consistency across domains. That is, the nature of the agencies that occupy central or peripheral positions and the nature of the relation-ships between the legislative and executive regions of the space shift from domain to domain depending on the content of current issues.

In three of the domains—energy, health, and labor—there is a clear separation between the legislative and the executive agencies. In the agriculture domain, however, agencies from the two branches are mixed together throughout the space. In all of the domains, the congressional leadership and committees are usually more central than are the executive agencies; but in two of the domains, agriculture and labor, the office of the Secretary of the lead cabinet department is the most central of all of the agencies. In the energy and the health domains, by contrast, the cabinet secretaries are surprisingly far from the center.

In searching for principles that might account for the structure of relationships among the agencies, we seized on the obvious proposition that agencies with broader jurisdiction might occupy the core of the space, where several constituencies overlap, while agencies with more specialized mandates would be found in peripheral locations. On the whole, the analyses do find such an effect—it would be very surprising if they did not. But the two agencies that have the broadest jurisdiction of all, the White House and the OMB, are not consistently found in the center of the space. They are central in the energy domain, but they are far from the center in both health and agriculture, and in a more moderate position in the labor domain. The truly peripheral agencies—the ones that are off the scale in the figures—are often independent regulatory commissions that have quasi-judicial functions, or they are the courts themselves. These findings reflect the high degree of separation between lawyer and nonlawyer representatives.

It is clear that the centrality of the agencies is strongly associated with the size of their constituencies. In all four domains, agencies that have a higher volume of contacts are significantly closer to the center of the space. Since larger constituencies are also likely to be more diverse, agencies that have a broader range of contacts are located in between the several more distinctive constituencies—that is, in a more central position. The relative isolation of the White House and the OMB in three of the four domains may be explained by this volume effect. That is, though those agencies have very broad jurisdiction, access to them is limited and perhaps available only to certain classes of representatives.

We speculated that the core agencies might serve as mediators among the competing interest groups or might resolve political conflict. This would suggest that the representatives who are in contact with the core agencies would be likely to report that their work is characterized by a higher level of conflict than that reported by the constituencies of more peripheral agencies. Insofar as there are any significant tendencies in our data, however, we find that the opposite is the case: in both the agriculture and the labor domains, representatives who are in contact with peripheral agencies are more likely to report high levels of conflict than are those who are in contact with the core agencies; and in the other two domains, there is no significant relationship between the centrality of the agencies and the level of conflict reported by their constituents. These findings suggest that the specialized policy niches that exist in the agriculture and labor domains are not iron triangles where the interest groups and their agency sponsors coexist in a harmonious, symbiotic relationship. Rather, these niches would appear to be specialized arenas of conflict where pitched battles are fought. The formal conflict-resolving agencies (the courts and quasi-judicial bodies) are usually located in the periphery of the space—suggesting, again, that high conflict issues may be resolved, insofar as they are resolved, around the margins of the space rather than in the core.

The varying core agencies of the several domains appear to perform for the most part a more neutral coordination or facilitation function. In the domains where the office of the Secretary of a cabinet department or the lead congressional committees are in the center of the space, it may be that all issues, great and small, move through these clearinghouses at some point, but that the real battles take place elsewhere, in more peripheral locations. The shifts in the content of the core across the four domains suggest that no one agency or set of agencies is consistently in a position to be able to mediate among the groups or to impose solutions. The White House has perhaps the greatest stock of authority that might be used to promote and enforce compromise, but we have seen that it is usually not central in these domains. Thus, the four domains we have considered appear to lack government agencies that consistently perform a mediation function or resolve the broad conflicts. More particular conflicts appear to be contested (and some, perhaps, resolved) in specialized regions of the space, around the outer edges of the circle. It may be that private elites, rather than government agencies, perform the central mediation function. We will consider that possibility in chapter 10.

Chapter 8

The Government Officials

It has long been an axiom of politics that access to government officials is the sine qua non of interest representation. Journalists and academicians agree that much of what interest groups do is designed to secure and maintain effective access; only the officials, after all, have the authority to act, to make policy decisions that can benefit or injure a group's interests. Lobbyists can offer reasons and arguments for or against action, but it is government officials who monopolize the legitimate power. Officials differ profoundly, however, in the extent and character of their power, and lobbyists must use their limited resources to try to reach those officials who can best help them. These strategic targets might well vary from group to group and from one policy domain to another. But selecting officials to concentrate on is a concern common to all interest group representatives.

Several plausible explanations of how groups structure their quest for access have been put forward. Political action committees are presumably designed to gain access to members of Congress through campaign contributions. Interest groups, drawing upon PAC resources, may concentrate on access to Congress and use that access, in turn, to influence decisions in the executive branch. Alternatively, it has often been alleged that organized interests tend to "capture" the bureaucracy that is charged with regulating them (Bernstein 1955, inter alia). This might mean that group representatives would pay special attention to lower-level bureaucratic and independent agency officials, developing friendly long-term relationships with them that could withstand the pressures for policy change brought about by fluctuations in electoral fortunes. Or, to take a third possibility, the quest for access might well follow an official's reputation for power and influence. Thus, if it is generally believed that the executive branch has come to dominate the policy process and that, within the executive branch, power has been increasingly centralized in the White House and the Executive Office of the President, it might be expected that lobbying access would be sought more and more often at that institutional level.

In order to explore these ideas empirically, we asked each of our interest representatives to name the five government officials they contacted most often. From these, we drew random samples of from 101 to 108 officials per domain. Interviews were completed with 301 officials, for an overall response rate of 71%. The refusal rate was only 8%; the remainder could not be scheduled for various reasons. Table 8.1 displays the distribution of respondent officials by policy domain and institutional location.

If we try to discern a broad pattern of interest group access by drawing inferences from the table, it is striking, first of all, that there is an equal division between the executive and legislative branches overall. There is some variation among the policy domains: agriculture interests, having cultivated the Agriculture Department agencies for many years, give greater attention to the executive branch; more of labor policy is determined in independent agencies such as the National Labor Relations Board or the Equal Employment Opportunity Commission. But the similarities in institutional focus are impres-

Table 8.1 Distribution of government officials, by policy domain and institutional location (percentages)

	Agriculture	Energy	Health	Labor	Total
Legislative branch					
Senate or House member	12	25	19	23	20
Member staff	15	4	7	1	7
Committee staff	18	26	22	27	23
Legislative branch subtotal	45	55	48	51	50
Executive branch					
White House/Executive Office	4	5	3	10	5
Top-level department	14	14	6	7	10
Mid-level department	34	16	37	16	26
Independent agency	4	10	7	16	9
Executive branch subtotal	56	45	53	49	50
N	74	80	73	74	301

sive. The data suggest that group contact is sought and attained across the full spectrum of policy-making authority. Moreover, despite popular images to the contrary, Congress is not more heavily subject to group interest contact than is the executive branch. What any particular contact may mean is another matter, of course. In one case, contact may be mainly informational, while in another it may carry connotations of political pressure.

When we look more closely at how group contacts are distributed within each branch, several items of significance can be noted. Congressional officials can be readily divided according to their positions as elected members, member staff, or committee staff, respectively, within each house of Congress. This procedure reveals that interest groups distribute their attentions broadly across the Hill types. Somewhat more individuals are chosen from the House than from the Senate (89 to 57); the latter is, after all, a much smaller body. Despite conjecture in recent years that congressional staff has virtually taken over the members' functions, we find that elected members of Congress are often the primary points of contact. It is interesting to note that on the Senate side, where at the time of our interviews Republicans had been in control for two years after nearly three decades of minority status, only 23 committee staffers were named as important contacts. In the House, 43 were named. The change in party control had been followed by a considerable shakeup in the committee staffs; the newer Senate staff may not have had time to develop a full complement of group connections.

Categorizing the executive branch officials in our sample is less straightforward. One group is easy to identify: those who work on the White House staff or in the Executive Office of the President. A second group is composed of people in independent agencies and regulatory commissions; these, too, are readily identified. But this still leaves two-thirds of the executive officials in our sample, who are employed in various positions with diverse labels in cabinet-level departments. We have divided them into two groups. One consists of people at the level of the office of secretary, the deputy or under-secretary, and the assistant secretaries. These we call top-level department officials. Anyone below this level is identified as a mid-level official. Many of the latter are the operating heads of programs or their deputies, however, and all of them are officials that interest group representatives chose to contact most often. None of them, therefore, is very far down the bureaucratic ladder.

The mid-level group is considerably larger than any of the others. It includes fully half of the executive branch officials. One-third of this set are career officials with civil service status and substantial tenure in the federal government. In none of the other three groups, by contrast, are more than occasional career officials to be found; most are "in-and-outers" (MacKenzie 1987) to one degree or another. Even noncareer officials among the mid-level appointees are likely to have spent considerable time in government, in comparison with the top-level officials. The latter are the most fully "political" of the appointees, and 80% of them report prior experience as representatives of private interests. The mid-level people, on the other hand, including in-and-outers as well as careerists, are more often the officials with whom interest groups can develop long-term relationships that could be the structural bases of so-called iron triangles.

In the agriculture and health domains, mid-level bureaucrats are especially prominent. We interpret this to mean that in those policy fields the more detailed concerns of program implementation are a larger part of the interest groups' concerns than are new policy initiatives. We have data bearing somewhat more directly on this issue, and indeed we find that health groups and health officials both report relatively high levels of concern with rules and regulations, higher than in the other domains. These activists in the health field are also more deeply involved in questions of program funding, and lobbyists may therefore focus more on program-level officials than on those with broader but less detailed responsibilities.

Compared to interest group representatives, officials tend to see their domains as somewhat less partisan and less conflictual, but the differences are quite small, and in the aggregate both sets of respondents see their domains in similar terms. Congressional officials perceive significantly more partisanship than do those in the executive branch (means of 2.5 versus 3.0 on a 5-point scale); this results from the substantially less partisan perceptions of the mid-level bureaucrats. Congressional committee staff, member staff, and elected members within each domain share essentially the same perspectives, and high-level executive branch officials also hold similar views. Mid-level bureaucrats and independent agency personnel, however, rate their policy areas somewhat lower not only in partisanship but in conflict, visibility, and number of contending interests. There appears, therefore, to be a narrowing in both the scope and embattledness of interest entanglement that is in rough congruence with the lesser range of policy responsibility of these officials. They may be sought out by group representatives as often as those above them in authority, but the purposes of contact appear to be narrower and less embedded in conflict.

Demographics and Background

The personal characteristics of the government officials targeted by interest group representatives might be compared to several other populations. It would be interesting to know whether officials contacted by groups differ in consistent and meaningful ways from other federal government personnel, but we lack much of the data necessary for this comparison. Our impression is that there are not many differences of importance (see MacKenzie 1987; Ornstein et al. 1987). We can say with certainty that the officials who interact with lobbyists are a highly educated elite, mostly white male, of upper socioeconomic status and with a mean age in the forties, nearly half of whom grew up on farms or in small towns.

Two lines of reasonably detailed comparison may be made with our data. First, let us examine the similarities and differences among officials in varying institutional locations. In its most general form, the question is whether the Hill-based officials are drawn from the same population elite as those "downtown" in the executive branch, but differences among bureaucratic levels or types of congressional staff may also be important. Domain differences provide a second comparative dimension. Do the personal characteristics of officials vary across the four policy areas in patterns that can be discerned? In both types of comparisons, we are also interested in whether variations among officials match those among private representatives.

As Table 8.2 shows, there are some differences between the two branches of government. On Capitol Hill there are larger proportions of women and Catholics, and fewer Jews and high-status Protestants. It seems reasonable (if a bit risky given the small numbers involved) to argue that the congressional world is somewhat more responsive to electorally driven mobilization and recruitment of its personnel than is the executive branch, where social prestige and/or meritocratic criteria might have greater effect. This tendency would give a more elitist cast to the executive branch. The tendency may be somewhat moderated in our data, however, since all of our officials were selected because lobbyists seek them out, perhaps minimizing both inter-

Table 8.2 Personal background characteristics of officials, by government branch and policy domain (percentages)

	Govt. branch		Domain			
	Legislative	Executive	Agriculture	Energy	Health	Labor
Women	12	7	12	5	18	4
Jewish	9	15	7	10	14	16
Catholic	24	13	10	18	25	21
Type I Protestant	14	27	17	18	22	26
Northeast origin	30	34	23	29	40	37
Southern/Western origin	37	42	47	49	28	34
Law degree	45	23	23	39	17	55
Other advanced degree	27	50	44	33	54	23
N (= 300)	150	150	73	80	73	74

Note: Percentage is of the officials who possess the designated characteristic, within each branch or domain.

branch differences and the social distance between the group representatives and the officials.

Most of the representatives do not concentrate on contacts in one of the two branches to the exclusion of the other, and lobbyists tend to seek out officials more or less like themselves. (We omit the judiciary from this discussion. As pointed out earlier, the judiciary is the institutional focus of a highly specialized set of actors: the lawyers.) For both of these reasons, strong differences between the two institutionally defined sets of officials should not be expected, and in fact few appear. Substantial differences among the policy domains may be more likely, however. We know that the interest representatives in each domain are somewhat distinct, and the domain differences are readily interpretable. If it is true that representatives tend to contact officials who are like themselves in social background, those same kinds of differences should appear among the officials in our sample.

The data in Table 8.2 show that although the profiles among officials are not identical to those among lobbyists in the same domain, the general patterns are similar. The health domain has a relatively large number of women, Catholics, and Jews. Catholics and Jews are also overrepresented in the labor domain, but agriculture has few of either. Health draws disproportionately from the Northeast quadrant of the nation, while more agriculture and energy officials come from the South and West—much the pattern found among interest representatives. And while the officials in all four policy domains are well educated, the type of education varies substantially. The labor domain is dominated by lawyers, while health has more people with postgraduate medical and scientific training.

Party and Ideology

Party identification and ideology are far more immediate indicators of political compatibility between officials and interest representatives than is social background. Indeed, for the most part we would expect that common social background is significant primarily because it is likely to generate a similar political orientation, not because it provides a common social identification or comparable social graces.

Table 8.3 indicates that, in terms of both partisan commitment and ideological orientation, the government officials display the patterns we would expect. On Capitol Hill, there are approximately equal numbers of Republicans and Democrats among the senators, but there are substantially more Democrats in the House. It is noteworthy that House committee staffers are quite strongly Democratic, while a plurality of Senate committee staff are Republican. At the time of our study, of course, the Republicans held a majority in the Senate. On the House side, the agriculture staffers contacted by lobbyists are nearly all Democrats, but in general the policy domains do not show much variation in partisan composition.

Essentially similar patterns exist with regard to ideological leanings. On our scale of economic liberalism—which, not surprisingly, is highly correlated with partisanship—senators rank somewhat lower than House members. At the staff level, the differences are much greater. The Senate staff, especially member staff, is more strongly conservative, while the House staffers are predominantly liberal. Each of the categories contains individuals of diverse points of view, but it does appear that lobbying initiatives containing ideologically freighted substance were likely to get a different reception in the House than in the Senate and that this difference was more pronounced at the staff level than among the elected members themselves.

The picture on the executive side is very different, but it too approximates what we might have expected. Liberals are scarce and Democrats are nearly nonexistent among either White House staff or those in top department positions. In the more densely populated mid-

Table 8.3 Party and economic ideology, by domain and institutional position (percentages)

	Republican	Independent	Democrat	Conservative	Moderate	Liberal	N
Domain							
Agriculture	49	14	37	47	33	20	71
Energy	50	14	36	33	35	32	78
Health	33	27	40	19	40	40	70
Labor	39	11	50	22	40	39	72
Institutional position							
Senator	48	0	52	25	31	44	21
Senate member staff	54	0	46	55	18	27	13
House member	32	0	68	7	52	42	38
House member staff	29	0	71	29	0	71	7
Senate committee staff	46	27	27	36	27	36	22
House committee staff	10	19	71	8	28	65	42
White House/Executive Office	75	19	6	67	27	7	16
Top-level department	82	11	7	67	22	11	28
Mid-level department	39	32	29	27	51	22	75
Independent agencies	58	8	35	31	46	23	26

Note: "Conservative" = economic liberalism score in the lowest third of the distribution; "Moderate" = score in the middle third; "Liberal" = score in the highest third.

department level, however, more than a quarter are Democrats, as are a third of those in independent agencies. The latter two groups also display liberalism scores that are quite centrist, while the White House and top-level administrators tend to be strongly conservative. There are a few more Democratic liberals in the labor domain, and energy domain officials are more often Republican conservatives, but the domain differences are not nearly as striking as those between the positionally defined groups. Clearly, the policy-sensitive positions in the core of the administration were staffed almost completely by those in ideological sympathy with the goals of President Reagan. Whatever the political sympathies of the lobbyists may have been, they had to accommodate to this reality. At secondary levels of the bureaucracy, however, there was considerably more pluralism. These positions, too, were virtually all of policy-shaping importance; lobbyists do not select obscure functionaries for their most active attention. Though the Reagan regime had not completely eliminated Democrats, even liberal Democrats, from the leadership of operating programs, it should be noted that most of these second-tier Democrats were weak rather than strong in their partisan commitment.

It seems likely that the relatively bipartisan character of the independent agency personnel is largely a consequence of the bipartisan design of the agencies. The National Labor Relations Board, the Nuclear Regulatory Commission, the Federal Energy Regulatory Commission, and others provide a haven for partisans who, though out of sympathy with the White House, hold on to their positions for several years. Had we conducted our interviews in 1988, we might well have found that, as the Reagan administration continued to pursue its policy of ideological purification, most of the liberal Democrats had been replaced.

Embeddedness in Washington

One inference that might be drawn from the iron triangle hypothesis is that many of the personnel presently in official roles and now the objects of interest group attention previously served as interest group representatives themselves. Perhaps they came into government through the same revolving door that served as the exit for so many of the alleged "peddlers of influence" who capitalize on their government experience in their work as private lobbyists. If so, it would follow that these officials did not come to the capital recently from elsewhere, but had spent substantial portions of their working lives in and around Washington. In view of the Reagan administration's rhetoric condemning the domination of American life by the federal establishment, we should especially examine the extent to which its appointees came from outside the Washington Beltway.

In the aggregate, the government officials in our study are veterans of the national policy wars. While they had not been residents of the D.C. area quite as long as the interest group representatives, the mean length of their time there was 13.5 years, and they had a mean length of experience with the federal government of 11.9 years. Since their mean age was in the mid-forties, a large part of their working lives had been spent in Washington.

There are some substantial differences in Washington longevity, however. Officials in the legislative branch were somewhat more often old Washington hands than were those in the executive branch. This difference is explained primarily by the group we have labeled top-level department personnel. These top officials report distinctly briefer Washington residence than the other groups, suggesting that the Reagan administration did, in fact, bring in substantial numbers of policy makers from outside the Beltway. When we asked how long people had held their present positions, officials in the legislative branch reported their tenure to have been twice that of those on the executive side. The mid-level department personnel in the executive branch, however, had held their positions about as long as had the congressional staff. Members of Congress, reflecting the reelection advantages of incumbency, had served in their positions much longer than their staff aides. Staffers are younger than the members, of course, but there is no such age differential between levels in the executive branch. Such advantage as may be derived from long experience, therefore, accrues to the top echelon in the legislative branch and to the lower ranks of the executive branch.

There are differences among policy domains on both residence in the D.C. area and time in present position, and these differences appear in both branches of government. Agriculture officials are the least deeply rooted. They are followed in order by officials in energy, health, and labor. Partisan differences are even more striking. Democrats had been around substantially longer than Republicans. Independents had resided in Washington even longer than Democrats, but had not held their current posts much longer than the Republicans.

One other measure of embeddedness in the Washington political community is the extent to which the officials were acquainted with a selected set of especially notable representatives of private interests. (See chapter 10 for a discussion of the notables.) Here we find a startling difference between officials on Capitol Hill and those in the executive branch. The latter group knew only about half as many notables as did the legislative operatives, probably because the executive officials had come to town more recently. Among the legislative officials, the elected members were the most widely acquainted, though their margin over their staff in this respect is not very large. Indeed, when we measure acquaintance with the notables by a stronger criterion, one that requires a closer connection, it is the staffers, especially in the Senate, who most often have such acquaintance.

Especially interesting in this regard are the top-level department officials. As noted earlier, this category on the average had less experience in Washington and shorter service in their current positions than did the other groups of officials. Nevertheless, the top department officials were substantially more widely acquainted with the set of notable private representatives. They also had much more experience in private sector public policy representation than did the other groups of executive officials. It would appear that, at least in the Reagan years, these top administrators were hardly outsiders. They were able to draw upon wide contacts among prominent interest group lobbyists.

What Government Officials Do

We did not set out to make a complete inventory of the tasks of government officials, but rather to examine the tasks that have particular bearing on the interaction between officials and interest representatives. Accordingly, we considered three sets of questions. First, we asked how much of their time officials spent on policy-related activities as compared with internal administrative tasks, interagency contacts, or constituency cultivation. Second, we looked at the extent of official participation in various forms of policy action. And, finally, we examined officials' involvement in a number of specific work tasks. Where possible, primarily in discussing the latter two sets of data, we will make comparisons with the private interest representatives.

Since the government officials in our study were all contacted by interest representatives regarding policy issues, we would assume that these officials devoted much of their time to policy-related concerns. This assumption is valid. More than half of the respondents reported that they spent 50% or more of their working time on policy issues. But constituency and other routine relations outside the government, interagency and other routine contacts inside the federal establishment, and administrative chores within their own offices each also claim a significant fraction of their total working time. There is little variation among policy domains, but there are several interesting differences among the differently positioned cohorts of officials. As expected, lower-level administrators spend more time on internal administration and a bit less on policy development or external cultivation of contacts and support. Intragovernment communication is a prominent part of the activity of Executive Office personnel. Elected members spend more time with outside groups, a finding that fits nicely with what we know about casework, endless campaigning, and incumbent reelection success (Fiorina 1977; Cain, Ferejohn, and Fiorina 1987).

We presented the officials with a list of eight different types of public policy action and asked how often they were engaged in each type—as we did with the interest representatives (see chapter 4). Their responses show substantial differences among both policy domains and governmental positions. Legislative initiatives are primarily the prerogative of the legislative branch, as we would expect, though it is intriguing to find that elected members give somewhat less attention than do their staff to developing new legislation. All of the categories of government officials devote more time to reacting to the legislative proposals of others than they do to initiating their own proposals. Reacting to rules and regulations proposed by others also ranks above taking the initiative for all but one subgroup. Regulations are developed primarily in the executive branch, but reacting to them is an important concern for everyone. There appears to be somewhat less emphasis on initiating legislation in the labor policy domain. This may reflect the fact that a substantial bipolar stalemate has existed in the labor domain for several years.

The main lines of difference indicate that the two branches of government have different profiles of activity, but that reaction is consistently more common than initiation. A closely related finding—that monitoring the activities of other officials and of extragovernmental interests is a central task—is detailed below. Private representatives, as we have already seen, also spend much of their time monitoring and reacting to others. In part, this is an inevitable consequence of a system containing large numbers of active individuals and groups. Even if each participant initiates only a few proposals, that participant will need to consider and react to the proposals of several hundred other groups. The expansion of congressional staff and of the number of organized groups represented in Washington have thus increased the need for monitoring, both inside and outside of government.

In an age when so much of the controversy surrounding public policy appears to involve spending levels and budget deficits, issues of funding claim high priority. Interestingly, this category of policy action reveals the greatest gap in relative effort between officials and interest representatives. The latter give substantially less attention to funding matters. Public officials give great importance to budgets, and understandably so, but most outside groups are less concerned with the largely incremental differences in annual appropriations than they are with questions of statutory authority and regulatory rules. Lobbyists are not indifferent to money, of course, but they do not focus their major effort on it. We are not sure how to interpret this difference in emphasis between those inside of government and those outside. The core policies in agriculture involve entitlements, which are not subject to annual appropriations decisions; perhaps that is why lobbyists in that domain tend to put their energies elsewhere. Energy policy issues have involved regulation more than the distribution of federal money. In the health domain, funding does appear to be of concern to both government officials and interest group representatives. Although Medicaid and Medicare are entitlement programs, other health issues such as medical research involve annual decisions on money. The labor field ranks last in the salience of money. As in the energy domain, labor policy issues focus on regulation, not distribution of funds. In general, Hill officials pay somewhat more heed to funding questions than do officials in the executive branch, but the differences are not very great.

Three other modes of policy action—structural or organizational change, uncontested service or administrative action, and "contested matters," either litigation or adversarial administrative processes—received less emphasis. The relatively low salience of structural issues does not vary greatly across either the policy domains or the categories of officials. This was also true among outside interest representatives.

Much the same can be said regarding uncontested administrative action. Only slight variations appear among policy domains, and most of the positionally defined groups of officials give about the same modest emphasis to this mode of action. There is an exception, however, and it is a striking one. Elected members of Congress, in both the House and the Senate, give substantial attention to what in that milieu is referred to as casework. Note that the members themselves report this allocation of time and effort, not their staff. Clearly, these data reflect what commentators on Congress have contended: serving the uncontested needs of constituents is an important part of the elected member's responsibility and helps to account for the very high success rate of incumbents seeking reelection.

Contested actions present a different pattern. Executive officials, especially those in independent agencies, are more heavily involved than those on the Hill. A good deal of the policy action in the labor domain is located in independent agencies such as the NLRB or EEOC, and a large share of their proceedings are adversarial. Hence, labor domain officials display a marginally greater frequency of activity in contested matters. The interest group activity on labor issues is also characterized by relatively sharp, bipolar conflict, and indeed this was perhaps an important factor in the creation of independent agencies and the use of adversarial decision processes. In any case, interest group configurations, organizational forms, and the relative importance attached to various modes of policy action are surely related.

Inventory of Tasks

Schlozman and Tierney (1986) presented their respondents with a list of twenty-seven specific tasks and sought to determine which functions attracted the greatest effort from lobbyists. We employed a smaller, though similar, list of eighteen items, thirteen of which were presented to both the interest representatives and the government officials. (Elected members of Congress were omitted from this phase of the study because their tasks are not comparable to those of appointees in either branch.) The task profiles of the interest representatives were analyzed in chapter 4.

We subjected the list of eighteen tasks to factor analysis for each set of respondents, officials and interest representatives. Four factors with eigenvalues greater than 1.0 were generated for each set, accounting for 41% and 46% of the total variance, respectively. The first factor for officials involves monitoring and contacting within government; these items closely match those on the interest representatives' first factor. The second factor for officials involves external relations with groups, press, and the public. Lobbyists display a counterpart factor of contacting the government. A third factor for officials is composed primarily of supervisory tasks. The equivalent for the outside representatives involves managing their organizations and representing them before the government. The fourth of the officials' factors involves intragovernmental advocacy. This factor has no counterpart among the group representatives. Instead, the representatives have a separate litigation factor. Thus, in general, the task structures of lobbyists and officials are quite similar. Some institutional factors do differentiate particular roles, however; congressional staff members seldom testify on proposed legislation, for instance, or supervise policy implementation. They do more campaign fund-raising than executive branch officials, but lobbyists do considerably more fund-raising than congressional staff do. Most functions, however, are undertaken with somewhat more frequency by government officials than by lobbyists. Among the officials, there are a good many differences, but what seems especially impressive is the degree to which similar task structures are reported by officials from both parties, in all four domains, and in each positional cohort.

Having said this, let us briefly discuss some of the differences. Agriculture officials were a bit less often involved in drafting legislation, providing information to officials, or persuading them on policy issues. Our study was conducted midway between the major farm bills of 1981 and 1985; hence, we might expect to find less legislative emphasis. In the labor field, the two contending coalitions struggled hard to shift the policy balance, largely without success. Thus, labor officials were active in developing policy and, as was the case among the interest groups, were much the most litigious. Labor officials were also active in commenting for the press and public and in supervising policy implementation. Energy officials were comparatively heavily engaged in drafting legislation and, as participants tried to bring this policy domain into a more stable equilibrium, in urging their views on other officials.

There are also some differences among positional groups, most of which are just as one would expect. Congressional committee staff members are active in developing policy, drafting legislation, preparing testimony, providing information to officials, and, especially, monitoring developments both inside government and among interest groups. Monitoring is not a salient task for midlevel bureaucrats or independent agencies, however. Their responsibilities are more routinized, less entrepreneurial. Informal contact with interest groups and mobilizing grass-roots support are undertaken primarily by top-level department officials, as we would expect from our findings regarding their previous interest group activities; and White House staff join them in emphasizing informal contacts with other officials. These two groups are also very active in persuading other officials on policy. Whether this reflects the character of the Reagan administration agenda or is inherent in the roles of executive branch leadership cannot be determined from our data, but we would expect that advocacy on behalf of the policy initiatives of most administrations would be dominated by the partisan core in the top echelons of the executive branch (see, for example, Martin 1989).

The lesser bureaucracy and independent agency personnel are comparatively quiescent on all those tasks that entail monitoring or advocacy outside the confines of their own agencies. The corollary is that they are very active in supervising the implementation of policy. The lesser bureaucrats in the executive branch also dominate one other function, the provision of technical information to officials. All these distinctions conform nicely to the expectations we would hold on the basis of classic principles of administrative relationships. They provide a certain comfort—that our data are reasonable reflections of the world as we thought it was. We should note, however, that all of the positions engage to a substantial extent in all of the tasks. As we found to be the case among the lobbyists, the division of function and responsibility is often loose. Except for litigation, which remains the special province of lawyers, everyone tends to do at least some of nearly everything there is to do.

Contacting Others

In a governmental system as fragmented and complex in its authority structure as that of the United States, it is necessary for most officials to collaborate with others in order to accomplish anything. Relatively few authoritative decisions can be made by a single person, save those within the zone of exclusive presidential prerogative. And even those, as a practical matter, usually entail consultation with and participation by numerous others. On the congressional side, the necessity of building and sustaining coalitions is a constant feature of action at every decision level, from subcommittee to floor. It follows that federal officials will be engaged in near-continuous interaction with others. Contact may be made to acquire information, to explore cooperative possibilities, to advocate a policy, to cut a deal, and often all of the above.

We asked both the interest representatives and the government officials to examine a list of more than fifty government institutions, from subcommittees to executive agencies to courts, that are relevant to their particular policy domains. The respondents then indicated whether they were in contact with each of those units occasionally, several times, or regularly. (Patterns of representatives' contacts were analyzed in the chapter 7.) In addition to the questions addressed to both sets of respondents, government officials were asked to identify particular interest representatives with whom they worked regularly. From these responses, we can construct a reasonably full portrait of the interaction patterns within the federal government and of how those patterns, in turn, are tied to private interests.

There are no benchmarks from previous scholarship to use in assessing the quantitative results of our research. Instead, we must rely on some elementary hypotheses about who would be expected to contact whom. In formulating these hypotheses, we work in both directions. That is, we focus both on the roles of the officials undertaking particular patterns of contacting and on the differences among them as targets of contacting activity, on which ones will receive what degree of attention from other officials.

We would expect to find that institutional boundaries matter, and that these boundaries both enhance contact within and inhibit contact across institutional borders. Thus, officials in Congress would display higher rates of interaction with others on the Hill than with people in the executive branch. Some institutional boundaries are more porous than others, however. Congress is a notoriously accessible institution, far more so than the White House. We would expect to see this difference reflected in the responses.

Since much contacting is undertaken in order to persuade consequential actors on a course of policy action, interest group representatives might make an effort to concentrate at the top of the governmental authority structure, where the greater power to affect outcomes lies. Thus, we might see more attention given to officials located in the office of the Department Secretary than to the bureaucrats below. Similarly, we would expect also that the elected members of Congress would receive much more attention than their staff.

But there are two factors that may confound these expectations. First, staff may often stand in as surrogates for their employers, maintaining a working relationship in which it is widely known that, at least on certain questions, the staff person authoritatively speaks and acts for the principal. In such a case, the staffer would draw many of the contacts from other officials, as well as from knowledgeable outside interest representatives. A second complication follows from the fact that not all contacting is undertaken with the purpose of advocating policy positions or persuading others how to vote. Rather, as the earlier part of this chapter emphasized, officials often act as monitors in search of information. It is not always obvious where the best-informed officials will be found. This uncertainty is compounded by the fact that there are many different kinds of potentially useful information. What a senator's assistant may need to know in order to assist a constituent with a social security problem, for example, might lead him or her to call someone in the midst of the bureaucracy rather than the Secretary of Health and Human Services.

In much of the federal establishment, the structure of authority does not conform to anything resembling neat hierarchical arrangements. Responsibility is often broad and diffuse, particularly in Congress, where each member has a vote on every issue that comes to the floor and a considerable array of committee responsibilities as well. The total volume of contacting undertaken by and directed toward the elected member would therefore be substantially larger than that of congressional committee staff or the bureaucrats in the executive branch. Since our research was directed toward activity within circumscribed policy domains, however, we may miss some of the breadth of the members' activity. In addition, the policy responsibilities of some officials, particularly senators, may be so broad and diffuse that it will be inefficient to contact such a figure directly. It might be more effective to work through a more specialized surrogate or subordinate.

One final consideration in advance of the data: we would expect that contacting would be more frequent among those of like mind. Republicans will more often talk with Republicans, and Democrats with Democrats. Our data permit us to assess the importance of the partisan dimension in shaping interactions among officials.

The Volume of Contacting

Table 8.4 shows the frequency with which government officials contact their colleagues. Several points are immediately apparent. First, congressional officials have more contacts at a low level of frequency than do executive officials. The latter, with the exception of top-level department personnel, are generally less active. As contacting intensity increases, however, the difference between the two branches diminishes. Elected members and their staffs experience particularly noteworthy declines, and top-level department officials report a higher rate of regular contacting than do any of the other groups. These top executive officials, whom we earlier found to be the most political of the executive officials, appear to have primary responsibility for establishing and maintaining the connections needed to advance administration policy initiatives within a given domain. Congress and the White House might have more contacts across all policy domains, but elected members of Congress have such diffuse formal responsibilities and are faced with such extensive demands for legislative performance and constituency service that it is hardly surprising

Table 8.4 Mean number of government units contacted, by categories of officials doing the contacting and by domain

	Occasional contact	Several times a year	Regular contact
Legislative officials	26	16	8
Senator	23	15	6
Senate member staff	30	18	7
House member	29	17	8
House member staff	20	11	4
Senate comm. staff	24	16	9
House comm. staff	25	17	10
Executive officials	19	13	7
White House/OMB	18	14	9
Top-level department	26	20	13
Mid-level department	18	12	6
Independent agencies	14	9	4
By policy domain			
Agriculture	27	17	8
Energy	24	17	9
Health	21	14	8
Labor	17	12	6

to find the scope of their contacts shrinking as we move up in frequency. In the aggregate, the member staffs behave like their principals. There is some division of labor not reported in the table, however: members of Congress maintain stronger contacts with executive officials, while their staff focus within the legislative branch.

It would seem reasonable to expect that officials would want or need to secure contacts with others in some rough proportion to the scope of their policy interests. That is, the number of policy fields, subfields, or issues in which they took an interest all might be expected to serve as effective predictors of their level of contacting. For executive officials, this is indeed the case. Each of those variables is significant; the broader the scope of their issue involvement, the more contacting they do. For congressional personnel, however, none of these factors approaches even a minimal threshold of statistical significance. Their contacts with other officials seem to be spread in relatively idiosyncratic patterns across the government landscape, no doubt because their responsibilities are complex and diffuse. In the aggregate, their interactions are less orderly—less defined by constraints that are operative across the whole population—than are those of executive branch officials.

The frequency of contact with other officials displays substantial variation by domain. It is especially striking at the occasional level of contact. Agriculture officials report a mean frequency that is 50% higher than it is in the labor domain. Labor remains low at each level of intensity, but those involved in farm policy lead only at the lowest level. Such aggregate figures conceal much of the interesting detail, of course, but even the aggregate position of labor policy officials may seem anomalous in view of the generally high level of conflict surrounding issues in the labor domain. What these numbers reflect, however, is that a somewhat smaller number of institutional targets are involved on questions of labor policy than, say, in the organizationally unsettled field of energy. There is also a relatively sizable group of labor officials in independent agencies, especially the NLRB, who have relatively little outside contact; this also depresses labor's level of contacting. Patterns of interaction among officials will reflect the levels of conflict surrounding the policy issues in a domain, but they will also be sensitive to the institutional configuration of the domain. When, as was the case in the energy field in 1978–82, there is great flux in the structure of authority and action, officials and interest representatives must broaden the scope of their contacts. As noted earlier, the difference in contacting levels between the labor and energy domains may also be a product of the policy stalemate in labor, which made it relatively useless to cultivate support from others, as compared to energy, where a new policy equilibrium was in the process of being created. Moe (1987) has described the Reagan strategy of altering the balance of labor policy through changes in NLRB personnel rather than through legislation, and our contact data may reflect the results of this strategy.

Let us now examine the frequency with which officials select particular targets for attention. The policy domains vary in institutional configuration. Agriculture and labor do most of their business through a single committee of each house of Congress, while energy and health issues involve at least two. In the labor domain, independent agencies loom large. In this analysis, we look at six sets of targets that are relevant to all four policy domains in essentially comparable ways. Table 8.5 indicates the percentage of the sample of officials that contacts each set at each level of intensity. We find that there are two target groupings, one composed of the policy leadership and the other containing institutions that have primary responsibility for more specialized policy action within a particular domain. About one-third of the officials report occasional contact with the principal congressional committees and the Secretary's office of the main cabinet department. This is about half again as many as the percentage that contact the policy generalists, the congressional leadership, or the White House, at that level. At higher frequencies of contacting, there are few differences among the targets selected, but the more extensive interactions appear to take place with the top department

Table 8.5 Government officials contacting specified targets (percentages)

	No contact	Occasional contact	Several times a year	Regular contact
Republican congressional leadership	55	20	15	11
Democratic congressional leadership	61	18	14	8
Main Senate committees	41	34	15	10
Main House committees	51	28	14	7
Executive Office of President	54	21	15	11
Office of Secretary, main department	36	32	17	15

officials who are the most involved in the substance of the policy issues of the particular domain.

A closer look at the contacting frequencies discloses differences between the legislative and executive branches. A good deal of this interbranch difference is the result of partisanship. As we saw earlier, most of the officials in our sample are committed to one of the two major parties. On Capitol Hill, the overall balance is fairly even, but Republicans controlled the Senate and Democrats held the House during our study. Hence, the committees leaned accordingly. On the executive side, there is a strong Republican bias among the Executive Office and top-level department personnel. This is clearly reflected in the relative frequency of their contacts with the congressional leaders of the two parties. The officials tended to select politically amenable targets, so that the partisan effect was registered twice, once as a characteristic of the official and once as a relevant aspect of his or her target.

Working with Interest Representatives

We asked the government officials whether they worked regularly with any representatives of private interests. Some 83% said that they did, so there is not much variance to analyze. We do find, however, that fewer officials in independent agencies (63%) report such interaction. This means, in turn, that the labor policy domain, which contains a large share of the independent agency officials, has a lower percentage than the other policy areas. The White House/Executive Office staff also has a somewhat lower frequency of contact with lobbyists, as we might predict in view of the somewhat greater protection afforded the presidential circle against unwanted interest group intrusion. Even so, however, fully two-thirds of the respondents in such positions say that they regularly work with outside groups.

On the congressional side, it is interesting that staffers report somewhat higher rates of contact with lobbyists than do the elected members themselves. The latter by no means lack such contact, but their aides are nearly unanimous in their acknowledgement of interdependent working relationships with private interests. One other factor is associated with the likelihood that officials will work with interest groups. The more that officials specialize in a particular policy domain, as indicated by the percentage of their time that they devote to the domain, the more contact they have with lobbyists.

Respondents who indicated that they were in contact with outside groups were asked to identify up to three such groups. Several hundred different organizations were named, many only once or twice. Those attracting multiple nominations were, in general, the obvious choices—for example, the AFL-CIO, the National Association of Manufacturers, the U.S. Chamber of Commerce, the American Farm Bureau Federation, the American Hospital Association, the American Medical Association, the American Petroleum Institute, and the Edison Electric Institute. What is surprising, perhaps, is that only ten of the large, visible interest groups received as many as ten nominations from the three hundred officials interviewed, and the most popular group, the AFL-CIO, was named only thirty times. From the perspective of the government, the interest group universe would seem to be diverse indeed.

Substantive Scope and Range of Involvement

We sought to determine the degree of specialization by government officials within the spectrum of policy issues, both in their primary domains and in other policy areas. We found that differences in scope of policy engagement are greater among the position categories than among domains. On the average, officials on the Hill are active in twice as many policy areas as are those in the executive branch (5.0 versus 2.6 fields receive at least 5% of the time that the officials devote to policy). Elected members display the broadest range, with member staff and committee staff following in that order. Surely this is what would be predicted. The members must vote across the full spectrum of policy concerns, and their personal staffs must aid them in whatever issues arise. Committee staff by definition have a restricted substantive jurisdiction, and it is a bit surprising that they spend time in as many distinct policy areas as they do (3.3 fields in the Senate, 3.7 in the House). Presumably this reflects the fact that many committee jurisdictions overlap policy fields and in some areas have imprecise and shifting boundaries. Executive officials are active in a smaller number of policy fields and, as we would expect, there is a strong relationship between status in the bureaucratic hierarchy and the number of policy fields of concern. Independent agencies, though their hierarchical position is often ambiguous, are the most narrowly focused (2.1 fields), while White House/OMB officials have relatively broad mandates (3.9 policy areas, on the average).

When we examine specialization within their principal domains, we find that congressional officials are involved in substantially more subfields than are those in the executive branch (3.9 subfields versus 2.5, on the average). In the executive branch, only the top department category reported extensive subfield participation. This pattern is displayed even more strongly if we examine the number of issue events in which respondents took part (see chapter 11).

What all these data seem to indicate is that, first, there is less substantive specialization in Congress than in the executive branch; second, engagement or interest in a domain's policy business narrows as one moves down the ladder of authority or into institutional units that have more circumscribed jurisdiction, such as committees or independent agencies; but, third, interest groups work with policy makers at all levels of specialization and involvement. This last point is, in a sense, a restatement of the finding that there is great variety in the nature and extent of policy engagement, regardless of position. Of course, all these officials were chosen from those nominated to us by interest representatives, and all therefore are representative of those whom the lobbyists seek out; but the variety of the officials who were nominated suggests that interest groups need access for many purposes and at many levels.

Issue Event Participation and Success

In our interviews with government officials, we asked them about their participation in twenty specific issue events in each domain. Respondents were asked about the degree of their professional interest in each issue, and the three issues in which they "were most involved in an official capacity" were then identified for further exploration. On each of the latter, they were asked to indicate the position they took and the degree to which they achieved their objectives. The officials report doing quite well. About 38% of them said that they obtained all of their objectives on the events that most concerned them, and 64% said that they achieved at least most of their objectives. There seems to be a tendency for officials to favor policy proposals more often than they oppose them and to obtain better results when they are for a proposal than when they are against it. This may reflect a tendency to select their success stories among our list of issues, but it runs counter to that long-established adage that, because of the institutional complexity of American politics and the weakness of such aggregative mechanisms as the political parties, it is easier to block action than to effect it. Whatever the explanation, the pattern is repeated in all four policy domains.

There are some fairly sharp distinctions in success rates by party affiliation and strength of party identification. Strong Republicans do best, and strong Democrats report the lowest scores. Weak Republicans do somewhat better than weak Democrats. The scores of independents fall between these latter groups. But the big difference is between the strong Republicans and the strong Democrats. These findings no doubt reflect the successes of the Reagan administration early in the first term.

Specialization in the policy domain is a consistently significant variable. Officials who devoted at least 25% of their efforts to the domain reported achieving all of their objectives in 44% of the events and all or most in 69%. The nonspecialists report comparable success rates of 31% and 55%. But officials who are even more highly specialized, devoting a majority of their time to one domain, do not report greater success rates. Specialization thus appears to improve success up to a point, but many of the most specialized officials are relatively low in the hierarchy of influence.

We also asked each official to identify three interest groups that were active on each issue and to tell us what positions the groups took on the issues, what degree of success they achieved, and whether they had contacted the respondent regarding the issues in question. In 29% of the officials' issue-by-issue reports, no contact had been made by any group. On the other hand, at least three groups contacted the officials in 53% of the cases. More than three-quarters of the time, all of the groups making contact were on the same side of the issue. Moreover, groups were more likely to contact officials when the official and the group were in agreement (73%) than when they were opposed (60%). (We omit here the cases in which one or both of the parties were ambivalent.)

Whether officials were contacted had no consistent effect on how pleased those officials were with the outcome. There was a significant difference, however, in how well the interest groups were perceived to have fared. As Table 8.6 shows, only two comparisons of group success fail to show greater success in cases in which the official was contacted than in those in which he or she was not: when both the official and the outside group favored a proposal, no contact was required in order to produce a successful outcome; and when the

Table 8.6 Interest group success as perceived by officials

Official–group issue position	Official was contacted (N)	No contact (N)
Official and group agreed		
Both were for	3.03 (503)	3.86 (92)
Both were against	2.21 (290)	.79 (29)
Both were ambivalent	1.69 (36)	.50 (22)
Official and group disagreed		
Official for, group against	1.74 (205)	1.47 (68)
Official against, group for	2.28 (102)	2.86 (14)
Mixed cases		
Official for, group ambivalent	1.56 (50)	1.14 (14)
Official against, group ambivalent	2.64 (14)	0 (4)
Official ambivalent, group for	2.55 (86)	2.42 (43)
Official ambivalent, group against	1.80 (71)	1.31 (26)

Note: Number given is mean level of success on the issue events where 0 = no objectives achieved and 4 = all objectives achieved.

group favored a proposal, even if the official opposed it the group was perceived to do quite well, and the group's success was not seen as greater when the official was lobbied (though there were few cases in which the official was not lobbied). In all of the other comparisons, lobbying appears to produce some increase in the groups' perceived success (see also Rothenberg 1992). Clearly, lobbyists do lobby, and it appears that such contact usually enhances the groups' success in achieving their policy objectives.

Conclusion

The government officials with whom interest representatives are most often in contact mirror, in many respects, the characteristics and patterns of behavior of the interest group lobbyists. A substantial number in each set have served at one time or another on the other side of the relationship, and it is therefore not surprising that they have many things in common. In each policy domain, they have broadly similar backgrounds, and the general profiles of their tasks are essentially parallel. Officials and interest representatives do much the same kinds of things in their efforts to affect public policy.

Two factors, closely interdependent, sharply differentiate the officials from the lobbyists, however. One is partisanship, and the other is institutional location. Though lobbyists have pronounced party attachments, party appears to be a substantially greater influence on the behavior of officials. Not only does it affect the policy positions they take and the contacts they seek, but it is very often a decisive factor in getting them their jobs. Partisanship and ideology are often involved when interest groups select their representatives, to be sure, but they are perhaps even more salient in the choice of officials, whether though election or appointment. Thus, the upper strata of the executive branch will nearly always be staffed almost exclusively by people of one party, and generally by those of a single ideological orientation; congressional staff reflect the party balance in the chamber. Institutional location, in turn, also affects official behavior. Congressional officials operate in a context that is less rigidly bounded than that of the executive branch. The executive is far more hierarchical, and this shows up in the narrower scope of policy involvement and more restricted contacting patterns of officials who are further down the pecking order. On Capitol Hill, hierarchy matters less. Both members and staff reach out widely and involve themselves in diverse policy substance. They too are constrained by institutional boundaries, however, so the bulk of their regular contacts are within Congress.

One set of officials, the leaders of cabinet departments, appear to have distinct backgrounds and responsibilities. They come to their positions more often from outside the narrowly defined Washington community, but with substantial interest group connections. Once in office, they carry on much of the administration's outreach both to Congress and to the interest groups, and they appear to constitute a distinct political cadre in what is altogether, of course, a highly political context.

Finally, we would underscore the structured nature of the contacting among various types of officials and between officials and interest representatives. We find clear patterns of reported contacts, revealing well-defined and readily understood structures of authority and accessibility, and we find also that this contacting is believed to enhance the success of the interest groups in achieving their policy objectives. Group access (Truman 1951) and communication (Milbrath 1963) have long been at the core of the conventional wisdom regarding politics and policy making. Our data provide systematic evidence confirming the continuing validity of that wisdom.

Part IV

Consensus
and Conflict

Chapter 9

Allies and Adversaries

Since 1965, when Mancur Olson demonstrated that interest groups may fail to form even when social deprivation or economic self-interest is clear, much important work has been done on the origins and maintenance of voluntary associations (inter alia, Berry 1977; Moe 1980; Salisbury 1969; Walker 1983). Concepts have been reformulated in order to encompass institutions within interest groups (Salisbury 1984). Much has been learned about lobbying tactics and strategy (Berry 1977; Schlozman and Tierney 1986). Development and change over time have been examined at the level of both the individual group and broader sectors of interests (Browne and Salisbury 1972; Hansen 1987; Laumann and Knoke 1987; Starr 1982; Walker 1983). And useful cross-national comparisons have been made of the structural ties among business, labor, and the state (Schmitter and Lehmbruch 1979; G. Wilson 1985). But here we propose to address a topic central to many fields of political science, yet little addressed by students of interest groups: the structure of conflict.

Whenever a more or less well-defined system of political interactions can be observed or inferred—in legislatures, electoral politics, or international relations, to take three good examples—we move quickly to characterize that system in terms of the conflicts over scarce resources that have so long been held to be the defining feature of politics. We may focus on particular episodes: the struggle over a bill in Congress, a specific presidential contest, or an overseas military engagement. Or we may select some feature of the overall structure for attention: the committee system, third-party challenges, or coalition patterns in the United Nations. Several theories exist regarding both generic conflict patterns and the operation of specific institutional systems. Though the linkages between abstract concepts and particular occurrences are sometimes weak, substantial progress has been made in our theoretical and empirical understanding.

Like other political systems, the structure of interest groups in the United States may be characterized in terms of the extent and shape of conflict among participants. This structure is not evident in every policy dispute, nor is it necessarily revealed by any particular example of interest group activity. But, as in studies of voting or congressional roll calls, the interest group system or systems can be discerned at more aggregated levels of observation.

It is ironic that it should have taken so long to examine the structure of interest group conflict. Since the conceptualizations of Arthur Bentley (1908) began to work their yeasty way into political science, it has been commonplace to put group conflict at the very core of our thinking. Having done so, however, we have usually been unable to go beyond examples to reach more comprehensive formulations of how group interactions are structured. Is there much conflict or little? Are the main group players divided into two opposing camps or fragmented among several parties? Does the structure vary from one policy area to another? The existing literature gives little attention to these questions. (For an exception, see Schlozman and Tierney 1986, 283–288.) Part of the reason for this may be the absence of readily observed defining behavior. Party systems can be examined by looking at the distribution of votes. So can legislatures. So can the Supreme Court. The executive branch is more difficult to characterize because actions that could be the basis for defining relationships are not always visible. Interest groups present the same difficulty.

We can identify and examine three distinct sets of data that bear on the structure of interest group conflict. One set consists of perceptions of conflict as seen by both Washington representatives and government officials in each domain. The second is patterns of alliance and opposition, as revealed by responses to questions asking the representatives to identify other groups that they worked with or against. A third set of data is drawn from questions regarding participation in specific events that occurred during the five years prior to our interviews. From these quite different data sets, we derive reasonably consistent pictures of the extent and shape of group conflict in each domain.

Some of the analyses treat respondents as individuals, though they are no doubt constrained by their roles within the policy domains. In other analyses, the individuals speak for the organizations that employ them. That is, the organizations are the actors. This is appropriate for examining the patterns of organizational conflict, but it generates an unfortunate side effect. Approximately 20% of our respondents are external lawyers and consultants. Each was nominated by an organization, but in a fair number of instances these lawyers and consultants also work for other clients. When asked about their allies and adversaries or about actions relating to specific events, these respondents gave replies that could not dependably be assigned to the nominating organization. Consequently, we determined to treat external lawyers and consultants as employees of their respective firms and not try to include them in analyses of ally–adversary structures.

Quite a few of the larger organizations are represented by more than one respondent in our sample; this is the case with the AFL-CIO, the Chamber of Commerce, and other organizations of comparable significance. State and local chapters or branches of national organizations are treated as part of the same category as the parent group.

Perceptions of Issue Characteristics

In assessing the nature of interest group conflict in the four policy domains, it is helpful to have some idea of how the representatives themselves characterize the politics of their issue areas. Here, we examine three dimensions: issue stability, scope of participation, and intensity of conflict. Our data are drawn from responses to pairs of opposing statements, in which the respondents placed themselves on a five-point scale ranging from strongly agree to strongly disagree. In the presentation that follows, we simply subtract the percentage of responses on the disagree side of the scale from the percentage of responses on the agree side, and disregard choices of the middle position. In no instance was there any discernible bimodality of responses; thus, we are satisfied that we have not lost or obscured anything substantial in opting for this simple procedure.

Table 9.1 presents two measures of stability, one on the longevity of issues and one on the stability of group coalitions. A large majority in each policy domain sees the issues as long lasting, and both government officials and interest representatives share this view. Indeed, the agreement is sufficiently great that it might be accepted as settled that most of the business of policy making involves working and

Table 9.1 Perceptions of issue characteristics (percentages)

Domain issue characteristics	Agriculture		Energy		Health		Labor		Total	
	Repre-sentatives	Govern-ment officials	Repre-sentatives	Govern-ment officials	Repre-sentatives	Govern-ment officials	Repre-sentatives	Govern-ment officials	Repre-sentatives	Govern-ment officials
Issue stability										
Issues are long-lived	68	52	78	88	71	59	68	56	72	64
Coalitions are stable	26	5	21	17	28	28	35	19	27	22
Scope of domain participation										
High public visibility	38	47	78	65	43	65	54	63	53	60
Large number of actors	17	35	52	53	33	61	34	47	34	49
Level of domain conflict										
High intensity of conflict	49	6	70	88	44	45	70	69	48	67
Strong partisanship	-18	-11	11	31	-7	3	37	46	4	15
N of respondents	189	74	181	80	214	73	190	74	774	301

Note: Figures are the percentage of positive responses minus the percentage of negative responses.

reworking issues with a long history. Not many new items get on the agenda, and few matters are disposed of quickly.

There is far less agreement regarding the stability of issue coalitions, though in each domain a modest majority perceives stability rather than flux. The size of that majority is reasonably consistent across policy domains, but it is higher in labor than elsewhere. Except in the health domain, government officials perceive substantially less stability than do interest representatives.

To assess the scope of interest group activity in each domain, we asked respondents to estimate the amount of attention given by the general public to their issues and the relative number of groups actively interested in them. Two points can be made about these findings: the energy domain is seen as broader than the others in both attention and participation; and agriculture is seen as the narrowest. Doubtless this reflects the excitement surrounding energy issues in the period of our inquiry, but it may also be true that there is a particularly wide array of substantive concerns in this domain. It is interesting that energy representatives were so likely to perceive broad attention and participation. In all of the other domains, the representatives give lower ratings on these questions than do the government officials. This suggests that the representatives in domains other than energy are more specialized than the officials, and hence encounter a smaller portion of the domain's business. Energy politics had been in such turmoil at the time of our survey that it is not surprising that both officials and representatives were exposed to a broad scope of activity.

We also investigated the perception of group conflict. We asked about the intensity of conflict in general and the extent to which domain issues were contested in partisan terms. The two questions draw sharply different responses: conflict was generally said to be high and partisanship low. As one moves from one domain to another, responses on the two questions move more or less together; and they display rather startling domain differences. Agriculture and health are seen to be less conflict dominated and much less partisan than energy and labor. The labor domain appears to be intensely partisan in comparison with the other domains. (Partisan conflict can be seen as essentially bipolar opposition, while the ubiquitous but less partisan disputes of the energy domain might be characterized as more dispersed and pluralistic.)

In an effort to delve more deeply into the sources of variation in the issue perceptions of individual representatives, we undertook an extensive probit analysis, employing a considerable number of independent variables. The results were not sufficiently robust to warrant their full presentation here, but they did generally support one important conclusion. We used several different indicators of individual characteristics, including organizational position, prior government experience, present degree of policy representation effort, and personal values. A second set of variables was the respondent's policy domain and the substantive type of organization represented (labor unions, farm groups, and so on). In virtually every case, the domain and organization type had much more substantial effects than did the individual characteristics. Agriculture is relatively quiet and nonpartisan; labor is noisy, conflictual, and partisan. Energy and health are highly visible domains, with many participants, while agriculture is perceived to be otherwise. Peak-association representatives see themselves as more embroiled in controversies of broad scope and attention (apart from the actual range of their issue involvement) than do those who serve more specialized interests. These differences give support to our hope of capturing some diversity through our choices of policy domains.

Who Works with (and against) Whom?

We asked the respondents whether the organizations employing them regularly encountered other organizations, as either allies or adversaries. If the respondent answered affirmatively, we asked him or her to name up to three of each. These responses allow us to describe in considerable detail the patterning of interorganizational relationships. It is possible to distinguish between organizations that are deeply embroiled in group conflict and those that remain on relatively friendly terms with others in the domain, and to examine how the domains differ in their conflict structures. The domain differences can, in turn, be examined in terms of the substantive differences among interests.

Overwhelming majorities in each domain were able to identify both allies (89.9%) and adversaries (74.8%). Labor is most completely defined in ally–adversary terms; health and agriculture somewhat less so. Responses do not differ much by organizational position, though government-affairs specialists were a bit more likely than others to name adversaries. More time spent in the domain also made the representatives more likely to name adversaries.

When we turn to the actual nominations, we find a very sizable array of organizations named. Table 9.2 presents the total numbers for each domain. The difference between the "total nominations" and the "organizations named" lines in the table is that the former double-counts the organizations that were named by more than one respondent, while the latter counts the number of unique organizations named. We cannot say whether the domain differences are large or small because we lack any comparative standard, but it is clear from the ratio of nominators to organizations named that players in the energy domain are somewhat more likely to focus on the same allies. In the labor domain, the adversary list is also relatively concentrated, but in agriculture and health both allies and adversaries are more diffuse.

In order to comprehend the specific alliances and antagonisms in each domain, we sorted the nominating organizations and their nominees into groups of similar organizational type. While we wanted to make the process parsimonious, we also felt it necessary to adjust the categories to take account of elements specific to each domain.

Table 9.2 Nominations of interest group allies and adversaries

Domain	Allies	Adversaries
Agriculture		
Total nominations	422	287
Organizations named	186	116
Nominators	161	133
Energy		
Total nominations	449	321
Organizations named	143	95
Nominators	165	142
Health		
Total nominations	497	244
Organizations named	215	96
Nominators	185	125
Labor		
Total nominations	446	349
Organizations named	184	99
Nominators	167	151

Many organizations defy easy categorization. Energy firms are often involved in the production or sale of more than one kind of fuel, for example, so classifying organizations based on fuel type, of critical importance in energy politics (Chubb 1983), can be difficult. In agriculture, some commodity groups are composed entirely of farmer-producers, but others include processors, shippers, commodity brokers, and so on (see Guither 1980). We do not claim to have escaped error, but we believe that the more than one thousand organizations named were sensibly classified.

The agriculture domain presents the simplest array, though not the plainest structure (cf. Bonnen 1980; Browne 1986; Hansen 1987). The four categories in Table 9.3 are farm peak organizations (the general organizations of farmers, and their subsidiaries); commodity groups (producers or producer-dominated organizations specializing in a single crop or farm commodity); trade associations (organizations of corporations not directly involved in agricultural production); and, borrowing Hadwiger's (1982) term, "externality" groups (including environmental, welfare, labor, and consumer groups concerned about the externalities of farm policies). The table presents the number of nominations received by organizations in each category (omitting the considerable number scattered across other kinds of groups). It shows several things of importance. First, the groups in each category tend

Table 9.3 Allies and adversaries in agriculture

Nominee organizations	Nominating organizations			
	Farm peaks	Commodity groups	Trade associations	Externality groups
Ally				
Farm peaks	30	26	9	6
Commodity groups	27	60	13	5
Trade associations	8	10	41	4
Externality groups	5	0	6	38
N of nominating organizations	26	35	27	24
Adversary				
Farm peaks	20	18	3	9
Commodity groups	12	3	2	5
Trade associations	2	6	1	15
Externality groups	6	25	41	9
N of nominating organizations	22	28	19	20

very strongly to find their allies among organizations of their own type. As we will see, this is true in every domain. Second, farm peak organizations are internally divided. Both friends and enemies are found there, by the peak organizations and by the commodity groups especially. Neither the commodity groups nor the trade associations, on the other hand, often find adversaries internally or in the other. Those two categories, thus, appear to have a considerable affinity of interest. Despite the real potential for conflict between, for example, feed producers and livestock interests, the reported organizational alignments do not suggest such conflict. The primary object of adversarial concern among the commodity groups and the trade associations is the externality category. Apart from the externality groups themselves, few organizations choose them as allies, but they loom large as opponents. As we will see, a comparable tendency can be observed in other policy domains.

The pattern in the energy field (shown in Table 9.4) is much like that of agriculture, with one major exception. In energy politics, the role of peak associations—those that transcend particular industries—is quite modest. Again, however, we see the specialized producers working closely with one another, with relatively few adversaries

Table 9.4   Allies and adversaries in energy

| Nominee organization | \multicolumn{5}{c}{Nominating organizations} |
	Business peaks	Oil and gas	Nuclear and electric	Trade associations	Environmental groups
Ally					
Business peaks	3	10	1	15	3
Oil and gas	11	57	4	23	0
Nuclear and electric	4	3	38	11	0
Trade associations	6	7	5	24	0
Environmental groups	0	1	8	1	18
N of nominating organizations	9	32	27	31	8
Adversary					
Business peaks	0	0	0	0	0
Oil and gas	1	14	0	5	4
Nuclear and electric	0	1	5	1	5
Trade associations	0	2	3	1	4
Environmental groups	14	37	51	46	3
N of nominating organizations	8	27	26	29	8

within the industry. Trade associations are less differentiated from producers in energy than they are in agriculture, though in both domains they seem to avoid making enemies among producer groups. Here the environmentalists play the role that was played by the externality groups in agriculture. Three-fourths of all the adversaries named by the energy groups included in Table 9.4 are environmental groups. Rarely were they said to be allies, except by other environmental groups.

In the health domain, too, we find that interests select their allies primarily from within their own categories. (See Table 9.5.) The externality groups (here, citizens' organizations of various sorts, including Nader-related groups and labor unions) are often the targets of adversarial relations. More than in the other domains, however, these groups are also chosen as allies, especially by the disease groups and nonfederal officials. We take this to mean that the health domain is somewhat less rancorous. We noted earlier that a smaller proportion of the health respondents indicated that they regularly encountered opposing groups, and that health representatives perceived their issues to be less conflictual and less partisan than did participants in other domains.

In the health domain, there are no genuine peak associations. The American Medical Association might be so regarded, but only for doctors, and doctors are only one among several sets of interest-group participants. No health group successfully transcends the several major categories of interested parties. It may well be that this very fact helps to account for the somewhat lower level of acrimony characterizing health politics. Indeed, in the era when the AMA did largely dominate the full agenda of health issues, the domain seems to have been considerably more conflict ridden (Starr 1982). Analogies to superpowers in international politics may be farfetched, but it is not implausible to argue that the existence of superpowers tends to polarize conflict and that polarization tends to lead to the intensification of conflict.

Academic groups and hospitals are especially reluctant to name any adversaries. Veterans (a group category not included in Table 9.5) carry this strategy to perfection; they claim to have no organized group opponents at all. The congressional politics of health issues is often strenuously contentious, of course, but these data reflect the fact that the conflict is not so much with competing interests represented by adversary organizations as with the more amorphous forces

Table 9.5   Allies and adversaries in health

Nominee organization	Nominating organizations					
	Medical associations	Academic groups	Hospitals	Disease groups and nonfederal officials	Trade associations	Citizens and labor
Ally						
Medical associations	41	10	6	3	0	6
Academic groups	15	39	8	0	0	0
Hospitals	14	10	42	3	2	4
Disease groups and nonfederal officials	6	1	0	29	0	10
Trade associations	1	0	0	0	46	1
Citizens and labor	5	5	6	8	6	50
N of nominating organizations	31	25	23	19	20	25
Adversary						
Medical associations	19	1	0	0	0	7
Academic groups	1	0	0	0	0	0
Hospitals	3	2	1	5	0	11
Disease groups and nonfederal officials	0	0	0	3	2	0
Trade associations	2	1	2	4	3	8
Citizens and labor	17	9	11	6	21	16
N of nominating organizations	21	13	14	10	16	19

of budget constraints and administration priorities. Group politics is an important, sometimes even decisive, part of the overall policy-making process, but it is seldom, if ever, all one needs to know to explain policy outcomes.

We turn now to the labor policy domain, where the bipolar conflict structure is plain (Table 9.6). The peak associations of labor and business dominate the poles, and there is almost no trafficking with the other side. Individual unions and trade associations are only slightly less implacable foes. The latter report that they have worked out some alliances with the unions, but the unions do not reciprocate. Citizens' groups in this domain are a diverse lot, primarily aligned with labor but including a significant number of antilabor groups, producing substantial intracategory conflict. In the conflict-charged climate of labor policy, unlike the other three domains, nearly every respondent was willing to name adversaries as well as allies.

The ally–adversary structure mapped in Table 9.6 is congruent with the perceptions of labor issues. These findings confirm the perception that labor issues generate the highest levels of conflict and partisanship. Additional evidence is provided by the patterns of event-specific activity reported by our respondents. Again, we find a clear bipolar structure in the positions taken on particular labor policy

Table 9.6 Allies and adversaries in labor

Nominee organization	Nominating organizations				
	Labor peaks	Unions	Citizens' groups	Trade associations	Business peaks
Ally					
Labor peaks	2	32	8	2	0
Unions	9	37	11	11	2
Citizens' groups	15	17	30	3	4
Trade associations	0	1	5	54	15
Business peaks	0	0	5	30	42
N of nominating organizations	10	35	26	43	23
Adversary					
Labor peaks	0	0	6	20	22
Unions	1	3	3	20	12
Citizens' groups	4	24	24	2	4
Trade associations	1	11	5	7	0
Business peaks	15	41	17	4	2
N of nominating organizations	10	33	24	33	21

issues. (For further discussion of these events-based data, see chapter 11.)

Conclusion

Specialized producers, with relatively narrow policy agendas, tend to avoid becoming embroiled in adversarial encounters. As the protagonists in a system of distributive politics, they try instead to confine their efforts to building support for their primary policy goals. These live-and-let-live efforts are complicated in some domains by the presence of peak associations, organizations that seek to transcend the limited membership potential of specialized groups like trade associations and to formulate broader policy agendas as they try to speak persuasively on behalf of an entire economic sector. Peak associations tend to express their policy goals in the more encompassing language of doctrine and ideology, using abstraction to rise above the tangible differences of interest among more specialized producers.

The more prominent and unified the peak associations in a policy domain, the more polarized its group structure and policy struggles become. The limiting case in our data is labor, where the peak associations of business and labor do battle and pull the more specialized groups into one orbit or the other. In agriculture, by contrast, the peak associations are themselves divided—though at one time they were the basis of cohesive bloc politics. Farm policy making tends now to be dominated by narrower and often shifting coalitions and to be articulated with less partisan or doctrinal fervor than was the case, say, in the 1950s.

In each of these policy domains, the role of externality groups—environmentalists, consumers, and other citizens' aggregations—is a kind of mirror image of the peak associations. In labor, where the peak associations are powerful, the externality groups are diverse, divided, and often serve as satellites to the "superpowers." Where peak associations are divided or nonexistent, the externality interests provide the principal focus of opposition and are perceived as getting in the way of the realization of specialized producer interests (see also Schlozman and Tierney 1986, 285–286). Externality groups often like to think of themselves as guardians of the "public interest" against the diverse claims of multifarious "special interests." With or without the normative language, we find that this structure does indeed characterize three of the four policy domains.

Our interpretation of the role of peak associations in structuring interest group conflict moves in a very different direction from the principal lines of argument regarding societal corporatism and from the widely discussed contention of Mancur Olson (1982) regarding the significance of encompassing groups. In the corporatist model, effective peak associations of labor and business are necessary elements along with the state in a tripartite structure of cooperative negotiation (Schmitter and Lehmbruch 1979). The singularity of the United States in failing to develop along these lines has been examined elsewhere (Salisbury 1979; G. Wilson 1982). In the case of the labor domain, where we do find reasonably effective peak associations, group relations are rancorous, not cooperative—though the perceived conflict level is even higher in the energy domain, where the peak organizations are relatively weak.

Olson's argument would also lead one to expect that the more encompassing the group (the more effective the peak associations), the more efficient (less dominated by narrowly focused producer interests) will be the policy decisions. Our finding that conflict is less intense when group politics is characterized by a fragmented, special-interest-dominated pattern (as in the agriculture domain) than when more encompassing groups are the main players (as in labor) does not seem compatible with most notions of efficiency. There may, of course, be a stage beyond bipolar group politics in which a single encompassing group is able to accomplish fully Pareto-optimal results, but at that point it would appear that we have passed beyond the sphere of democratic politics.

We believe that our findings are relevant to the ongoing debate concerning the validity of pluralist models of U.S. politics. Our research design was based on the assumption that a multiplicity of groups compete in meaningful ways for the rewards at stake in public decisions, but the patterns of group action that we have reported go well beyond that. In his classic study of New Haven, Robert Dahl (1961) rests much of his pluralist interpretation on the discovery that business interests (and other interests also) pursued agendas that stopped far short of the full range of public issues and policy decisions. Consequently, their resources, though imposing, did not come into play on many issues. In his more recent statements, characterized by a considerable degree of recantation, Dahl (1985) and his colleague Lindblom (1977, 1983) place less emphasis on the theme of selective participation as the crucial factor limiting power and protecting pluralism. They stress instead the structural distinctiveness of business interests and the inherent political advantage derived therefrom.

Our data probably cannot illuminate the debate regarding the more abstract properties of business power in a capitalist order. They do show, however, that there is great variety in the forms of politically active business interests (as well as of labor, farmers, professional groups, and others) and that the variety of form is systematically related to the agendas and strategies of action. Trade associations and specialized producers are not simply smaller, narrower segments of a larger class or sector. They often have different goals and operate in different ways, not as anomalies or deviations from some class-defined normalcy but through rational strategy calculated to advance genuine interests.

The structures of conflict and cooperation are built from the particular configurations of interest organizations that participate in domain politics. Unless we know who the organizational players are, how they relate to one another, and what dynamics of organizational development and change are at work, we are unlikely to secure an adequate grasp of the policy process. American government texts should not talk in the present tense about "the farm bloc," the dominant role of the American Medical Association, or the unity of "business" interests long after events have rendered those propositions empirically invalid.

In the end, of course, we must be concerned not only with the structures of interest group relations but with their policy outcomes as well. What is the reflection in substantive decisions of the fragmented politics of agriculture or the bipolar conflicts over labor issues? Who wins and who loses? Does a "play it safe" trade association accomplish more of its objectives than a contentious citizens group? After analyzing the place in the national policy process of certain influential elites, we will return to questions such as these.

Chapter 10

Elite Networks in
National Policy Making

Because elites share an interest in the preservation of the system that made them elites (Carr 1951, 77; Field and Higley 1980, 5), they are thought likely to work together to produce a sufficient degree of integration of political demand to permit the polity to function. The integration may be achieved either by accommodating or by subjugating seriously disaffected groups. Not only will the social, economic, and political interests of elites tend to converge, but, in some views at least, elites will often be recruited from similar social backgrounds and will be likely to know one another (Baltzell 1958, 1964; Domhoff 1974, 1983). Through overlapping memberships in a variety of institutions, public and private, they will come into contact with other elites, and the contacts will promote a shared perspective on social events and provide a basis for compromise and accommodation. In the sympathetic pluralist view, therefore, elites serve to bring the divergent views of a multiplicity of social groups into greater harmony, furthering societal cohesion. In a more critical view, elites manage political conflict so as to preserve order and thus also preserve their own privileged positions.

In either view, elites occupy a position near the center of the political system. A depiction of the relationships among participants in a set of political issues might, then, show conflicting interest groups aligned in opposing ranks, with the elites between, varying in proximity to the respective sides but tending to bridge the gulf. The elites would be relatively tightly clustered, drawn close by their mutual involvement in mediation, bargaining, or conspiracy, have it as you will (see, for example, Useem 1984, 13–17, 192–196).

Some elites may well be more central than others, of course. Some are more intensely identified with their clients—or, in fact, *are* the clients (for example, the executive officers of trade associations). Others are more independent. These latter elites may possess special expertise or special access to government offices, either of which may permit them to be relatively autonomous from their client groups. (Indeed, distance from their clients may help them to maintain their special assets. Undivided loyalty to the client may be inconsistent with political allegiances or professional ideology.) In a graphic representation that includes both less autonomous and more autonomous political actors (perhaps the employees of trade associations, unions, or corporations versus the external lawyers and consultants retained by such organizations), we would expect to find the more autonomous actors nearer the center of the space. Thus, representatives who perform a mediative function would be located in a more central position in the system. Representatives found in oppositional alignments that are clearly associated with the interests of distinct groups, however, are more likely to be partisans than mediators, instructed delegates rather than free agents.

After analyzing networks of communication among national elites drawn from several sectors of American society, including business, news media, labor unions, and political leadership, Gwen Moore (1979, 689) suggested that the evidence "indicates that considerable integration exists among elites in all major sectors," and she termed this cohesive group of national elites the "central circle." She concluded:

> [T]he structure of the central circle—broad and inclusive, rather than narrow and exclusive—suggests that one of its main functions is the negotiation of conflict among major organized groups in American society. Crucial then are the ways in which the central circle directly and indirectly integrates leaders of a wide variety of institutions into a network capable of discussion and resolving issues of national concern. (690)

This chapter addresses much the same issues. We examine the acquaintance networks of a set of representatives who are especially prominent, referred to below as "the notables." This analysis considers the extent to which Washington policy elites function as a coherent community. The structure of relationships may reflect, in part, the degree to which the notables possess the freedom to plot their own courses of action and, thus, power that is independent of the resources of their clients. If any set of private Washington representatives is able to operate autonomously, it should be these especially prominent practitioners. Their expertise, contacts, experience, and general wisdom in the ways of Washington are resources that may constitute an independent base of power or influence. If their services are in demand by a wide variety of interest groups that seek to influence the decisions of the federal government, and the representatives can thus pick and choose their clients, they may refuse to advocate positions that would endanger their access to government officials in the future. They would, then, exercise a moderating influence on the policy demands of clients (Horsky 1952, 10). The client that takes an extreme or unreasonable position on an issue would be faced with the choice of modifying the position or looking elsewhere for representation—in the latter case, perhaps, losing some potential impact on public policy.

The Data

The set of notables consisted of a total of 72 private representatives, 18 from each of the four policy domains. Though many government officials no doubt hold positions of great importance in the networks, our objective here was to examine the roles of private agents in national policy making. Most of the notables had held federal jobs at one time or another during their careers, and the analyses make it possible to distinguish the network positions of those who had held high office. In a sense, then, we may assess the extent to which officials are able to take their influence with them when they leave office. The exclusion of current officials from the list of notables does, however, have significant implications for the nature of the networks, and those implications are discussed below.

The notables on the list were selected through extensive fieldwork. During the process of design of the survey, over the course of two years, the principal investigators conducted informal, open-ended interviews with more than a hundred government officials and Washington representatives of various types—lawyers, lobbyists, officers of trade associations, and so on. These discussions included questions about the most prominent or noteworthy representatives in the four policy areas. The names selected for the final list were among those mentioned most often.

An effort was made to include representatives working in a number of the different subfields within the four areas, some serving corporate clients, some serving labor unions, some from trade associations, and some from public interest organizations. We also sought to represent notables who deal primarily with Congress and those who focus more exclusively on the executive branch. The list includes several women, but no blacks or other minorities, a situation that we believe to be representative of the composition of the pool (see Figure 3.1). We wanted the list to include both lawyers and nonlawyers, but we did not have a clear view about the appropriate proportion of each because, in advance of doing the survey, we did not know how prevalent lawyers were among Washington representatives generally. As it turned out, 45 of the 72 notables included on the list were law school graduates, while only a third of the random sample of Washington representatives held law degrees (chapter 3). This over-representation of lawyers among the notables may suggest that representatives who are lawyers tend to attain greater prominence than those who are not. We have explored this possibility, however, and we find that the lawyer notables on our list were not, on the average, as widely known among the representatives as were the nonlawyer notables (Nelson and Heinz 1988). Thus, it is probable that in selecting among the candidates for inclusion on our list we selected some lawyers who are "less notable" than the nonlawyers.

We do not believe that the overrepresentation of lawyers is a significant threat to the validity of the findings. We make no claim that the Washington representatives included on our list are the *most* notable practitioners working in these four policy areas, however "notable" might be defined. There are surely other representatives working in these fields who have prominence, expertise, and access that is equal to or greater than that of some of the persons we included. Notability was not the only criterion used for selection. Thus, while our set of notables is not a random sample of a population of notables (assuming that one could define a true population of notables), the list does reflect the kinds of representatives who were mentioned as important actors by numerous informants. The appendix at the end of this chapter briefly identifies each of the persons on the final list. Readers who are familiar with Washington policy making may recognize many of the names and, we hope, acknowledge the appropriateness of their inclusion.

The respondents were presented with a list of the full set of 72 notables (including those from all four policy areas) and were asked two questions. First: "Would you please place a check in column A next to the names of people with whom you are personally acquainted?" Then: "Please place a check in column B by the names of

people you know well enough to be confident that they would take
the trouble to assist you briefly (and without a fee) if you requested."
Thus, we sought to measure two levels or degrees of acquaintance,
the first being a minimal level and the second calling for a somewhat
stronger connection. We analyzed the structure of acquaintance at
both levels of association. Smallest space solutions were computed
using both measures, and their similarity was then assessed by corre-
lating the interpoint distances in the two solutions. In the four policy
areas, these correlations range from .7 to .9. The principal difference
is that the stronger connection (the second question) produces somewhat clearer patterns, no doubt because the likelihood of chance
acquaintance is reduced.

The Notables' Networks of Acquaintance

Washington representatives actively engaged in work on federal policy concerning agriculture, energy, health, or labor issues are not
likely to be personally acquainted with many of the notables. At
the weaker level of acquaintance, the median number known by
respondents in our sample is 6. At the stronger level, the median is 3.
For both questions, the modal number of notables known is zero:
173, or 22% of the respondents were connected to none of the
notables at the stronger level of acquaintance; and 111, or 14% were
connected to none even at the minimal level. One representative
claimed to be acquainted with 39 of the notables at the minimal level,
but only 9 of the 776 representatives claimed to know more than 30,
and 80% of the representatives knew 13 or fewer. At the stronger
level of acquaintance, only 5 representatives claimed connections to
more than 20 notables, and 80% claimed eight or fewer. There are
no significant differences in these patterns among the four policy
domains. Thus, only a small percentage of the representatives indicated that they had close ties to any substantial segment of the notables.

It may be instructive to examine the characteristics of the representatives that are associated with the likelihood of knowing notables.
Table 10.1 indicates differences in the characteristics of representatives who are acquainted with more or fewer than the median number
of notables. Because younger representatives would have had less
time in which to establish a wide range of contacts, we might expect
older representatives to be more likely to know the notables. Some-

Table 10.1   Comparison of selected characteristics of representatives, by extent of acquaintance with notables

	Representatives knowing 2 or fewer notables	Representatives knowing 3 or more notables
Number of representatives	339	437
Mean age	48	49
Mean number of years of residence in D.C.**	8	14
Mean number of policy fields pursued**	3.6	5.4
% of subfields pursued*	49	58
% with 1982 income of $65,000[a] or more**	42	60
% who attended elite college	26	20
% with Northeast origins	34	35

Note: The number of notables known is divided at the median. Acquaintance is measured at the stronger level of connection.

a. $65,000 is the median income. The mean is $90,489.

* $p < .01$. ** $p < .001$.

what surprisingly, we do not find this to be the case. Representatives who have resided in Washington and environs for a longer period of time, however, are likely to know more notables. Members of one political party are not significantly more widely acquainted with notables, but there is no reason to expect such a difference since the notables are distributed between the parties in about the same proportions as are representatives in general. Not surprisingly, we find that representatives who pursue a narrow specialty are likely to know fewer notables than are representatives who cover a broader range of issues; and the familiar observation that elites are more than ordinarily likely to know other elites is supported by the relationship between representatives' incomes and the likelihood of knowing the notables. The median income of the random sample of representatives in 1982 was $65,000, but the median income of the notables was $137,500. Representatives who knew three or more notables had a mean income of $100,407, while those who knew fewer than three had a mean of $76,753 ($F = 16.2$; $p < .001$). The more economically successful representatives, then, are clearly more likely to know the notables—who are themselves big earners.

Although the representatives who know more notables appear to be an economic elite, they may not be especially elite in other respects. We find that Washington representatives who attended elite colleges and universities are less likely to know the notables than are other representatives (see Table 10.1; in an analysis of variance, $F = 4.38$, $p < .05$). This pattern is not explained by the notables' own places of schooling. A slightly larger percentage of them than of the representatives in the random sample attended such elite colleges or universities (25.4% versus 22.8%).

Nor does our data provide evidence that an "Eastern establishment" among Washington representatives enjoys special access to those in positions of prominence. Popular literature and political rhetoric include many references to the supposed influence—by definition, an unhealthy influence—that Easterners have on Washington decision making. But we find that representatives who resided in the Northeast during their high school years are not especially likely to be acquainted with notables. We have noted that representatives active in health and labor policy issues are more often recruited from the Northeast, while those active in agriculture and energy are drawn disproportionately from the South and West (see chapter 3). Analyses done separately in each of the four policy domains, however, disclose no significant differences between representatives from the Northeast and those from elsewhere in the level of acquaintance with notables. The only significant relationship between a regional origin and the number of notables known is that representatives who come from the West are somewhat less likely to know the notables (chi square = 8.18, significant at .004).

In sum, then, our analyses suggest that representatives who have connections to a greater number of notables tend to earn high incomes, but that they are not unusually likely to have been raised in the East and they are less likely than are other representatives to have attended an elite college or university. While we find some evidence for the existence of an economic elite among Washington representatives, therefore, these data do not provide support for the proposition that an inbred social or educational elite occupies a favored position. In a multivariate analysis evaluating the contributions of these variables to the explanation of the number of notables known by the representatives, we find that only income ($F = 23.9$, $p < .001$) and the scope of policy activities ($F = 59.6$, $p < .001$) have substantial effects.

Looking at these measures the other way around, we may gauge the prominence of individual notables by the extent of their acquaintance with the sample of representatives. Using the minimal level of connection, the median notables are known by 85 representatives. On the average, somewhat more than half of the representatives knowing each notable are active in the notable's own policy domain. If we measure acquaintance at the stronger level, the median notables are known by 52 representatives, and acquaintances within the notables' own domains again account for more than half. Five of the notables were selected by 100 or more of the representatives at the stronger level of acquaintance.

Table 10.2 is a list of the fifteen notables most widely known by the random sample of representatives. In spite of the overrepresentation of lawyers on the list of notables, only five of these fifteen are lawyers—Boggs, Bagge, Bayh, Post, and Rogers. Moreover, if we rank-order the notables from most to least widely known, there are twice as many lawyers in the bottom half of that list as there are in the top half. Nine of the ten least-chosen notables are lawyers. We have written at some length on the place of lawyers within the system of Washington representation (see chapters 3 and 4), and the data

Table 10.2 Notables most widely known by the sample of Washington representatives

	Number of acquaintances
1. Evelyn Dubrow	121
2. Robert Georgine	107
3. Thomas Boggs	105
4. Lane Kirkland	101
5. Carl Bagge	100
6. Charles DiBona	92
7. Birch Bayh	89
8. Arnold Mayer	85
9. Bertram Seidman	85
10. Carol Foreman	84
11. William Timmons	84
12. Frederick Webber	84
13. John Post	83
14. Ray Denison	81
15. Paul Rogers	77

Note: The numbers reported in this table are measured at the stronger level of acquaintance. The correlation between the order of the 72 notables ranked by the stronger measure and the order as ranked by the weaker level of connection is .94.

previously presented, taken together with the finding that notables who are lawyers are less likely to be known by the representatives, suggest that lawyers do not occupy an especially central place among Washington representatives.

Another striking feature of the list of notables in Table 10.2 is that six of them, including half of the top ten, are labor union officers—Dubrow, Georgine, Kirkland, Mayer, Seidman, and Denison. This is greatly out of proportion to the number of union officers on the list of notables. Of the original list of 72 notables, only 11 were employees of organized labor or outside counsel employed primarily by unions—and more than half of those 11 are found among the 15 most widely acquainted notables. Two of the others in the top ten, Bayh and Foreman, have very strong ties to the Democratic party and often represent consumers or public interest clients. Bayh is the former Democratic senator from Indiana, and among the clients of his law firm is the American Cancer Society. Foreman was the director of the Consumer Federation of America, was subsequently Assistant Secretary of Agriculture for consumer affairs in the Carter administration, and continues to represent consumer interests. The remaining 7 notables among the 15 most widely-known represent primarily corporations or trade associations composed of corporations. The best-known representative among that group, however, is Thomas Boggs, who also has very strong ties to the Democratic party. Overall, notables who are Democrats are not significantly more likely to be widely known than are those with other political affiliations, but notables with ties to organized labor or the Democratic party appear to do particularly well at the upper end of the acquaintance distribution.

After inspecting the frequency distribution of the notables on the two acquaintance measures, we decided to drop from the further analyses those who were only narrowly acquainted. In a sense, these persons were misspecified; they proved to be less notable than we had supposed. An additional reason for dropping these persons from the list is that we wanted to analyze the characteristics of the constituencies of the individual notables. Basing these analyses on a very small number of respondents would, of course, produce unreliable estimates. The criteria we adopted for including the notables in the analyses were a minimum of 20 acquaintances measured at the weaker level, and at least 12 at the stronger level. Of the 72 notables on the original list, 4 failed to meet one or both of these criteria. The analyses that follow, therefore, report findings on the remaining 68 notables.

Smallest Space Analyses of the Notables' Networks

To reveal the structure of the notables' networks of association with other Washington representatives, we again use smallest space analysis. The proximities of the notables in these analyses are based on the extent of overlap in their circles of acquaintance among the representatives, measured at the stronger level of acquaintance.[1] Notables who are known by many of the same representatives will be located close together, and notables who share few acquaintances will be far apart. Notables widely acquainted with varying constituencies will therefore be placed where the circles of acquaintance overlap, usually near the center of the space. A notable who is known by very few representatives will also be located near the center, however, if that notable is equally unknown to all of those surrounding him or her. This does not often happen because few people (especially notables) are equally isolated from everyone. Notables who are known only by a narrower subset that is highly homogeneous in key social characteristics will tend to be set apart, and thus will usually be located near the periphery of the space. If many representatives know notables A, B, and C and many also know X, Y, and Z, but there is no overlap between the two groups—that is, none of the people who know A, B, or C also know X, Y, or Z—then notables A, B, and C will tend to be grouped close together, as will X, Y, and Z, but the two groups will be widely separated. Thus, social groupings that are mutually antagonistic or repellent will tend to be located on opposite sides of the space.[2]

The points in Figure 10.1 are arranged on the first two dimensions of a three-dimensional smallest space solution.[3] The solution represents the structure of the acquaintances of all 68 notables in all four policy domains. The three-dimensional solution has stress of .20, which is minimally acceptable ($R^2 = 70.9$). Though not a very good fit, the solution can certainly be interpreted in ways that appear quite persuasive, as we shall see below. The third dimension is shown in this figure by arrows placed in parentheses next to the names of notables who are located markedly in one direction or the other on

Figure 10.1 Patterns of acquaintance of the sample of representatives with 68 notables (three-dimensional smallest space solution; relative position on third dimension indicated by arrows in parentheses)

that dimension. Notables who have no arrow are located near the middle of the third dimension.

The solution is essentially a spherical structure with a hollow center. Though some of the notables occupy more central positions, none of them appears to be primarily a broker, located in the core, approximately equidistant from all of the intense partisans and playing a role as mediator or peacemaker. There may be some message carriers in the center of the system of Washington representation, but those persons were probably not likely to be included on our list of notables. Those who are more central in the space tend to be generalists who are highly visible in Washington, like Clark Clifford, Charls Walker, Thomas Boggs, and Paul Rogers. Notables who are leaders of particular constituencies are located near the centers of those constituencies rather than near the center of the space, no matter how prominent they may be—for example, Lane Kirkland in the lower left quadrant of the space.

The principal factor organizing the networks of association of these notable Washington representatives appears to be the specialization of their work, which might be interpreted either as specialization in an area of substantive expertise or as specialization in a particular type of client. Each of the notables was selected in one of the four policy domains (on the original list, 18 each from agriculture, energy, health, and labor). Figure 10.2 presents the same smallest space solution as that in Figure 10.1, that is, the same configuration of points, but here the points are labeled with a letter indicating the policy domain in which the notable was selected—A for agriculture, E for energy, and so on. As is apparent from the figure, the four quadrants of the space tend to represent the four policy domains. Thus, the networks of acquaintance of these notables are clearly structured by the issues they work on or the clients they represent.[4] Those two variables are, of course, closely intertwined. Is it possible to distinguish their effects?

In some cases, it may be. To illustrate the structure of the relationships, let us look again at Figure 10.1, focusing on the notables selected from the labor policy domain. We can see that the notables

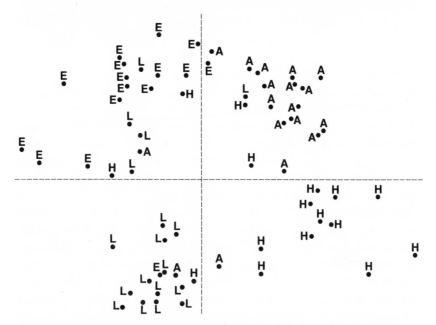

Figure 10.2 Policy domain affiliations of the 68 notables, as located on the first two dimensions

who represent labor unions are rather clearly separated from those who represent management. All of the union officers are at the bottom left of the figure—Georgine, Dubrow, Mayer, Denison, Jarvis, Kirkland, Warden, Bredhoff, Connerton, Gold, and Seidman—with Kirkland near the center of that group. Most of the management representatives are also located on the left side of the space, but higher on the vertical dimension, and all but one of them are far below the plane on the third dimension. (Note that, because of the third dimension, White, Nash, and Pantos, who represent management, are located farther from the union officers than appears to be the case in Figure 10.1.) Tysse, Hale, and Post, who represented the U.S. Chamber of Commerce, the National Association of Manufacturers, and the Business Roundtable, respectively, are not located in the labor quadrant of the space, but are found in the area populated by representatives engaged in energy issues. This is understandable because most of the energy representatives work for corporations or trade associations composed of corporations. Thus, this is an example of the influence of client type on the structure of relationships. The remaining labor notable, Fields, is found in the agriculture quadrant, which is similarly appropriate since Fields was employed by the American Farm Bureau Federation, specializing in immigration and farm labor issues. In the case of Fields as well, then, the client affiliation prevails.

The labor quadrant includes one notable from each of the other three domains. Mayer, from agriculture, was the vice-president and director of governmental affairs of the United Food and Commercial Workers (a merger of the meatcutters' and the retail clerks' unions). He worked on consumer protection and nutrition issues. Flug, from energy, is a Harvard Law School graduate who was a legislative assistant to Senator Edward Kennedy, then served as chief counsel of a Senate subcommittee and was special counsel to the Kennedy for President committee. His principal involvement in the energy domain was as a lawyer for claimants in oil overcharge refund matters, which placed him in opposition to the major oil companies. Bayh, the former senator from Indiana, is a lawyer who was in private practice with the Washington office of an Indianapolis firm. He devoted much of his time to biomedical research policy, but he also dealt with a broader range of concerns. Thus, of the three notables from other domains who are found in the midst of the labor union officers, Mayer is himself a labor union officer and Flug and Bayh have both been deeply involved in Democratic party politics and liberal causes, which would tend to align them with the representatives of unions. These examples suggest the importance of political ideology in structuring the networks of at least some Washington representatives.

The analyses that follow are performed within each of the four policy domains, considered separately, thus permitting us to evaluate the effects of client affiliations, political ideology, and other variables in a context where all of the representatives are working on similar issues. In these analyses we may examine the structure of relationships absent the overwhelming effect of substantive specialization that we observe in Figures 10.1 and 10.2. Our hypothesis is that the notables' attachments to particular clients or groups of clients are the principal determinant of the structure of these networks of acquaintance, and that economic ideology and political party affiliation are strongly associated with the differences among types of clients. We use quantitative measures of economic liberalism, partisanship, and income in analyzing the networks, but we have not attempted to quantify the client-type variable. Because the conflicts or affinities among the client organizations are based on interests that are specific to the content of particular issues, no set of categories of client organizations arrayed along a single dimension can hope to capture the complexity of the connections and antagonisms among the groups. To interpret the positions of the notables in these networks of acquaintance, therefore, we will identify the client organizations that employ the notables and observe whether particular interest groups are associated with segments of the networks in ways that might be explained by affinity or opposition among the groups (Stinchcombe 1989).

The Agriculture Domain

Figures 10.3 through 10.6 all display a two-dimensional smallest space solution representing the networks of acquaintance of the notables among representatives who are active on agriculture policy issues (stress = .16, R^2 = 84.7). Because the analysis does not consider their connections with other representatives who are not involved in agriculture policy, notables who have broader-ranging concerns may be less centrally located in the space.

The notables who represent the interests of agricultural producers—farmers and ranchers—are mostly found on the left side of the space. These include, among others, Healy, of the National Milk

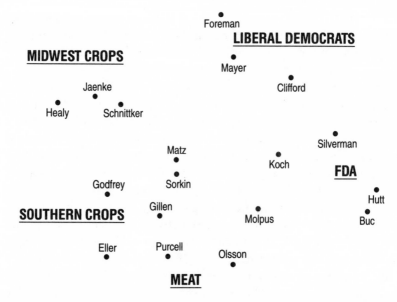

Figure 10.3 Patterns of acquaintance in the agriculture domain (two-dimensional smallest space solution based on representatives' connections to notables)

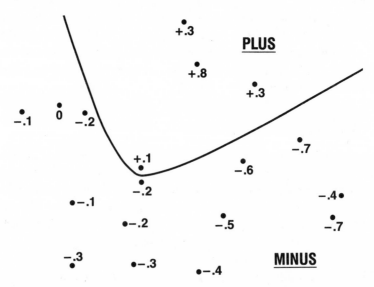

Figure 10.4 Economic liberalism scores of notables' acquaintances in the agriculture domain; differences from mean of 2.9

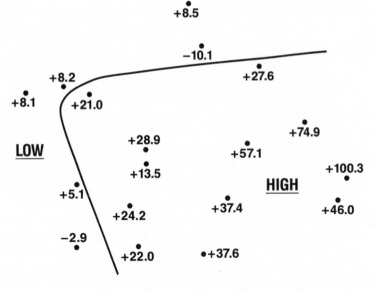

Figure 10.5 Income of notables' acquaintances in the agriculture domain, 1982 (in thousands); differences from mean of 86.9

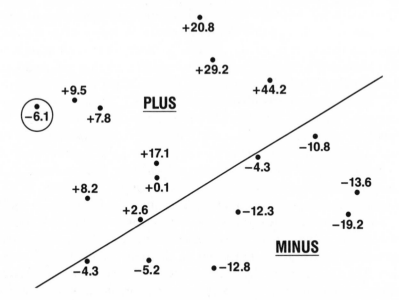

Figure 10.6 Percentage of Democrats among notables' acquaintances in the agriculture domain; differences from percentage among all agriculture representatives (total = 35.8%)

Producers Federation; Eller, of the National Cattlemen's Association; and Godfrey, a private consultant who represents sugar interests. To the right are the notables who represent consumers, processors, and distributors of agricultural commodities. These include Foreman, who was formerly the director of the Consumer Federation of America; Koch, of the Grocery Manufacturers of America; Molpus, of the American Meat Institute (representing meatpackers); Mayer, of the meatcutters' union; and Clifford, whose law firm represents General Foods, the Australian Meat and Livestock Corporation, Warner-Lambert, and Parke, Davis. Clifford, Foreman, and Mayer are all involved, to one degree or another, in liberal politics, and this appears to have an important impact on their circles of acquaintance. The three form a distinct group at the top of the space. Another distinct grouping is found at the far right of the space—Silverman, Hutt, and Buc had all served as counsel to the Food and Drug Administration, and all of them continued to work on food safety and food labeling issues as lawyers in private practice.

The conventional wisdom is that the members of a permanent Washington establishment seek to maintain contact with both allies and adversaries (see Goulden 1972; Green 1975; H. Smith 1988). Their work requires that they closely monitor developments in government and politics and that they be aware of the positions that are taken on the issues of the day by a wide variety of interest groups. It may therefore be in their mutual interest to exchange information. Because these Washington insiders intend to spend their careers there, they would seem to have good reason to preserve cooperative relationships and make as few enemies as possible. Thus, they might be expected to de-emphasize partisanship and political ideology, to be sophisticated (or perhaps cynical) about politics, not doctrinaire, and to present themselves as experts or professionals. Their contacts and communication would therefore cross partisan lines rather freely, whatever their own political affiliations and origins. Is this wrong?

To examine the role of ideology in the creation and channeling of Washington notables' networks of acquaintance, we superimposed an economic liberalism dimension on the same smallest space solution. The data used are the mean scores of the acquaintances of each of the notables on a series of economic ideology items (see chapter 6 for an explanation of the economic liberalism scale). The means are: agriculture, 2.9; energy, 2.7; health, 3.2; and labor, 3.5. There is, thus, considerable variation among the domains in economic ideology. In

Figure 10.4, the number next to each point is the difference between the overall mean score of all representatives active on agriculture issues, including those who did not know any notables, and the mean score of the agriculture representatives who reported that they knew that particular notable. Plus scores indicate that the economic values of the persons who knew the notable were, on the average, more liberal; minus scores indicate the opposite.

The most conservative scores are located on the lower right of the space, among the FDA group and those closest to them. The three notables in the FDA group are all lawyers, as noted above, and the value positions of their acquaintances probably reflect client interests. The most liberal scores, not surprisingly, are found at the top, among the three notables engaged in liberal politics. The only other notable on the plus side of the line, Matz, represents the American School Food Service Association and is concerned with nutrition issues.

Figure 10.5 presents an analysis that uses the same technique to consider the representatives' individual incomes. The labels on the points in Figure 10.5 show the extent to which the mean 1982 income of the representatives who know each notable differs from the mean of all representatives active on agriculture policy, which was $86,900. For example, the representatives who know Hutt have a mean 1982 income that is $100,300 above the overall mean—that is, the mean for Hutt's acquaintances is $187,200. Note that the acquaintances of all but two of the notables have average incomes that are above the overall mean. This finding no doubt reflects the prominence of this group of notables. That is, people who know these notables are themselves likely to be financially successful. Because only two points have negative scores, we have divided the space somewhat arbitrarily into areas of high and low incomes. The highest incomes are found where the economic liberalism scores are the most conservative, among the acquaintances of the FDA group and the notables closest to them. The lowest incomes are found among the acquaintances of the notables at the top and the left margin of the space. These are the notables who represent union labor, consumers, and producers' groups (as opposed to processors and distributors).

The last of these analyses, Figure 10.6, shows the extent to which the acquaintances of the notables differ from the overall level of affiliation with the Democratic party. There is, again, considerable variation among the domains on this variable. The percentages of the representatives in each who are Democrats are: agriculture, 35.8%;

energy, 28.8%; health, 48.5%; labor, 51.3%. That is, for example, although 35.8% of all representatives in the random sample who are active on agriculture policy are Democrats, 56.6% of Foreman's acquaintances in the agriculture domain are Democrats. The area of the space that has an above-average representation of Democrats can be divided by a straight line from the area where they are underrepresented—with only one exception, Healy, the head of the National Milk Producers (circled in the figure). The percentage of Democrats is highest, as expected, among the acquaintances of Foreman, Mayer, and Clifford. It is lowest, again as expected, among the FDA group and two of the notables located close to them.

The structure of these networks within the agriculture domain is, then, very orderly. Ideological differences, which are related to differences in clientele, appear to play an important part. As might be expected, the ideological differences are also clearly related to income and party politics. These variables mutually reinforce the patterns of selective association that we observe among Washington representatives.

The Energy Domain

Figure 10.7 presents the first two dimensions of a three-dimensional smallest space solution for the patterns of acquaintance with notables in the energy domain (stress = .11, R^2 = 88.8). As before, the third dimension of the solution is represented by arrows placed next to the points that have extreme scores on that dimension. Like the analysis of the agriculture domain, the solution uses only the acquaintances reported by representatives active in this policy area. The analysis includes one notable who was originally selected for the labor domain—Post, then the executive director of the Business Roundtable. Post is included here as well as in the labor domain analyses because he was active on both labor and energy policy issues.

The structure of the networks in the energy domain appears to be organized primarily by energy source, with a secondary distinction between the producers and the distributors of oil and gas. The whole left side of the space is populated by notables who are concerned with oil and gas policy issues, but those at the lower left are distinguishable from those at the upper left. (Oil and gas go together because gas production is often a by-product of oil exploration and drilling, and the two fuels are sometimes produced in the same fields by the same

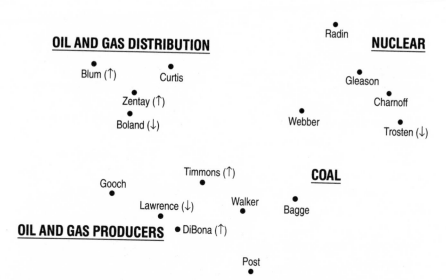

Figure 10.7   Patterns of acquaintance in the energy domain (three-dimensional smallest space solution based on representatives' connections to notables)

companies.) At the lower left, we find Gooch, a partner in a Houston-based law firm that represents Pennzoil, among other clients; Lawrence, the president of the American Gas Association; DiBona, the president of the American Petroleum Institute (API); and Timmons, a private consultant who represents API and Standard Oil of Indiana. Thus, all of these notables represent oil and gas producers. At the upper left, Blum, Curtis, Zentay, and Boland are all lawyers in private firms who represent clients engaged in the distribution and marketing of oil and gas. Flug, at the top of the space, is removed from the others. As noted above, he represents claimants in oil overcharge refund matters and is an associate of Senator Edward Kennedy. Note that Flug is on the opposite side of the space from Post, of the Business Roundtable.

At the upper right, we find Radin, the executive director of the American Public Power Association, which represents government-owned generating and distribution facilities. Flug is, thus, approximately equidistant from the oil distribution notables, to whom he is

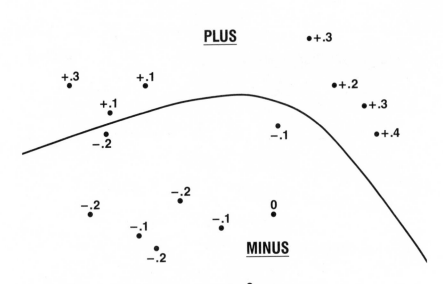

Figure 10.8 Economic liberalism scores of notables' acquaintances in the energy domain; differences from mean of 2.7

apparently drawn by his work on oil matters, and Radin, with whom he may have a political affinity. Farther down on the right, we come to Gleason, of the American Nuclear Energy Council; and Charnoff, a private lawyer who specializes in nuclear energy issues and who was formerly on the staff of the Atomic Energy Commission. Still farther down, we come to Trosten, a private lawyer who represents both nuclear and coal interests. Just to the left of these is Webber, of the Edison Electric Institute. Farther down again, we see Bagge, the president of the National Coal Association. Thus, Webber, who represents electricity generating and distribution companies, is approximately equidistant from the representatives of nuclear and coal interests. This seems appropriate, since electric companies use both nuclear and coal generating plants. Finally, Walker, a private consultant whose principal expertise is in tax and monetary policy and who formerly held the top staff position at the American Bankers' Association, is located at the lower middle of the space, near the center of the notables who represent the interests of the largest corporations.

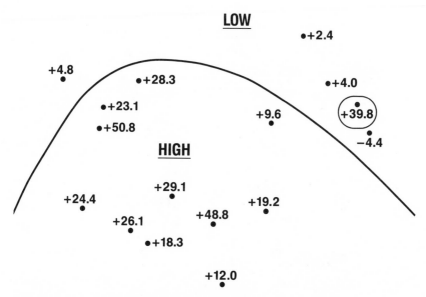

Figure 10.9 Income of notables' acquaintances in the energy domain, 1982 (in thousands); differences from mean of 104.6

Figure 10.8 shows the extent to which the economic liberalism scores of the notables' acquaintances diverge from the mean for the energy domain. Note that the scores here are, on average, the most conservative of the four domains. The most extreme economic liberalism score in the energy domain—the acquaintances of Flug, at +.8—would be only an average score in the labor domain. The overall pattern in Figure 10.8 is quite clear, and there are no exceptions. The notables who represent the largest private business enterprises have the most conservative average scores. It is interesting to note that the three notables who deal primarily with nuclear energy policy—Gleason, Charnoff, and Trosten—are all on the plus, or liberal, side of the line, perhaps because of the role of government in nuclear power.

Figure 10.9 shows the differences in mean 1982 income for the acquaintances of each of the notables. As in Figure 10.5, we have divided the space into relatively higher and lower income areas, but the acquaintances of almost all of the notables have average incomes

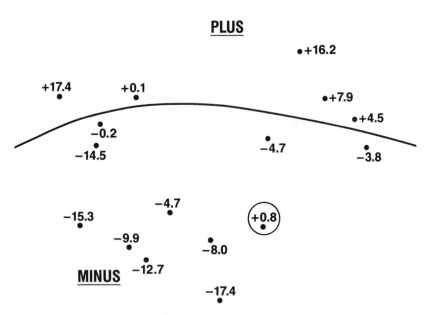

Figure 10.10 Percentage of Democrats among notables' acquaintances in the energy domain; differences from percentage among all energy representatives (total = 28.8%)

that are above the mean for the energy domain as a whole. There is an obvious correlation between economic liberalism and income level: all five of the points that have lower average incomes are on the liberal side of the line in economic ideology. But one of the points in the lower income area of Figure 10.9, Charnoff, does not fit. Charnoff's acquaintances have an average income that is considerably above the norm (+39.8), though they scored on the liberal side in economic values. Two other points that had relatively liberal scores (though not markedly so) also had high average incomes—Curtis and Zentay. What do these three notables have in common? All are lawyers in private practice with major Washington law firms. Perhaps because there are both Republican and Democratic officeholders to whom such firms need to have access, the firms include at least some lawyers who embrace liberal economic values. For the most part, however, high incomes among the constituencies of the energy notables are associated with conservative economic values—and, as we shall see, with political party preference.

Figure 10.10 presents the extent to which the notables' acquaintances differ from the overall level of affiliation with the Democratic party. The same general division between the top and the bottom of the space that we saw in the economic liberalism and income distributions also prevails in the percentage of Democrats among the notables' acquaintances. Only one point is out of place, which is circled: Bagge, of the National Coal Association, has a slightly higher percentage of Democrats among his acquaintances even though he is located well on the minus side of the line. Flug's acquaintances, once again, have the most divergent score (63.6% of his acquaintances are Democrats); Post's score, directly across the space from Flug, is the most extreme in the opposite direction (only 11.4% Democrats).

Thus, as before, we see that economic and partisan differences appear to organize the structure of these networks in highly interpretable ways. Contrary to assertions that we heard time and again during our fieldwork in Washington, ideology and political party loyalties do appear to have an important impact on the networks of Washington representatives. The representatives' patterns of contact with notables suggest that they are not one community but several, separated by the interests and partisan allegiances of their clients. The persons with whom representatives talk are, presumably, the ones with whom they exchange information and the ones they might persuade or be persuaded by. These linkages—shaped and channeled by economic ideology and partisan politics—determine the flow of information about policy options and strategies and, perhaps, the flow of influence.

The Health Domain

Figure 10.11 presents a three-dimensional smallest space solution for the networks of acquaintance in the health policy domain (stress = .14, $R^2 = 83.2$). The data are somewhat more difficult to fit in the health policy area than in the other domains, but a satisfactory solution is achieved in three dimensions. As before, the third dimension is represented by arrows. At the upper left of the space, we find notables who represent physicians and hospitals, including Donelan of the American Medical Association, Epstein of the American Hospital Association, and Bromberg of the Federation of American Hospitals. Jenckes, who is located just above them, represents the Health Insurance Association of America and is primarily concerned with the regulation of payment plans. She formerly represented Blue Cross/

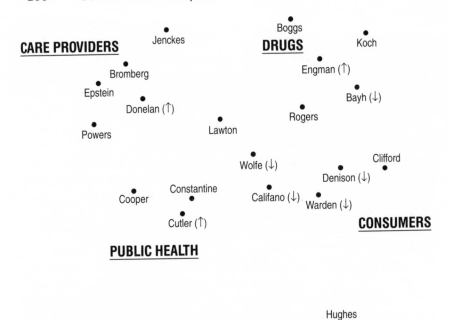

Figure 10.11 Patterns of acquaintance in the health domain (three-dimensional smallest space solution based on representatives' connections to notables)

Blue Shield. On the lower left of the space, we see Cooper of the Association of American Medical Colleges; Cutler of the American Psychiatric Association; Constantine, a consultant representing the American Nurses Association; and Califano, a lawyer who represents the National Association of Public Hospitals. The affinity among these notables may be that public financing is especially crucial to their clients and that they are all concerned with public health issues. Wolfe, who is just above Califano, is an advocate for consumer protection or patients' interests in health care regulation and is also very much involved with public health issues. Wolfe and Califano are located near Denison and Warden, both of whom are labor union officers. Denison is the Director of Legislation for the AFL-CIO and Warden holds the same position at the United Auto Workers. We selected them as notables in the labor domain but found that both were also active on health policy, especially on health insurance and benefit issues and public health matters. The proximity of Califano, Wolfe, and Clifford to these labor union notables suggests the salience

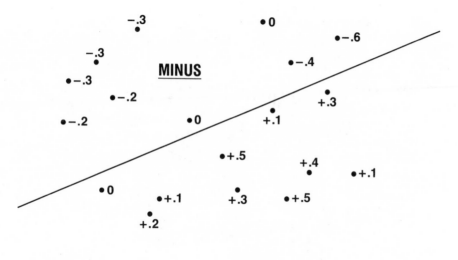

Figure 10.12 Economic liberalism scores of notables' acquaintances in the health domain; differences from mean of 3.2

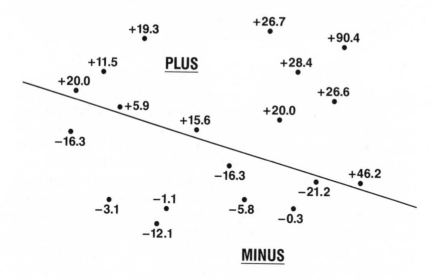

Figure 10.13 Income of notables' acquaintances in the health domain, 1982 (in thousands); differences from mean of 87.8

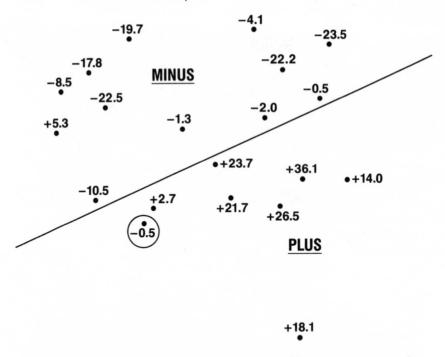

Figure 10.14   Percentage of Democrats among notables' acquaintances in the health domain; differences from percentage among all health representatives (total = 48.5%)

of the liberal policy agenda in organizing this region of the space. (See Figure 10.12.) Also in this consumer interests region, though much closer to the lower margin of the space, is Hughes, a representative of the American Association of Retired Persons. He is primarily concerned with health care payment and insurance plans.

At the upper right of Figure 10.11 we find Boggs, who represents the Retail Druggists Association and the National Association of Chain Drug Stores (as well as the American Hospital Association); Engman, the president of the Pharmaceutical Manufacturers Association; and Koch, the president of the Grocery Manufacturers of America. Koch was selected as a notable in the agriculture policy domain, but he is much involved in food and drug regulation, including labeling, packaging, and safety issues. Bayh is also found in this region of the figure. Note, however, that Bayh is located substantially lower on the third dimension, as are Wolfe, Califano, Denison, and Warden. All five of those points are in close proximity on the third dimension of the space, and Bayh's Democratic party and liberal affiliations are probably the source of the acquaintances that draw him into this group. Lawton, who is closer to the middle of the space, is a lawyer who represents a variety of health care clients—thus, his central location.

Figure 10.12 confirms the salience of economic ideology to the organization of these networks. The acquaintances of Hughes, Wolfe, Warden, and Denison have the most liberal values, and Califano and Bayh come next. At the other end of the spectrum, the most conservative scores are found among acquaintances of the representatives of pharmaceutical and grocery manufacturers. The next most conservative scores are those of acquaintances of the representatives of health insurers and hospital associations. We should remind ourselves, however, that even these scores are liberal compared with those in the energy policy domain.

Figure 10.13 shows that the income differences among the acquaintances of these notables also display a division between the top and the bottom of the space, though the slant of the dividing line is in the opposite direction. The principal difference is that the acquaintances of Bayh, Rogers, and Clifford are on the liberal side of the line in economic ideology but have incomes that are substantially above average. These three notables are all Democrats, all formerly held high office in the federal government, and all were prominent lawyers in private practice at the time of our survey. If there is a liberal establishment, the three should be members in good standing; the characteristics of their circles of acquaintance seem to be consistent with that status. Note that in the health domain, unlike the agriculture and energy domains, the average incomes of the acquaintances of several of the notables are substantially below the norm. This is so in spite of the fact that the overall average is substantially higher among the energy representatives than it is here. This difference may reflect the greater involvement of representatives of minority group and nonprofit associations in health issues than in energy issues.

Figure 10.14, which shows differences from the overall percentage of Democrats, is obviously highly congruent with the distribution of scores on the economic liberalism scale. The only difference between the two is that the line dividing the plus and minus areas is slightly higher in the space in Figure 10.12, so that Bayh and Rogers are on the liberal side of the line. In Figure 10.14, the acquaintances of Bayh and Cutler differ from the overall percentage of Democrats by only a trivial amount, and several of the other points also have percentages that are close to the norm—Constantine, Lawton, Rogers, and Boggs, especially. All of these are located close to the dividing line, except Boggs. Boggs's position in the space thus appears to be determined by his corporate clientele rather than by his ties to the Democratic party (including family ties).

Thus, ideological differences and political party affiliation, both of which generally correspond to the nature of the clients represented by the notables, are reflected in the structure of these networks of acquaintance within the health domain, as they were in the agriculture and energy policy areas. But these effects are even more apparent in the labor domain.

The Labor Domain

The story of the labor domain is a short one. All of the union representatives are on one side, all of the management representatives are on the other, and there is a gulf between them. A one-dimensional smallest space solution would, in fact, fit the data quite satisfactorily. For the two-dimensional solution presented in Figure 10.15, stress = .08, R^2 = 98.2. The fit is nearly that good in one dimension, but the two-dimensional solution is easier to see because many points are piled

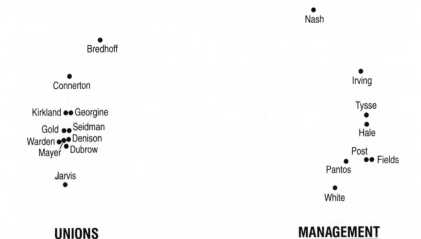

Figure 10.15 Patterns of acquaintance in the labor domain (two-dimensional smallest space solution based on representatives' connections to notables)

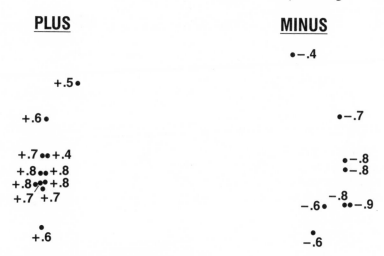

Figure 10.16 Economic liberalism scores of notables' acquaintances in the labor domain; differences from mean of 3.5

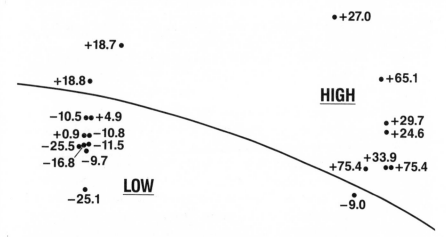

Figure 10.17 Income of notables' acquaintances in the labor domain, 1982 (in thousands); differences from mean of 84.0

on top of each other in a one-dimensional representation. Thus, in interpreting the figure, we should not give much importance to the vertical dimension of the space.

The organization of the three diagnostic variables is not subtle here. The economic liberalism score (Figure 10.16) and the percentage of Democrats (Figure 10.18) correspond exactly to the division between

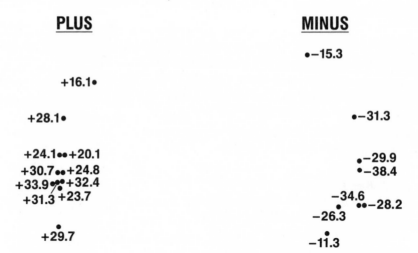

PLUS   **MINUS**

•−15.3

+16.1•

+28.1•   •−31.3

+24.1••+20.1   •−29.9
+30.7••+24.8   •−38.4
+33.9•••+32.4
+31.3 +23.7   −34.6
                                            •   ••−28.2
                                            −26.3
+29.7
•   −11.3
                                            •

Figure 10.18   Percentage of Democrats among notables' acquaintances in the
labor domain; differences from percentage among all labor representatives
(total = 51.3%)

the labor and management sides of the space. Only the income distribution (Figure 10.17) needs any explication.

In Figure 10.17, we see that the acquaintances of all but one of the
management notables have incomes that are substantially above the
norm for the field. The exception is White, who is vice-president
of the American Retail Federation. His trade association represents
smaller businesses, for the most part, and this may bring him into
contact with representatives who are less highly compensated than is
typical on the management side of the space. On the union side, two
notables have acquaintances with substantially higher incomes—
Bredhoff and Connerton. Among the union notables, they are the
only lawyers in private practice. Both are leading partners in Washington law firms specializing in labor law; their law practice probably
brings them into contact with highly compensated representatives,
including other lawyers.

The external lawyers serving the labor and management sides are
closely aligned with their respective client groups, however, rather
than found between them. The three external lawyers on the management side, Nash, Irving, and Pantos, are closer to Post of the Business
Roundtable, Tysse of the Chamber of Commerce, and Hale of the
National Association of Manufacturers, than they are to Connerton
and Bredhoff, who in turn, are closer to the union officers. It was not

inevitable that we would find this to be the case. If the external lawyers were go-betweens, serving to enhance cohesion by promoting bargains and compromise, we might have seen the principals of labor and management lined up in opposing ranks, but with their lawyers occupying a more intermediate position. The union lawyers would tend toward the union side, of course, and the management lawyers would be located nearer their management clients, but both sets of lawyers would be found between the client groups. That is not what we observed.

In fact, although the patterns in the other three policy domains are more complex and diffuse than is the case in labor, in none of the four areas do external lawyers or prominent politicians appear to function as intermediaries. Rather, they are closely aligned with particular client groups. The health policy domain is the least clearly segmented, but we nonetheless see in Figure 10.11 that such "super-lawyers" as Clifford, Califano, Bayh, and Boggs are embedded in particular regions of the space. They are *not* located in the center.

Though the labor policy domain is the clearest example of an oppositional structure, the principles that organize the networks of association are the same as those observed in the other three domains. The most difficult problem of interpretation is to unravel the effects of client type, economic ideology, and political affiliation. Those three variables are, as one can see in our smallest space analyses, thoroughly entangled. For our present purposes, however, we need not sort them out. The important lesson is that Washington representatives do not constitute one community in which the players keep in close touch with adversaries as well as allies. Rather, the adversarial lines are sharply drawn.

Connections among the Notables

If we look at the connections among the notables themselves rather than at the relationships among them as determined by their constituencies, would we then find a structure that has a central core? That is, are there some notables who have a greater breadth of connections among the other notables, and who thus appear to be in a position to act as mediators or deal-makers? Or is it possible that virtually all of the notables active within a particular policy domain might be in regular contact with each other, so that the notables would in effect constitute a core, regardless of where their constituencies might be located? This latter possibility, especially, would seem to be plausible, perhaps even likely. After all, the notables active on a particular range of issues are highly visible practitioners of essentially the same art, working on much the same subject matter, within a limited range of government institutions. It would be remarkable if they did *not* bump into each other in the hallways, hearing rooms, and cocktail-party fund-raisers.

To address these issues, we have done smallest space analyses of the notables' reports of their association with other notables active in their domains.[5] As before, the connections are measured at the stronger of two levels of acquaintance. In the solutions presented in Figures 10.19 to 10.22, the points are not labeled with the names of individual notables. Because these analyses are based upon information gathered in interviews with the notables themselves—rather than, as above, on reports by a random sample of representatives—it would in some cases be possible to draw a strong inference from the figures that a particular notable reported a connection with another specific notable. In order to safeguard confidentiality, therefore, we have omitted the notables' names.

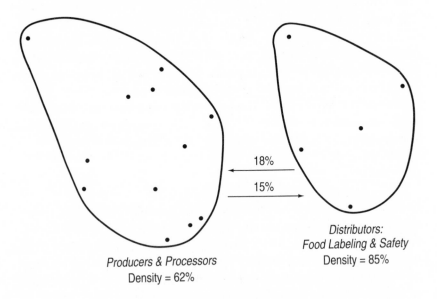

18%

15%

Producers & Processors
Density = 62%

Distributors:
Food Labeling & Safety
Density = 85%

Overall Density = 43%

Figure 10.19 Connections among the notables in the agriculture domain (two-dimensional smallest space solution; stress = .09, R^2 = .96)

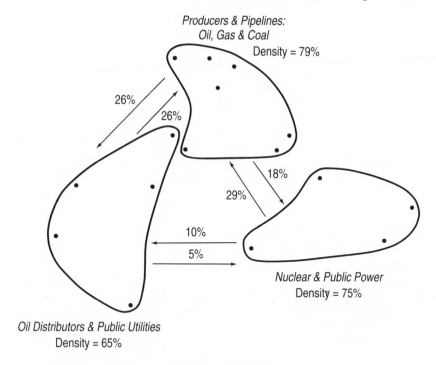

Producers & Pipelines:
Oil, Gas & Coal
Density = 79%

26%

26%

18%

29%

10%

5%

Nuclear & Public Power
Density = 75%

Oil Distributors & Public Utilities
Density = 65%

Overall Density = 37%

Figure 10.20 Connections among the notables in the energy domain (two-dimensional smallest space solution; stress = .09, R^2 = .96)

In addition to the smallest space analyses, we have computed block models of the relationships among the notables (see White, Boorman, and Breiger 1976; Boorman and White 1976). The objective is to reduce the complexity of the network to a set of interpretable relationships between groups. The blocks are indicated on the figures by irregular curves that enclose the points within each block, and we have labeled the blocks to indicate the predominant character of the interest groups represented by the notables located within them. The figures also indicate the density of connections among the notables overall (that is, the percentage of all possible connections), the density of connections within each block, and the density across blocks (the percentage of cross-block ties). The last of these may differ depending upon the direction in which the ties are measured (that is, whether going from block A to block B or from B to A), since the notables' choices of each other are not always reciprocated. For example, in the labor domain (Figure 10.22) the management notables are

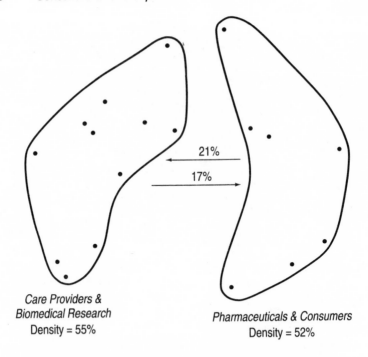

Care Providers &
Biomedical Research
Density = 55%

Pharmaceuticals & Consumers
Density = 52%

Overall Density = 39%

Figure 10.21 Connections among the notables in the health domain (two-dimensional smallest space solution; stress = .12, R^2 = .93)

somewhat more likely to report connections to the union notables than are the union notables to report association with management notables. We have therefore computed these ties viewed from both directions, and we note both in the figures.

The two most important findings in these analyses are:

1. The density of contact among the notables is far less than total—in all four domains, the notables have connections to fewer than half of the other notables, on the average.
2. The density of connections within each of the blocks is quite high (usually in excess of 60%), but there are relatively few ties across the blocks (usually less than 20% density).

Thus, even among the notables, the networks of relationships are divided. Most notables have instrumental connections to other notables who represent interests similar to their own, but they lack such

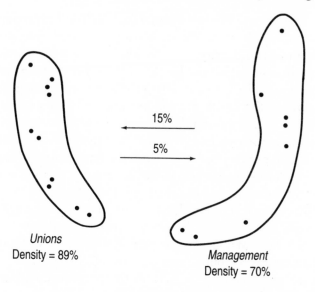

Overall Density = 44%

Figure 10.22 Connections among the notables in the labor domain (two-dimensional smallest space solution; stress = .10, R^2 = .96)

connections to notables representing contrary interest groups. No notable is connected to all of the other notables in his or her domain. The most connected notable, who was located in the agriculture domain, reported ties to 77% of the notables in that domain. In the other domains, the most connected individuals had ties to only 56% of the notables in the energy domain, 61% in health, and 67% in labor.

In three of the four domains, the notables can be divided into two blocks; in the fourth domain, energy, there are three blocks. The divisions among the blocks appear to reflect the broadest sorts of differences among the active interests, such as differences between producers of commodities and the distributors of those commodities, or differences between labor and management. In the labor domain, the division between the union block and the management block is clear and without exception. The number of cross-block ties in that domain is also quite low, especially from the vantage point of the union notables. The few ties that exist between the two blocks in the labor domain are mostly between outside counsel for the respective sides (see Nelson and Heinz 1988, 291–293). The health domain is somewhat more diffuse or less clearly differentiated than the other three domains. The density of ties within the two health blocks is lower than that in any of the blocks in the other domains, and the number of cross-block ties is relatively great, suggesting that the divisions within the health domain are not well defined. The other places where we find substantial percentages of cross-block ties are in the energy domain—between oil distribution interests and notables representing oil producers, and between the latter notables and those representing nuclear and public power interests (probably because of the substitutability of various fuels in the generation of electric power). By contrast, the low level of ties between the nuclear and public power block and the notables representing privately owned utilities and oil distribution companies suggests the antagonism between advocates for public and private enterprise.

There are substantial differences in the partisan composition of several of these blocks. In the agriculture domain, for example, three-quarters of the notables in the producers and processors block are Democrats, while only one of the five notables in the distributors block is a Democrat. In energy, the percentage of Democrats in the oil producers and pipelines block is substantially lower (14%) than in the other two blocks (60% and 50%). In health, there are fewer Democrats in the care providers and biomedical research block (36%) than among the notables representing pharmaceutical companies and consumer groups (71%). And in labor, as might be expected, there is a far higher percentage of Democrats among the union notables (78%) than among management (13%). Though the number of notables in each block is small, the differences in both the agriculture and the labor domains are statistically significant.

These analyses of the connections among the notables reinforce the conclusion that the four policy domains lack core actors. The overall rate of connection seems surprisingly low, given the notables' common concern with a range of issues that have at least a broad similarity. We should recall, however, that the question used as the measure of connection asked the respondent to indicate the individuals that "you know well enough to be confident that they would take the trouble to assist you briefly (and without a fee) if you requested." Since the question uses assistance as the criterion for the presence or absence of a tie, this may bias our data against finding that adversaries are in contact with one another.

But perhaps we should not begin by assuming the existence of adversarial divisions among Washington elites. C. Wright Mills, as noted in chapter 1, asserted that men "from the great law factories and investment firms . . . are almost professional go-betweens of economic, political and military affairs . . . By the nature of their work, they transcend the narrower milieu of any one industry, and accordingly are in a position to speak and act for the corporate world or at least sizable sectors of it" (1956, 289). Now if Mills were right, we ought to find some of our notables functioning as go-betweens or brokers. Thus, we need to pose the question in a form that will permit us to determine the extent to which the elites divide along adversarial lines versus the extent to which they (or some of them) serve as mediators or "transcend" one industry and speak for all (or most) of the "corporate world."

Since information is a principal medium of exchange in Washington, our question about the potential for assistance by other Washington representatives might be interpreted as asking whether the respondent could contact the target person and get an informative answer to a factual inquiry. A typical case might be something like this: Respondent represents the Amalgamated Avocado Producers. His clients are opposed to proposed labeling regulations dealing with vegetable fats. He therefore calls his opposite number at the Cottonseed Oil Processors Association and asks whether this matter is going to be an important priority for them—that is, whether they are going to expend substantial resources on it. He wants to know this, of course, in order to assess his chances for success. Now, he might ask this question of the Cottonseed Association regardless of whether he thought that their position on the matter was likely to be the same as his own. It might be mutually beneficial to share this sort of information even if the two groups were on opposite sides. But, as it turns out, adversaries appear to be in contact relatively seldom.

Notables, or for that matter other Washington representatives, could play three rather different roles, any of which might bring them into contact with opposing parties: information-gatherers; advocates; and mediators or deal-makers. Information-gatherers would find it useful to maintain the widest possible range of contacts, as the example given above suggests; advocates might sometimes need to meet with their opponents in order to try to negotiate settlements; and mediators must presumably be in touch with all (or most) of the contending parties, or at least with the advocates for those parties. The contact patterns of the advocates should be readily distinguishable from those of the mediators and information-gatherers, however. Though some of the advocates may be in touch with some of their adversaries from time to time, advocates would probably have far closer and more regular contact with their allies (see chapter 9). The contacts of the mediators and information-gatherers should be more evenly spread across adversarial lines. Thus, in our smallest space analyses of the notables' networks, if some of the notables were performing the advocate role and others were functioning as mediators, we should find the advocates aligned with their varying constituencies, while the mediators should be found in a more central position.

How, then, do these three roles relate to the formulation of the question that we used to measure the connections—whether the person would assist without a fee. For the information-gatherers, the question seems appropriate. Persons playing that role have good reason to cultivate disparate contacts, and they regularly call upon their acquaintances for assistance of this sort. Mediators are also in close contact with a range of parties, and they may call upon those parties for assistance when necessary. Note that the question did not ask respondents to identify people from whom they had actually requested assistance in the past, but only those from whom they would be in a position to request assistance if they needed to do so. The question should therefore uncover the strong connections of the mediators reasonably well, if there were mediators to be found. Of the three roles, therefore, it is only the advocates who might be likely to think of assistance in adversarial terms. If the advocates are averse to cultivating contacts with their adversaries or seeking information from them, our measure should disclose that. But that is a salient fact about the organization of their work, and it is indeed what we set out to discover.

By these measures, then, the notables appear to function as advocates rather than as mediators, deal-makers, or information-gatherers. We find close affinity among notables who share economic or political interests and a common partisan identification, but we do not see evidence that there are networks of multiple ties that bridge these interest boundaries.

Hollow Cores

Figure 10.1, the analysis that includes all four domains, displays a roughly spherical structure with a hollow core, but the empty center of that figure may be a consequence of the substantive specialization of the representatives. That is, if notables are not equally likely to know representatives who are active in each of the four policy areas, they will not be located in the center of the space. If such heavy hitters as Clifford, Boggs, Timmons, and Walker were true generalists, however, they would be likely to be located near the middle.[6] Even though our list of notables includes Washington representatives of great prominence, accomplishment, and reputed influence, we find no identifiable set of core actors. This suggests that autonomous brokers who have the capacity to bridge the four policy areas either do not exist or we were not able to find them.

The analyses of the individual policy domains, however, provide less ambiguous tests of the proposition that these policy-making structures lack core actors. Because the health domain is the most diffuse, the conclusion is less clear in that policy area, but even in health none of the notables is located at the center of the space with the exception of Lawton (see Figure 10.11). Each of the analyses displays a substantial gap or open area near the middle of the structure. In the labor domain, of course, the structure is not circular. Rather, the hollow center is more like a gulf between the two opposing camps. But in all of the domains we find little evidence to suggest that a powerful role is played by intermediaries—by more or less autonomous actors who are able to use their personal influence to promote compromise or impose settlements. Our set of notables, selected to represent the most prominent and influential of Washington representatives, does not appear to include persons who often play such roles. This suggests that the intermediaries, if they exist, function more as messengers than as deal-makers.

The overall characterization of the notables that emerges, then, is that they exercise influence as organizational advocates and mobilizers rather than as mediators whose contacts and connections facilitate the resolution of issues. Communication among influentials takes place mostly with the elites of adjacent, politically compatible interest groups. They deal with their allies, not their adversaries.

If these powerful elites are not engaged in mediating disputes and do not serve to bring the conflicting interest groups together, how is that essential function accomplished? We are not among those who would argue that the American political system has ceased to function. The communication necessary to produce political decisions does take place, but it takes place among the principals of the organizations and among agents who are closely associated with the organizations. If the network structure is a rough sphere, then communication occurs on the surface of the sphere among parties that are in relatively close proximity to one another, rather than through the center. Thus, the cohesion that makes the system function is produced incrementally, step by step around the sphere.

This suggests that the policy-making structure is held together not by the magnetism of a dense core but by surface tension, like a soap bubble. If this analogy implies instability, that is probably appropriate. Social networks of this kind are more fragile than are highly integrated structures (Blau and Scott 1962, 126–127, 198–199). The overall policy-making system has not burst, but on particular issues, from time to time, some ruptures occur. The system apparently has regenerative capacity, however. When a breakup takes place, new alliances may subsequently be formed and, thus, new bubbles created.

We return, therefore, to the question posed above: If the authority of elites does not provide a significant moderating influence on the demands of interest groups, how does the polity overcome the divisive effects of economic specialization? A possible answer is that government officials act as the mediators who bind the system together. Our data do not permit us to address this directly since government officials were not included on the list of notables, but we think it is plausible that officials would sometimes be found at the core of policy networks. The "issue networks" discussed by Hugh Heclo (1978) include government officials as key participants, and officials made up more than half of the "central circle" found in Moore's (1979) study of national policy elites, referred to above.

There are at least four different roles that a government official might play in policy decisions: (1) a mediator among the interest groups; (2) a partisan or advocate for particular interests, closely aligned with one side of the issue; (3) a competitor for the spoils, or a self-interested party, sometimes representing interests of the state, itself, or of segments of the state (Tullock 1965); or (4) an arbiter who listens to argument and chooses among the interest groups' positions, or a ministerial authority who simply implements the interest group bargain (Latham 1952, 390; Landes and Posner 1975, 894). The first and last of these roles would be likely to place the official near the center of the decision-making networks, but the other two would not. All government officials do not play all of these roles, but all of the roles are played by some officials some of the time.

We might speculate that there are certain issue areas in which officials would be likely to play central roles, either as mediators or as arbiters, and other fields in which they would be more likely to act as aligned partisans or competitors. The areas of national domestic policy chosen for this study, for example, are all primarily areas of private enterprise where numerous, well-funded interest groups are active. Criminal justice policy, by contrast, is almost a government monopoly, with relatively little involvement by private interest groups, apart perhaps from the ACLU (Heinz, Gettleman, and Seeskin 1969). It may be, therefore, that government officials are more likely to be found at the center of policy making in criminal law or in other fields that are primarily areas of government activity rather than of private enterprise. The centrality of government may also vary by historical period, as well as by issue area. According to Moe's (1987) history of the National Labor Relations Board, for example, there was a long tradition of bipartisan cooperation in the selection of NLRB members, which usually placed the agency at the center of labor policy, until the Reagan administration began to make more ideological appointments.

We should point out that most of the notables on our list had previously held government office, some of them quite recently. Those who served at the highest levels of government—such as Clark Clifford, Joseph Califano, Charls Walker, Paul Rogers, and Lewis Engman—seem to be nearer to the center of the space (Figure 10.1) than are those of equal prominence, such as Lane Kirkland, who did not hold office. But the principal finding remains that none of these notables in federal agriculture, energy, health, and labor policy, regardless of prior government service, is found in the middle of these policy networks. If these private elites do not serve as mediators, and government officials do not play that role on all issues, at all times, then how is the requisite consensus built?

Another possible answer is that the divisive tendencies of narrow interests are not overcome—the interest groups fight it out, and the strong win. Decisions would then be arrived at through sheer power, unmoderated by "other-regarding" evaluations of the public weal. There are several different conceptions of this interest group–dominated polity. Theodore Lowi (1967, 1969) has labeled one version "interest group liberalism," where diverse groups focus on relatively narrow slices of the policy pie and neither the interest groups nor public officials take a more encompassing view of the "public interest." A slightly different version of the same dynamic is said to occur in Congress when broadly applicable norms govern the allocation of constituency-specific benefits, such as post-offices, or river and harbor improvements (Ferejohn 1974; Arnold 1979). The choices of who will get what are then governed not by efficiency criteria or the power of committee chairs, but by the decision rule that every district should receive a share. Obviously, such benefits must be divisible and sufficiently abundant to go around. When these conditions obtain, political conflict is minimized and mutual accommodation may be accomplished without explicit mediation.

But many policies cannot be expressed in terms that permit such friendly disaggregation and broad distribution. There is often not enough to go around. Partisan hostilities intrude. If the policy options are characterized by zero-sum conflicts, with winners and losers clearly identified, then group battles group. Resolution of issues in this manner will, of course, produce greater bitterness and, perhaps, instability than will a system that places greater emphasis on the achievement of consensus or "well-integrated" decisions. Is there greater bitterness in American politics now than at some earlier time? Is the structure of the Washington policy-making elites that we have observed typical only of this post-Watergate era? Would it have looked different in the time of Dean Acheson and John McCloy (Steinfels 1971; Brinkley 1983)? Perhaps, but we are not sure that "Tommy the Cork" Corcoran, Thomas Austern, and Abe Fortas would have been found to be any less partisan than the present incumbents (Goulden 1972; Irons 1982).

In the final chapter of *Private Power and American Democracy,* Grant McConnell (1966, 339) observed:

> The first conclusion that emerges . . . is that a substantial part of the government in the United States has come under the influence and control of narrowly based and largely autonomous elites. The elites do not act cohesively with each other on many issues. They do not "rule" in the sense of commanding the entire nation. Quite the contrary, they tend to pursue a policy of noninvolvement in the large issues of statesmanship, save where such issues touch their own particular concerns.

Our findings support the thesis that American political elites have only relatively narrow constituencies and do not act cohesively, but we do not find that they are "autonomous." Rather, the elites' networks appear to be based in their client organizations or in constellations of such organizations (Coleman 1973; Laumann and Knoke 1987). Some of the notables gained their prominence through positions of leadership in trade associations or other private organizations, while others had formerly held high federal office. Even these latter notables, however, were found to be clearly aligned with particular client groups.

The dominance of the organizational base may explain why the American polity enjoys relative stability in spite of the lack of unity or cohesion among elites. That is, the elites are constrained by their organizational bases. Unless the nature of a representative's organizational base is altered—which may occur through technological or social change—the representative's positions on issues and consequent patterns of alliance and opposition will shift only within narrow limits. Thus, such cohesion and peace as we manage to achieve may be the product of organizational authority, not of personal influence (Salisbury 1984).

Why?

In their classic *Formal Organizations: A Comparative Approach*, Blau and Scott (1962) reviewed several experiments that had manipulated the communication networks in small groups (citing Bavelas 1950; Leavitt 1951; and Guetzkow and Simon 1955). Some of the groups used centralized "wheel" or "X" structures of communication in which one person could communicate with all group members but the other members could communicate only with the central person. Other groups used decentralized "circle" or "O" communication structures in which every person communicated with two neighbors. Blau and Scott's review concluded that, in solving coordination problems, "the performance of wheel groups has been consistently found to be superior to that of circle groups" and that this was the case because "the wheel imposes . . . hierarchical organization on a group, since the person in the central position naturally assumes the dominant role of coordinator" (126).

The analyses that we have presented suggest that the structure of communication among elites in most of these national policy domains resembles a circle with an empty center (or a sphere with a hollow core) rather than the wheel structure with a hub and spokes. It is easy to understand why a wheel would be a more efficient communication structure than a circle. The obvious question, therefore, is *why?* Why do we observe a network structure that is more like a circle or a hollow sphere than like a wheel or a sphere with a dense core?

There are two parts to this question: Why is it circular? And why are there no central mediators? A plausible and perhaps sufficient reason for the circular form is that the structures need to be continuous so that no significant players will find themselves at the end of a chain of groups. If the structure were not continuous, some groups would be located at a dead end. To the extent that the structure is stable, an end group would be dependent upon its adjacent neighbors; it would be able to communicate with other participants in the system only through a single intermediary or set of intermediaries. To avoid this dependency, the group would have an incentive to form additional connections—to create neighbors in another direction, thereby completing the circle or tending toward the creation of a continuous structure. Thus, the general imperative to avoid isolation or dependency tends to lead to circular or spherical structures.

The explanation for the lack of central mediators may be more complex. Let us start with the proposition that uncertainty about who will win and who will lose, and how much, is a functional element in democratic politics. If there were certainty, the parties that consistently lose would have a strong incentive to violate the rules of the game, to threaten drastic action in order to bring about a change in the rules, or to exit from the game if the situation permits (that is, to withdraw from this arena and seek to have the issues resolved by other means or in another forum). Now, as Blau and Scott observed, "the central position naturally assumes the dominant role." That is, the occupants of the core, or inner circle, hold a highly advantaged position. If other participants are dependent upon them for efficient communication, or if the core actors can form a winning coalition by choosing to side with one alliance or another, these core actors will be disproportionately powerful. In effect, they will always be winners. Surely the other participants would prefer to occupy that position themselves. Thus, there will be a strong tendency to push actors out of the core, or not allow them to occupy such a position for very long, so as to avoid dependency. Democratic political structures will therefore tend to have a preference for the circle rather than the wheel configuration because the hub position is too empowering.

An alternative line of argument leads to the same result. Representatives, including notables, are all people who are for hire. That does not mean, of course, that they are all available to work for just anyone (typically, in fact, they have strong ideological allegiances), but there is a market for their services. They have not taken vows of impartiality or of poverty. If certain representatives were, then, observed to be in the central position consistently—that is, if they were regularly able to use their positions as mediators to create a winning coalition or to control communication with decision makers—their services would be greatly in demand. Indeed, it seems likely that the market would bid up the price of their services until they were converted from mediators into advocates. That is, they would be hired by one side or the other. The result is that they would be moved out of the center, becoming aligned with one of the antagonists. Thus, the position in the core would not be a stable equilibrium.[7]

The experiments on small groups, referred to above, provide supporting evidence. In some variations of the experiments, the subjects were permitted to organize themselves for more efficient communication. The finding was that few of the circle groups adopted a hierarchical form of organization (Shaw 1954; Guetzkow and Simon 1955; Guetzkow and Dill 1957). The apparent reason for this is that the participants in the decentralized, circle networks were more satisfied with the process of communication and decision than were the participants in hierarchical groups. This has been confirmed by direct measures of the degree of their satisfaction (Leavitt 1951; Shaw 1954; Shaw 1981). Thus, networks that are circular in form may not be likely to evolve naturally into centralized wheel structures because the participants will not voluntarily yield their autonomy or cede their control over the process of communication.

On the other hand, a considerable amount of testimony about European democratic politics asserts that decision making there is, or at least was, quite clearly organized around established inner circles, or cores, of elites (Schmitter and Lehmbruch 1979; Lehmbruch and Schmitter 1982; Lehmbruch 1984; Western 1991; but see also Knoke and Pappi 1991). But important differences between the political contexts in Europe and the United States may affect the manner and extent of coalition formation. In comparing this country to other Western democracies, W. D. Burnham (1974) has observed that the "vast size" of the United States "is a major determinant of one of its most important political characteristics, that of coalitional heterogeneity" (653). The degree of the cultural, racial, and ethnic diversity of the United States and the variety of its economic base distinguishes its politics from that of European countries. But a functionalist argument would suggest that greater heterogeneity or complexity of interest groups would tend to make the mediators' contribution to efficient communication more important or useful, while broader aggregation of the interest groups would diminish the communication problem and thus make the mediators less necessary. Insofar as our data address this issue, we find no evidence that differences in the breadth of the interest aggregations alter the likelihood of finding a hub-like pattern. Where the aggregations are broadest in our sampling—on labor versus management issues—we find a bipolar oppositional structure without notable mediators. We should note, again, that it is entirely possible that communication links may be provided by message carriers who are not themselves reputed to be persons of substantial influence and who would not therefore have been nominated for our list of notables. But the inclusiveness of the interest groupings, from the evidence available in our study, does not appear to enhance the probability that influentials will occupy a central, mediational position.

Perhaps a more telling difference between the European and American political systems is that the United States is a relatively "weak state" (Skowronek 1982). That is, the government apparatus is less powerful in the United States and is thus less able to modify the groups' perceptions of self-interest. Note that we are not arguing that European governments function as neutral mediators. Rather, we believe that they act as major players in political struggles. But the power of the European governments may be sufficient to alter the calculations of advantage of the business and labor interest aggregations, so that they perceive mutual benefit in a settlement of the policy issues. The result of this sort of "corporatism" would, of course, be a more centralized decision-making structure with a relatively dense network of influentials in the core.

In sum, our findings concerning the acquaintance networks of elites active in four broad areas of domestic policy in the American national government suggest that the structure of these networks resembles a sphere with a hollow core. Interest groups are connected to others with similar interests, but not to their adversaries. Communication with opposing groups, if it exists, takes place only through a chain of other groups. We do not find a central core or inner circle of elites, capable of mediating among opponents.

APPENDIX: Notables' Positions, 1983–84

CARL E. BAGGE. President, National Coal Association.

BIRCH E. BAYH, JR. Lawyer: clients include American Cancer Society.

JACK A. BLUM. Lawyer: represents Independent Gasoline Marketers Council.

THOMAS HALE BOGGS, JR. Lawyer: clients include National Association of Chain Drug Stores, Retail Druggists Association, and American Hospital Association.

CHRISTOPHER T. BOLAND. Lawyer: clients include Texas Gas Transmission Corporation.

ELLIOT BREDHOFF. Lawyer: general counsel to the industrial union department of AFL-CIO; special counsel to United Steelworkers.

MICHAEL D. BROMBERG. Executive Director, Federation of American Hospitals.

NANCY L. BUC. Lawyer: clients include National Retail Merchants Association.

JOSEPH A. CALIFANO, JR. Lawyer: clients include National Association for Home Care.

GERALD CHARNOFF. Lawyer: clients include Duquesne Light, Indiana and Michigan Electric, Northern States Power, and Union Electric.

CLARK M. CLIFFORD. Lawyer: clients include Australian Meat and Livestock Corporation, General Foods, McNeil Pharmaceuticals, Phillips Petroleum, IBM, and the Government of Mexico.

ROBERT J. CONNERTON. Lawyer: general counsel to the Laborers International Union, AFL-CIO.

JAY CONSTANTINE. Consultant: represents American Nurses Association.

JOHN A. D. COOPER. President, Association of American Medical Colleges.

CHARLES B. CURTIS. Lawyer: clients include General Public Utilities Corporation.

JAY B. CUTLER. Director of Government Relations and Special Counsel, American Psychiatric Association.

RAY DENISON. Director of Legislative Department, AFL-CIO.

CHARLES J. DIBONA. President, American Petroleum Institute.

PAUL R. M. DONELAN. Director of Federal Affairs, American Medical Association.

EVELYN DUBROW. Vice-President and Legislative Director, International Ladies Garment Workers Union.

J. BURTON ELLER, JR. Vice-President for governmental affairs, National Cattlemen's Association.

LEWIS A. ENGMAN. President, Pharmaceutical Manufacturers Association.

RICHARD L. EPSTEIN. Senior Vice-President and General Counsel, American Hospital Association.

C. H. (CHUCK) FIELDS. Assistant Director for National Affairs, American Farm Bureau Federation.

JAMES F. FLUG. Lawyer: specializes in oil overcharge refund matters.

CAROL TUCKER FOREMAN. President of consulting firm: specializes in food safety and welfare issues.

ROBERT A. GEORGINE. President, Building and Construction Trades department of AFL-CIO.

NEAL P. GILLEN. General Counsel, American Cotton Shippers' Association.

GEORGE L. GLEASON. Executive Vice-President and General Counsel, American Nuclear Energy Council.

HORACE D. GODFREY. President of consulting firm: represents Florida Sugar Cane League and Rio Grande Valley Sugar Cane Growers Cooperative.

LAURENCE GOLD. Special Counsel to the AFL-CIO.

GORDON R. GOOCH. Lawyer: represents Pennzoil and Houston Lighting and Power.

RANDOLPH M. HALE. Vice President, National Association of Manufacturers.

PATRICK B. HEALY. Chief executive officer, National Milk Producers' Federation.

PETER W. HUGHES. Legislative counsel, National Retired Teachers Association and American Association of Retired Persons.

PETER BARTON HUTT. Lawyer: clients include Grocery Manufacturers of America and Hershey Foods.

JOHN S. IRVING, JR. Lawyer: represents management in labor-management relations issues.

EDWIN A. JAENKE. President of consulting firm: represents California and Hawaii Sugar, Farmland Industries, and Land O'Lakes.

JOHN T. JARVIS. National legislative representative, United Mine Workers.

LINDA JENCKES. Vice President for Federal Affairs, Health Insurance Association of America.

LANE KIRKLAND. President, AFL-CIO.

GEORGE W. KOCH. President, Grocery Manufacturers of America.

GEORGE H. (BUD) LAWRENCE. President, American Gas Association.

STEPHAN E. LAWTON. Lawyer: represents Infectious Disease Society of America, Genentech, and National Association for Biomedical Research.

MARSHALL L. MATZ. Lawyer: represents American School Food Service Association and Affiliated Food Processors.

ARNOLD MAYER. Vice-President and Director of Governmental Affairs, United Food and Commercial Workers International Union.

C. MANLY MOLPUS. President, American Meat Institute.

PETER G. NASH. Lawyer: represents Minnesota Mining and Manufacturing.

PHILIP C. OLSSON. Lawyer: clients include National Turkey Federation.

GEORGE J. PANTOS. Lawyer: represents ERISA Industry Committee (pensions).

JOHN POST. Executive Director, Business Roundtable (to 1983).

GALEN D. POWERS. Lawyer: represents hospitals and health care financing clients.

GRAHAM B. PURCELL, JR. Lawyer: clients include Nabisco Brands, American Rice, Pesticide Producers Association, Planters Manufacturing Division of Standard Brands, Iowa Beef Processors.

ALEX RADIN. Executive Director, American Public Power Association.

PAUL G. ROGERS. Lawyer: clients include Merck and Company.

JOHN SCHNITTKER. President of consulting firm: clients include Heinold Commodities.

BERTRAM SEIDMAN. Director, AFL-CIO's Department of Occupational Safety, Health and Social Security.

RICHARD S. SILVERMAN. Lawyer: clients include National Association of Convenience Stores and American Frozen Food Institute.

MARTIN SORKIN. Consultant to agribusiness: clients include Archer Daniels Midland and Amway.

WILLIAM E. TIMMONS. Chairman of consulting firm: clients include American Petroleum Institute, State of Alaska, Standard Oil (Indiana), H. J. Heinz Co., and G. D. Searle and Company.

LEONARD M. TROSTEN. Lawyer: clients include Exxon Nuclear, Electric Utility Companies' Nuclear Transportation Group, and Public Service Company of Indiana.

G. JOHN TYSSE. Director of Labor Law Department, U.S. Chamber of Commerce.

CHARLS E. WALKER. President of consulting firm: clients include AT&T, Bechtel Power Corp., Bethlehem Steel, General Electric, Union Carbide, and W. R. Grace and Company.

RICHARD D. WARDEN. Legislative Director, United Auto Workers.

FREDERICK L. WEBBER. Executive Vice President, Edison Electric Institute.

DONALD F. WHITE. Vice President, American Retail Federation.

SIDNEY M. WOLFE. Director, Health Research Group.

JOHN H. ZENTAY. Lawyer: clients include Northeast Petroleum Industries, True Oil Purchasing, and Western Crude Oil.

Chapter 11

Participation and
Success in Policy Decisions

Washington representatives may influence policy merely by monitoring government activity and then alerting their clients to potential threats or opportunities, or they may take a more direct role in attempting to persuade government officials. Some representatives are active on a relatively broad range of issues; others are content to occupy narrowly circumscribed policy niches (Browne 1990). And some specialize in particular strategies or techniques, such as policy-oriented litigation or public relations campaigns designed to mobilize opinion, while others pursue a considerable range of techniques in their efforts to shape government policy.

Are some of these representatives notably more successful than others in influencing policy outcomes? If so, is success achieved by a narrow concentration of resources, or are the successful players likely to pursue a broader range of interests? The breadth of the interest portfolio might, of course, be a function of the extent of the resources available to the organization, and greater resources probably facilitate success, other things being equal. But breadth of activity might also be a function of the extent and nature of the ideological motivation of the interest group. That is, a group such as Public Citizen may address a broader set of issues than does General Motors, even though Public Citizen possesses fewer resources. Rather than pursue a broad ideological agenda, General Motors might restrict its activity to matters that particularly affect its business interests.

To assess the activity of Washington representatives on specific issues, we selected a set of twenty policy events in each of the four domains. All of these events occurred during the period 1977–1982, the latter years of the Carter administration and the first years of the Reagan administration. In each case, we identified a particular action taken during the course of consideration of the issue: for example, in December 1982 the Secretary of Agriculture proposed the payment-in-kind (PIK) program of subsidies for farmers. (See the appendix at the end of this chapter.)

Respondents were given the lists of events in their respective domains and were then asked a series of questions. First, they were asked to indicate their level of professional interest in each event—great, moderate, some, or none. Then, for the five events in which they had expressed the greatest interest, they were asked: (1) whether the controversy surrounding the event involved little conflict, some conflict, considerable conflict, or intense conflict among opposing parties; (2) whether the actions that they took regarding the event included contacting congressional representatives or staff, contacting executive branch or independent agency officials, helping to mobilize public opinion, working with representatives of other organizations, or helping to conduct litigation; (3) whether their client or organization favored the proposal, opposed it, was ambivalent (or favored parts of it but opposed other parts), or took no position; (4) whether their interest in the matter concerned the central policy issue itself, or only more peripheral or technical subissues; and (5) given their client's or organization's objectives on this issue, whether they would say that it achieved all of its objectives, most, about half, few, or none.

The Structure of the Activity

We did not find that identifiable groups or clusters of issues were associated with distinct strategies or profiles of political activity. Rather, the analyses suggest that the character of the politics of the issues is determined simply by their size or inclusiveness. That is, the issues differ according to how encompassing they are. On the biggest issues, the conflict is great, the number of participants is high, and the representatives pursue a multiplicity of strategies or tactical options—contacting government officials, contacting the representatives of other organizations, and seeking to mobilize public opinion. All of the issues we included, however, were relatively major ones. They were all among the small percentage of policy proposals that managed to receive serious consideration on the public agenda (Kingdon 1984; Polsby 1984). All of them had been given considerable attention by the *Congressional Quarterly* or other journals that cover national policy making, which is how they came to our notice. In this respect, therefore, our sample of issues is relatively homogeneous. If we had used a set of issues that was more representative of the full range of major and minor, successful and unsuccessful issues, presumably we would have observed even greater salience of this size effect.

Thus, the principal finding in these analyses is that the issues tend to separate into two groups—one with relatively high values on all of the variables, and the other with low values on all of them, though there are some issues that lie between these extremes.

The identity of the interest groups that become active, however, is largely determined by the content of the issues. Distinct subject matter activates distinct "issue publics" (Laumann and Knoke 1987). In broadest outline, this can be seen by examining the extent to which various kinds of organizations express interest in the four policy domains. Recall that the respondents were asked to indicate their level of interest in each of the issues in their domains. If we compute the mean interest score for the representatives employed by each type of organization, the patterns in the several domains are clear and not surprising. Trade associations, including the farmers' organizations, have the highest levels of interest in agriculture issues; in the energy policy domain, businesses express the greatest interest; professional associations and nonprofit organizations, such as public hospitals, are the categories that have the highest interest in health issues; and unions and consulting firms express the highest interest levels in the labor domain. Respondents who are employed by law firms have relatively low levels of interest in all four policy domains. Analyses that divide the issue events into smaller substantive categories disclose similar patterns.

Multiple regression models of the interest levels of the individual representatives confirm that these organization-type categories have significant effects even when other variables are taken into account. In addition, however, some of the other variables are also important predictors of interest levels. Models were computed for each of the four domains, separately, on the twenty events specific to each domain, and then on the entire sample of representatives and the entire set of events across the four domains. The dependent variable was the mean interest level of the individual representatives. Mean interest level, of course, depends both upon the number of events in which the representative is interested and the extent of his or her interest in those events. The fourteen variables used in the analyses were:

The respondent has been engaged in political fund-raising during the past two years

The respondent distributes PAC money

The respondent has a law degree

Percent of respondent's work time devoted to the particular domain (that is, specialization)

Number of professionals employed in the respondent's organization (a measure of organizational resources)

Number of years of respondent's government experience

The square of years of government experience (to measure curvilinear effects)

Number of respondent's acquaintances among the notables

Percent of events in which respondent pursued a strategy of congressional contact

Percent of events in which respondent pursued a strategy of contact with executive agencies

Organization type

Economic liberalism

Democrat

Republican

Rather than present all five full models, with all the variables in each, we will merely summarize the principal findings.

The amount of variance explained by the models (R^2) ranges from 24% to 27% in the agriculture, health, and labor domains, but reaches only 16% in the energy domain and in the overall (four-domain) model. As one would expect, the respondent's employment by a union is a significant predictor of interest level in the labor domain, as is employment by a professional association in the health domain and employment by a business organization in the energy domain. In the overall model, only employment by a professional association is associated with a higher interest level. None of the organizational categories has a significant effect in the agriculture domain.

Other variables that make significant contributions to the models are:

Number of notables known (in agriculture and in the overall model)

Law degree (*negative,* both in agriculture and in the overall model)

Pursuit of contact with executive agencies (in health and in the overall model)

Domain specialization (in agriculture and, more marginally, in the overall model)

Organizational resources (makes a marginal contribution only, and only in the overall model)

Political fund-raising, a role in distributing PAC funds, government experience, economic ideology, and political party identification all make no significant contribution to any of the models.

Thus, the overall picture that emerges is that the interest measures identify the more central players in the field—those who are connected to the notables active on such issues, those who specialize in the field, and, to a lesser extent, those who work for organizations that have substantial resources to expend on pursuing a broader range of issues or on pursuing them in greater depth. The analyses also confirm that lawyers are less central to these policy-making processes. This supports our earlier observation (chapter 4) that lawyers usually become involved only episodically or only when more technical matters are at issue. We should emphasize, however, that these variables, taken together, explain only a quarter or less of the variance in the mean interest levels. Thus, there is a substantial amount of individual variation that is not captured in these analyses.

We have also done smallest space analyses of the relationships among the issues in each domain based on the extent to which the same representatives express either high or low interest in the issues. That is, issue events are proximate in these analyses to the extent that they share a constituency that has interest in them. We find that there are some clearly identifiable groupings in all four of the domains (see Figures 11.1–11.4).

In the agriculture domain (Figure 11.1), environmental and conservation issues are located at the left of the figure—the Water Reclamation Act; the use of overgrazed federal land; the reauthorization of the Federal Insecticide, Fungicide, and Rodenticide Act (FIFRA); and the proposed increase in the timber harvest from Bureau of Land Management forests. Three food safety issues are quite tightly and distinctly grouped at the top right. The remaining issues are generally bread-and-butter economic issues—price supports, foreign trade

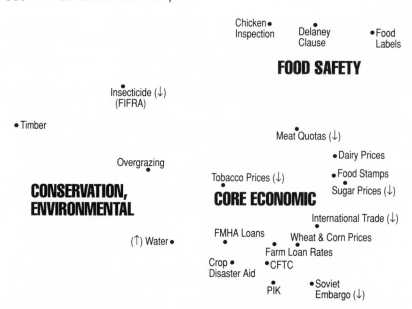

Figure 11.1   Agriculture domain issue space (three-dimensional smallest space solution; stress = .11, R^2 = .92)

restrictions and tariffs, farm loans, and futures trading. These are located in a larger, more diffuse mass toward the center and lower right of the space. The findings suggest that the constituencies for environmental and food safety issues are relatively narrow and coherent, while the more purely pocketbook issues activate a broader range of interest groups, including farmers' groups, agribusiness trade associations, unions (sometimes representing consumer interests and sometimes representing the interests of organized labor employed in agricultural production, processing, and distribution), grocery manufacturers, foreign governments, and fast food chains.

In the energy policy domain (Figure 11.2), we find the three nuclear power issues located in close proximity at the left of the space. Another grouping that is quite clearly associated with a particular energy source, coal, is located in the upper left quadrant of the space. These are issues dealing with a proposed tax on coal to provide benefits to miners afflicted with black lung disease, sulphur emission standards for coal-fired power plants, subsidies for the conversion to coal of oil-fired utility plants, and surface mining regulations. At the far right of the space, we find a clearly identifiable group of oil and gas issues: the Federal Energy Regulatory Commission (FERC)

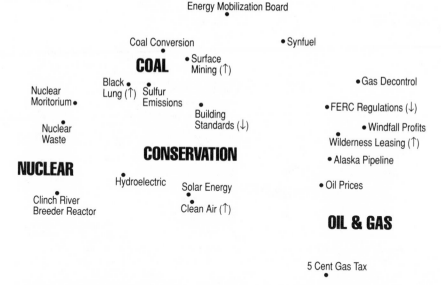

Figure 11.2   Energy domain issue space (three-dimensional smallest space solution; stress = .09; R^2 = .94)

regulations dealt with natural gas rates; the windfall profits tax was to be imposed on profits from the sale of decontrolled oil; the wilderness leasing issue was a proposed ban on oil and gas leasing in federal wilderness areas; and the remainder of those issues require no further explication. Between these groups, running diagonally across the center of the space from the lower left toward the upper right, are a number of conservation and environmental issues, including reauthorizations of the Clean Air Act and of Solar Energy Banks, subsidies for municipal development of hydroelectric power sites, energy performance standards that set limits on total energy consumption in new buildings, and development of the synthetic fuel industry. The clusters that are based in particular fuels—nuclear, coal, and oil and gas—are relatively tight. The environmental and conservation issues, however, appear to have a more diffuse constituency; they draw participants from several of the fuel-type interest groups and thus are located between them.

The analysis of the health issues displays at least three distinct groups (Figure 11.3). At the upper left of the space, we find four issues that deal with food and drug regulation—the proposed repeal of the Delaney clause banning carcinogens in food, the Carter admin-

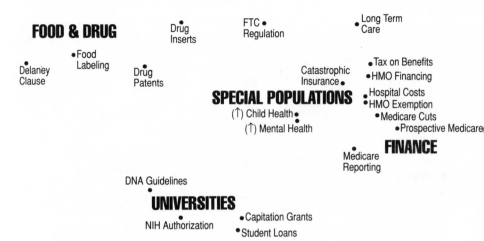

Figure 11.3 Health domain issue space (three-dimensional smallest space solution; stress = .08; R^2 = .96)

istration's package of food labeling regulations (both of these issues are also included in the agriculture domain, and thus the left boundary of the health figure might be thought of as its intersection with the agriculture domain), FDA proposals for mandatory information inserts in all packages of prescription drugs, and a proposal to extend the patent protection period for prescription drugs. In the lower left quadrant, we see a cluster of four issues that deal with biomedical research and funding for medical students. These are of interest to universities and to nonprofit hospitals that are often affiliated with universities. At the right side of the space are several issues dealing with the financing of medical care—hospital cost containment, cuts in Medicare, other changes in Medicare and Medicaid regulations, proposed changes in the taxation of health insurance benefits, and so on. Just to the left of these are a few issues dealing with "special population" groups—the Child Health Assurance Program (CHAP), authorization for new grants for community mental health centers, and the catastrophic health insurance plan (which, appropriately, is closest to the finance issues). Again, the food and drug issues and the universities' issues seem to be quite clearly defined, though the food and drug issues are relatively widely spread within their region of the space, and the health-care finance issues appear to be the basic core of the domain. This is more like the situation in agriculture, where the price support and more purely economic issues are the core, and less like the energy domain, where environmental and conservation issues are found toward the center of the space because all of the various fuel groups participate in them to one degree or another. In energy, the primary activity may take place in the separate fuel groups rather than in a unified constituency.

The labor domain also contains some distinct issue groupings (Figure 11.4), but the relative absence of tight clusters suggests that interest groups active in the domain, especially unions, participate in a broader range of substantive issues. At the left of the space, we find several issues dealing with full employment and income maintenance. The CETA program, the bailout of the Chrysler corporation, the regulation of migrant labor, the gas tax to support the reconstruction of the interstate highway system, and the domestic content bill (which required the use of goods produced by U.S. workers) all directly affect employment opportunities for American labor. Unemployment benefits and social security payments, of course, affect the income level of unemployed and retired workers. Inspection of the lists of organizations active on these issues reveals that this is relatively

Figure 11.4 Labor domain issue space (three-dimensional smallest space solution; stress = .14; R^2 = .86)

uncontested terrain for labor unions. Apparently because these issues involve distributive programs—that is, they do not affect the particular interests of specific segments of business, but instead involve claims on the government's fiscal resources—business groups are not active on them. The issues in the upper right portion of the space (minimum wage policies, immigration reform, and affirmative action obligations imposed by federal contracts) are of special concern to civil rights and urban poverty groups, on the one hand, and to business groups such as fast food chains that employ large numbers of relatively unskilled, service workers, on the other.

Just below these points are two core proposals in labor-management relations—to limit the Davis-Bacon Act's requirement that government contractors pay "prevailing" wage rates (that is, union scale) and to change federal labor laws to strengthen penalties against employers guilty of unfair labor practices and allow unions broader rights to strike through common situs picketing. (Note that the Davis-Bacon issue is adjacent to the other wage issues on the two-dimensional representation in Figure 11.4 but, as the arrow indicates, is far removed from them on the third dimension.) The lower middle of the space contains a set of issues concerning occupational safety and health. In the far right corner are two pension issues that elicit the interest of groups specializing in compensation and investment planning, in addition to unions and business groups.

The issue space in the labor domain is, thus, reasonably well ordered by subject matter. But once again the labor domain represents an interesting departure from what we find in other arenas. Our data on the constituencies of notables and the patterns of alliance among interest groups suggest that labor is an exceptionally polarized domain, effectively split between union and business groups. This stable oppositional structure tends to blur the distinctiveness of the issue publics. While there are still some specialized issue constituencies, such as employers of service workers, civil rights groups, and pension specialists, the labor domain is characterized by generalized opposition between labor and management on a wide range of fiscal and regulatory matters, rather than by contests within distinct issue publics.

These analyses look only at the patterns of activation; they do not take into account the respondents' positions on the issues. Thus, antagonists have been treated as members of the same "constituencies" in the sense that they are activated by the same issues. For that reason, "issue publics" is probably a better term to use to refer to these aggregations. But what are the patterns of alliance and opposition among the interest groups active in each domain, and the degree of the conflict or cooperation among them?

The Structure of the Interest Groups

In chapter 9, we noted that the four policy domains differ in the degree to which the interest groups confront each other in intense, sharply defined conflict and that they also differ somewhat, though less, in the degree of stability of the coalitions of interest groups. Those analyses were based on the respondents' characterizations of their positions in relation to two pairs of polar opposite statements. The statements dealing with the level of conflict were:

> The matters on which I work often generate intense conflicts among the contending parties, with each side devoting substantial amounts of their energies and resources to the battle.

> *versus*

> The nature of my work is such that the controversies seldom become intense and the decisions are more often characterized by accommodation and consensus than by conflict.

The statements concerning the stability of interest group coalitions were:

> In my work, the issues on which different parties or groups cooperate are characterized by stable coalitions in which the same leaders or groups are usually found together advocating the same side of the issue.

> *versus*

> In my work, on the issues that mobilize many parties or groups, the alignment of those groups usually changes from issue to issue, so that the controversies are characterized by constantly changing coalitions.

The mean response scores on these items in all four of the domains are on the intense conflict and stable coalitions sides of the scales, rather than toward consensus and changing coalitions. There are, however, some differences among the domains (see Table 11.1).

We find that the conflict dimension is more strongly skewed toward the high end of the scale than is the coalitional stability distribution. But there is some tendency for the two variables to move in the same direction. Conflict and stability are both high in the labor domain, while in agriculture and health both are relatively low or moderate. This suggests that conflict and stability are really one dimension—that is, if conflict is intense, then alliances and antagonisms are likely to be rigid. But the findings for the energy domain negate this thesis. In the energy domain, the conflict rating is even higher than it is in labor, while the stability of coalitions is the lowest of any of the domains (though this latter difference just misses the .05 level of statistical significance). The scores in the energy domain, thus, are at the opposite extremes of the two dimensions.

Conflict and coalitional stability are, then, two separate dimensions. They may, however, be likely to move together except in unusual circumstances. The energy domain was in a state of considerable flux at the time of our study (see chapter 2). The OPEC oil embargo and the consequent gasoline shortages were fresh in memory; the Department of Energy had only recently been established and was threatened with dismemberment. Uncertainty about the future was high, as was the level of conflict, but the domain on the whole had not coalesced into an established pattern of interest group interrelationships (Chubb 1983).

Table 11.1   Variation among domains in perceived conflict and coalitional stability

			N
Mean response			
Conflict[a] = 3.89			743
Stability[b] = 3.42			739
Differences from remainder of sample for:			
	Conflict	Stability	
Agriculture	−.30***	−.02	179
Energy	+.38***	−.15	171
Health	−.30***	.00	205
Labor	+.24**	+.16*	184

a. Intense conflict = 5, consensus = 1.
b. Stable coalitions = 5, changing coalitions = 1.
* $p < .05$. ** $p < .01$. *** $p < .001$.

Perhaps, therefore, intense conflict that continues for an extended period, as in the labor policy domain, will tend to cause the interest group alignments to become more stable. That is, the groups will eventually be forced to choose sides because the antipathy among potential sets of partners will make it impossible for the groups to switch back and forth. They will become tainted by past associations. The energy domain at the time of our observations, however, may not yet have been operating as an arena of common activity for a sufficient time to bring this process to fruition.

To what extent do the conflicts within these domains reflect broader ideological divisions in American politics between liberals and conservatives? The difference in the economic liberalism scores of the proponents and opponents of each of the issue events (twenty per domain) can be used as a measure of the degree to which the opposing sides are drawn from distinct ideological camps (see Table 11.2). We find that the agriculture domain has the fewest issues that manifest a clear difference between the two sides of the question, while the labor domain has by far the most such issues and, on the whole, larger differences. Though the level of conflict was rated highest in the energy domain, energy issues appear to be more like those in health or even agriculture in the extent of their ideological divisiveness. Thus, it appears that the conflicts on energy issues are, for the most part, battles among ideologically similar businesses pursuing the interests of competing fuel types. It may be that the greater instability of the interest group coalitions in the energy domain, as compared to labor, is related to the relatively nonideological character of energy politics—that is, conflicts are more often based in issue-specific competitive stakes than in dogma or ideological principle. This is also true more generally. Labor has by far the most stable coalitions and, in all of the domains except labor, a majority of the issues do not display significant ideological differences. This suggests that, on most issues, most of the time, conflicts among the active interest groups are motivated not by the conservative agenda or the liberal agenda but by more narrow concerns raised by the particular proposals at issue. The markedly higher stability of the interest group coalitions in the labor domain is no doubt associated with the much more ideological character of the politics of labor issues.

The analyses discussed thus far have been conducted at the level of the individual representative. To assess the alignments of the interest groups, however, we should examine the structure of the relationships among the client organizations themselves. We can do this if we

Table 11.2   Issue events with significant differences in the economic liberalism scores of representatives favoring and opposing the proposal

Issue event	Mean liberalism score		Significance level
	For	Against	
Agriculture			
Water reclamation	2.4	4.0	****
Food labeling	3.6	2.4	**
Delaney clause repeal	2.5	4.3	****
Farm debt ceilings	3.4	2.2	**
Payment in Kind (PIK)	2.6	3.2	*
Energy			
Nuclear moritorium	3.7	2.8	**
Synfuel development	2.6	3.2	*
Energy Mobilization Board	2.7	3.6	*
Windfall profits tax	3.4	2.4	****
Hydroelectric applications	3.9	2.5	**
President's emergency powers	3.1	2.1	****
Clean Air Act	3.3	2.6	**
Wilderness leasing ban	4.0	2.2	****
Health			
Hospital cost control	3.7	3.0	**
Medicare reporting	3.4	2.7	**
Food labeling	4.1	2.7	*
Drug patents	2.7	4.7	***
HMO financing	2.9	3.4	**
Delaney clause repeal	2.7	4.0	*
Limits on FTC	3.2	4.1	**
Labor			
Common situs picketing	4.4	2.5	****
Minimum wage	4.3	2.4	****
Youth subminimum wage	2.4	4.6	****
Davis-Bacon waiver	2.5	4.3	****
Chrysler aid	4.0	2.0	**
OSHA inspection exemption	2.6	4.2	****
OSHA employee records	4.2	2.6	****
Cotton dust	4.3	3.2	**
Unemployment aid cuts	2.4	4.3	****
CETA termination	2.9	4.5	****
Social Security cuts	2.2	4.4	****
Affirmative action exemptions	2.5	4.2	****
Multiemployer pensions	2.7	4.1	****
5 cent gas tax	3.6	2.5	*
Domestic content	4.4	2.4	****
Immigration reform	4.1	3.1	*

Note: For more complete descriptions of the issue events, see appendix at end of chapter.
* $p < .05$. ** $p < .01$. *** $p < .001$. **** $p < .0001$.

attribute to the respondent's employer the position that the respondent took on the matter. The assumption that this requires is surely not heroic.[1] The respondents told us what positions they took on the five issues in which they were most active. Because we often have in our sample more than one representative employed by a particular organization, however, we often have information on the positions taken by the organizations on a larger number of issues.[2]

The relationships among the organizations can be assessed by the use of smallest space analysis where the proximity measure is the correlation of the positions taken by the groups on the several issues. The correlations might be based on: (1) an affinity matrix, counting instances of agreement or matching in positions; (2) an antagonism matrix, counting instances of opposition in position; or (3) stacked matrices, combining the affinity and antagonism approaches. We opted for the third of these procedures.[3] Some political situations are characterized by a high degree of consensus, and agreement alone will not tell us much then. In such circumstances, opposition may be much more significant. We therefore decided to take both agreement and opposition into account.

The smallest space solutions were computed on each of the four domains separately, using the twenty issues that were drawn from each. In presenting the solutions, we show the positions of only a "diagnostic set" of the interest groups active in each domain (see Figures 11.5–11.8). The total number of organizations for which we have data exceeds one hundred per domain, but the solutions would not be comprehensible if we attempted to show so many points. The analyses were computed using the full set of organizations; the locations of the organizations shown in these figures are therefore determined by their relationships to all of the interest groups represented in the sample. We believe that the substance of the findings is accurately reflected in these partial presentations.

The analysis of the structure of interest group relationships in the agriculture domain (Figure 11.5) reveals that all of the unions active on agriculture issues are found in a tight cluster, relatively low in the space, toward the front of the box. Just above these, somewhat more spread, are a group of distributors of agricultural products—the Food Marketing Institute, the Foodservice and Lodging Institute, Kraft, the Grocery Manufacturers of America, General Foods, the American Meat Institute (an organization of meat packers and processors), and McDonald's. Both the unions and the distribution companies (which

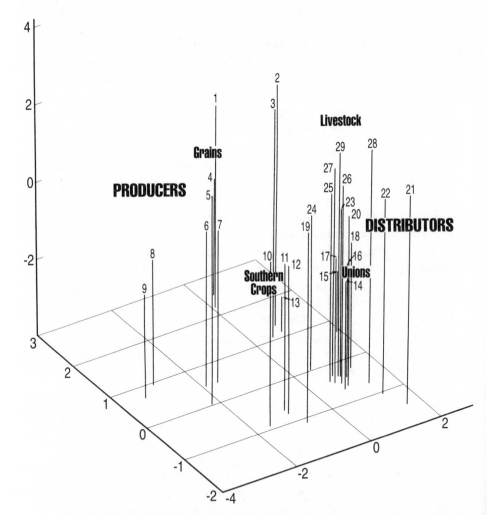

1 U.S. Feed Grains Council	11 Universal Leaf Tobacco Co.	21 Nat'l Milk Producers Ass'n
2 United Egg Producers	12 Nat'l Cotton Council of America	22 Nat'l Meat Ass'n
3 Livestock Marketing Ass'n	13 Nat'l Farmers Union	23 Food Service Institute
4 American Soybean Ass'n	14 Int'l Longshoremen's Union	24 Chicago Board of Trade
5 Nat'l Ass'n of Wheat Growers	15 AFL-CIO	25 Grocery Manufacturers of America
6 Nat'l Corn Growers Ass'n	16 Food and Beverage Workers	26 General Foods Corp.
7 Grain Sorghum Producers Ass'n	17 United Farm Workers	27 American Meat Institute
8 American Agriculture Movement	18 United Food and Commercial Workers	28 Nat'l Cattlemen's Ass'n
9 American Farm Bureau Federation	19 Kraft, Inc.	29 McDonald's Corp.
10 Western Cotton Growers Ass'n	20 Food Marketing Institute	

Figure 11.5 Agriculture domain organizations, located by positions on policy issues (three-dimensional smallest space solution; stress = .17; R^2 = .85)

are the employers of most of the unionized workers) have interests that are at odds with those of the farmers. Even higher in the space, above many of the distributors but overlapping some of them, are a number of livestock production and distribution interests. These include the National Meat Association (an organization of meat packers), the National Milk Producers, the National Cattlemen's Association, and the Livestock Marketing Association, as well as McDonald's and the American Meat Institute, which were already mentioned. The U.S. Feed Grains Council is located closer to these livestock interests than are the other feed grain interests. Unlike the other feed grain organizations, the U.S. Feed Grains Council represents grain processors and exporters as well as producers, and it thus shares with the livestock groups a direct interest in enhanced international trade. The remainder of the organizations representing grain interests are located lower in the space, toward the left—the American Soybean Association, the National Association of Wheat Growers, the National Corn Growers Association, and the Grain Sorghum Producers Association. Even farther to the left of the space are two of the three "peak" associations of agricultural producers, the American Farm Bureau Federation and the American Agriculture Movement. The membership of both is drawn primarily from grain-producing areas. The remaining peak association, the National Farmers Union, is located low in the middle of the space, closer to the labor unions, probably reflecting the historical alliance between the NFU and organized labor (see chapter 2). Finally, three associations that represent cotton and tobacco interests (Southern crops) are located on the left side of the space, toward the front, about halfway up on the vertical dimension. Generally speaking (though not without exception), the organizations on the right side of this space represent interests engaged in the distribution of agricultural commodities, and the organizations on the left represent producers.

The energy domain includes three large clusters, one much broader than the other two (see Figure 11.6). The most distinct of these clusters is the group of "externality" interests located at the lower right front of the space—including the National Association of Counties, the Natural Resources Defense Council, the National Governors Association, the Center for Auto Safety (founded by Ralph Nader), and the Sierra Club. Above and behind this cluster, and somewhat to the left, is a much larger collection of business interests. At the top of these are a number of oil companies—Phillips Petroleum, Union

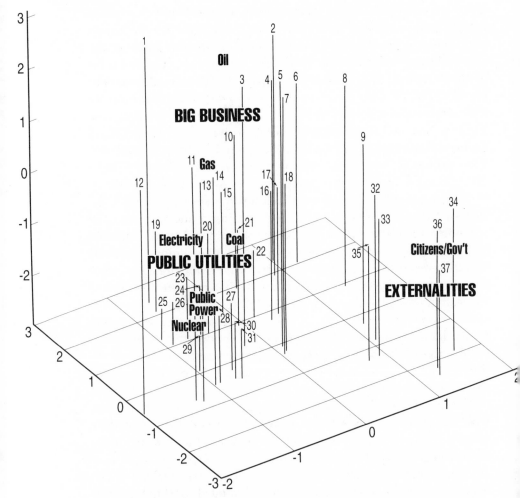

1 Phillips Petroleum
2 Union Oil Co. of California
3 Chemical Manufacturers Ass'n
4 Gulf Oil Corp.
5 Council for a Competitive Economy
6 American Petroleum Institute
7 Heritage Foundation
8 Independent Petroleum Ass'n
9 Nat'l Petroleum Refiners Ass'n
10 Nat'l Ass'n of Manufacturers
11 American Gas Ass'n
12 Atlantic Richfield Co.
13 Transco Energy Co.

14 Interstate Natural Gas Ass'n
15 Chamber of Commerce of the U.S.A.
16 Ford Motor Co.
17 Motor Vehicle Manufacturers Ass'n
18 Business Roundtable
19 Consumers Power Co.
20 Slurry Transport Ass'n
21 General Electric Co.
22 United Mine Workers of America
23 Hunton & Williams
24 Edison Electric Institute
25 Electric Power Research Institute

26 Commonwealth Edison Co.
27 American Public Power Ass'n
28 American Nuclear Energy Council
29 Nat'l Rural Electric Cooperative Ass'n
30 Atomic Industrial Forum
31 American Mining Congress
32 Chrysler Corp.
33 Sierra Club
34 Center for Auto Safety
35 Nat'l Governors Ass'n
36 Natural Resources Defense Council
37 Nat'l Ass'n of Counties

Figure 11.6 Energy domain organizations, located by positions on policy issues (three-dimensional smallest space solution; stress = .17; R^2 = .78)

Oil, Gulf Oil, the American Petroleum Institute, the Independent Petroleum Association, and the National Petroleum Refiners. Mixed in with these are the Heritage Foundation and the Council for a Competitive Economy, which are devoted to the promotion of free enterprise and limited government. Just below these is the National Association of Manufacturers, and a bit further down is the Chamber of Commerce. Just to the left of the NAM and the Chamber is a tight cluster of organizations representing natural gas interests—the American Gas Association, Transco Energy Company (a natural gas pipeline and production company), and the Interstate Natural Gas Association. To the right of the NAM and the Chamber are some auto manufacturing interests—Ford, the Automobile Manufacturers Association, and Chrysler. In the same area as the auto manufacturers, we also find the Business Roundtable, the members of which are officers of the largest corporations. At the lower left of the space is a quite cohesive cluster of public utilities and other organizations involved in the production of electricity. The lower half of that cluster is composed primarily of public power and nuclear power interests, while the top half appears to be more oriented toward coal-generated electricity and includes the Slurry Transport Association and the United Mine Workers.

Thus, the energy domain displays a fairly clear division between oil and gas, on the one hand, and coal, electricity, and nuclear power on the other, while the citizen/government groups form a cluster of their own. The conflicts among the fuel types are not as clearly displayed here as in some of the other analyses, although the position of oil (at the upper right) is quite clearly in opposition to nuclear power (at the lower left). Gas and coal are in a more intermediate posture, gas being closer to oil and coal being closer to nuclear power, which makes good sense because gas and oil are sometimes produced by the same companies and coal and nuclear power are sometimes used by the same utilities as alternative fuels. Laumann and Knoke (1987) observed a quite similar structure of interests in the energy domain, using an entirely separate data set and a different operationalization of the structure of the space.

The clusters in the health domain are, on the whole, rather less distinct (Figure 11.7). At the right side of the space, we find organizations representing the interests of a number of populations with special needs for health services—the American Foundation for the Blind, the Veterans of Foreign Wars, the Paralyzed Veterans of

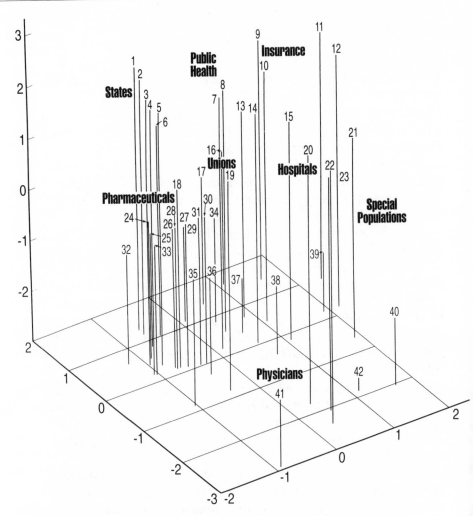

1 Nat'l Conference of State Legislatures
2 New Jersey Dep't of Human Services
3 Nat'l Governors Ass'n
4 State of New Jersey, Washington Office
5 State of Virginia Dep't of Health
6 American Ass'n of University Affiliated Programs for the Developmentally Disabled
7 Nat'l Ass'n of Public Hospitals
8 Nat'l Ass'n of Area Agencies on Aging
9 Health Insurance Ass'n of America
10 Blue Cross/Blue Shield
11 Nat'l Council of Senior Citizens
12 American Public Health Ass'n
13 Miles Laboratories
14 American Physical Therapy Ass'n

15 Ass'n of American Medical Colleges
16 United Mine Workers
17 United Auto Workers
18 Equitable Life Assurance Society
19 Nat'l Ass'n of Pharmaceutical Manufacturers
20 Federation of American Hospitals
21 Veterans of Foreign Wars
22 American Hospital Ass'n
23 Healthcare Financial Management Ass'n
24 Public Citizen
25 Covington & Burling
26 Monsanto Co.
27 Grocery Manufacturers of America
28 U.S. Brewers Ass'n

29 Nat'l Abortion Rights Action League
30 Nat'l Abortion Federation
31 Proprietary Ass'n (proprietary drugs)
32 Ass'n of American Universities
33 Abbott Laboratories
34 American Dental Hygenists Ass'n
35 American Legion
36 Nat'l Council on Alcoholism
37 American Academy of Orthopaedic Surgeons
38 Nat'l Ass'n of State Universities and Land Grant Colleges
39 American Foundation for the Blind
40 Paralyzed Veterans of America
41 American Medical Ass'n
42 American Psychiatric Ass'n

Figure 11.7 Health domain organizations, located by positions on policy issues (three-dimensional smallest space solution; stress = .17; R^2 = .85)

America, and the American Psychiatric Association. Just to the left of these, we see interest groups representing hospitals—the American Hospital Association and the Federation of American Hospitals. The Association of American Medical Colleges is in this same region, as is the National Association of State Universities and Land Grant Colleges, though the latter organization is much lower on the vertical dimension. At the top of the space, to the right, we find a number of public health and insurance interests. These include the American Public Health Association, Blue Cross/Blue Shield, the Health Insurance Association of America, and the National Association of Public Hospitals. Mixed in with these are the National Council of Senior Citizens and the National Association of Area Councils on Aging, probably because the elderly have such a strong interest in publicly financed health insurance. At the far left of the top of the space, we find a tight cluster of organizations representing state governments. This reinforces the point that the upper region represents the public sector.

The American Medical Association is located about as far away from the public sector as it could possibly be—very low on the front edge of the space, widely separated from all of the other groups. This suggests that the AMA continues to pursue positions that often place it in opposition to those who seek public funding for health care. It also appears to play a quite independent role.

On the left side of the space, around the middle of the vertical dimension, we see a group of interests concerned with "food and drug" issues. These include the Proprietary Drug Association, the U.S. Brewers Association, the Grocery Manufacturers of America, Monsanto, Abbott Laboratories, Public Citizen (a Nader affiliate), Covington & Burling (a large law firm that has an extensive practice before the Food and Drug Administration), and, somewhat farther to the right, the National Association of Pharmaceutical Manufacturers. A bit lower on the vertical dimension and somewhat closer to the front of the space, we find the American Legion and the National Council on Alcoholism. Two unions—the UAW and the UMW—are located approximately equidistant between the public health and the food and drug sectors, reflecting the positions that they adopt on publicly funded health plans and the consumer interests that they pursue on food and drug issues.

With the exception of the cluster of state government organizations, these groupings in the health domain are somewhat more diffuse than those in the other domains. This could be a consequence of shifting coalitions, but the respondents do not tell us that the health domain is especially characterized by instability. Its mean score on the coalitional stability dimension is exactly in the middle of the distribution (Table 11.1). There is certainly no evidence to suggest that the coalitions are less stable in health than, say, in the energy domain. We thus have no satisfactory explanation for the relative lack of clear patterning of the organizational positions on health issues. It may be that we simply lack sufficient knowledge of the characteristics of the organizations and the particulars of the issues to permit us to comprehend the subtleties of the relationships. If so, other scholars who are better informed may be able to provide a more complete explanation of our findings.

The labor domain displays a classic oppositional structure (Figure 11.8), but it is somewhat more differentiated than a simple division between labor and management. On the right side of the space, toward the front and relatively low on the vertical dimension, we see a group of three unions—the United Steelworkers, the Machinists and Aerospace Workers, and the Communication Workers. Note that these are primarily industrial unions, as opposed to craft unions, and that they tend to be more militant or more consistent in their adherence to liberal ideology. The craft and service workers' unions, by contrast, are found higher in the space, mostly toward the rear and also mostly toward the right. These include the ILGWU, the Clothing and Textile Workers, the Bricklayers, the United Food and Commercial Workers, and the United Mine Workers. The Kamber Group is a consulting firm that does work for the unions. The AFL-CIO is found, appropriately, at the intersection of the craft unions and the industrial unions.

Across the space from the industrial unions, on the left side, toward the rear and higher in the space, are a number of organizations that represent the interests of large corporations, especially those engaged in heavy industry. These include the National Association of Manufacturers, the Business Roundtable, the Committee for Economic Development, General Motors, and the Chamber of Commerce. Their location in the space suggests that these organizations pursue policy positions that are in opposition to those of the industrial unions, but note that some of the business groups (for example, the Business Roundtable) appear to adopt more moderate positions than do others (for example, the Chamber of Commerce).

Chamber of Commerce of the U.S.A.
General Motors
Nat'l Federation of Independent Business
Committee for Economic Development
Business Roundtable
Nat'l Ass'n of Manufacturers
Nat'l Roofing Contractors Ass'n
American Trucking Ass'n
Nat'l Small Business Ass'n

10 Foodservice and Lodging Institute
11 Nat'l Restaurant Ass'n
12 General Mills
13 The Kamber Group
14 Int'l Union of Bricklayers and Allied Craftsmen
15 United Food and Commercial Workers Int'l Union
16 United Mine Workers of America
17 Amalgamated Clothing and Textile Workers Union
18 Int'l Ladies Garment Workers Union

19 AFL-CIO
20 Communications Workers of America
21 Int'l Ass'n of Machinists and Aerospace Workers
22 United Steelworkers of America
23 American Arbitration Ass'n
24 NAACP
25 United Automobile, Aerospace, and Agricultural
      Implement Workers of America
26 American Civil Liberties Union

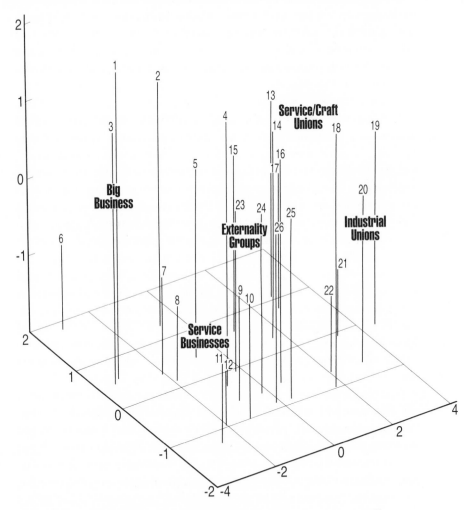

Figure 11.8 Labor domain organizations, located by positions on policy issues (three-dimensional smallest space solution; stress = .13; R^2 = .92)

Across the space from the service and craft unions, at the front of the left side of the space, lower in the vertical dimension, we see a number of organizations representing service businesses and small businesses—the National Roofing Contractors Association, the American Trucking Association, the National Small Business Association, the Foodservice and Lodging Institute, and the National Restaurant Association. Thus, the industrial unions are located in opposition to the big business organizations, and the service and craft unions are opposed to the smaller, service businesses, while the two sorts of unions are relatively close to each other. There is a greater separation of the two parts of business, but the businesses are nonetheless clearly distinct from the unions.

In the center of the labor domain space, we see two organizations that represent interests concerned with the externalities of labor policy—the American Civil Liberties Union and the NAACP Legal Defense Fund. The United Auto Workers is somewhat closer to the industrial unions but clearly aligned with the civil rights groups, reflecting its social agenda. Also in the center of the space, not because of its social agenda but because it did not take a position for or against any of the issues, is the American Arbitration Association. It did, however, pursue an active monitoring role on six issues.

We can see, then, that the degree to which the conflicts on the issues are based in broader ideological positions (Table 11.2) bears little relation to the clarity of the structure of interest group alignment in these policy domains. In the agriculture and energy domains, the alignments are quite clear even though most of the issues do not appear to draw their supporters and opponents from distinct ideological camps. Health, where the structure is less clear, has more issues with significant ideological differences than does agriculture. Nor is the clarity of the structure related to the respondents' perceptions of the degree of stability of the interest group coalitions. In health, coalitional stability is rated average. In energy, where the coalitions are perceived to be less stable, alignments are relatively clear. Thus, even though most of the conflicts in three of the four domains are nonideological, the alignments produced by these narrow, particular conflicts (in combination with some ideological ones, to be sure) are strong enough and stable enough to result in interpretable patterns. These more specific conflicts occur, for example, between producers, distributors, and consumers of a particular commodity (feed grains versus livestock interests, or farmers versus grocery distributors), or between entrepreneurs seeking competitive advantage when their products are substitutable in certain markets (for example, competing fuel sources). These conflicts are robust enough to cut through the strongly ideological character of labor issues and to produce noticeable further differentiation even in the structure of the labor coalitions.

To illustrate the manner in which specific alliances and antagonisms generate the structures in each of these domains, let us examine a few more figures. These use the same smallest space solutions, but present only the first two of the three dimensions and include only the organizations that took a position either favoring or opposing a particular issue event. We indicate the position that each organization took by including either a plus sign (for the proposal) or a minus (opposition), but we do not identify the specific organizations.[4] The general character of the organizations occupying particular regions of the space is indicated, however. Other organizations were often active on a policy proposal without taking a clear position for or against it. Organizations could, for example, provide factual testimony on the matter without taking a clear position, favor parts of the proposal but oppose other parts, or simply monitor the progress of the issue, pursuing a watching brief. None of these latter roles are indicated in the figures.

The Secretary of Agriculture's proposed Payment in Kind (PIK) program, a payment for retiring land from production and thus reducing the supply of agricultural commodities (Figure 11.9), was supported by producer interests (located in the lower half of the space) and opposed by consumer and distributor interests (in the top half), including the consumers of feed grains. The Delaney clause issue (Figure 11.10), by contrast, splits the space from right to left. That proposal would have softened the language of the 1958 Food Safety Amendment to permit the FDA to weigh the risks and benefits of food additives that are potentially carcinogenic, such as saccharin, rather than simply banning them. Two labor unions (located on the left of the space) opposed the bill, presumably reflecting consumer interests, while all of the producer and distributor interests (on the right of the space) supported the bill.

The division of the energy interest groups on the proposed reauthorization of the Clean Air Act (Figure 11.11) also shows a very clear split—oil companies, public utilities, and their corporate allies (on the right of the space) opposed the reauthorization, while government and citizen groups (on the left) favored it. Issues like this one and the

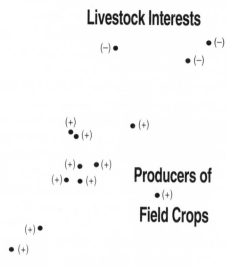

Figure 11.9   The Payment in Kind (PIK) program

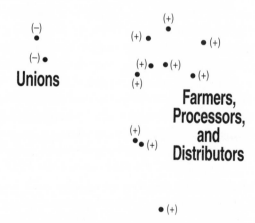

Figure 11.10   The Delaney clause regarding food additives

PIK proposal have considerable influence on the overall patterning of the smallest space solutions because they involve large numbers of interest groups and create sharp divisions.

The Environmental Protection Agency's tougher sulphur emission standards for new coal-fired power plants produced a pattern that is less sharply divided, but still quite clearly interpretable (Figure 11.12).

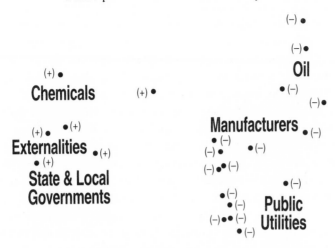

Figure 11.11 Reauthorization of the Clean Air Act

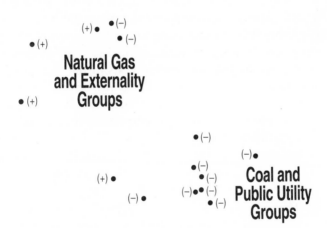

Figure 11.12 Sulphur emissions from coal-fired plants

Two of the organizations located just to the left of the center of the space (near the supporters) opposed the proposal. The locations of these two organizations are obviously determined by their positions on other issues. Patterns like this are not uncommon among the eighty events; we do not want to give the false impression that all of the issue events display clean splits.

Another common pattern is exemplified by the division on the proposed ban of oil and gas leasing in federal wilderness areas (Figure

11.13). Of the nine organizations among the diagnostic set that were active on this issue, only one supported the proposal. Nonetheless, the wilderness leasing ban was passed by Congress and signed by the President. Other private interest groups in fact supported the ban, as did interest groups located within the federal government. The active support of some well-situated members of Congress was no doubt important to the success of the proposal.

Two issues in the health domain were even more one-sided. On these, *all* of the active organizations in our diagnostic set opposed the proposals. The issues were the proposed budget cut in the Medicare program's periodic interim payments to hospitals and the proposed cut in low-interest loans to medical students. Both of these proposals were supported by the Reagan administration and opposed by Democrats in Congress. Though several of the organizations in our sample were active on these issues, none supported the proposals. The Medicare cut was adopted, but the student loan cut was not. Thus, knowing the number of organizations supporting a proposal may not permit us to predict the outcome with any great confidence. This point is treated more fully and more formally in the next section of this chapter, where we analyze the determinants of the success of policy proposals. Though our sample excludes some private organizations that may well have played important roles, probably a more substantial reason why the number of supporters bears little relation to the success of the proposals is that these analyses leave the activity of

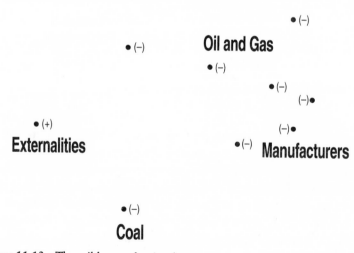

Figure 11.13   The wilderness leasing ban

federal officials entirely out of account. The Reagan appointees were vigorously pursuing their agendas, and Reagan's power and popularity, especially relatively early in his first term, were undoubtedly important in determining the outcome of these proposed budget cuts.

Not all health issues are of this character, however. The Carter administration's proposed mandatory controls on hospital costs, for example, produced an almost complete split between the right and left sides of the space (Figure 11.14). Only one organization (located just to the right of the midline near the top) is out of alignment on this issue. All of the hospital associations and medical associations (on the left of the space) opposed the proposal. They were joined by some of the special population groups, who may have feared that the cost controls would bring a reduction in the quality of care. The insurance organizations were split, some supporting and some opposing the proposal. Groups on the right of the space, including state governments, public health groups, and a union, supported the proposal.

The Reagan administration's prospective payment system for Medicare reimbursement of hospitals divided the space in the other direction, from top to bottom (Figure 11.15). The proposed plan was to pay hospitals a fixed, standard amount for the treatment of a

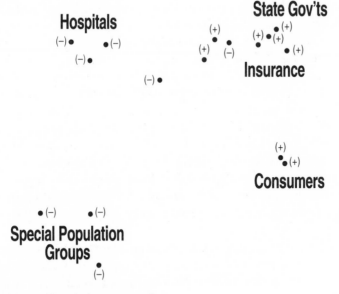

Figure 11.14 Hospital cost controls

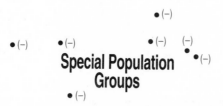

Figure 11.15   Prospective Medicare reimbursements

patient with a particular disease or condition rather than paying per day of hospitalization or per procedure performed. This proposal was ultimately supported not only by the insurance industry and state governments, which bear a substantial part of the cost of welfare payments, but by hospital associations, some of the medical professionals, and some of the special population groups. It was opposed, however, by other groups representing high-risk or intensive-treatment patients and their physicians.

The organizations in the labor policy space that were active on the proposed increase in the minimum wage illustrate a division that is typical of most issues in the labor domain (Figure 11.16). All of the active unions (the top half of the space) favored the proposal; all of the active business organizations (the lower half) opposed it. Fourteen of the twenty labor issues display this pattern. The unions and business groups that were active differ from proposal to proposal, of course, but the split between labor and management is absolute in all of those cases. Other issue events display only minor or individual exceptions to the pattern.

The externality groups active on labor issues are in the middle of the space not so much because they sometimes side with unions and sometimes with management as because they often take an ambivalent or middle position. On the proposal to raise the threshold of the

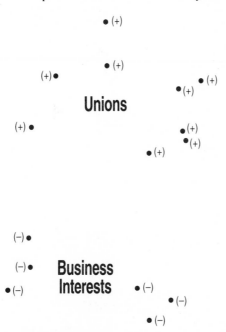

Figure 11.16   Increase in minimum wage

size of government contracts requiring an affirmative action plan, however, most of the active opponents in our diagnostic set are externality groups (Figure 11.17). Of the unions, only one large organization took an active opposing role. The organizations support-ing the proposal are all business groups; all of the active business groups in our diagnostic set were aligned in support.

Thus, the splits in the labor domain are much more consistent than are those in the other domains. Our measure of the perceived degree of coalitional stability gives the labor domain the highest stability score by a significant margin (Table 11.1), but the smallest space analyses of the agriculture and energy domains (and, to a lesser degree, health) also display clear alliances and antagonisms. This is not inconsistent with the respondents' perceptions since the perceived degree of stability in these other three domains was on the stable rather than on the changing coalitions side of the scale. The degree of structure that is present in the alignments, therefore, is sufficient to produce strong patterns.

In sum, the agriculture, energy, and health domains are character-ized by positions that are highly specific to the issues and that are

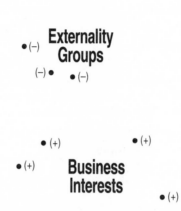

Figure 11.17   Exemption from affirmative action

technical rather than ideological, but that produce splits recurring often enough to produce distinct lines of division. The issues in the labor domain much more often reflect the broad ideological divisions between labor and management. But many of the labor issues are also quite narrow and specific in content, most activate only a limited range of groups, and some produce defections on one side or the other for issue-specific reasons.

Our sample of issues is almost certainly more visible and more controversial than the general run. It is probable, therefore, that the level of conflict on these issues is also higher than the average. But the respondents characterized the usual issues involved in their work as being well toward the conflict side of the conflict/consensus dichotomy. Perhaps, then, our set of issues is not so atypical. Competition for scarce resources can produce pitched battles even if the stakes are not defined in broad ideological terms.

The Structure of Success

The title of one of Harold Lasswell's books suggests that the essence of politics is who gets what, when, and how (Lasswell 1936). Certainly, both politicians and students of politics devote much of their attention to identifying winners and losers and to speculating about what caused them to win or lose. There is equal reason for us to address those issues. Lasswell began the same book by saying that "the study of politics is the study of influence and the influential," and he defined the influential as "those who get the most of what there is to get" (3). Who, then, got the most on these issues of federal agriculture, energy, health, and labor policy?

We asked the respondents to evaluate the degree of their success on the five issue events in which they had the greatest interest. Specifically, with respect to each of the five, we asked: "Given your client or organization's objectives, would you say that your client or organization achieved (1) all of its objectives, (2) most of its objectives, (3) about half of its objectives, (4) few of its objectives, or (5) none of its objectives?" These data, then, give us a success score for each representative on the five issue events in which he or she was most active.[5] The scores permit us to compare both the success of different sorts of representatives on the same issue and the success of the same representative or organization from issue to issue. In addition, since we have data on the strategies pursued by each representative on these issues, we can also assess the extent to which some strategies appear to be more successful.

To evaluate the validity of these self-reports of success, we have used data from the interviews with the sample of government officials. During those interviews, we asked the officials to identify the organizations that won and lost on the issue events on which the officials were active. Using those responses, we constructed lists of the winning and losing organizations on each issue, and we then tested for differences between the mean success scores reported by representatives of winning organizations and those reported by representatives of organizations identified as losers. These means are significantly different in all four of the domains, in the predicted direction. They are more highly significant in the energy, health, and labor domains than they are on agriculture issues, where there was a greater degree of consensus on the issue events.

Relatively few events have heavily one-sided support. There are only three events on which more than three-quarters of the representatives who were active supported the proposal. Two of those three are in the agriculture domain. Similarly, only four of the eighty proposals were opposed by more than three-quarters of the active representatives. Three of those four are in the health domain. Only one of the twenty events in agriculture was opposed by a majority of the active respondents, but there was majority opposition to four events in the energy domain and to six events each in health and in labor. The mean percentage of active respondents supporting the proposals in the four domains ranges from 47% in the agriculture domain to 35% in health. The mean percentage opposing the proposals ranges from 38% in health to 27% in agriculture.

The relationship between the extent of support for a proposal and the likelihood of its success can be assessed by examining either the number of representatives or the number of organizations supporting the proposal. We did both, and we find that neither has a significant relationship to the success of a proposal, as measured by the success scores reported by the proponents of the proposal. The number of representatives and the number of organizations *opposing* a proposal, however, do have significant negative relationships ($p < .005$) with the level of success reported by the proponents. It appears, then, that the support of only a small number may be sufficient to procure success as long as there is no significant opposition, but that the number of opponents does affect the likelihood that a proposal will succeed. Thus, we have also found that the *percentage* of active players supporting a proposal is significantly associated with success ($p < .008$).

When the five-point scale used to evaluate success is constructed so that a higher score indicates higher success, the mean level of reported success is 3.24—just on the high side of the midpoint. Though one might expect some tendency toward inflation in self-reports of success, there does not appear to be much bias of that kind in these data. The mean scores in the four policy domains range only from a low of 3.15 in the labor domain to a high of 3.35 in health. These domain differences are not significant in an analysis of variance, but there are some significant differences in the kinds of organizations that report higher or lower success in the domains. In the agriculture domain, representatives employed by law firms and business organizations report especially high levels of success, while those employed by citizen or government organizations report the lowest success levels ($p < .006$ in an analysis of variance). In the health domain, representatives employed by trade associations and professional associations report high success, while those representing not-for-profit organizations, such as public hospitals, are the least successful ($p <$

.003). There are no significant differences in the success rates of the various types of organizations in the other two domains.

Though law firms report high success on agriculture issues, their interest level was especially low in such matters (see the beginning of this chapter). It appears, therefore, that representatives employed by law firms participate only in a narrow range of issues within the agriculture domain, especially food safety and food labeling issues, but that they enjoy relative success in that agenda. The professional associations, by contrast, have both high interest and high success in the health domain, while the not-for-profit organizations combine significantly high interest in health issues with their low reported success, a combination that must be especially frustrating. The success of trade associations on health issues is, like that of law firms in the agriculture domain, achieved in the context of low levels of interest, indicating limited involvement.

The questions regarding success, positions taken, and strategies pursued were asked only on the five events on which the respondent was most active. We have 30 or fewer responses on about half of the issue events in each domain, from 31 to 50 on about another third of the events, and more than 50 responses on only three to five of the twenty events per domain. The mean number of respondents on each issue event ranges from 39 in the health domain to 35 in agriculture.

If we examine the characteristics of the representatives and of their organizations that appear to be associated with greater or lesser success, we find that few of the variables appear to have marked effects (using t-tests and analyses of variance). Representatives of organizations that have greater resources (as indicated by the number of their representatives appearing in our sample) or that are more prominent (as indicated by the number of times that the organization appeared in the nominations in our sampling procedure) do not have significantly different levels of success in the agriculture, energy, or labor domains. In the health domain, however, their success is marginally *lower* than that of other organizations. Respondents who were included in our set of notables (chapter 10) are not significantly more successful than other representatives in any of the four individual domain analyses, but that is probably a result of the relatively small number of notables present in each of the domains. If we compare the success of notables and non-notables across the full sample, pooling the four domains, we find that the notables do have significantly higher reported success ($p = .011$). Representatives with government experience report significantly greater success in the energy and health domains, but not in agriculture or labor. In all four of the domains, however, the representatives with government experience do have higher scores. Specialization, measured by the percentage of time that the representative devotes to the domain, enhances success only in the energy domain. It is not significant elsewhere.

Organizations pursuing particular strategies are more successful in some domains, but the general pattern is that doing more of anything produces greater success than doing less, regardless of the strategy. The exception to this is the pursuit of litigation. In the agriculture, health, and labor domains, representatives who use litigation to advance their policy objectives have somewhat lower success scores.

In the health domain, representatives who have levels of activity that are above the mean on any of the strategic options other than litigation—that is, contacting Congress, contacting executive agencies, mobilizing public opinion, and contacting representatives of other lobbying organizations—have significantly higher success scores than those who are at or below the mean. But in the labor domain, the only strategy that is associated with greater success is contacting Congress. This may be attributable to the fact that the Democrats controlled the House of Representatives during all of this period and the Senate as well until 1981, and unions have an affinity for Democrats.

The labor domain, however, is not unusual in rewarding contact with Congress. Representatives who more often use that strategy report significantly greater success in all of the domains except energy. The only strategy associated with higher success on energy issues is contacting the executive agencies. The situation in energy, then, is rather the opposite of that in the labor domain—Republicans controlled the executive branch during much of the period, and business groups are the dominant players in the energy domain. In the agriculture domain, like the health domain, doing more of anything other than litigation tends to enhance success.

The findings of these bivariate analyses, however, are placed in better perspective by multiple regression models that assess the relative effects of several variables on the success scores. These give us a somewhat different picture. In these analyses, we included the same fourteen variables that were used in the regressions on the levels of interest (see the beginning of this chapter). The most important finding here is that we are able to explain only a very modest amount of the variance in the success scores (Table 11.3). Thus, the processes that determine the success of the representatives' efforts on these issues, whatever those processes may be, do not appear to be captured adequately by the variables included in the analysis, and that is so even though these variables reflect the most obvious hypotheses about the determinants of influence. One might suppose that a role in political fund-raising or in the distribution of PAC money might enhance influence and, therefore, success; that the amount of the resources possessed by a respondent's organization would be related to the amount of effort that the organization could expend on an issue; that specialization in a substantive field would enhance expertise or contacts, and therefore enhance success; that legal expertise or the authority conferred by a lawyer's credentials might make lawyers influential; that a party affiliation either as a Democrat or as a Republican might ease access to particular networks of decision makers; or that the pursuit of certain strategies, such as contact with Congress or contact with executive agencies, might enhance success. But none of these variables makes a significant contribution in the overall regression model.[6] Distributing PAC money and contacting executive agencies do contribute significantly to an analysis of success in the

Table 11.3 Multiple regression of selected variables predicting success in issue events over four domains

Independent variable	Beta	T	Significance of T
Years in government	.24	2.48	.01
Square of years in government	−.19	−2.00	.05
Economic liberalism	−.14	−2.92	.004
Number of notables known	.14	3.30	.001
Employed by professional association	.13	3.29	.001
Law degree	.06	1.67	.10
Contact executive agencies	.06	1.27	.21
Specialization in domain	.05	1.24	.22
Number of professionals in organization	.05	1.20	.23
Political fund-raising	.05	1.04	.30
Distribute PAC money	.03	.76	.45
Contact Congress	.03	.68	.50
Republican	−.02	−.34	.74
Democrat	.02	.33	.74

$R^2 = .11.$ $F = 5.38.$ $p < .001.$ $N = 655.$

health domain, but that is true only in that domain. It is not clear why health policy issues should be exceptional in this regard.

The number of years of the respondent's experience in a federal government position is among the variables that have the most important effects on the level of success (Table 11.3). Spending at least a few years in the federal government is associated with higher success on these issue events, but the effect appears to be curvilinear. Since the square of the years of government experience is *negatively* associated with success, as the number of years increases (and the square becomes much larger), success declines. There is, then, not only a point of diminishing returns in government experience, but a point at which more becomes counterproductive. It may be that longer-term government employees spend most of that time in lower-level positions, and they may thus have failed to acquire high-level contacts.

High-level contacts do appear to be of some value in achieving success. The number of notables known by the respondent—a measure of connections with people who count—has a significant association with success. The employment of the respondent by a professional association also has a significant positive value, indicating that professional associations enjoy relatively high levels of success when they are active. Their activity, however, is largely restricted to the health domain.

Economic liberalism has a significant negative association with success—that is, the more liberal the respondent, the lower the success score. About half of the issues were drawn from the first two years of the Reagan administration, when the conservatives were vanquishing all foes, but the other half were drawn from the latter years of the Carter administration. We devote some attention below to the question of whether liberals fared notably better under Carter than under Reagan.

In regression analyses done separately on each of the four policy domains, the amounts of variance explained range from a high of 22% in the energy domain to a low of 16% in both agriculture and labor. With the exception of the health domain (which is deviant, as was noted above) the variables that make significant contributions to the regression equations in each of these domains are some combination of those that were significant in the overall, four-domain model.

The findings of these regression analyses, then, suggest that federal government experience is useful in the work of Washington representatives up to a point, that those who have frequent contact with influential representatives are themselves likely to be influential, and that economic ideology is significantly associated with success even though most of the issues are essentially nonideological in character, perhaps because ideology indicates one's location in relevant decision-making networks.

The most important point, however, is that so much of the variance in success is not explained by these analyses. This suggests that the determinants of success are usually situation specific. The outcomes appear to turn less on the presence or absence of broad variables—organizational resources, political finance activity, partisan political affiliation, lawyers' skills, or the pursuit of a congressional or an executive branch strategy—than on much more particular factors that vary from issue to issue.

The issues examined were, of course, among those that had reached the public agenda for decision, a set that constitutes a relatively small percentage of all issues. These issue events had therefore been preceded by a great deal of winnowing, redefinition, and trading on matters of both substance and priority. They were followed by further political activity. They are therefore snapshots taken at a particular point during the course of a much longer series of events. It is not correct to think of them as end games. Battles remained to be fought on almost all of these matters.

The representatives' choices or options were therefore highly constrained by the interaction of the events with other events—past, present, and future. An interest group may choose to concede the outcome of a given matter in order to achieve strategic advantage elsewhere. Thus, it may choose to lay down a sacrifice bunt. It is an out, but it advances the cause. Should we construe that as a success or a defeat? For most interest groups, the top priority is survival. The outcome of any particular issue will be less important than that the group lives to fight again. Given the surrounding circumstances, therefore, success might be defined in any number of ways. It will not necessarily mean that the group "won." Presumably, when we asked the respondents to assess the extent to which their client or organization had achieved its objectives on an issue event, they are likely to have perceived the matter in terms of the overall context, in terms that took into account the benefits, risks, and losses that both preceded and followed the event.

All of this suggests that one of the reasons why it is difficult to account for success may be that the meaning of success is uncertain or ambiguous. It is certainly a function of expectations; if one does better than was expected, that is often perceived as success. We have some evidence of these varying perceptions. Different representatives of the same organization sometimes gave us different assessments of the success of the organization on an event. In 94 (or about 21%) of the 442 instances where we have reports from more than one representative of an organization on the same event, the assessments of success differ substantially. Partly, then, the modest level of the explained variance may be attributable to the fact that success is so much a matter of perception, and different observers assess the same situation differently. But it is no doubt also low because the factors that determine success vary from issue to issue.

Veto Groups and Agenda Control

We explored the obvious hypothesis that liberal representatives might be more successful during the Carter administration and conservatives relatively more successful during the Reagan administration. We divided the representatives into three categories based on their economic liberalism scores: those who had scores higher than 3.25 were categorized as liberals; those who had scores lower than 2.75 were labeled conservatives; and those between were placed in the moderate category. We then computed the reported success of these three groups on issue events that took place in the Carter administration versus those that occurred during the Reagan administration (Table 11.4).

In the agriculture domain, conservatives appear to fare better than liberals. In both administrations, the success scores increase as the economic liberalism scores decrease across the three categories. There is a decline in the success of all three liberalism categories from Carter to Reagan, but the rank order of the three categories is unchanged and all three decline by approximately the same amount. This suggests that success on agriculture issues was more difficult to achieve during the Reagan administration, for everyone, possibly because the politics of agriculture became more unsettled.

The labor domain displays a similar pattern. There, success also declines in all three categories from Carter to Reagan, but the amounts of decline are more unevenly distributed—indeed, the conservatives' success is essentially unchanged, and the rank order of the categories reverses. Conservatives are the least successful group under Carter

Table 11.4 Success on the issue events, by economic liberalism categories, in the Carter and Reagan administrations

	Carter administration		Reagan administration		
	Mean Success[a]	N	Mean Success[a]	N	Change
Agriculture domain					
Liberals[b]	3.18	34	2.81	39	−.37
Moderates[c]	3.22	37	2.92	43	−.30
Conservatives[d]	3.62	65	3.30	75	−.32
Energy domain					
Liberals	2.86	32	3.56	33	+.70
Moderates	3.25	39	3.17	39	−.08
Conservatives	3.15	69	3.45	75	+.30
Health domain					
Liberals	3.02	60	3.27	62	+.25
Moderates	3.86	40	3.35	55	−.51
Conservatives	3.74	37	3.01	41	−.73
Labor domain					
Liberals	3.45	61	3.02	87	−.43
Moderates	3.45	18	3.09	26	−.36
Conservatives	3.24	32	3.18	47	−.06

a. Higher score = greater success: 1 = client achieved "none of its objectives"; 5 = client achieved "all of its objectives."
b. "Liberals" = score of 3.26 or greater.
c. "Moderates" = score of 2.75 to 3.25.
d. "Conservatives" = score of 2.74 and below.

and the most successful group under Reagan, while liberals move from the top of the heap under Carter to last place under Reagan. This might have been expected.

In the energy and health domains, however, we see some surprising findings. In both of those domains, liberals report greater success under Reagan than under Carter. In fact, the liberals and the conservatives actually exchange positions in those domains—conservatives being the more successful group in both during the Carter administration, and liberals becoming the more successful group in the Reagan administration. In the energy domain, the success rates of both liberals and conservatives improve from Carter to Reagan, but the success of liberals improves far more. In health, the liberals' scores improve while the conservatives' scores decline markedly.

What, then, is the salient difference between the energy and health domains, on the one hand, where the liberals' success increases under Reagan, and the labor domain, where the relative position of the liberals weakens during the Reagan administration? The pattern could be explained if the Reagan forces gained control of the policy agenda in the energy and health domains, while the unions continued to control the agenda in the labor domain. If that were the case, then the increased success of the liberals on energy and health issues might have been success in blocking Reagan policy initiatives—that is, success in defeating Reagan proposals rather than success in advancing their own policies—while the liberals in the labor domain were still trying, with diminishing success, to advance their own initiatives. Then the pattern would be the result of veto group politics: whoever was playing defense was successful. This observation, however, also makes it clear that the success scores give us only a partial or particular view of success. No matter how effective the defense, one cannot ultimately win a contest if one remains on defense during the entire game. Thus, agenda control is as essential to victory as is success on the individual events.

To explore this further, we examined the difference between the success scores of proponents and opponents of the policy proposals during the Carter administration and during the Reagan years, further divided by economic liberalism categories. The findings for all of the health and labor issues on which there is a significant difference in the economic liberalism scores of the proponents and opponents are reported in Table 11.5. (For the mean economic liberalism scores of the respondents favoring and opposing these proposals, see Table 11.2.) In the health domain during the Carter administration, the three proposals on which there was a clear ideological difference between proponents and opponents were all sponsored by liberals. During the Reagan administration, all of the proposals with a significant ideological split were sponsored by conservatives. This is consistent with the thesis that liberals moved from control of the agenda under Carter to a more reactive role under Reagan. But the proponents lose on six of these seven health issues. (On the seventh—the attempt to restrict the Federal Trade Commission's jurisdiction over state-licensed professionals, including physicians—the outcome was more ambiguous or more evenly balanced.) Since the proponents almost always lost, regardless of whether they were liberal or conservative and regardless of the issue, liberals would achieve higher success scores merely by moving from the role of proponent to the role

Table 11.5   Success scores of proponents and opponents of liberal and conservative policy proposals in the health and labor domains

	Sponsors[a]	Success scores (N) Proponents	Opponents	Proponents minus opponents
Health				
Carter administration				
Hospital cost control	liberal	1.9 (16)	4.6 (39)	−2.7
Medicare reporting	liberal	3.0 (9)	4.1 (11)	−1.1
Food labeling	liberal	2.0 (2)	4.2 (9)	−2.2
Reagan administration				
Drug patents	conservative	2.2 (8)	5.0 (3)	−2.8
HMO financing	conservative	2.7 (25)	3.4 (25)	−0.7
Delaney clause	conservative	1.8 (9)	4.6 (5)	−2.8
Limits on FTC	conservative	4.0 (19)	3.9 (8)	+0.1
Labor				
Carter administration				
Common situs picketing	liberal	2.2 (41)	4.8 (27)	−2.6
Minimum wage	liberal	4.2 (29)	2.8 (14)	+1.4
Youth subminimum wage	conservative	1.2 (9)	4.5 (18)	−3.3
Davis-Bacon waiver	conservative	1.9 (7)	3.9 (11)	−2.0
Chrysler aid	liberal	4.7 (10)	3.0 (3)	+1.7
OSHA inspection exemption	conservative	2.7 (18)	3.9 (19)	−1.2
OSHA employee records	liberal	4.3 (11)	3.1 (10)	+1.2
Reagan administration				
Cotton dust	liberal	4.8 (14)	3.7 (3)	+1.1
Unemployment aid cuts	conservative	4.4 (10)	2.3 (23)	+2.1
CETA termination	conservative	4.0 (10)	1.8 (19)	+2.2
Social Security cuts	conservative	3.0 (3)	3.0 (20)	0
Affirm. action exemption	conservative	3.2 (16)	2.7 (11)	+0.5
Multiemployer pensions	conservative	1.8 (25)	4.0 (14)	−2.2
5 cent gas tax	liberal	4.4 (19)	1.6 (5)	+2.8
Domestic content	liberal	3.0 (16)	2.6 (8)	+0.4
Immigration reform	liberal	1.8 (10)	4.1 (14)	−2.3

a. See Table 11.2.

of opponent—by moving from offense to defense. Thus, the pattern of success is accounted for by agenda control in a context of veto group politics.

The evidence in the labor domain, however, is less clear. To support the veto group thesis, we should find that liberals retained substantial control of the agenda. The relative success of conservatives under Reagan might, then, be attributed to their ability to veto liberal proposals. But our findings on the labor issues are more equivocal. On the issues with a clear ideological split, liberals do appear in the proponent role during both the Carter and Reagan administrations, but they are slightly more often proponents under Carter and opponents under Reagan. This is not consistent, therefore, with the thesis that organized labor maintained dominant control over the agenda during the entire period.

Moreover, we find that, although conservatives lost on all three of the proposals they sponsored during the Carter administration, liberals scored clear wins on three of the four proposals they sponsored during the Carter administration, and they suffered only one clear loss in the four initiatives that they backed during the Reagan administration. The conservatives scored clear wins on two proposals and suffered only one clear loss in the five proposals that they sponsored during the Reagan administration. Thus, the liberals did not lose under Reagan because they were predominantly in the role of proponent. They won some and they lost some—as both proponents and opponents. So did the conservatives. But the conservatives simply won more often under Reagan and the liberals more often under Carter. This observation does not require any arcane explanation.

The question remains, however, why the energy domain is not like this—why did the liberals have greater success there under Reagan than under Carter? This certainly cannot be explained by agenda control. Liberals are found in the opponent role on energy issues more often under Carter than they are under Reagan, and the increase in liberals' success during the Reagan years is clearly attributable to their success as proponents rather than as opponents (Table 11.6).[7] Moreover, conservatives move from predominantly being proponents under Carter to predominantly being opponents under Reagan!

Proponents prevailed more often than did opponents on the energy issues, except in the case of liberals during the Carter administration (Table 11.6). This suggests that, unlike the situation in the health domain, veto group politics was not the norm on energy issues. In fact, there appears to be a clear difference between, on one hand, the agriculture and energy domains, where proponents more often prevail, and health and labor issues, where the opponents are somewhat more successful. The mean success scores in the domains (Table 11.7) suggest that, overall, the policy-making process in the agriculture and energy domains functioned so as to permit policy change. That is, one could propose a policy initiative in those contexts and

Table 11.6   Mean success scores of liberal and conservative respondents on twenty energy policy issues, by role as proponent or opponent

	Liberals[a]		Conservatives[b]	
	Success score	N	Success score	N
On 11 issue events during the Carter administration:				
Proponents	2.7	(33)	3.7	(87)
Opponents	3.1	(28)	2.3	(58)
On 9 issue events during the Reagan administration:				
Proponents	3.7	(35)	3.9	(41)
Opponents	2.5	(13)	3.0	(54)

a. Liberals = economic liberalism scores above 3.25.
b. Conservatives = economic liberalism scores below 2.75.

Table 11.7   Mean success scores, by domain, proponents versus opponents, on twenty issue events in each domain

	Proponents	Opponents	Proponents minus opponents	Significance
Agriculture	3.61	2.55	+1.06	***
Energy	3.62	2.71	+.91	***
Health	3.32	3.57	−.25	*
Labor	3.16	3.39	−.23	N.S.

* $p < .05$ (using t-test). *** $p < .001$ (using t-test).

have a reasonable chance of getting it adopted. In the health and labor domains, fewer proponents report success. Thus, in agriculture and energy the political process appears to have resulted in policy product, for better or worse, while in health and labor the situation was more often a standoff among the competing interest groups, and the status quo therefore prevailed.

All four of the domains display distinct patterns. In agriculture, the conservatives are in control, both under Carter and under Reagan. In health, it appears to be a clear case of veto group politics—the liberals have agenda control under Carter and the conservatives have it under Reagan, but the proponents lose whether they are liberal or conservative. In energy, liberals surprisingly appear to have more agenda control under Reagan than they did under Carter, and the proponents win more often than do opponents. In labor, the pattern is more mixed—liberals and conservatives do not differ markedly in their propensity to sponsor initiatives during the Carter and Reagan administrations, though liberals are somewhat more likely to win under Carter and conservatives are more likely to win under Reagan.

The lessons in all of this appear to be that success on these events is determined by issue-specific variables and that agenda control cannot be assumed to flow inevitably from control of the White House. If conservatives are so emboldened by Reagan's election victory that they seek to repeal the Delaney clause's ban on carcinogens in food, they lose. If liberals mobilize to ban oil and gas leasing in federal wilderness areas, they win, even during the Reagan years. We are of necessity modest, therefore, about our ability to predict wins and losses through the use of broad categorical variables of the sort that social scientists are accustomed to measure. We may, to be sure, make some unexpected observations along the way. We certainly did not expect to find liberals reporting greater success under Reagan in any of the domains. But we cannot claim to possess generalizations that will account for all of these findings.

Conclusion: The Uncertainty of Influence

Though there is clearly some structure in these data, the principal finding of the various sorts of analyses is that there is a considerable degree of uncertainty both in the nature of the decision process and in the outcome of issue events:

> The degree of conflict on the issues and the stability of the interest group coalitions are often directly related, but this is not always the case. It is not the case, in our findings, in the energy domain, where the two appear to be inversely related.
>
> Most of the issues do not significantly involve broad principles of economic ideology, except in the labor policy domain. If ideological divisions were more common, then the alignments of interest groups might be clearer and more stable, but we do find some clear and stable alignments even when the issues are nonideological.

Most important, though the outcomes of individual events may sometimes be foreseen, the respondents' overall rates of success in achieving their objectives cannot be adequately explained by categorical variables. We cannot account for much of the variance in those rates even though we have good measures of several variables that one might expect to enhance influence.

We should therefore consider the possibility that the more important part of the story is not the structure that is undoubtedly present, but the uncertainty or lack of structure. There may be good reasons to think that uncertainty is a necessary part of the policy-making process. Some degree of uncertainty is no doubt essential to the legitimacy of any democratic political system, and, probably, of many nondemocratic systems. The game must not appear to be rigged. Indeed, if winners and losers were known in advance, the losers would not play, and there would thus be no game. Policy making is not an idle pastime. The cost of playing is usually substantial. If the participants did not believe that there was a reasonable likelihood that they could win enough to recover the investment they make in the game, they would not invest. They sometimes have the option of seeking to move the decision into another forum. If they know that they cannot expect to win in the legislature, they may try to have the matter decided in the courts. If they cannot win in the courts, they may take the dispute to the streets. They always have the option of sitting out and "lumping it" (Galanter 1974).

Not all outcomes are uncertain, of course. There are bounds to the uncertainty, and many issues are not contested precisely because there is too much certainty about the outcomes. The contested issues, therefore, take place within the area of uncertainty (Priest and Klein 1984).

There is an important distinction to be made, however, between uncertainty with respect to outcomes and uncertainty regarding strategies or the means used to pursue those outcomes. Game theory makes it clear that there are some situations in which it will not be optimal to play a consistent, or "pure," strategy. Rather, the individual player will optimize his or her position by playing a "mixed strategy"—that is, random moves. Indeed, there are some games in which all players pursue mixed strategies in the equilibrium state. It is possible that Washington representatives deliberately vary their strategies from issue to issue so as to make it more difficult for their opponents to anticipate the moves; but we doubt that, in the all-too-real world of Washington policy making, representatives vary their tactics randomly. No doubt they would articulate some reason other than randomness for the moves they made.

Though we do not find clear patterns of strategy associated with the particular content of the issue events, what we see for the most part is that larger issues differ from smaller ones. On large issues, the interest groups tend to do everything they can. That is, they expend considerable resources and they pursue multiple strategies—presumably, all of the strategies or options that are open to them. On smaller issues, the groups do less. They expend fewer resources and they pick their shots. This is, of course, a quite rational way to proceed.

The uncertainty that we are principally concerned with, then, is uncertainty about outcomes rather than uncertainty about means or process, though it is no doubt the case that representatives are often uncertain about which of several possible strategies might best advance their interests. They must decide what to do—indeed, decide whether to play the game or not—under conditions of quite limited information and in a highly dynamic context where the conditions may change very rapidly.

One of the tenets of pluralist theory, at least as articulated by Nelson Polsby, is that there is "uncertainty about the distributions of payoffs of political actions" (Polsby 1980, 136). But we do not want to be understood as suggesting, as Polsby did not, that our findings paint a happy view of a pluralist heaven in which every citizen has a decent chance of having his or her voice heard, or at least of having his or her needs and wants considered. With rare exceptions, the truly dispossessed are not represented by organized groups. They may occasionally be represented in the health and labor domains, but they seldom are in agriculture or energy. (Perhaps this is part of the reason why it is more difficult to reach the requisite degree of consensus in the former two domains.) Essentially all of the players we have studied are powerful. Some, no doubt, are more powerful than others. But all had enough power to get onto the playing field, which distinguishes them from many other persons and groups. In contests within this set of relatively powerful actors, outcomes are difficult to predict or even to account for after the fact. The uncertainty before the fact may well be essential to the maintenance of the system.

APPENDIX: Policy Events, 1977–1982

Agriculture Events

1979

April
1. USDA's Food Safety and Inspection Service establishes a "modified traditional inspection procedure," increasing the maximum rate at which chicken carcasses pass inspectors to seventy birds per minute.

May
2. House Agriculture Committee reports HR 2172, increasing federal sugar price supports. (Measure is defeated by full House in October.)

May
3. Senate reauthorizes FIFRA (Federal Insecticide, Fungicide and Rodenticide Act). (House passes similar measure in November.)

June
4. House Ways and Means Committee approves HR 4537, a measure to allow implementation of the Geneva Multilateral Trade Negotiations agreement, which reduces tariffs and expands quotas on imports in exchange for assurances that Europe will not subsidize exports to Third World agricultural markets.

September
5. Senate clears S 14, reforming sections of the 1902 Water Reclamation Act, increasing by four times the amount of federally irrigated land a farmer can own, and exempting California farms from any acreage restrictions. (Measure before House Interior Committee at year's end.)

November
6. Senate Finance Committee approves HR 2727, establishing a countercyclical formula for meat import quotas.

November
7. Conference Committee amends HR 4930, the Interior-Energy appropriations for fiscal year 1980, to allow ranchers greater access to federal courts to challenge restrictions on the use of overgrazed federal land.

December
8. The FDA, the FTC, and the USDA announce a joint initiative in food labeling, including declaration of ingredients and extended open-date and nutritional labeling in standard food items.

1980

March
9. Congress clears HR 3398, raising wheat and corn target prices by 7%.

September   10. Congress clears S 1125, suspending federal disaster aid payments after 1981 and expanding Federal Crop Insurance Corporation coverage of crop losses.

September   11. Senate votes to cut off funds necessary to continue Soviet grain embargo.

1981
March   12. Congress clears S 509, canceling a 90-cent-per-hundredweight increase in dairy price supports enacted the previous year.

May   13. Congress considers replacing the Delaney clause's ban on carcinogens in food by establishing tolerance levels and a gradual phaseout of suspect additives.

July   14. Congress clears HR 3982, the Omnibus Budget Reconciliation Act of 1981, including provisions to raise interest rates on federally guaranteed farm loans.

1982
July   15. Congress clears HR 6590, requiring tobacco growers to repay the federal government for losses in price support loans and rejecting a move to subject tobacco price supports to periodic congressional review.

August   16. Congress clears HR 6955, the Omnibus Budget Reconciliation Act of 1982, cutting billions of dollars in federal aid in food stamps, feeding programs for the aged, and school lunches.

September   17. Congress clears HR 5831, deferring certain FMHA loans and raising the debt ceiling for total farmer indebtedness.

October   18. The Bureau of Land Management considers plans to increase the timber harvest from the "old growth" stands it manages in western Oregon.

December   19. Congress clears HR 5447, reauthorizing the Commodity Futures Trading Commission, strengthening state enforcement against fraud, allowing the CFTC to charge the industry for services, and defining the jurisdiction of the SEC and the CFTC on financial instruments.

December   20. Agriculture Secretary Block proposes "Payment in Kind" (PIK) plan, under which farmers who retire up to one-half of their cropland in 1983 will be reimbursed in surplus crops. (Congress later approves the program.)

Energy Events

1978

October   1. Congress passes HR 5289, allowing prices of newly discovered natural gas to rise 10% per year until complete decontrol in 1985.

1979

May   2. House Interior Committee votes for a six-month moratorium on nuclear plant construction following Three Mile Island. (Amendment to the NRC authorization is killed in November.)

May   3. The EPA adopts tougher sulphur emission standards for new coal-fired power plants.

June   4. The House Banking Committee proposes development of the synthetic fuel industry. (Congress passes S 932 in March 1980.)

August   5. House Committees report bills to create an Energy Mobilization Board. (Passed by Senate but eventually killed in conference in March 1980.)

September   6. Senate passes S 1403, exempting state plans from direct regulation by the Office of Surface Mining regulations and requiring instead that states meet the goals of the 1977 surface mining act.

1980

March   7. Congress passes HR 3919, a Windfall Profits Tax on decontrolled oil.

May   8. House passes HJ Res 655, overturning FERC regulations imposing higher natural gas rates on industrial users than on other consumers.

May   9. The DOE considers issuing building energy performance standards that set limits on total energy consumption in new buildings and set different costs for various energy sources.

June   10. Senate Energy Committee reports a bill to subsidize the conversion of 80 oil-powered utility plants to coal. (S 2470 passed by Senate.)

December   11. Conference committee reports S 2189, leaving responsibility for low-level nuclear waste to the states.

1981

July   12. In the Budget Reconciliation Act, Congress clears a three-year reauthorization for Solar Energy Banks.

September   13. FERC announces that state and local governments have to apply for hydroelectric power sites without private co-signers to qualify for municipal preference benefit.

October   14. Senate clears S 1053, empowering the president to allocate and set prices for oil in an energy emergency. (Passed in 1982, vetoed by President Reagan.)

December   15. Congress clears SJ Res. 115, authorizing waivers for private financing of the Alaska natural gas pipeline and permitting early billing of potential consumers for pipeline construction.

December   16. Congress passes HR 5159, the Black Lung Disability Trust Fund Bill, which increases tax on coal to provide benefits to miners.

1982

August   17. Senate Environment and Public Works Committee reports S 3041, reauthorizing the Clean Air Act.

December   18. Congress clears HR 6211, the Transportation Assistance Act of 1982, placing a five-cent-per-gallon tax on gasoline.

December   19. Congress clears HR 7359, banning oil and gas leasing in federal wilderness areas until September 1983.

December   20. Congress clears HJ Res. 631, continuing funding for the Clinch River Breeder Reactor program.

Health Events

1979

May   1. The House Ways and Means Committee indefinitely postpones consideration of HR 2626 (S 570), Carter's hospital cost control bill, providing mandatory revenue controls if the industry fails to hold revenue increases to 9.7% in 1979.

June   2. The Senate Finance Committee approves the $6.4 billion, $3,500 deductible, "catastrophic" health insurance plan of Russell Long.

October   3. Congress passes S 544, reauthorizing health planning and exempting HMO's from Certificate of Need processes.

October   4. The FDA proposes mandatory package inserts for all prescription drugs.

October   5. HEW proposes eliminating capitation grants.

November   6. Under authority of PL 95-142, the Health Care Financing Administration proposes uniform cost reporting for Medicare and Medicaid programs.

December   7. The FDA, the FTC, and the USDA announce a joint initiative in food labeling, including declaration of ingredients and extended open-date and nutritional labeling in standard food items.

December   8. The House approves HR 4962, upgrading and expanding CHAP (Child Health Assurance Program).

1980
February   9. The National Institutes of Health change guidelines on recombinant DNA research, exempting many researchers from NIH registration procedures.

May   10. The Senate Labor and Human Resources Committee reports a bill (S 988) proposing specific authorization procedures for each of the eleven National Institutes of Health, including "sunset" provisions for authorizations and the establishment of a presidential commission to set funding priorities.

September   11. Congress approves the Mental Health Systems Act (S 1177, HR 4156) extending the Community Mental Health Center Act through fiscal 1981 and authorizing states to award new grants.

1981
April   12. The Congressional Office of Technical Assessment proposes longer-running patents for prescription drugs.

April   13. The Reagan administration proposes phasing out health planning, PSRO's, and federal financing for HMO's.

May   14. Congress considers replacing the Delaney clause ban on carcinogens in food by establishing tolerance levels and a gradual phaseout of suspect additives.

June   15. Congress considers a $500 to $700 million cut in Medicare by repealing periodic interim payments.

July   16. The Reagan administration proposes reducing the availability of low-interest loans to medical students.

December   17. The Reagan administration proposes relaxing federal legislation regarding patients in long-term care facilities.

1982
October   18. The Department of Health and Human Services proposes a prospective payment system for Medicare based on diagnosis-related groups.

December   19. Reagan administration aides urge changes in the taxation of health insurance benefits, including ceilings on tax-exempt coverage.

December   20. The House votes to restrict the FTC's jurisdiction over state-licensed professionals, including medical doctors.

Labor Events

1977

October   1. The House clears the Labor Reform Bill (HR 8410), giving labor additional remedies against employers who block unionization and legalizing common situs picketing. (Died in Senate at end of 1978.)

October   2. Minimum wage increase with indexing to 1980 receives final passage (HR 3774).

October   3. Move to amend HR 3774 with subminimum wage for youth fails in House.

1979

July   4. The Senate Armed Services Committee reports the Military Construction Bill (S 1319) waiving the Davis-Bacon Act prevailing wage requirements for military construction. (The waiver is deleted before final passage.)

December   5. The Chrysler financial aid package (HR 5860) receives final passage.

December   6. Senator Schweiker proposes S 2153, which would exempt many U.S. businesses from OSHA investigation.

1980

May   7. The Labor Department issues final regulations requiring employers to maintain employee health records for at least thirty years and allow workers, their representatives, and OSHA officials access to the records.

July   8. The House passes HR 6613, barring the Federal Maritime Commission from regulating collective bargaining in the maritime industry.

1981

June   9. The Supreme Court upholds OSHA's cotton dust standard against a challenge by the textile industry.

July	10. HR 3982, the Omnibus Budget Reconciliation Act of 1981, cutting federal-state unemployment programs by $3.1 billion, receives final passage.
July	11. The Budget Reconciliation Act terminates CETA Title IID and VI public service jobs programs.
July	12. The $122-per-month Social Security minimum benefit is eliminated by the Budget Reconciliation Act. (Restored by HR 4331 in December.)
July	13. Senator Nickles introduces S 1541, a bill changing the reporting requirements and investment rules imposed on single-employer pension plans and prohibiting companies from dumping pension disabilities on the PBGC.
August	14. The OFCCP proposes raising the threshold amount of government contracts requiring a written affirmative action proposal from 50 workers and $50,000 to 250 workers and $1,000,000.
October	15. Senator Hatch introduces S 1748, exempting firms in most multiemployer pension plans from the liabilities that PL 96-364 imposed upon withdrawal from plans.
December	16. Congress passes HR 5159, the Black Lung Disability Trust Fund Bill, which increases tax on coal to provide benefits to miners.

1982

December	17. Final passage of HR 6211, the Transportation Assistance Act of 1982, which places a five-cents-per-gallon tax on gasoline.
December	18. The House passes HR 5153, the Domestic Content Bill.
December	19. The House defeats HR 7357, the Immigration Reform Bill.
December	20. Final passage of HR 7102, which replaces the Farm Labor Contractor Registration Act with a new set of federal protections for migrant and seasonal workers.

Chapter 12

Conclusion:
Structure and Uncertainty in
Private Interest Representation

The representation of private interests poses a central paradox. Although greater numbers of organizations of all types—business corporations, unions, public interest groups, trade and professional associations, state and local governments—actively monitor and participate in the making of national policy, and although the scope and intensity of their efforts has increased significantly, the returns on these efforts are not at all clear. No single category of interest groups, be it business organizations, labor unions, or professional associations, proved more successful than others in achieving policy objectives in the events we analyzed in the period from 1978 to 1982. Nor did any group unambiguously seize control of the agenda for policy making during this period.

While some may argue that the installation of the Reagan presidency marked the triumph of business and conservative interests, the evidence of a conservative victory in national policy making is weak. The Reagan administration won some notable battles over tax and fiscal policies, but other conservative initiatives—on the environment, food safety, civil rights, employment standards, and entitlement programs—were defeated. The much-heralded shift toward more conservative federal policies was far more a product of Reagan appointments to the courts and executive agencies than of any change in the system of private representation. If anything, the politics of interest representation within policy domains tended to resist and modify the Reagan program.

Given the uncertainty of the benefits, why then should interest groups continue to invest in private representation? Why have we seen substantial growth in the number of representatives? Is it possible that even though there are more representatives—working in larger and more sophisticated organizational units and commanding higher incomes—they in fact possess less power than in earlier periods? In this chapter we examine this seeming paradox and speculate about its implications.

Structure and Uncertainty: An Organizational Theory of Interest Representation

Our findings reveal what appears to be a curious combination of structure and uncertainty in the social organization of interest representation. In many respects, the policy domains we have studied reflect a high degree of structure: the social characteristics and behaviors of both individual and organizational actors exhibit clear, sociologically interpretable patterns (Giddens 1984). One might expect such highly structured systems to produce relatively stable, predictable policy outcomes. Yet our analyses of a large set of policy events from 1977 to 1982 reveal considerable uncertainty in the policy-making process, both in terms of what items received serious consideration and in terms of who won and lost.

This pattern could be explained in relatively straightforward game-theory fashion. Many games are designed to have a stable set of rules and players and yet produce a series of changing outcomes. Civil litigation appears to work in a similar fashion, in that plaintiffs and defendants who go to trial win in roughly equal proportions (Priest and Klein 1984; but see Gross and Syverud 1991). One could construct a parallel argument for the case of interest representation: policy events that reach some kind of discrete decision point often are highly contested. While this makes it difficult to predict the outcome in any single event, there is an overall stability in the set of outcomes produced by the system. Each of the contending parties will win some and lose some.

The simplicity of a game model is appealing and may have some validity here. But such an approach has some serious limitations in this context. First, interest representation presents very different possibilities for outcomes than do civil trials. In civil litigation, cases in which one side has clearly inferior odds of success are likely to settle, with the result that most tried cases will be among the most uncertain. There is no parallel mechanism in the policy-making process that maximizes uncertainty in individual outcomes while establishing a stable result in a series of events. It is common for some policy measures to be adopted by one-sided majorities, often because the "settlements" are ratified by the legislature (Steiner and Gove 1960). The proposals we studied varied enormously in the number of participants and the level of conflict and consensus among the participants. Nor was there a clear correspondence between these patterns and the likelihood of adoption of the policy proposals, either in particular cases or as a series of outcomes. Second, game-theoretic conceptions typically assume a fixed set of parameters in terms of the number and character of players and the rules or conventions that govern play. But it is exactly these dimensions that are the fastest changing, least studied, and potentially most important aspects of the system of interest representation. Why are so many players drawn to these systems? Why have the players expanded the scope and intensity of their involvement? Why do their strategies for representation follow set patterns?

To account for the patterns we observe, it is necessary to develop a theory that explains the relationship between structure and uncertainty in terms of the organizational dynamics of representation. Our findings and the literature on interest representation suggest that structure and uncertainty are mutually reinforcing processes. In the attempt to deal with bigger stakes and rising uncertainty in the policy-making process, interests have organized their representational activities to reinforce control over their agents, to increase the amount of policy-relevant information they process, and to expand their capacity to participate in policy deliberations. It is now widely accepted as legitimate, indeed necessary, for organizations to devote significant resources to interest representation. Most major corporate actors employ a group of specialists whose work consists of monitoring the risks and opportunities posed to the organization (or its constituencies) by the policy-making process. Yet, in the process of creating structures to control or adapt to uncertainty, they have contributed to the development of a more complex and rapidly changing policy-making environment. Interest representation has thus become a self-reproducing organizational field.

The Structural Tendencies of the Interest Representation System

We speak of "structural tendencies" of the system of interest representation to emphasize the probabilistic and evolving character of the structures. The structures are probabilistic in the sense that not all organizations manifest the same characteristics in the same degree, and they are evolving because the organizational context is in flux. Though our principal findings are based on cross-sectional measures, both the historical indicators contained in our data on individual careers and organizational origins and those found in other sources demonstrate that the overall size and the organizational patterns of the interest representation system have changed significantly.

Many of the features of interest representation are quite plausibly seen as organizational responses to uncertainty. It is not necessary to argue, however, nor do we intend to argue, that uncertainty is the only force driving these tendencies. Some of these characteristics would tend to reproduce themselves regardless of the level of uncertainty in the system. In the absence of adequate longitudinal data, it is impossible to test a strong version of our thesis directly—that is, to test whether increasing uncertainty in policy-making processes has called forth the structural patterns we observe. Nonetheless, it seems quite likely that uncertainty accentuates these trends.

PRINCIPAL–AGENT RELATIONSHIPS

In contrast to the historically dominant conception of Washington representatives as free agents, based in law or consulting firms and retained by clients on an episodic basis, we found that organizational employees outnumbered freestanding professionals four to one. Even the freestanding professionals typically had represented their clients for three years or more, which suggests that their work is not episodic. The representatives who were most active in policy-making activities and in formulating the objectives of client organizations were the government affairs officers employed directly by client organizations. Only about a third of the client organizations utilized external representatives for advice on policy positions. Our analyses of tasks performed, specialization by subfield, and patterns of contact with government agencies indicate that external lawyers were primarily used for specialized legal functions, such as advocacy before courts or administrative agencies. Thus, the representatives with the most involvement in determining the goals and strategies of interest organizations were, if not principals themselves, a set of agents under direct and continuous monitoring by their principals.

The preference for organizational employees over external representatives might be explained in part by cost. External lawyers report the highest median incomes among our sample, which implies that their hourly charges are substantially higher than the per-hour costs of internal personnel. Given sufficient demand for monitoring and other services, therefore, it will cost less for organizations to hire their own representatives than to rely on outside producers. But client organizations may also prefer employees over whom they have greater control. One of our early informants in this research, a law firm partner who had relocated from the firm's main office to the firm's Washington office, reported that his institutional clients were delighted to have a "main office partner" in Washington. They had expressed concern that old Washington hands might have been "co-opted by the process" and thus might not identify with their positions. Whether the pattern is motivated by cost or control, interest representation is now dominated by agents who are tightly linked to specific client organizations. This structure of principal–agent relationships should minimize one kind of uncertainty—whether clients can trust their representatives to pursue the organization's interest without compromise.

RECRUITMENT PATTERNS

The manner of recruitment of representatives produces social and ideological differentiation *across* categories of interest organizations, and social and ideological similarity *within* categories of organizations. Ethno-religious identification, father's occupation, and political party affiliation are significantly related to the probability that representatives will work for liberal groups or for business interests. Jews, the children of the working class and the professional class, and Democrats are far more likely to represent unions or citizen/government groups than are representatives from other social backgrounds. Protestants, the children of owners or managers and of sales and clerical workers, and Republicans are far more likely to work exclusively for businesses or trade associations. We also found a close correspondence between the regional origins of representatives and the types of organizations that employ them. Professional associations and labor unions draw a large proportion of representatives from the Northeast, while trade associations, especially in agriculture and energy, recruit primarily from the South and West. Women are more likely to be found in professional associations and citizen-government groups than in other contexts; racial minorities hardly appear in our sample, but the few who do tend to be concentrated in nonprofit organizations and unions.

In our preliminary fieldwork, we often heard assertions that political party affiliation and social background rarely mattered in the sophisticated world of Washington representation. We, too, had assumed that these representatives were a relatively homogeneous group—uniformly well-educated, from a narrow range of social backgrounds, serving clients that consisted overwhelmingly of large corporate actors. Certainly, we thought that Washington representatives would be far less stratified by class and ethno-religious lines than Heinz and Laumann had found to be the case among Chicago lawyers (1982). While the stratification was less pronounced than that among Chicago lawyers and while Washington representatives were homogeneous in some respects, especially with respect to race and gender, we found that the social and political characteristics of representatives were important dimensions of the social structure of representation. Representatives were not, apparently, hired primarily to maximize either skill or access to government officials. Rather, representatives were selected to match the characteristics of their clients. Organizations often "grow their own" representatives. But, even when representatives change employers, there is a strong tendency for them to work for the same type of organization. Rarely did our respondents "cross sides" in the sense that they moved from representing a business or trade association to representing a union or public interest group, or vice versa.

Organizational recruitment along class, ethnic, or gender lines is hardly an unusual phenomenon. There are some suggestions that ascriptive characteristics play a more significant role in hiring and promotion decisions at the top of organizations, where the costs of indulging preferences for socially similar workers are relatively small in proportion to overall labor costs and where close working relationships are required (see, for example, Kanter 1977; Cohn 1985). These processes may well be operating here. Trust or confidence is highly valued in the choice of Washington representatives. Some 70% of the sample of representatives agreed with the statement "The matters on which I work tend to require a strong identification between the interests of the client organization and their representatives, such that representatives do not 'switch sides' by moving from one organization to another with opposing views." Interest organizations prefer representatives who have grown up in their own industry or organization, or who at least share their social characteristics. This tends to minimize dissonance within the organization's decision-making councils. Given the conflictual and uncertain nature of the work of interest representation, client organizations apparently attempt to minimize both the conflict and the uncertainty by assembling socially and ideologically similar individuals.

COLLEAGUE NETWORKS

When asked to name the three individuals with whom they were most likely to discuss their work, our sample typically listed persons who worked in the same organization and shared social and political characteristics. This is more evidence that information predominantly flows within interest alliances rather than among them. Thus, while the literature on policy networks tends to emphasize interorganizational exchange and the wide diffusion of policy information among the various segments of a policy community, our data on collegial networks indicate that most exchange does not cross boundaries of group interest, social characteristics, or political ideology. Instead, policy discussions primarily take place with persons who can be trusted: employees of the same organization or persons with similar social and political characteristics. The density of within-group ties may enhance the sense of solidarity within a group, but it may also accentuate the sense of antagonism with other actors in the policy system. Indeed, the configuration of interorganizational relationships and elite networks suggests that interest groups rely primarily on direct representation or on relatively narrow coalitions of allies rather than on brokering institutions or centrally located elites.

THE RISE OF DIRECT PARTICIPATION BY INTEREST GROUPS

The interest representation system may once have been dominated by peak associations or umbrella groups—such as the American Farm Bureau in agriculture, the American Petroleum Institute in energy, the American Medical Association in health, and the Chamber of Commerce, the National Association of Manufacturers, and the AFL-CIO in labor—but today a much more diverse set of actors participates directly in policy-making processes. Individual businesses and nonprofit organizations continue to work through established associations, but now also monitor policy issues themselves, develop more specialized interest coalitions, and pursue their own strategies. The number of major business corporations operating offices in Washington increased from 50 in 1961 to 545 in 1982 (Yoffie 1985).

This trend is apparent in our sample. Some 43% of the representatives were employed by organizations that had opened Washington offices after 1970, some 26% as recently as 1977. Most numerous among these organizations were business and professional associations, who had presumably relied on peak organizations for a Washington presence before they established their own Washington offices. The peak associations are now joined by specialized associations—such as the American Cotton Shippers, the Western Cotton Growers, and the U.S. Beet Sugar Association in agriculture; and the National Association of Area Councils on Aging, the Health Insurance Association of America, and the American Association of Medical Colleges in health—as well as major business firms and institutions such as Cargill, Archer-Daniels-Midland, and Quaker Oats in agriculture; and Blue Cross/Blue Shield, Miles Laboratories, and Mt. Sinai Hospital in health.

The principal reason for the growth of direct representation is straightforward. As accounts of the collapse of the farm bloc illustrate (see Heinz 1962; Browne 1988), peak associations cannot always satisfy the policy preferences of their diverse constituencies. Larger associations tend to take positions that minimize internal conflict, thus encouraging specialized interests to develop independent strategies (Berry 1984, 202–205; Lynn and McKeown 1988, 110–112). Peak associations can no longer prevent individual members from breaking ranks and thus are unable to deliver the support of major constituencies. As a result, contestants find it more difficult to assess the level of support or opposition that policy proposals are likely to face. The fragmentation of interest aggregates thus increases the uncertainties of the policy-making process.

A corollary of the growth of direct representation is that organizations with similar interest portfolios form alliances. We found that interest organizations are far more likely to name organizations of the same type as their allies (for example, oil and gas companies naming other oil and gas companies), while they typically identify organizations of a different type as adversaries (for example, oil and gas companies naming environmental groups). This can be seen as an analogue at the organizational level of our finding about the nature of collegial networks: organizations are more likely to form ties with organizations like themselves.

A distinct but related phenomenon appears with respect to governmental and public interest groups. While consumers, welfare claimants, environmentalists, and other public interest constituencies formerly relied on indirect representation by organized labor or the political parties, these groups are now represented by recently created citizen groups. Some 76% of citizens' organizations and 79% of welfare groups with offices in Washington in 1981 had come into existence since 1960 (Schlozman and Tierney 1986, 76; Walker 1983). Although these groups are still considerably outnumbered by other types of organizations, they occupy a distinctive place in the interest representation system. Such externality groups were most frequently named as adversaries by the representatives of business, trade, and professional associations. But it is not just the presence of externality groups that destabilizes the policy process; their tactics are also upsetting to the more established interests. Externality groups of the mass-citizen variety, lacking the stable institutional bases provided by business interests or organized labor, often attempt mass public mobilization and use dramatic, headline-grabbing strategies rather than the inside strategies of negotiation. Their interventions and accusations, even if not effective in the long run, disturb existing relationships between officials and interests.

ELITE NETWORK STRUCTURES

Contrary to assertions that mediating elites integrate the demands of conflicting interest groups, we found that the networks of representatives are arranged in spheres with hollow cores. Elites are positioned around the surface of the sphere, in proximity to their client groups. Such configurations probably form because the participants are unwilling to cede power to a central broker. The exchange of information thus proceeds around the surface of the sphere, which slows the rate at which decisions are processed but reduces the likelihood that any one group will manipulate the decision-making process.

One might explain this pattern by postulating a core consisting of government officials. Because our research design did not permit us to include government officials in the network analyses, one could argue that we have simply failed to identify the central actors. This would suggest that the balkanized character of interest groups empowers government officials, who can play contending groups against each other and select policy positions compatible with their own interests and ideology. Accordingly, the interest representation system may appear uncertain from the perspective of contending interest groups, but more controlled and certain from the vantage of government officials.

As the preceding sentence indicates, the centrality of government officials would not contradict the thesis we are advancing—that the social organization of representation has developed in response to perceived uncertainty in the policy-making process. If government officials are autonomous from interest group demands, that will make the system more uncertain for the groups. "Captured" government agencies, by contrast, would be more predictable in their behavior toward dominant interest group constellations. For reasons discussed below, we believe that government officials are more independent from the constraints of the interest group environment now than in the past. We doubt, however, that they have become central brokers in the policy-making process. The most direct data we have on this issue deal with the patterns of contact between representatives and government agencies. We found only weak and inconsistent indications of centrally positioned governmental actors. The offices of the Secretary of Agriculture and the Secretary of Labor are the government units closest to the center of spatial analyses in their fields, but the energy and health secretaries are distant from the center in their fields. The White House and OMB are central only in the energy domain. The most consistent presence in the centers of the domains are the leading congressional committees, such as the Senate Natural Resources Committee in energy and the Senate Labor and Human Resources Committee in health, but each of those bodies is itself composed of members with diverse partisan and constituency attachments. The predominant patterns of contact with government institutions were analogous to the configurations of elite representatives and interest groups—they were differentiated into specialized institutional and substantive sectors. We therefore think that there is, in most situations, an absence of brokers of either the private or government variety, and that this contributes to the fluidity of policy-making processes.

THE EXPANDED SCOPE OF INTEREST GROUP ACTIVITY

The dominant view of the interest representation system in the 1960s posited a set of tight linkages among specialized interest groups, congressional subcommittees, and regulatory agencies. In a system of iron triangles, an unchanging cast of policy actors controlled specific policy debates, and these closed circles produced predictable, self-interested policy outcomes (Cater 1964). Thus, most organizations saw themselves as having a relatively limited portfolio of policy concerns, which they could effectively manage by participating in a narrow set of institutional arenas. More recently, the metaphors used to describe these relationships suggest looser structures. For example, Jones refers to "sloppy hexagons" (Jones 1979) and Heclo speaks of "issue networks" (Heclo 1978). The shift in terminology reflects a recognition of the greater number of direct participants and the organizations' expanding portfolios of policy concerns.

We found that interest groups devote considerable resources simply to monitoring the Washington scene. Contrary to the conventional image of representation as consisting primarily of advocacy, our sample of clients reported that they most often used representatives to keep track of developments and maintain contacts with allied organizations. (See Milbrath 1963 and Schlozman and Tierney 1986 for similar findings.) Representatives typically monitor a wide range of issues. When we presented respondents with a list of twenty policy events that had occurred in their domain in the preceding four years, they indicated at least "some" interest in eleven events, on average. We found that no fewer than 53 respondents and an average of more than 100 respondents had been interested in each event. While many of the events we employed in our interviews were highly visible, we sought out some that were not. Yet even these "smaller" issues were within the watching briefs of a broad range of interest organizations.

Patterns of specialization tell the same story. Representatives do not usually focus on a particular committee or administrative agency; they report regular contact with four or five separate government agencies on average, typically including both executive and legislative branch agencies. Moreover, the average representative spends time in more than half the subfields within his or her policy domain and, in addition, in some four other major policy fields. The revolving door between government employment and work as an interest representative—one of the mechanisms through which interest groups are thought to influence the agencies that regulate them—appeared in the career histories of only 5% of our sample. Few among this small number of cases fit the stereotype of moving from the role of regulator to the role of regulated that gives rise to concerns about conflict of interest and influence peddling. The absence of both institutional and substantive specialization suggests that much representational work is dictated by the scope of client interests.

As Salisbury notes: "[T]he descent upon Washington of so many hundreds of associations, institutions, and their agents does not mean that these private interests have acquired greater sway or even a more articulate voice in the shaping of national policy. In many ways, the opposite is true. Washington is, after all, the main source of information about what government officials are doing or planning to do. To get that information in a timely way, a continuous and alert presence in the capital is vital. Moreover, in this quest for information the interest representatives are very often in a position of profound dependence. They need access to officials not so much for purposes of applying pressure or even of policy advocacy but in order that they will be told when something important is brewing . . . Their dependence on information requires interest representatives to go wherever they can learn something useful. This may well mean that watchful attendance at hearings and markup sessions is the more modal lobbying task than position-taking or policy advocacy in whatever form" (1990, 25–26).

Broad monitoring also corresponds to broad activation on policy issues. Agricultural price support issues are no longer left exclusively to farm groups. Major consumers of food products, such as restaurant franchisers, lobbied against the PIK plan. Labor unions opposed the weakening of the Delaney clause ban on carcinogens in foods. Debates on the Clean Air Act not surprisingly activated environmental groups, peak business associations like the Chamber of Commerce, and major oil companies. But other groups with less obvious and direct interests also participated. For example, the American Institute of Chemical Engineers provided technical information concerning the issue. The Council for Auto Safety and the National Association of Counties were also involved. Groups concerned with public power, nuclear energy, and natural gas participated in policy debates on whether to tighten restrictions on sulphur emissions from coal-fired plants. And representatives of the Gray Panthers, the National Council of Senior Citizens, and other special population groups were active in the debates on the proposal for prospective Medicare reimbursements. These examples underscore two aspects of the modern interest representation system: that major policy decisions are not made by closed circles of interest groups and, the necessary corollary, that numerous interest groups monitor any given policy question and consider taking a more active role in the debate.

The breadth of monitoring and participation is both a response to and a cause of uncertainty in the interest representation system. Interest groups organize representation to reduce the risk of surprise;

hence, extensive monitoring. Then, given the investment in staff to monitor a broader range of issues, the marginal cost of advocacy on additional policy debates is reduced, thus contributing to the development of broader, more diverse patterns of interest activation. The efforts of individual interest groups to reduce uncertainty, then, may have the opposite effect in the aggregate.

INTEREST REPRESENTATION AS A TYPIFIED RESPONSE TO UNCERTAINTY

Scholars identified with the institutional school of organization theory argue that much of the formal structure of modern organizations should be understood as "rational myths," that is, as structures that are produced by the rules, belief systems, and relational networks of organizational environments. "The beliefs are rational in the sense that they identify specific social purposes and then specify in a rule-like manner what activities are to be carried out (or what types of actors must be employed) to achieve them. However, these beliefs are myths in the sense that they depend for their efficacy, for their reality, on the fact that they are widely shared, or are promulgated by individuals or groups that have been granted the right to determine such matters" (Meyer and Scott 1983, 14). Legitimating myths are more likely to emerge in organizational sectors with uncertain technologies, where the link between work processes and results is difficult to assess. In the absence of clear methods for evaluating performance, organizations make "typified" responses that derive from accepting a particular social construction of the situation rather than from a means-ends calculus (Meyer and Rowan 1977). Typified responses often mimic the approaches of similar or leading organizations in an organizational field. Professionals are depicted as especially important actors in this scheme; it is in the terrain of problems with uncertain solutions that professional groups tend to dominate. Professional training provides both practical skills and cultural authority for dealing with intractable difficulties. Professionals often promote the diffusion of organizational practices as they import "professional standards" into the organizations that employ them (DiMaggio and Powell 1983).

Interest representation manifests several of these tendencies. Just as most large corporations develop relatively standardized personnel departments in response to government mandates and the rise of professionalized personnel management, it is apparent that the business organizations in our sample have developed similar structures to organize the government affairs function. Humphries' (1990) analysis of the political strategies of Fortune 1,000 manufacturing firms found that roughly 90% of the 100 largest firms (measured by annual sales) maintained a Washington office in 1982–83, retained additional agents (trade associations, law and consulting firms), and had political action committees. Among the next 150 firms in sales, not quite two-thirds had this full complement of representation. The proportion declines sharply for smaller firms.[1] Humphries also found a significant relationship between the extent of government regulation in an industry and the proportion of firms with Washington offices. In our sample, we found that the establishment of Washington offices occurred in discrete waves (see Table 12.1). While a majority of the labor unions and trade associations had already opened Washington offices by 1960, most of the professional associations, businesses, and law firms did so in the sixties and seventies, during the period of greatest growth in federal regulation. The variation in the timing of these waves across domains and organization types suggests that organizations create representation capacities in response to major changes in the intensity of government policy. Note that the professional associations opened Washington offices in the period when Medicaid and Medicare were created.

Interest organizations followed a convergent path; they expanded the representational function by creating government affairs departments and opening Washington offices. Their behavior could be explained in part on objective grounds, as necessary for monitoring the activities of trade associations and external representatives. Yet as organizational institutionalists suggest, it may also have resulted from imitative behavior. Certainly the entrepreneurial efforts of representatives have played a role in creating this expansion. We found more than one Washington law firm that creates and houses trade associations that are nominally "clients" of the lawyers but are in fact something closer to wholly owned subsidiaries of the law firm. In these cases, the law firm typically was instrumental in organizing the trade association. The headquarters of the association is often located in the lawyers' offices, one of the lawyers serves as executive secretary or director of the association, and the law firm performs management services for the association—sometimes organizing its annual meeting and editing its newsletter. One lawyer told us that he devised a new form of government financing for a particular type of

Table 12.1 Percentage of respondents in each organization type, by date at which organization established a D.C. office

	1960 or before	(1960–1970 change)	1970 or before	(1970–1976 change)	1976 or before	(N of respondents)
Business	26	(+19)	45	(+20)	65	(96)
Nonprofits	22	(+ 9)	31	(+16)	47	(49)
Trade associations	55	(+15)	70	(+13)	83	(233)
Unions	73	(+ 8)	81	(+ 6)	87	(74)
Professional associations	28	(+27)	55	(+23)	78	(76)
Citizen/government	22	(+27)	49	(+25)	74	(108)
Law firms	30	(+21)	51	(+19)	70	(109)
Consulting firms	10	(+20)	30	(+20)	50	(30)

housing, drafted the regulation that authorized such funding, brought together the companies that moved into the market created by the new regulation, organized those companies into a trade association, housed the association in his law firm, provided management services to the association, and served as its "general counsel," monitoring developments in Washington that might affect the companies and representing their interests. This is the model of the lawyer as Dr. Frankenstein.

Certainly, this is an extreme case, but representation has a significant entrepreneurial dimension. The government affairs officers of corporations, the executives of trade associations, and the heads of citizen-government groups must justify the cost of their operations to their respective organizational constituencies—whether the constituency is the CEO, industry members, or contributors. They must walk a fine line, arguing on the one hand that the complexities and risks of the policy process require specialized management, and on the other hand trying to demonstrate effectiveness in producing results. The uneven record of success of the interest groups in our sample suggests that both the risks and the opportunities are real. But we should be aware that interest organizations relate to national policy making in terms of a social construction of how policy making operates. Interest representatives are, in a sense, double agents. In projecting an image of policy making as an unpredictable high stakes game, they contribute to the reality of the image.

Sources of Uncertainty in National Policy Making

Having set out the argument that the structural tendencies of the modern system of interest representation reflect the uncertainties of national policy making, we now turn to a brief survey of the sources of uncertainty in the policy process. Some of these sources quite clearly originate outside the system of interest representation; they are exogenous variables. But, as we have already suggested, others are part of the interest representation system itself.

THE EXPANDED SIGNIFICANCE OF FEDERAL POLICIES

Federal policies reach into so many sectors of organizational life, with such potentially dramatic effects, that many interest organizations view the direction of those policies as a critical determinant of their fate. If it were not so, the unpredictability of policy outcomes would be of little concern to them. But, by almost any measure, the federal government plays a vastly larger role today than it did twenty-five years ago in the early days of the Great Society programs. The size of the *Federal Register,* a rough measure of the degree of regulatory change, almost tripled from about 30,000 pages in 1970 to just under 90,000 in 1980, though the deregulation of the Reagan era reduced this bureaucratic output to 50,000 pages by 1985.

Perhaps more important than the quantitative expansion that these numbers document is the qualitative shift in regulation. In the old paradigm, regulatory structures were developed for specific industries—the ICC for trucking and rail transportation, the FAA for air transport, the FCC for radio and television communications. The new paradigm of regulation that emerged in the late sixties was for cross-industry administration (see generally Weidenbaum 1980; Meidinger 1985). Rules governing occupational safety and health, environmental protection, pension benefit programs, equal employment opportunity, energy conservation, product safety, and truth in lending applied to a broad array of organizational sectors. Not only did many industries confront federal regulation on an unprecedented scale, but they confronted regulatory bodies that had no close political-economic links with their industry, as the old administrative agencies did. Established relationships between regulators and regulated were disrupted by new cross-cutting jurisdictions. Energy companies, for example, had to deal with the EPA and the multiple layers of the Department of Energy in addition to the successors to the Federal Power Commission and the Atomic Energy Commission.

By the late seventies, policy domains had become complex environments populated by substantially increased numbers of private interest representatives and a multitude of executive branch agencies, independent regulatory bodies, the courts, and a greatly expanded congressional staff, all of which were processing a daunting volume of legislation, regulation, and litigation. Policy making had become more significant for more groups, but less controlled by the groups it affected. The growing sense of uncertainty may have led business interests to back the electoral campaign of Ronald Reagan with more than the usual zeal (Ferguson and Rogers 1986). But the Reagan presidency did not bring greater stability to the policy process, nor did it slow the continuing expansion of interest representation. Two-thirds of our sample interviewed in 1983 and 1984 reported that demand for their services had *increased* since 1981; only 1 in 10 said that demand had declined since Reagan's inauguration. Indeed, the Reagan presidency continued a period during which the nature of presidential politics tended to destabilize the domains of policy making.

THE WILD CARD OF PRESIDENTIAL POLITICS

The priorities and ideological orientations of presidential administrations are a major source of uncertainty for policy making within specific domains. The administration controls appointments to policy-making positions in executive agencies and independent commissions, and appointments draw the keen attention of interest groups for both symbolic and practical reasons. If the administration selects appointees with clear ideological positions or strong identification with particular interests, this amounts to a public endorsement of their ideas and a recognition of the political power of their sponsors. For example, President Carter appointed Carol Tucker Foreman, the director of the Consumer Federation of America, to the position of Assistant Secretary for consumer affairs in the Department of Agriculture. This clearly signaled the administration's support of consumer perspectives on food safety issues and, by placing a consumer advocate in control of the agency, virtually assured that it would promulgate regulations and enforcement strategies favored by consumer groups. President Reagan's appointment of James Watt as Secretary of the Interior was a clear gesture to the New Right, and predictably led to efforts within Interior to reverse many public lands policies.

In addition to appointments, the administration exercises substantial influence on domain politics by its ability to shape legislative priorities and the budget. Peterson's study of the role of presidential initiatives in Congress (1990) demonstrates the enormous political resources that the White House can deploy to pursue its legislative agenda. One of the main priorities of the Carter administration, for example, was energy policy. Against staunch opposition, President Carter proposed a sweeping set of programs, some of which gained congressional approval. Similarly, the Reagan administration achieved legislative successes in the Economic Recovery Act of 1981 and the Tax Reform Act of 1986. If the administration targets a specific policy domain for major changes, then, it may dramatically alter the political balance within the domain. But our analysis of the issue events, which we report in the next section, suggests that presidential initiatives do not in fact prevail as often as do more routine policy proposals, though they often pose more dramatic and threatening policy shifts. Unlike other repeat players, the administration has an incentive to sacrifice support from a particular set of the "usual" interests within a domain in order to "go public" and muster support from a broader constituency (Kernell 1986).

Changes in presidential priorities are hardly a new factor in the policy process. Such shifts may have more significance now as a source of uncertainty for interest representation, however, because the power and initiative of the executive branch have become increasingly centralized in the White House, and presidential politics have become increasingly ideological and decoupled from the interest group politics of specific policy domains. Interest groups enjoy more access to the line agencies and independent commissions situated squarely within the policy domains than they do to the Executive Office of the President. Only one-third as many of our sample reported contacting the White House as contacting the leadership of the Cabinet Department in their domain.

Byron Shafer (1988) has described a major shift in the process of nominating presidential candidates that began in the 1960s. Interest groups of several kinds have come to play an increasing part in sponsoring delegates, lobbying on the platforms, bargaining over the nominations, and mobilizing support in the election campaigns. The strong support of the National Education Association for Jimmy Carter in 1980 and of groups from the religious right for Reagan in that same year illustrates a development of long-term importance. Shafer contends that in this process it is mainly the ideologically motivated groups that are active, not the more pragmatic interests who are willing to bargain and compromise. As a result, presidential campaigns are now more radicalized than in the days when party organizations were stronger and could play a more effective brokering role. If presidents owe stronger allegiances to ideological groups than to the more pragmatic interests that dominate specific policy domains, it is not surprising that presidential politics have become a wild card in the policy process.

Terry Moe (1987) provides an excellent analysis of such an instance in the labor domain. Moe documents how the politics of appointments to the National Labor Relations Board had for many years operated as a repeated game. The party in control of the White House was recognized as having the power of appointment, but with the tacit understanding that the selections would reflect a balance of viewpoints and so be broadly acceptable to both the business and labor communities. The Reagan White House broke with this tradition by nominating a series of conservative Board members who were anathema to organized labor. These ideological appointees introduced new uncertainty into the politics of the Board, raising the prospect that the Board would consider significant changes in the direction of its decisions. With the collapse of the traditional standard for appointments, it became unclear what, if any, rules would restrain conflicts over NLRB policy.

THE DIFFUSION OF POWER IN CONGRESS

The weakening of seniority, the increase in subcommittee power, and the expansion of staff have all contributed to a more diffuse distribution of influence within Congress. Members are now in a position to participate in a much larger number of issues than once was possible (Salisbury and Shepsle 1981). The growth of staff lessens the need for specialization by members, and substantive expertise is not as much deferred to by others in any case (Patterson 1978; Oppenheimer 1980, 12; but see Hall 1987). On any particular set of policy concerns, groups can seek support in Congress through multiple points of access. But the corollary is that none of the interest groups is likely to carry decisive weight in shaping policy. Most of the iron triangles have been weakened or destroyed. The several congressional power bases often compete in position taking and credit claiming, which often means that ultimately no action is possible in any direction. Whether the ultimate result is action or inaction, the structures of command by seniority and committee that once imposed stability on the legislative process no longer exist.

THE ELECTORAL SAFETY OF INCUMBENTS

The diffusion of power within Congress has been accompanied by a widely remarked increase in the electoral success of incumbents. Although part of that success has come from the superior access to PAC contributions enjoyed by incumbents, election safety helps to undermine dependence of the member on any particular group or coalition. As members of Congress find themselves increasingly secure beneficiaries of name recognition and case work, they learn that they can afford to stand aloof from many parts of the interest group community. There are important exceptions, but in the Congress of the 1980s interest groups were better supplied with access to present their arguments than with influence resources that would assure their success (Fenno 1978).

SYSTEMIC DEMANDS OR CRISES

As we saw in chapter 11 and as we discuss in more detail in the next section, the policy agenda is sometimes shaped by dramatic crises, or what Kingdon (1984) called "focusing events." Certain circumstances—natural disasters, environmental accidents, the threatened financial collapse of major economic institutions—generate intense demand for a government response. These events are an inherent source of uncertainty in national policy making. Due to their nature, interest groups cannot plan to deal with them. Yet because various interests are often differentially affected by such problems and the solutions proposed for dealing with them, interest groups must be in a position to react to the political situations these crises produce.

AN ABUNDANCE OF INFORMATION

The growth in the activity of the federal government and in the armies of interest representatives who work in its shadows has led to a profusion of published information about policy making. Our sample of representatives reported using a wide range of information sources—daily newspapers, specialized newsletters, the *Federal Register,* the *Congressional Record,* trade and professional journals, judicial opinions, and other government publications. The diversity and volume of information produced on policy developments probably exceeds the capacity of most organizations to absorb and analyze it in any useful way. Feldman and March (1981) suggest that organizations often collect more information than they can process, in part because it expresses an organizational commitment to certain values. The self-reported behavior of interest representatives, though it may be exaggerated, suggests that they seek information avidly because they perceive that the policy process can produce unexpected risks or opportunities at any time. In our preliminary fieldwork, one representative reported how the routine perusal of the *Federal Register* had triggered an alarm and saved a group of client organizations from a potentially damaging disclosure of business secrets. Such stories tend to confirm both the difficulty of anticipating problems in the Washington context and the need to have representatives reviewing vast amounts of information.

THE ACCELERATING PRODUCTION OF NEW APPROACHES

Kingdon's (1984) analysis of agenda setting assigns relatively little significance to the power of ideas—especially policy initiatives that originate with academics. The notable exception in his study of transportation and health policy was the deregulation of transportation, an idea that originated with economic critiques of the inefficiencies of regulation in competitive markets. Kingdon's research makes clear that only a few ideas, typically those that happen to converge with the interests of officials and interest groups, make their way onto the policy agenda. Yet the current Washington policy process produces more and more proposals that vie for a spot in the public debates. One source of increased production of proposals is government itself. As members of Congress become more entrepreneurial, seeking to achieve distinction in the eyes of colleagues and constituents, they search for initiatives they can claim as their own. In each Congress over the last forty years, more than 10,000 bills have been introduced (Ornstein, Mann, and Malbin 1987, 165–167) and the number of amendments offered has tripled (S. Smith 1989, 93). On the private side, we see a similar trend. Think tanks have become prominent in the Washington landscape. The American Enterprise Institute, the Brookings Institution, the Heritage Foundation, the Urban Institute, and many others publish and publicize policy analyses and recommendations (Derthick and Quirk 1985; J. Smith 1991). Interest representatives themselves, particularly the consulting firms dubbed the "beltway bandits," are engaged in much the same activity, even though for more specialized purposes and for profit as well. The issue networks that Heclo (1978) describes are more than just patterns of acquaintance; they are structures created to facilitate the rapid movement of ideas among policy specialists.

The circulation of new policy proposals further enhances the fluidity of the policy-making process. Given the substantial support that conservative think tanks have enjoyed from business interests and the visible role they played in laying the ideological groundwork for the Reagan presidency, it seems clear that they have had an effect on the direction of policy making. The broader point is that such intellectual activity has become another moving force in the Washington context that interest groups can ignore only at some risk.

THE PERVASIVENESS OF COUNTERVAILING POWER

We close this inventory with three factors that are simultaneously causes and effects of the uncertain nature of national policy making.

Although our data suggest that interest groups have substantial power to organize the process of representation, the outcomes of particular policy issues are not adequately explained by interest group characteristics such as organizational resources, political fund-raising, PAC activity, and political party affiliation. Why?

The power of interest groups is not, of course, exercised without opposition. The typical issue has some interest groups on one side and some on the other, or many interest groups on many sides, not necessarily with an equal balance of power. On some issues, the principal opposition to the private groups comes from within the government itself. But all of the issues we studied were *contested* issues. Matters that are approved by acclamation or that sneak through without notice are not the subject of intense interest group lobbying, and they were not what we investigated. We did not study "non-issues" or "non-decisions" (cf. Bachrach and Baratz 1962). Though we gave some attention to the ideological character of the sponsors of issues that secured a place on the agenda for decision, we did not attempt to determine what the potential issues might have been that never got on the agenda, or what matters were foreclosed by the hegemony of the prevailing political order. A part of the reason for the uncertainty in outcomes that we observed, then, is that power countervailed power. In any real contest, it is problematic to predict outcomes with certainty. This permits bookmakers to earn a steady living.

THE COMPLEXITY OF INTEREST GROUP DECISIONS
ON PREFERENCES AND STRATEGY

A typical assumption in the analysis of interest groups is that they hold clear and relatively unchanging preferences. This is not always the case. First, interest organizations must define the nature of their interests in any particular issue. Many corporations consist of collections of subsidiaries in different industries, with different interests. Trade associations must make judgments about the potentially divergent needs of their members. Individual interests of all kinds must decide what coalitions to join, and on what issues. Second, as noted in chapter 11, each of the issues is considered in the context of a broad array of other issues. The position that an interest group adopts, therefore, is conditioned by the positions that it takes on other issues being considered at the same time, by events that preceded this issue event, and by yet others that are expected to follow. All of this occurs within a highly dynamic context, and changes in the political situation may require the balance of political risk and advantage to be recalculated. Moreover, participants in the process will often act without sufficient information about the several variables that would affect their choices. That is, they will often be making decisions under conditions of highly imperfect information, and this may distort their preference orderings (March and Olsen 1976). Interest representation involves learning. A group's understanding of its interests may change as a result of improved analysis or reflection on past experience. The consequent difficulty of predicting how interest organizations will behave on particular questions therefore contributes to the complex, fluid character of the policy-making context. Thus, uncertainty is likely to beget more uncertainty.

INTEREST GROUP PREFERENCES
FOR AMBIGUOUS OUTCOMES

The preceding paragraph may suggest that uncertainty is simply the result of misunderstanding or miscalculation—that, if actors could grasp the full complexity of the situation and had perfect information about it, they would be able to order their preferences consistently and the political world would then become predictable. But that is probably not the case. There are good reasons to believe that participants in the policy-making process (or some participants, at least) may prefer uncertainty. That is, they may prefer ambiguous outcomes, and some of the uncertainty may therefore be a consequence of this calculated ambiguity. The reasons are something like this:

One of the salient characteristics of the policy-making system is that most of the potential participants are, at any given time, inactive and largely indifferent. It is in the interest of elites that this be so. Elites are, by definition, the usual players in the process; they are active more or less continuously within whatever range of issues concerns them. If a larger share of the potential participants were to become active, that would dilute the influence of the elites and perhaps even endanger their control. It would certainly complicate their lives. Greater participation by occasional players would mean that decisions settled among the regulars might become unsettled, and that the manner in which the regulars were accustomed to handle business among themselves might be upset. Elites, therefore, want to avoid moves that might stir up these inactive potential players and bring them into the process.

One thing that might awaken the sleeping interests is a loud outcry about policy decisions. Elites will therefore prefer that the outcomes of the issues be at least minimally acceptable to the major contending parties, tolerable enough that no party is motivated to raise the alarm. Sometimes this may be accomplished by spreading the benefits or deprivations around a bit. Another and perhaps more reliable way to secure tranquility is to arrange for the outcomes to be sufficiently ambiguous that the deprived parties cannot be quite certain that they have lost. Put another way, if the outcome is not too definite and conclusive, the deprived parties may calculate that they have more to lose by unsettling the process than they would by working within the framework of the decision. If the outcomes are unclear, complicated, or ambiguous, it will also be difficult to communicate the substance of the decision clearly enough to explain to a broader public why they should be concerned about it. Thus, it may be in the interest of elites that one side in a dispute not prevail so clearly over another that the losers are able to see how much they have lost, thereby causing them to mobilize and perhaps enabling them to raise broader perceptions of unfairness.

This line of argument need not presuppose any sort of conspiracy or concerted action among the elite contestants. It will often be in the interest of individual players to cultivate ambiguity, and they may therefore individually pursue such outcomes.

The activity of interest organizations that we have observed, then, can be understood as a product of mutually reinforcing tendencies toward structure and uncertainty. But we have yet to address the implications of such a system. We turn next to some comments on the relationship between private and public power.

Private Interests and Governmental Power

One of the classics of the political science literature, E. E. Schattschneider's *Politics, Pressure, and the Tariff,* asserted, "Influence is the possession of those who have established their supremacy in the invisible empires outside of what is ordinarily known as government" (1935, 287). And from at least Adolf Berle and Gardiner Means (Berle and Means 1932) to Ralph Nader and Mark Green (Nader and Green 1973; Green 1975), social critics have viewed with alarm the power of "private governments." Some of this writing has fewer scholarly adornments and some has more, but it all makes much the same point—that private interest groups have a substantial, usually central, role in setting the government agenda (Bachrach and Baratz 1962; Lukes 1974, 10) and determining the outcomes of issues on that agenda.

Economic theorists of interest group politics have elaborated this perspective with the aid of formal deductive theory. In an influential essay that parallels the work of Stigler (1971, 1974) and Becker (1983, 1985), Richard Posner summarizes the "interest group theory of legislation" as an assertion that "legislation is a good demanded and supplied much as other goods, so that legislative protection flows to those groups that derive the greatest value from it, regardless of overall social welfare" (1982, 265). In this view, government is seen as a neutral marketplace within which interest groups bargain among themselves. Changing policy outcomes can be treated as shifts in the equilibrium level that balances the preferences of competing interest groups. Accordingly, there is little need to attend to the ideology or interests of government officials in their own right. Even the institutional forms and rules that dictate how policy is made are seen as endogenous to the interest group system, the product of some earlier bargain among private interests. They too will change, given sufficient demand.

Another branch of rational choice theory takes a very different tack on the role of government actors in policy making. Working from the premise that policy making could not achieve stability under conditions of free competition among interest groups, it posits that institutional frameworks play an essential role in structuring policy decisions (see, for example, Shepsle 1986). "The positive theory of institutions" (Moe 1987) sees institutional rules and processes, such as congressional procedures for bringing bills to a vote or committee oversight of regulatory agencies, as fundamentally transforming the politics of government decision making. To understand policy making therefore requires an analysis not only of the underlying economic interests of private parties, but also of the interests and resources of the governmental actors who construct and operate the institutional structure. As Chubb (1983) and others have pointed out, government institutions often set the range of strategic options open to interest groups. Indeed, government sometimes creates new interests (inside and outside of government), which then participate in subsequent policy-making deliberations.

Many critical scholars also assert that the state in a capitalist society occupies a position of considerable autonomy from the demands of particular factions within the capitalist class. Poulantzas (1978) observed that the conflicting objectives of various business interests, combined with the recognition by capitalists that it was in their long-term interest that the state be seen as legitimate, gives state actors considerable room for maneuvering (see also Nordlinger 1981). Skocpol (1985) suggests that the relative power of state and private actors varies by industrial sector and historical period and calls for research that attempts to map such variation.

Conflict among the interest groups within the government can result in a neutralization of governmental power, just as the conflict among private interests can result in a neutralization or counterbalancing of the power of private groups. Therefore, the concentration of government power varies from situation to situation or context to context, as does the power of the private interests. That both vary on the same sort of dimension suggests the possibility of employing a device that is all too prominent in the pitiful armamentarium of social science, the fourfold table (see Figure 12.1).

Schattschneider, Berle, Nader, et al. argue that the concentration of private power in the United States is high and the government is relatively weak, and that the outcome is often private government. In the four domains that we examined, however, both the power of

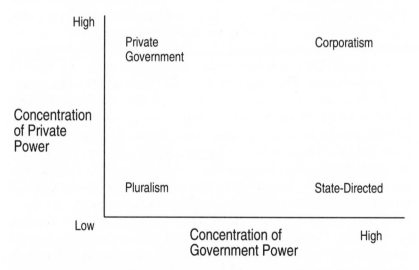

Figure 12.1   Relationship between degree of concentration of private and government power and types of governmental systems

the private interests and the authority of the government agencies appeared to be relatively dispersed overall, and the outcomes would probably be more accurately characterized as pluralist. The United States is commonly classified as a case of a weak state, and we would not therefore expect to find many examples of either corporatism or purely state-directed policy. William Coleman (1991) argues that monetary policy in both the United States and Canada is state-directed, with relatively little participation by private interests in decisions made by the Federal Reserve Board or by the Bank of Canada. Other fields, such as defense policy or foreign affairs, also may be relatively closed to participation by private groups. Yet, as Coleman recognizes, such areas are departures from the "normal" U.S. condition of pluralist politics. In most spheres of domestic politics, participation involves many groups and policy outputs are broadly distributive in character, spreading around the benefits or deprivations.

Political relationships among private and governmental actors are subject to sudden change, even in highly institutionalized arenas. We have already alluded to Moe's (1987) historical analysis of the breakdown of stability in the politics of appointments to the NLRB. In 1977, concerned about their declining ability to organize American workers and given Democratic control of both the White House and Congress, organized labor mounted a major effort to amend labor relations law to strengthen their bargaining position with employers. The effort failed, and a by-product of the attempt was renewed hostility with business interests. Business had mobilized so effectively in response to the threat that business groups gained a new sense of political strength. While this set the stage for what followed during the Reagan years, the most significant element in the destabilization of the NLRB appointments process was the pursuit of an "outsider's" strategy by the Reagan administration. Rather than adhere to the well-established pattern of making appointments that met the criteria of "professionalism," thus insuring that NLRB policy would change only incrementally, Reagan appointed ideologues who rapidly overturned prior Board precedents to establish a more conservative vision of labor relations. Moe suggests that business interests had not asked for this shift. Nothing in the institutional order of the NLRB or its constituencies had changed that would have predicted such a turn. It was the novel assertion of an ideological agenda by a governmental actor that transformed the politics of this field.

Another particularly telling instance of the unpredictable character of interest group influence is the Tax Reform Act of 1986. Salisbury (1990) characterized the defeat of the lobbyists at the "Battle of Gucci Gulch" as a "startling event." It came at a time when the number of lobbyists in Washington was at an all-time high, in a policy area famous for adopting bizarre loopholes designed to benefit specific groups, and it defied the predictions of local political pundits. Salisbury read the success of tax reform as an indication of a broad structural trend—the declining ability of interest groups to control government policies directly affecting their interests.

But in an analysis of major shifts in U.S. tax policies from 1960 to 1986—some that directly benefited business interests and some that did not—Martin (1989) argues that tax policy outcomes cannot be understood simply in terms of the relative power of state or private actors, but must be explained through a more complex coalition model in which factions within the federal government mobilize segments of the business community to support a policy shift. According to Martin, a specific set of circumstances led to the Tax Reform Act of 1986, including the strong support of a popular Republican president, which tended to defuse business opposition, and the electoral interests of key members of Congress. A critical ingredient was the rift between high-technology, small-business, and service-sector business groups on one hand, who saw themselves as benefiting from tax simplification, and capital-intensive firms, which traditionally had taken the lead in defending existing business deductions (Martin 1989, 209). Thus, the fragmentation of business interests combined with the ideological and electoral interests of government officials to produce an unexpected result.

What appears uncertain and unpredictable to participants involved in an ongoing stream of events may, in retrospect, form a well-ordered historical pattern. Viewed post hoc, the eighty policy events we analyzed yield an interpretable history of the politics of the four domains in the Carter and Reagan presidencies. In search of an interpretive framework for the analysis of the events data, and stimulated by Kingdon's (1984) and Polsby's (1984) work on agenda setting, we discovered that the events appeared to be of three types: those significantly identified with the ideology and programmatic priorities of the presidential administration, those that arose from systemic demands or crises, and those that reflected ongoing, relatively routine issues within a domain. Given the potential value of a such a typology for understanding variations in agenda setting and policy outcomes across domains and presidential administrations, we proceeded to classify the events in terms of these categories. The results are reported in Tables 12.2 through 12.4.

Placing policy events into mutually exclusive categories is a perilous enterprise. As Peterson discusses in detail (1990, 32–75), there are considerable complexities in determining whether a piece of legislation is a presidential initiative. Seldom do proposals actually originate within an administration. Often the president claims as his own a piece of legislation submitted by a member of Congress at an earlier time. Similarly, while there are some crises, such as natural disasters, that are so dramatic that they instantly prompt a government response, most crises are social constructions that depend on the mobilization of political actors. Moreover, even given the recognition of a crisis, the nature of the government response is seldom foreordained. How much money should be included in a disaster relief bill, for example?

To classify the eighty events, we relied on a set of dossiers assembled for each event consisting of reports from the *Congressional Quarterly,* the *National Journal,* and, less frequently, the *New York Times* and *Washington Post.*[2] If these materials explicitly identified the proposal in question with the president's program or with government officials closely identified with the president's announced preferences in a policy area (such as James Watts's position on federal lands), we classified the event under "administration politics." If a proposal was connected specifically to a dramatic event or the imminent collapse of an institution or government infrastructure, the event was classed as "systemic demands." All other events were called "domain politics."

These decisions required several difficult judgments. For example, many of the budget cuts in farm price supports proposed by David Stockman in 1981 and 1982 could be seen as agricultural politics as usual. Republican presidents typically prefer lower price supports than do Democratic presidents; Reagan's proposals differed from Carter's in much the same way that philosophies shifted between Truman/Brannan and Eisenhower/Benson. Given the salience of budget cutting proposals during the first two years of the Reagan administration, however, we chose to treat all of the Reagan/Stockman budget cuts as part of the Reagan program and thus as instances of administration politics. (Peterson made a parallel decision by including all of

Reagan's proposed budget cuts as presidential initiatives, even though presidential statements seldom referred to specific cuts; see Peterson 1990, 312.) The *Congressional Quarterly Almanac* supports a similar view. A typical report characterized one of the budget-cutting events as "a significant victory" for "Reagan's ambitious economic program" in that it had limited what Reagan considered potentially "budget-busting" farm legislation (1981, 550–551).

Another example of these complexities is posed by the health policy events concerning medical costs. Rising medical costs were a major problem for both Carter and Reagan. Kingdon uses health care costs as an example of an issue that forces its way onto the policy agenda because of the budgetary pressures it exerts. As one of his respondents put it: "It is on the agenda because ... the increasing costs of Medicare and Medicaid just hit you over the head with a two-by-four" (1985, 96). On that basis, we might have classified both Carter's hospital cost control proposal and the Reagan administration proposal to use a prospective payment system for Medicare as responses to systemic demands. But we decided to treat the Carter proposal as an instance of administration politics, and the prospective payment proposal as a response to a systemic demand. The distinction is based on the particularity of the solution Carter proposed and the prominence it had in Carter's pronouncements on health policy (Peterson 1990, 18–19). The prospective payment plan, in contrast, came in response to a congressional directive (*Congressional Quarterly Almanac* 1982, 471–476). That proposal was not so much a Reagan initiative, therefore, as a response to a widely recognized budgetary exigency.

After dividing the policy events into the three categories (the note to Table 12.2 reports the coding decisions), we examined how the categories were distributed by domain, presidential administration, and proposal success. While the difficulties of coding decisions and the nonrandom process of event selection demand caution, the results are quite striking. Table 12.2 indicates that all three types of events occur with some frequency, but that there is significant variation by domain and administration. Overall, domain politics generated the largest share of events (37 of 79), followed by administration politics (27 of 79). Not surprisingly, systemic demands are rarer (15 of 79). Domain politics are far more dominant in agriculture than in the other domains, a pattern that is consistent with the history of agricultural policy. Browne (1990) argues that, despite a considerable loosening of iron triangles, agricultural interest groups tend to concentrate

Table 12.2   Event type, by domain and presidential administration

Domain	Administration politics		Systemic demands		Domain politics		Total
	Carter	Reagan	Carter	Reagan	Carter	Reagan	
Agriculture	0	5	1	1	10	3	20
Energy	5	2[a]	3	3	3	4	20
Health	4	6	1	1	6	2	20
Labor	1	4	1	4	5	4	19
Total	10	17[a]	6	9	24	13	79

Note: The events, as numbered in the appendix to chapter 11, were coded as follows.
Administration politics: agriculture events 12, 13, 14, 15, 18; energy events 1, 5, 7, 9, 10, 12, 19; health events 2, 5, 8, 13, 14, 15, 16, 17, 19; labor events 1, 10, 11, 12, 14. Systemic demands: Agriculture events 11, 20; energy events 2, 4, 11, 15, 18; health events 6, 18; labor events 5, 13, 16, 17, 19. Other events were coded as domain politics.

a. Includes one reversal of a feared unilateral action by administration officials and one adoption of a funding request the administration had excluded from its proposed budget.

on narrow policy niches. We also found that agriculture representatives expressed "some interest" in an average of only 9 policy events, compared to means of 11 to 13 events for representatives in the other three domains ($p < .0001$). This suggests that the agriculture representatives pursued somewhat more specialized portfolios and that such specialization is possible when the regular players in the domain exert control over a large portion of the policy agenda.

It also is apparent that, during the first two years of the Reagan administration, the agenda was more dominated by administration proposals than had been the case in Carter's final years. The pattern varies by domain, however. Carter was most active on energy matters. Reagan, pursuing a market-oriented approach, offered no positive initiatives that showed up in our energy events. Two events involving administration politics did occur in energy policy during Reagan's presidency, but these were both congressional proposals seeking to reverse Reagan policies—authorizing continuing funding for the Solar Energy Bank (contrary to Reagan's proposal to terminate funding), and a ban on the granting of oil and gas leases in wilderness areas. In agriculture, health, and labor, domains in which the federal government makes outlays for price supports, food aid, health and unemployment insurance, and social security, Reagan's budget cuts figured prominently on the policy agenda.

Table 12.3   Proponent success, by event type and domain

Domain	Administration politics			Systemic demands			Domain politics			Total
	Win	Lose	Unclear	Win	Lose	Unclear	Win	Lose	Unclear	
Agriculture	3	1	1	2	0	0	11	1	1	20
Energy	4[a]	3	0	5	0	1	5	1	1	20
Health	1	8	1	1	1	0	2	4	2	20
Labor	3	1	1	3	2	0	4	4	1	19
Total	11	13	3	11	3	1	22	10	5	79

Note: If the proponents' mean success score on the event exceeded opponents' mean success score by .5, it was coded a win; if it was .5 less, it was coded a loss; if the absolute difference was less than .5, it was coded unclear.

a. Includes one reversal of a feared unilateral action by administration officials and one adoption of a funding request the administration had excluded from its proposed budget.

Table 12.4   Proponent success, by event type and presidential administration

Admin.	Administration politics			Systemic demands			Domain politics			Total
	Win	Lose	Unclear	Win	Lose	Unclear	Win	Lose	Unclear	
Carter	3	6	1	4	1	1	16	7	1	40
Reagan	8[a]	7	2	7	2	0	6	3	4	39
Total	11[a]	13	3	11	3	1	22	10	5	79

Note: If the proponents' mean success score on the event exceeded opponents' mean success score by .5, it was coded a win; if it was .5 less, it was coded a loss; if the absolute difference was less than .5, it was coded unclear.

a. Includes one reversal of a feared unilateral action by administration officials and one adoption of a funding request the administration had excluded from its proposed budget.

Tables 12.3 and 12.4 reveal major variation in the success of different types of proposals.[3] Not surprisingly, the chances of clear victory are best for proposals stimulated by systemic demands. Eleven of fifteen proposals of this nature succeeded by our measure. Two that did not, immigration reform and changes in single-employer pension programs, led to legislation at a later time—and, thus, eventually succeeded. Proposals produced by domain politics as usual also are likely to win (22 wins, 10 losses, 5 unclear). The pattern is particularly striking in the agriculture domain, where 11 of 12 proposals associated with domain politics succeeded. Energy's domain politics also produced winners (5 of 6). Overall, energy was a more contentious and unsettled domain, in part because more of the policy agenda was defined by external influences—Carter's ambitious attempts to reorganize energy production, and unforeseen or intractable problems such as the Three Mile Island disaster, the disposal of nuclear waste, and cost overruns on the Alaska pipeline. But intradomain politics in both agriculture and energy during this period consistently yielded victories for proposals that made it onto the agenda.

The internal domain politics of health and labor appear far more divisive. Only 2 of 8 health proposals succeeded. Most of the failed events involved issues that divided consumers and segments of the health care industry. Labor domain proposals split down the middle, with 4 of 9 proposals succeeding; the uneven record of success appears to reflect the continuing skirmishes between labor and business. Unions did not control the agenda; 4 of the 9 domain politics proposals were put forward by conservatives. Yet labor won most of these battles. They blocked business initiatives for a subminimum wage and for reducing the scope of the Davis-Bacon Act, and they succeeded in raising the minimum wage, tightening requirements for employers to keep employee health records, and upholding OSHA cotton dust standards against a legal challenge. They were less successful in resisting administration proposals or in gaining passage of their own highest priority, labor law reform. And our events do not reflect the NLRB's move in a decidedly anti-labor direction (Moe 1987, Rogers 1990).

The proposals with the least chance of success were those identified with administration politics. Only 11 of 27 proposals in this category gained clear victories. Indeed, 2 of the 11 were reversals of presidential policies and might more properly be seen as losses for the administration. Again, the pattern of success varies by domain. Only 1 in 10 administration proposals on health policy—the Carter administration's elimination of capitation grants to medical schools—prevailed. Six Reagan administration proposals (to reduce funding for medical programs, to relax food and drug guidelines or regulations for health care, and to tax health benefits) were defeated. Reagan was far more successful on budget cuts in agriculture and labor. Though Carter's energy policies met considerable opposition (see Peterson 1990), Carter succeeded in 2 of the 5 energy events sponsored by his administration.

Table 12.4 presents our version of the Carter and Reagan scorecards. Consistent with the conventional assessment of their political accomplishments, Reagan won a greater proportion of these contests than did Carter. But what is more important, perhaps, is the finding that the proposals of both administrations received a far less congenial reception than did responses to systemic demands or the proposals generated by more routine domain politics. Administration initiatives are often of greater consequence than other proposals and for that reason may encounter more resistance. The largely incremental proposals of domain politics are less likely to upset settled interests. Proposals generated by systemic demands may be perceived either as unavoidable necessities or as onetime interventions.

Carter's war on energy interests ended in frustration, and Reagan fared no better in health. These defeats are attributable to the power of interest groups to defend against incursions from actors outside the domain, even presidents. Kingdon's (1984) analysis of agenda setting found that government officials often are in a superior position to interest groups in putting items on the agenda, but frequently are unable to control the specific solutions selected to deal with a problem or to gain ultimate adoption. Organized interests play a more prominent role in the latter two stages. The proposals that emerge from the regular course of domain politics, then, may already have passed hurdles that are critical to eventual adoption.

These findings underscore a major theme in this research. Policy-making systems must be seen as historically situated social structures. Who controls the issue agenda and determines ultimate policy outcomes varies by domain, by presidential politics, and by historical circumstance. In agriculture, which has a long tradition of segmented, logrolling politics, and which was not a policy-making priority for either Carter or Reagan, a high proportion of policy proposals was accepted. The politics of energy was more chaotic due to Carter's ambitious proposals in response to the oil crisis and a series of other emergencies requiring government action. Health politics was particularly unsettled. Only 4 in 20 proposals achieved clear successes, as health constituencies battled the Reagan and Carter administrations over budget cuts and policy changes and as consumers battled drug companies and care providers over regulatory issues. While the labor policy agenda was also influenced by the Reagan presidency (union interests confronted governmental proposals to cut back unemployment insurance, social security benefits, and wage standards legislation), the agenda continued to reflect the bipolar conflict between business and labor, a pattern of conflict that generally results in a stalemate on major policy issues.

The findings also make clear that there are multiple arenas of politics and multiple forms or methods of interest representation. We have given little attention to electoral politics, but it is clear that control of the White House can have important consequences for the politics of the domains. Even though Carter's energy program suffered some defeats, and even though Reagan's health budget cuts were rebuffed, they became the focus of representational efforts. The decision by business interests to invest heavily in Republican campaigns for the presidency and for Senate seats in 1980 (Sorauf 1988) contributed to significant changes in the direction of policy proposals. That business interests reverted in succeeding elections to supporting incumbents, a majority of whom are Democrats, suggests that the political behavior of business is guided more by pragmatism than by ideology.

Return again to the fourfold table on which we plotted the relationship between public and private power (Figure 12.1). While the predominant pattern of policy making is still pluralist, it may well be that the expansion of group participation has reduced the concentration of private power in recent decades, while the concentration of government power has increased. We would expect, in that case, to find that policy outputs had shifted on an axis from private government toward state-directed policies. In an earlier time, much of the national policy-making apparatus was controlled by relatively narrow, entrenched groups of government and private actors. It was this pattern that inspired what has been the dominant conception of policy systems, Lowi's interest group liberalism (1969). Our data indicate that this is no longer an accurate description. Interest groups now participate in a broad range of events and institutional arenas. No doubt some closed circles of private interests and government officials persist. But the more common pattern today is for interest groups to pursue their interests in a variety of relatively open, competitive political arenas. As our event typology suggests, the government itself is often a major actor with which private interests must contend. As presidents have grown more autonomous from political parties, as they have amassed more resources and budgetary control in the Executive Office of the President, and as they have been held increasingly responsible for the performance of the economy, presidential priorities have assumed an increasingly significant role in defining the policy agenda. Similarly, as congressional incumbents have become more immune to electoral challenges and as congressional staff has grown, Congress too has become more autonomous from any single set of interests. While private interests are seldom excluded from policy deliberations, the balance of power may have shifted in favor of governmental actors.

Is Influence an Individual Attribute?

What, then, can we conclude about the nature of influence wielded by individual representatives? Is it possible to analyze influence as an individual trait? That is, can the capacity of lobbyists to shape policy be explained by their particular characteristics? In the preceding chapter, we saw that we were largely unable to explain self-reported success on policy events. But influence of a more general sort, which is not well expressed by success reports, may nonetheless exist in policy-making systems.

Students of community power (see, for example, Hunter 1953; Dahl 1961; Polsby 1980) have sharply disagreed about the methods appropriate to their task. Some have insisted that power can only be examined in its exercise, and have chosen to study discrete decision processes to determine who influenced whom. Others have relied on reputational measures of influence; the more votes an individual receives from the group polled, the greater his or her influence is assumed to be. Our data permit us to follow the latter strategy. Each of the respondents was asked to name three representatives who were regarded as "most effective" in shaping national policy in the relevant domain. In addition to these effectiveness votes, we can use the number of votes each representative received as a named ally or adversary. (See chapter 9 for a discussion of the allies and adversaries questions.) We include the latter because these mentions also reflect the prominence of the representatives. Nomination as an adversary might be thought to be negatively associated with the other two measures, but this was not the case. All three measures were strongly positively correlated. (Effectiveness correlates with allies, $r = .65$, and with adversaries, $r = .67$. The correlation between ally votes and adversary votes is .37.) Given the statistical advantages of having more votes to analyze, we pooled the three questions and examined the total number of mentions of each representative.

Many of the representatives who were mentioned are, of course, not present in our sample, but a significant portion of our sample received at least one vote. Some 263 respondents in the random and nonrandom samples, or one-third of the total representatives, received votes. Not surprisingly, the selected sample of notables garnered many more votes than did other respondents. Of the notables, 89% were mentioned, as compared to 28% of the remaining respondents. Almost two-thirds of the notables attracted 5 or more votes, but only 6% of the non-notables achieved a similar level of notice.[4]

We computed regression analyses seeking to account for the number of mentions by using independent variables concerning the work of representatives (percent of time spent contacting Congress, percent of time spent contacting executive agencies, percent of time spent in the domain), career attributes (years in government, law degree), characteristics of the employing organization (organization type, number of professionals in the organization), and political activities and party affiliation (whether they were an active Democrat or an active Republican, whether they had helped distribute PAC money, whether they had engaged in political fund-raising in the past two years, and their score on the economic liberalism scale). We also included two other variables that arguably are alternative measures of influence rather than independent determinants of it: the number of notables known and the average level of self-reported success on events.

The regression model in which the four domains were combined explained 20% of the variance in the number of mentions. Only three variables had statistically significant effects (at the .10 level): self-reported success on events and the number of notables known had positive effects net of other variables, and being an active Democrat had a significant negative effect. The number of notables known had the greatest effect by far; the standardized coefficient for this variable was .34 versus coefficients of .10 and −.08 for the success and Democrat variables, respectively.

The explanatory power of the regression models and of the specific measures differs across domains. The same model explains 21% of the variance in agriculture, 31% in energy, 22% in health, and 34% in labor. Only one variable, number of notables known, has significant effects in all four domains. Self-reported success is significant (p = .10) only in the labor domain, although it comes close to achieving conventional significance levels in agriculture ($p = .13$) and energy ($p = .18$). Being an active Democrat has a significant negative effect only in energy, although it approaches significance in health ($p = .12$). Active Republicans receive significantly more mentions in the labor domain, but nowhere else. Economic liberalism is positively related to the number of mentions in agriculture and health, but negatively related in labor. Possessing a law degree significantly increases mentions in the energy domain, as does political fund-raising. These effects do not hold elsewhere. The percent of time spent contacting executive agencies is positively related to mentions in the energy and labor domains, but not in agriculture or health.

These findings suggest that a general reputation for influence, like success on particular events, is not well explained by individual characteristics of the broad sort measured here. Organization type, career variables, work characteristics, political ideology, and political activities do not provide consistent returns in notice or recognition. The two variables that had the strongest relationship with the number of mentions could themselves be construed as measures of influence. A track record of success on policy events in the four years preceding the interview might well have increased reputation, but we have no way of knowing whether the reputation preceded the success. It also is not possible to say whether connections to notables led to a reputation for effectiveness or vice versa.

If we could effectively explain event success, we might be better able to understand the bases for reputed influence in Washington. But as we reported in chapter 11, we did even worse in accounting for the variance in success. Nor does our measure of reputed influence do much to improve the prediction of event success. Although the number of mentions has a statistically significant effect on average success, adding this variable to the regression models does not significantly increase the variance explained.

Researchers should be wary of celebrating null findings. The absence of striking effects may result from the failure to develop adequate measures. But we think that the absence of strong effects here is not a methodological failing so much as a reflection of the uncertain and situational nature of influence in national policy-making systems. We were able to select a list of notable representatives in each domain, and the notability of these people has been validated through both quantitative and qualitative means. But the standing of these individuals is apparently based on the unique characteristics of their careers in government and in interest representation. Even the elaborate data that we gathered about the characteristics of the representatives and their work do not explain much of the variance in reputed influence.

These findings suggest—in quantitative, systematic terms—much the same lesson that we saw in the story of the lawyer and the heavyweight, with which we began this book. It is possible to talk about "Washington heavyweights." One can construct a list of notable representatives who will be recognized as prominent players in the policy process. But the characteristics of these elites, and the occasions on which their influence is effective, vary by domain, by issue, and by historical period. The search for influential individuals will no doubt continue. It is fed by journalistic interest, and there is a market for reputed influence. Clients who are well heeled, if somewhat uninformed, will no doubt continue to seek out expensive talent in the hope of achieving a policy-making coup. But we doubt that the search for individual influence is likely to produce many theoretical insights into the nature of the national policy-making process.

Implications

Several theoretical issues, discussed in chapter 1, shaped the design of this research, but much of the ambition of the project has been avowedly empirical. Despite all that had been written about the nature of private influence in Washington, about the roles of lawyers and lobbyists in shaping national policy, and about the inner circles of American political elites, many prominent features of the interest representation system had not been subjected to systematic observation. While we had considerable experience with the methods employed, we could not accurately forecast our findings about the nature of national policy systems in these particular contexts—indeed, some of our forecasts were wrong (see Laumann and Heinz 1985). Thus, our project has been a kind of probe into the inner space of the American policy system. Many of the findings we have brought back are not radically divergent from those of preceding studies; others challenge important elements of previous conceptions of interest representation.

It is conventional to conclude enterprises of this sort with some assessment of the significance of the findings, and we are nothing if not conventional. We close, therefore, by considering whether these policy systems allow democratic participation and whether they have the capacity for rational planning.

Democracy

We can say little about two critical questions: What segments of the polity go unrepresented? And what is the universe of questions that is open for discussion and debate? Our sample can be taken, we think, as a reasonable approximation of the variety of interest groups that are active in the four domains. The composition of the represented interests varies by domain, but organized groups predominate. Many of these are traditional power holders: major corporations, trade and producer associations, professional associations, and unions. Also present, although in smaller numbers, are representatives of more recently and less fully organized groups: civil rights advocates, environmentalists, consumers, and special claimant populations such as veterans, the aged, and victims of various diseases. We have no way to catalogue the segments of society that lack a voice in discussions of policies affecting them or that are unable even to initiate discussion of their concerns. Thus, despite the great range and diversity in the political orientations of the interest groups in these domains, we cannot conclude that national policy systems have overcome the problems of exclusiveness and limited participation noted by so many scholars. Indeed, our individual-level data contain some evidence of exclusion. Women and minorities constitute only a small proportion of representatives. We have no measure of their availability among the pool of qualified individuals, and we are not sure that such a measure would be an appropriate yardstick in any event, but it is obvious that, despite the increased participation by women and minorities in politics and in the work force, most of the voices speaking on national policy are those of white men.

Nor can we offer original insights regarding the range of alternatives that are considered. Most of the policy proposals we analyzed dealt with incremental changes in current policies. This is consistent with the argument of many theorists that fundamental, systemic alternatives do not appear on the agenda, and that the most pervasive form of power in decision-making systems is largely invisible—the power not only to determine what issues enter the realm of discussion, but to define the features of society that will be recognized as issues (Lukes 1974; Bachrach and Baratz 1962; Alford and Friedland 1985). We acknowledge these critiques and recognize that broader comparisons of political systems across historical periods and societal contexts might reveal deeper conflicts (Higley and Burton 1989; Tilly 1984).

Yet it would be odd to dismiss the contests we have studied as trivial tinkering within otherwise well-settled policy-making systems. Certainly, the client organizations considered the issues important enough to require the expenditure of very substantial resources, and the representatives themselves were convinced that they were involved in substantively significant debates that were often highly conflictual. The careers of representatives, the social and political values they embrace, the networks in which they move, and the alliances and antagonisms they form make it clear that the system of interest representation reflects fundamental social and political divisions in our society. Debates about the level of government price supports for agricultural commodities, about the extent to which national energy policy should be centrally planned or left to market mechanisms, about the financing and distribution of medical care for the poor and the aged, and about the legal empowerment of management and labor in collective bargaining disputes are, we would assert, matters of considerable systemic importance.

The policy domains vary in the degree to which they are divided by basic political ideologies. Labor policy, because it consistently pits unions against management, is the most ideologically conflictual domain. Agriculture, which retains the residual effects of compromises worked out by the farm bloc, is the least divided ideologically. We are not specialists in the substantive policy debates that take place in these domains and cannot address the political subtleties of how policy options are defined and debated, and how alternative perspectives are suppressed or advanced. Policy representation in these domains may not be completely inclusive, but the domains are not assembly lines of ideological uniformity.

Given the considerable diversity of participants in Washington policy making, how are the diverse interests brought together to produce policy? Some accounts argue that closed circles of elites perform this function. Critical scholars characterize these elites as coordinating the interests of the capitalist class; functionalist scholars view elite governance as an inherent, necessary tendency of group political life. Our data do not support either version. No cohesive private elite consistently occupies a central, mediating position in the networks among representatives. Some elites may be in the center on some issues, at some times, but this is not a stable equilibrium. Nor do any government institutions, such as the White House, the leading cabinet departments, or the congressional leadership, consistently occupy the center of the contact structure between representatives and government agencies. The visual metaphor we have offered to describe the structure of policy-making networks is the hollow core. In this conception, elite representatives are instructed by the clients that retain them. The composition of dominant coalitions changes from issue to issue, and coalitions thus form and re-form at various points around the circle of interests.

Some may be inclined to celebrate these findings as additional evidence that democracy is alive and well. But the absence of an inner circle of powerful elites is no guarantee that the constantly emerging and shifting coalitions produce desirable outcomes. According to some versions of democratic theory, a correct outcome is one that does not distort the aggregation of individual preferences (Olson 1982). Yet, as Kenneth Arrow has demonstrated, even straightforward systems of rule by majority vote often result in such distortions (Arrow 1951). Even if we ignore the problem of unequal participation, in the absence of data that somehow measure the true preferences of participants it is impossible to establish empirically that policy systems with hollow cores produce outcomes that are better likenesses than those produced by other structures.

Coherence

Many scholars have expressed concern about the capacity of our national government to develop and pursue long-range strategies (for example, Lowi 1969; Olson 1982). Some of our findings may reinforce these concerns; policy domains that are segmented by interest group sectors and that lack mediating elites may not have sufficient stability to permit planning and coordination. As we noted above, however, the system of interest representation may give government agencies a substantial degree of autonomy in policy making. If the government is relatively autonomous, it may have sufficient flexibility to be able to produce coherent government policies. But changes in the procedures for nominating candidates for the presidency may have resulted in the executive branch becoming more ideologically extreme (Shafer 1988), and presidential appointees may therefore be more likely to pursue agendas that diverge significantly from those of preceding administrations.

While presidents can push their proposals onto the agenda, however, they often cannot control the final form that legislation will take, nor can they insure its adoption. The policy proposals that we analyzed were of three predominant types. Some were crises that demanded government reaction. This reactive component of the policy agenda enjoyed the highest level of legislative success. Incremental policy proposals that maintained existing programs also enjoyed high levels of adoption. Presidential initiatives were least likely to succeed and most conflictual.

Given the structure of policy making, both private and public organizations have little incentive to look beyond short-term interests. Private groups must constantly be aware of the uncertainty of the policy-making process. Their resources are expended in monitoring policy developments, reacting to events in the political and economic environment that are largely beyond their control, and responding to the political initiatives of Congress or the administration. Contrary to the image of the lobbyist as strategic planner, most of what interest representatives do is reactive. Government officials, both elected and appointed, also focus primarily on immediate political gains, such as the consolidation of an electoral base or the accommodation of political constituencies. Because national policy-making systems process an immense volume of proposals, contested by a large and diverse universe of interest groups that present and manipulate a daunting array of information about the options, it is not surprising that the actors have time for little more than the most immediate and urgent decisions.

One of the dangers of the hollow core, therefore, may be that the pursuit of immediate interests by individual representatives and officials will produce policies that go around in circles. Though the velocity and volume of policy-making activity may be great, the ultimate product may be a return to the place at which one started. Thus, the policy system may move very little despite escalating effort. The issues remain in much the same form over long periods of time.

New proposals look much like the old. The participating groups and their representatives are, or soon become, old hands. Though changes do occur, innovation is generally meager and exceedingly gradual. It may seem a paradox, but the principal result of the vast amount of interest group activity may be stability in the systems of policy formation.

Notes

1. The Lawyer and the Heavyweight

1. The federal statute requiring registration of lobbyists applies only to persons who act "for pay or for any consideration for the purpose of attempting to influence the passage or defeat of any legislation by the Congress" (U.S. Code, Title 2, chapter 8A, Section 267, 1989). Thus, lobbying of the executive branch is not included within the definition.
2. Mark Twain observed, "It could probably be shown by facts and figures that there is no distinctly native American criminal class except Congress" (from "Pudd'nhead Wilson's New Calender" in *Following the Equator,* 1897).
3. Much of the research on lobbyists has been done at the state level, using lists of registered lobbyists (Zeigler and Baer 1969; Devries 1960; Patterson 1963; Kolasa 1971; Zeigler and Van Dalen 1971). While such lists may be appropriate at the state level, the deficiencies of the lobbyist registration lists as rosters of those actively engaged in attempts to affect federal policy are well known (U.S. Congress, Senate Committee on Governmental Affairs 1983).
4. James Q. Wilson's analysis of political organizations devotes a chapter to organizational representation (1973). Although it raises some salient issues about the representative–organization relationship, it does not attempt to develop a comprehensive analysis of the relationship (305–325). Terry Moe's analysis of the internal politics of interest organizations distinguishes among the major participants in the organization and recognizes the potential influence that the representatives may have on organizational goals and tactics through their control of information and expertise, but it contains no empirical data that address the issue (1980, 97–100). Cherington and Gillen (1962, 49–51), Bauer et al. (1963, 330–331), Dexter (1969, 143–145), and Berry (1977, 79–109) comment on the relationships between representatives and organizations but do not attempt to generalize beyond their particular subject matter. Milbrath (1963), again, is the most comprehensive analysis. He asked lobbyists about their personal histories and present activities, as well as about the organization that employed them.
5. Students of legislative bargaining have tended to slight the role of interest

groups in the process and to treat it as though it occurred entirely within the legislative institution. In fact, negotiations among groups as well as between groups and officials regularly characterize the quest for effective legislative coalitions.

6. Each of the policy domains was given an operational definition; for these, see the appendix at the end of this chapter.

7. The data were compiled from The Information Bank of the New York Times Information Service. To compensate for regional effects, we included the Chicago *Tribune,* the Houston *Chronicle,* the Los Angeles *Times,* the New York *Times,* the San Francisco *Chronicle,* the Seattle *Times,* the Washington *Post,* and *Time* magazine.

8. Because of the enormous number of hearings covered in the Congressional Information Service data base, we restricted the search to the first sessions of the Ninety-fifth, Ninety-sixth, and Ninety-seventh Congresses and to a selection of the major committees active in each domain.

9. For the number of organizations identified in each domain through each of these sources, see Nelson et al. 1987, 196.

10. Slightly more than two-thirds of the respondents were based in Washington and were personally interviewed there. Another 15%, based in other major cities, also were interviewed personally. The remainder of the sample was interviewed by telephone using an adapted format that was more appropriate for the telephone.

2. The Policy Domains

1. This section draws on the substantial recent literature concerned with the politics of agriculture. Especially valuable are Browne (1988) and Hansen (1987). Heinz (1962) provides a baseline for more current analysis. Hadwiger (1982) and Guither (1980) are useful sources. For a more comprehensive background, see Cochrane (1979).

2. This section draws primarily on Rosenbaum (1987), A. McFarland (1976), Nivola (1986), Uslaner (1989), Jones and Strahan (1985), Chubb (1983), and Laumann and Knoke (1987).

3. Comprehensive reviews of the development of U.S. health policy are Stevens (1971) and Starr (1982). In addition, this section draws upon Marmor (1983), Campion (1984), and Laumann and Knoke (1987).

4. Material for this section has been drawn from Lipset, ed. (1986), Moe (1987), Meier (1985), Gerston et al. (1988), and Goldfield (1989).

3. Representatives and Their Clients

1. We discuss measures of professional autonomy in chapter 6.

2. Milbrath's sample is not directly comparable to ours. We have defined representatives more broadly. Executives, internal lawyers, and other internal staff are less likely to register as lobbyists than are government affairs personnel or external lawyers, and this may account for the somewhat lower proportion of lawyers in our sample. Other research on lobbyists has found similar

percentages. Of Berry's (1977) sample of public interest group lobbyists, 35% had law degrees. Zeigler and Baer's four-state study of state lobbyists found a low of 10% lawyers in Utah and a high of 42% lawyers in North Carolina (1969, 44).

4. The Organization of Work

1. Respondents were asked to indicate how they had allocated their time among these activities over the past twelve months by checking whether they had spent 0%, 1%–5%, 6%–25%, 26%–50%, or more than 50% of their time in each activity. The responses were converted to continuous-variable, maximum-likelihood estimates of percentages of time that sum to 100% using a computer program originated by Charles Cappell and written by Kent Smith. Respondents were instructed to differentiate between conventional law practice and policy activity as follows: "Please include [under conventional law practice] all time spent on regular legal work, including case by case matters that do not shape policy to a significant extent. Test cases, administrative rulemaking, legislative advice and advocacy—work that shapes policy—should be included under policy activity." A small number of respondents reported spending no time in policy activity, even though their responses to other questions indicated substantial involvement in various policy issues and with government agencies and officials. These cases were assigned a minimum value of 1%–5% on federal policy time.

2. The following fields were presented: agriculture, civil rights, communications, consumer rights, defense, domestic economics, education, energy, environment, foreign affairs, health, housing, international trade, labor, law enforcement, rural development, social welfare/social security, tax, transportation, and urban development. Representatives were asked to add other fields as necessary.

3. In addition to time spent on the main policy areas, time spent in closely related policy fields also was included in the total for the domain. Rural development, the environment, and international trade issues were included in agriculture. To energy, we added transportation and environment. Health included social welfare, consumer rights, environment, and housing issues. Social security, civil rights, and international trade concerns were added to labor.

4. The lists were as follows. *Agriculture:* price supports, foreign trade, commodities trading, food safety, food welfare, land use, agricultural finance. *Energy:* nuclear energy, oil, natural gas, coal, alternative energy sources, general energy conservation issues and regulations, electric power, energy-related tax policies. *Health:* regulation of health care providers, regulation of health professionals, health care payment and insurance plans, food and drug regulation, funding and policies on biomedical research, public health care delivery systems, manpower and training. *Labor:* labor-management relations, employment standards, jobs programs, immigration and farm labor, occupational safety and health, private pensions, social security and public pension

programs, equal employment opportunity and civil rights, international trade questions affecting employment. Representatives could add other subfields.

5. The number of government agencies in each domain varies somewhat, from a low of 38 in labor to a high of 56 in agriculture. As a result, responses are not strictly comparable across domains. Nonetheless, given the very low percentage of agencies that are regularly contacted in any of the domains, we simply report the mean number of contacts without adjusting for domain.

6. The loadings can be interpreted as the degree to which the items are related to the unobserved factors, whereas the marginal percentages reveal the relative prominence of the items for the representatives. The four-factor solution, estimated with the unweighted least-squares method, explained 46.2% of the total variance, the sum of within-task variation for the eighteen tasks. As usual, the solution is not unique. The loadings reported in Table 4.4 were determined through varimax rotation, a technique that spreads out the squares of the loadings on each factor as much as possible and allows the identification of groups of large and small coefficients for each factor. Our purpose in applying factor analysis here is to make sense of a complicated set of correlations among the eighteen tasks. To that end, we adopted the liberal stand that a five-point scale of task importance can be treated as a continuous scale and assumed that other standard statistical conditions of a common factor model hold.

7. The factor scores are the estimates of the scores of each representative on the four unobserved factors. To fix the scale measurement, the standard deviation of each factor has been set equal to 1. A multidimensional scalogram analysis consistently found that trade association executives were more similar in their task profiles to government affairs representatives than to other executives. Therefore, in Table 4.5 we have grouped trade association executives with government affairs personnel.

8. Readers who are not content with the brief summary presented here will find a more complete presentation of the data in Nelson and Heinz (1988, 258–259, Table 6).

5. The Careers of Representatives

1. Note that the recoded data do not reflect all individual job changes. Unless a job change also amounted to a move from one of the seven categories to another, we did not include it in the final analysis. For example, moving between different legal positions within the federal government or changing from government affairs work in one organization to government affairs work in another is not counted as a transition. Initially, for the last three categories we distinguished between present employers and previous employers. Although we make some use of the data in this less reduced form, in the interest of reducing complexity and increasing the statistical stability of results, the tables we present do not differentiate between similar positions held with different employers.

2. The result could also be produced by other factors. For example, government affairs officers might be younger or relatively recent entrants to the system.

If those holding government affairs positions in earlier years left the system disproportionately, as their positions were refilled it would create the appearance of an increase in government affairs positions in the seventies and eighties. Cross-sectional data cannot eliminate these possibilities. But we found no information indicating such a disproportionate exit rate from government affairs work.

3. Before analyzing career states by age for the sample as a whole, we conducted statistical tests to determine whether the younger and older cohorts exhibited different career profiles. After dividing the sample into three equally large age groups, we employed log linear analyses to compare the career transition tables of the groups. We found no significant cohort differences for tables that included a main diagonal (which contains cases that did not change career states from the beginning state to the ending state). When we divided our sample in half at age 46 and above, we found that the younger segment had more career moves (2.38) than the older half reported before age 46 (1.83). While younger representatives are somewhat more mobile than were older representatives in their earlier years, the basic career patterns did not vary by cohort. We concluded that the differences did not warrant splitting the sample by age.

4. Mean reported success on policy events is discussed in chapter 11. Chapter 10 analyzes the patterns of a selected set of especially prominent representatives, referred to there as the "notables."

5. For other analyses in this chapter, military duty and judicial clerkships were excluded from the category of government service. The analyses presented here conform to those published in an earlier article; see Salisbury et al. 1989.

6. This is a peculiarly American view. The percentage of lawyers in the legislatures of other nations, even other Western democracies, is notably lower than in the United States. See Rueschemeyer 1973, 71–75; Rueschemeyer 1989, 309–311.

7. The original categories for the variable were 0%, 1%–5%, 6%–25%, 26%–50%, and more than 50%. Given the number of variables and categories used in the analysis, it was advantageous to dichotomize time spent on federal policy, but we carefully considered the impact of doing so. The results of the model selection procedures described in the text were the same when we trichotomized the time variable (0%–25%, 26%–50%, and more than 50%). Moreover, in the analysis of models that did not include the four-category organizational position variable, we included models using a four-category time variable. In moving from a two- to four-category variable, we again found no change in results.

8. In constructing the organizational position variable in this fashion, we again recognized the similarity in the tasks performed by trade association employees and government affairs officers (see chapter 4). Also, we chose to split that portion of the sample that did not hold an executive or government affairs position into internal staff and external representatives rather than divide them between legal and nonlegal positions. If we had defined some of the categories of the organizational position variable according to whether they were legal or nonlegal positions, it would have created a greater overlap

in the information contained in the measures of law degree and organizational position. This would have posed technical problems due to the presence of zero cells in the table (because only individuals with law degrees can hold law positions). The approach we have followed allows us to study the effects of both law degree and the employment relationship more effectively than if we used the occupational characteristics of representatives to define organizational position.

9. Some 13% of the representatives who held both federal jobs and law degrees attended law school after starting federal employment. Similarly, 22% of those who held federal jobs and who had been politically active were first actively involved in a campaign after they started working for the federal government. For the sake of simplicity, we have pointed the causal arrows to indicate the more frequent sequence of events.

10. The chi-square values for selected models pertaining to this system of variables are contained in Tables 5.A3, 5.A4, and 5.A5 in the appendix to this chapter.

11. The model represented in Figure 5.3, on which we rest our interpretation, might be questioned on three grounds. First, federal policy time might be confounded with organizational position as we have defined it so that, because organizational position is more temporally proximate to current behavior than are the other background variables, the finding of a strong relationship between the two variables is trivial. Second, given the strong association between federal policy time and organizational position, the absence of direct effects between some of the background variables and federal policy time might be a statistical artifact of the system of variables. Third, there might be plausible alternative conceptions of the causal ordering among federal policy time, organizational position, and the background variables.

With respect to the first of these issues, we should note that our definition of organizational position does not logically imply given levels of policy activity. All of the persons included in the sample had been identified by their clients as key representatives, and we thus might expect that prior career experience, more than formal title, would determine the level of time spent on policy work. Indeed, we found substantial variance in federal policy time within each organizational position. Hence, even though we knew from the analysis of time allocation patterns that organizational position was an important correlate of policy involvement, without a multivariate analysis we did not know whether organizational position had an effect independent of other variables.

Second, the strong relationship between organizational position and federal policy time does not dictate that other variables in the system have no direct effect on federal policy time. Government experience has as strong an effect on federal policy time as organizational position; each variable explains 22 units of chi-square per degree of freedom. Moreover, there are some 20 units of chi-square left unexplained in the selected model. If either law degree or political experience had explained 4 units of chi-square, the effect of removing the variables from the model would have been significant at the .05 level. Because the direct effects of these variables on policy time fell far short of this level of explanatory power, they were dropped from the final model.

Third, the causal model set out in Figure 5.3 is the only model that fits the data. One might pose as alternative causal models that either (1) background variables determine federal policy time, which in turn determines organizational position (as a kind of ex post facto recognition of an individual's activity); or (2) organizational position determines background variables in the sense that individuals with a given set of background experiences are selected into particular organizational positions, and then the background variables in turn determine federal policy time. In a set of analyses in which we dropped organizational position, however, we replicated the findings reported in Figure 5.3. That is, only government experience had a direct effect on federal policy time.

6. Ideology, Colleague Networks, and Professional Autonomy

1. The items in the scale are the same as those used by Heinz and Laumann (1982, 139). In Table 6.1, they are shown as items a, d, e, f, h, i, j, and k. The scale achieved an acceptable level of reliability (Alpha = .82).
2. In chapter 10, we examine networks of association with a selected set of notable representatives. In this chapter, we examine an entirely different set of questions dealing with the collegial networks of the cross-sectional sample.
3. The research strategy is similar to that employed in other studies of collegial and friendship networks (see Laumann 1973; Laumann and Pappi 1976; Heinz and Laumann 1982). Rather than ask respondents subjective questions about collegial relationships, we emphasized the more objective characteristics of colleagues and respondent-colleague interactions. For example, instead of asking why respondents selected their colleagues, which is unlikely to produce complete and candid responses, we asked questions that would allow us to compare the characteristics of respondents and colleagues. From these data, we draw inferences about the bases on which respondents select colleagues, including the tendency to select colleagues who possess political and social characteristics similar to their own.
4. There were also higher rates of missing data on the colleague questions than on other questions because interviewers were instructed to drop these items if the time available did not permit completion of the entire interview schedule.
5. In chapter 10, we examine the networks of association of a selected set of especially notable Washington representatives. Those findings are consistent with the ones reported here. Notables who embrace a liberal welfare state ideology are more likely to have widely ramifying social ties than are persons who hold conservative views (see also Laumann, Tam, and Heinz 1992).
6. It may seem remarkable in the context of the Washington policy-making community that so many respondents reported that they did not know the political leanings of their colleagues. Given the gap between the proportion of independents among respondents and colleagues (23% versus 8%), it appears that many of the unidentified are independents. Apparently, indepen-

dents have a relatively indistinct political identity, making it difficult for respondents to classify them politically. Claiming ignorance of a colleague's political party identification may also be a socially preferred response, however, for it implies the irrelevance of partisan politics to a professional relationship. Independents and Republicans failed to specify their colleagues' party affiliations at a much higher rate than did Democrats (31% and 28% versus 19%, $p < .001$). Party affiliation thus appears to be a more salient aspect of the networks of Democratic representatives.

7. We recommend to future researchers that they ask respondents to speculate about the political, ethnic, and religious characteristics of colleagues, rather than allowing them the easy option of disposing of the matter by saying that they do not know.

8. Each colleague set consists of the respondent and up to three colleagues. The homogeneity index is the percentage of pairs within the colleague set that match on the characteristic of interest. The values vary between 0, indicating that none of the pairs consists of individuals with matching characteristics, and 100, indicating that all pairs contain individuals possessing matching characteristics. Pairs containing missing data were dropped from the colleague set.

9. Multiple regression models of the homogeneity indices support these findings. Using three broad categories of independent variables—organizational characteristics, social background characteristics, and political characteristics—we were able to explain 17% of the variance in organizational homogeneity, 18% of party homogeneity, 8% of ethnic homogeneity, and 9% of religious homogeneity. Controlling other variables, we found that unions and public interest groups are more homogeneous in organization type and political party, while independents and Republicans are less homogeneous politically than Democrats. Women and both Protestant groups are significantly less homogeneous with respect to religion.

10. See Nelson (1985) for an extended discussion of the methodological problems with a similar measure.

11. We doubt that this is a significant problem. It would only exaggerate the reported incidence of refusals, and less than a third of the sample report refusals. Since representatives have been with their current employers for an average of 12 years, a major portion of their exposure to assignments is in the same organization, if not the same job. Given the follow-up probes about the frequency and context of refusals and the location of the question among a series of questions concerning their current work, it is likely that representatives would have noted that the problems arose in a different context. A small number of respondents did so, and these cases were dropped from the analysis.

12. For a table reporting a detailed breakdown of the responses, see Nelson et al. 1988, 289.

7. *Contact with Government Institutions*

1. A two-by-two table can be constructed that represents four possible combinations: contacting government target X or not contacting target X, cross-

classified by contacting government target Z or not contacting target Z. If *a* refers to the frequency of the upper left cell, *b* to the frequency of the upper right, *c* to the lower left cell, and *d* to the lower right, then Yule's $Q = ad - bc/ad + bc$. It varies between +1 and −1. The size of Yule's Q tells us how much more probable it is that an observation will fall into a diagonal cell than into an off-diagonal cell (Bishop, Fienberg, and Holland 1975). Since it is a ratio scale measure, it can be averaged and compared across domains.

2. Because some government targets attract too few representatives to sustain a meaningful statistical analysis, we dropped any government target that had a constituency of fewer than 18 representatives. The smallest space analyses reported thus include only 42, 39, 38, and 31 government targets for the agriculture, energy, health, and labor domains, respectively. The fit of the representation to the full set of data may be assessed using Kruskal's stress (Kruskal 1964) and the Guttman-Lingoes coefficient of alienation (Guttman 1968; Lingoes 1973; Kruskal and Wish 1978). For the solutions presented here, we report Kruskal's stress. In all domains, we present three-dimensional solutions, though a satisfactory fit could be achieved in the labor domain in only two dimensions.

10. Elite Networks in National Policy Making

1. The proximity estimator used in these analyses is Yule's Y. Like Yule's Q, which was discussed in chapter 7, this is a monotonic function of an odds ratio.

2. But one can say only that this will "tend to" be the case because A, B, and C may share a number of acquaintances with J, K, and L; and X, Y, and Z may also have a substantial overlap of acquaintances with J, K, and L, which will draw all of those points into closer proximity. Thus, we are dealing with a very large and complex set of relationships that are interdependent.

3. A perfect depiction of the degree of overlap in the acquaintances of two notables that simultaneously represents the relationships of those ties to the acquaintances of each of 66 other notables is unlikely to be accomplished in only two or three dimensions. The full complexity of the relationships among 68 points can always be accurately represented in a space of 67 $(N - 1)$ dimensions, but that would be difficult to comprehend. We may need only a few dimensions, however, if the structure of the data is very orderly—for example, if all the boys in the fourth grade know all of the other boys and all the girls know all the other girls, but no boy knows any girl and vice versa. The number of dimensions that are required in order to represent the relationships among a large set of points with an acceptable degree of accuracy is, thus, a measure of the degree to which some underlying structure organizes the data. The amount of distortion in the representation of the relationships that is regarded as acceptable is a matter of judgment and varies with the nature of the relationships that are being considered, but there are statistical tests available for use in assessing the fit of the representation to the full set of data. Two of these measures are Kruskal's stress (Kruskal 1964) and the Guttman-Lingoes coefficient of alienation (Guttman 1968; Lingoes

1973; Kruskal and Wish 1978). For the solutions presented here, we report Kruskal's stress.

4. There is a third possible explanation for this pattern: specialization in particular government institutions or agencies, which themselves have a substantive specialization. For the reasons given in chapter 4, we think that this third hypothesis is less plausible.

5. These analyses are based on graph theoretic measures, which count the number of steps or connections that are required in order to get from one person in the network to a designated other. That is, notables A and B might be directly connected (they know each other), but to get from A to C it might be necessary to go through an intermediary (a mutual acquaintance). This analytic technique obviously cannot be used unless all of the persons have been interviewed, and we therefore drop from these analyses 5 notables whom we were unable to interview. The data in this section of the chapter, therefore, are drawn from interviews with 63 notables.

6. Though no notables are located at the center of the space in Figure 10.1, the most centrally located of the notables are Clifford and Boggs. Note that, of the points located around the inner circle of the space, only Clifford and Boggs do not have an arrow. Thus, they are closer to the center on the third dimension.

7. We are indebted to John Donohue for suggesting this line of argument.

11. *Participation and Success in Policy Decisions*

1. For the four-fifths of the representatives in our sample who are full-time employees of their organizations, there is little or no ambiguity in the attribution of their positions. For the representatives who are employed by law firms or consulting firms, however, this procedure means that the law or consulting firm will be identified as the organizational actor rather than the client represented by the firm. This is unfortunate but unavoidable, since client confidentiality prevented us from inquiring about the positions pursued on behalf of particular clients. An alternative would have been to attribute the positions of the respondents to the organizations that nominated them (see chapter 1) rather than to their employers, but that would have been even more problematic. Many of the lawyers and consultants in independent firms represent numerous clients, and we could therefore not be sure that the positions they took on issues were taken on behalf of the client organizations that had nominated them to us.

2. In a few instances, there was disagreement in the reports given us by representatives of the same organization concerning the positions they took on an event. In such cases, other internal evidence in the interview sometimes made it clear that one of the reports was simply an error, such as an interviewer or recording error. Where we could not be certain that one of the reports was erroneous, we reinterviewed the respondents by telephone to clarify the matter. In all instances, these procedures eliminated the inconsistencies.

3. We are grateful to Tony Tam for his work on these analyses. The following statement by Tam describes the procedures that he followed: The proximities

were estimated in three stages. First, for each of the twenty events in a domain, we constructed two social dissimilarity matrices: one corresponding to the affinity in positions (shared preferences in outcomes) between pairs of organizations, and the second corresponding to their opposed positions. For the affinity matrix, the element (i, j) will be 0 if the positions of organizations i and j are not missing and if their positions match; otherwise the element will be 1. For the antagonism matrix, the element (i, j) will be 1 if either i or j is for while the other is against; otherwise the element will be 0. In both matrices, 0 means similar and 1 means dissimilar. Second, we stacked the 40 binary matrices, 20 for affinity and 20 for opposition (that is, two for each columnwise Pearson correlation) to generate the N by N proximity of the twenty events, to form a comprehensive matrix of N by $40N$ in size, where N = the number of organizations in the domain. We then computed columnwise Pearson correlations to generate the N by N proximity matrix. Third, the proximity matrix estimated in stage 2 was submitted to ALSCAL (Schiffman et al. 1981) in SAS for nonmetric multidimensional scaling.

4. Most of the positions taken by these organizations were made public, but some of the organizations may have acted quietly or behind the scenes. We therefore are not free to disclose the positions taken by all of the organizations. Because the axes of the smallest space solutions were rotated in Figures 11.5 through 11.8 in order to permit a clearer grasp of the characteristics of the structures (that is, the first dimension is not always presented in the same orientation), and because not all of the points are shown in these figures, it will not be possible for the reader to identify the locations of particular organizations with confidence.

5. Some representatives might choose to participate only in issues where there was a high degree of consensus, thereby minimizing their risk of failure. We therefore computed a second success measure in which the average level of success on the particular issue was subtracted from the individual representative's rating. This measure creates a score that is either positive (above average) or negative (below average). Our findings when we use the second measure are not substantially different from those produced by the simple success scores, and we therefore report only the simple measure here.

6. To determine whether an *active* affiliation with one or the other of the political parties might be more significant than mere party membership, we constructed a variable that combined party membership with a history of participation in one or more campaigns for political office. We then ran the same regressions using these new "active Democrat" and "active Republican" categories (the residual category then being composed of inactive members of both parties and nonidentifiers). The new variables also did not approach significance in either the overall model or the four individual domain analyses. To assess the possibility that Democrats may have been more successful during the Carter administration and Republicans more successful during the Reagan administration, and that these effects cancel each other when events from the two periods are combined, we ran separate regressions on the Reagan period events and the Carter period events. Again, neither political party variable was significant.

7. We did the same analysis on each of the other three domains, and none of the findings was inconsistent with the conclusions drawn from Table 11.5.

12. Conclusion: Structure and Uncertainty
in Private Interest Representation

1. Only 17% of the firms ranking from 251 to 500 had Washington offices; 3% of those ranking from 501 to 1,000 had a Washington presence.
2. One event, legislative proposals on maritime bargaining, was dropped because it had too few responses to be considered a valid case.
3. See chapter 11, pp. 344–352.
4. Unfortunately for purposes of this analysis, the notables list was presented to respondents prior to the questions about the most effective representatives and about their allies and adversaries. The sequence of questions may thus have inflated the number of votes received by notables.

References

Abbott, Andrew. 1988. *The System of Professions: An Essay on the Division of Expert Labor.* Chicago: University of Chicago Press.

Abel, Richard. 1989. *American Lawyers.* New York: Oxford University Press.

Alford, Robert R., and Roger Friedland. 1985. *Powers of Theory: Capitalism, the State, and Democracy.* New York: Cambridge University Press.

Arnold, R. Douglas. 1979. *Congress and the Bureaucracy: A Theory of Influence.* New Haven: Yale University Press.

Arrow, Kenneth. 1951. *Social Choice and Individual Values.* New Haven: Yale University Press.

Auerbach, Jerold S. 1976. *Unequal Justice.* New York: Oxford University Press.

Bachrach, Peter, and M. S. Baratz. 1962. "The Two Faces of Power." *American Political Science Review* 56:947–952.

Baltzell, E. B. Digby. 1958. *Philadelphia Gentlemen: The Making of a National Upper Class.* New York: Free Press.

———. 1964. *The Protestant Establishment: Aristocracy and Caste in America.* New York: Random House.

Bauer, Raymond, Ithiel Pool, and Lewis Dexter. 1963. *American Business and Public Policy.* New York: Atherton.

Baumgartner, Frank, and Bryan Jones. 1990. "Interest Groups and Agenda Setting in the United States." Paper presented at Conference on Organized Interests and Democracy, Cortona, Italy, May 29–31.

Bavelas, Alex. 1950. "Communication Patterns in Task-Oriented Groups." *Journal of the Acoustical Society of America* 22:725–730.

Becker, Gary S. 1983. "A Theory of Competition among Pressure Groups for Political Influence." *Quarterly Journal of Economics* 98:371–399.

———. 1985. "Public Policies, Pressure Groups, and Deadweight Costs." *Journal of Public Economics* 28:329–347.

Bell, D. 1976. *The Coming of Post-Industrial Society.* New York: Basic Books.

Bentley, Arthur F. 1908. *The Process of Government.* Chicago: University of Chicago Press.

Berle, A. A., and G. C. Means. 1932. *The Modern Corporation and Private Property.* New York: Macmillan.

Bernstein, Marver D. 1955. *Regulating Business by Independent Commission.* Princeton: Princeton University Press.

Berry, Jeffrey. 1977. *Lobbying for the People.* Princeton: Princeton University Press.

———. 1984. *The Interest Group Society.* Boston: Little, Brown.

Bishop, Yvonne M. M., Stephen E. Fienberg, and Paul W. Holland, with Richard J. Light and Frederick Mosteller. 1975. *Discrete Multivariate Analysis: Theory and Practice.* Cambridge, MA: MIT Press.

Blau, Peter M., and W. Richard Scott. 1962. *Formal Organizations: A Comparative Approach.* San Francisco: Chandler.

Bok, Derek, and John T. Dunlop. 1970. *Labor and the American Community.* New York: Simon and Schuster.

Bonnen, James T. 1980. "Observations on the Changing Nature of National Agricultural Policy Decision Process, 1946–76." Pp. 309–327 in *Farmers, Bureaucrats, and Middlemen: Historical Perspectives on American Agriculture,* ed. Trudy Huskamp Peterson. Washington, DC: Howard University Press.

Boorman, Scott A., and Harrison C. White. 1976. "Social Structure from Multiple Networks. II: Role Structures." *American Journal of Sociology* 81:1384–1446.

Bottomore, T. B. 1964. *Elites and Society.* Harmondsworth, England: Penguin Books.

Bourdieu, Pierre. 1977. *Outline of a Theory of Practice.* New York: Cambridge University Press.

Brinkley, Alan. 1983. "Minister without Portfolio." *Harper's* 266:30.

Browne, William P. 1986. "Lobbyists, Private Interests, and the 1985 Farm Bill." Pp. 148–159 in *Increasing Understanding of Public Problems and Policies.* Oak Brook, IL: Farm Foundation.

———. 1988. *Private Interests, Public Policy, and American Agriculture.* Lawrence: University of Kansas Press.

———. 1990. "Organized Interests and Their Issue Niches: A Search for Pluralism in a Policy Domain." *Journal of Politics* 52:477–509.

Browne, William P., and Robert H. Salisbury. 1972. "Organized Spokesmen for Cities: Urban Interest Groups." Pp. 255–278 in *People and Politics in Urban Society,* ed. Harlan Hahn. Beverly Hills: Sage Publications.

Browne, William P., and Charles Wiggins. 1978. "Resolutions and Priorities: Lobbying by the General Farm Organizations." *Policy Studies Journal* 6:493–498.

Burnham, Walter Dean. 1974. "The United States: The Politics of Heterogeneity." Pp. 653–725 in *Electoral Behavior: A Comparative Handbook,* ed. Richard Rose. New York: Free Press.

Cain, Bruce, John Ferejohn, and Morris Fiorina. 1987. *The Personal Vote: Constituency Service and Electoral Independence.* Cambridge, MA: Harvard University Press.

Campion, Frank D. 1984. *The AMA and U.S. Health Policy Since 1940.* Chicago: Chicago Review Press.

Carr, E. H. 1951. *The New Society.* London: Macmillan.

Carter, Terry. 1988. "The Capitol Hill Revolution." *The National Law Journal,* December 26, p. 24.

Cater, Douglass. 1964. *Power in Washington.* New York: Random House.

Cherington, P. W., and R. L. Gillen. 1962. *The Business Representative in Washington.* Washington, DC: The Brookings Institution.

Chubb, John E. 1983. *Interest Groups and Bureaucracy: The Politics of Energy.* Palo Alto, CA: Stanford University Press.

Clausen, Aage. 1973. *How Congressmen Decide: A Policy Focus.* New York: St. Martin's Press.

Clausen, Aage, and Richard B. Cheney. 1970. "A Comparative Analysis of Senate-House Voting as Economic and Welfare Policy: 1953–64." *American Political Science Review* 64:138–152.

Clawson, Dan, and Alan Neustadtl. 1989. "Interlocks, PACS and Corporate Conservatism." *American Journal of Sociology* 94:749–773.

Cochrane, Willard W. 1979. *The Development of American Agriculture: A Historical Analysis.* Minneapolis: University of Minnesota Press.

Cohn, Samuel. 1985. *The Process of Occupational Sex-Typing: The Feminization of Clerical Labor in Great Britain.* Philadelphia: Temple University Press.

Coleman, James. 1973. "Loss of Power." *American Sociological Review* 38:1.

Coleman, William D. 1991. "Fencing Off: Central Banks and Networks in Canada and the United States." Pp. 209–234 in *Policy Networks: Empirical Evidence and Theoretical Considerations,* ed. Bernd Marin and Renate Mayntz. Frankfurt, Germany: Campus Verlag.

Congressional Quarterly. 1981. *Congressional Quarterly Almanac 1981.* Washington, DC: Congressional Quarterly.

———. 1982. *Congressional Quarterly Almanac 1982.* Washington, DC: Congressional Quarterly.

———. 1983. *Congressional Quarterly Almanac 1983.* Washington, DC: Congressional Quarterly.

Dahl, Robert A. 1961. *Who Governs? Democracy and Power in an American City.* 2d ed. New Haven: Yale University Press.

———. 1985. *A Preface to Democracy and Power in an American City.* 2d ed. Berkeley: University of California Press.

Davis, David H. 1982. *Energy Politics.* 3d ed. New York: St. Martin's Press.

Deakin, James. 1966. *The Lobbyists.* Washington, DC: Public Affairs Press.

Denzau, Arthur T., and Michael C. Munger. 1986. "Legislators and Interest Groups: How Organized Groups Get Represented." *American Political Science Review* 80:89–106.

Derthick, Martha, and Paul Quirk. 1985. *The Politics of Deregulation.* Washington, DC: The Brookings Institution.

Devries, W. D. 1960. "The Michigan Lobbyist: A Study in the Bases and Perceptions of Effectiveness." Ph.D. diss., Dept. of Political Science, Michigan State University.

Dexter, Lewis Anthony. 1969. *How Organizations are Represented in Washington.* Indianapolis: Bobbs-Merrill.

DiMaggio, Paul J., and Walter W. Powell. 1983. "The Iron Cage Revisited: Institutional Isomorphism and Collective Rationality in Organizational Fields." *American Sociological Review* 48:147–160.

Domhoff, William G. 1974. *The Bohemian Grove and Other Retreats: A Study in Ruling Class Cohesiveness.* New York: Harper and Row.

———. 1983. *Who Rules America Now?: A View for the 80's*. Englewood Cliffs, NJ: Prentice Hall.

Dye, Thomas R. 1976. *Who's Running America?* Englewood Cliffs, NJ: Prentice Hall.

Edsall, Thomas B. 1985. "Cashing in on Connections." *Washington Post Weekly Edition*, Nov. 11, p. 809.

Eulau, Heinz. 1964. "Lobbyists: The Wasted Profession." *Public Opinion Quarterly* 28:27–38.

Eulau, Heinz, and John Sprague. 1964. *Lawyers in Politics*. Indianapolis: Bobbs-Merrill.

Fararo, Thomas J., and Morris H. Sunshine. 1964. *A Study of a Biased Friendship Net*. Syracuse, NY: Syracuse University Youth Development Center.

Feldman, Martha S., and James March. 1981. "Information in Organizations as Signal and Symbol." *Administrative Science Quarterly* 26:171–186.

Fenno, Richard F. 1978. *Home Style: House Members in Their Districts*. Boston: Little, Brown.

Ferejohn, John A. 1974. *Pork Barrel Politics: Rivers and Harbors Legislation*. Stanford, CA: Stanford University Press.

Ferguson, Thomas, and Joel Rogers. 1986. *Right Turn*. New York: Hill and Wang.

Field, G. Lowell, and John Higley. 1980. *Elitism*. London: Routledge and Keegan Paul.

Fienberg, Stephen E. 1980. *The Analysis of Cross-Classified Categorical Data*. Cambridge, MA: MIT Press.

Fiorina, Morris. 1987. *Congress: Keystone of the Washington Establishment*. New Haven: Yale University Press.

Freidson, Eliot. 1986. *Professional Powers: A Study of the Institutionalization of Formal Knowledge*. Chicago: University of Chicago Press.

Friedman, Lawrence. 1985. *Total Justice*. New York: Russell Sage Foundation.

Fritschler, A. Lee. 1983. *Smoking and Politics*. Englewood Cliffs, NJ: Prentice Hall.

Galanter, Marc. 1974. "Why the Haves Come Out Ahead: Speculation on the Limits of Legal Change." *Law and Society Review* 9:95.

Gerston, Larry N., Cynthia Fraleigh, and Robert Schwab. 1988. *The Deregulated Society*. Pacific Grove, CA: Brooks/Cole Publishing Co.

Giddens, Anthony. 1984. *The Constitution of Society: Outline of the Theory of Structuration*. Berkeley: University of California Press.

Gold, David. 1961. "Lawyers in Politics." *Pacific Sociological Review* 4:84.

Goldfield, Michael. 1989. *The Decline of Organized Labor in the United States*. Chicago: University of Chicago Press.

Goodman, Leo A. 1972. "A General Model for the Analysis of Surveys." *American Journal of Sociology* 77:1035.

———. 1973a. "The Analysis of Multidimensional Contingency Tables When Some Variables Are Posterior to Others: A Modified Path Analysis Approach." *Biometrika* 60:179.

———. 1973b. "Causal Analysis of Data from Panel Studies and Other Kinds of Surveys." *American Journal of Sociology* 78:1135.

Goulden, Joseph. 1972. *The Superlawyers*. New York: Weybright and Talley.

————. 1973. "The Washington Legal Establishment." *The Washingtonian* (October) 84.

Green, Mark. 1975. *The Other Government: The Unseen Power of Washington Lawyers.* New York: Grossman Publishers.

Greenstone, J. David. 1969. *Labor in American Politics.* New York: Knopf.

Gross, R. Samuel, and Kent D. Syverud. 1991. "Getting to No: A Study of Settlement Negotiations and the Selection of Cases for Trial." *Michigan Law Review* 90:319–393.

Guetzkow, Harold, and William R. Dill. 1957. "Factors in the Organizational Development of Task-Oriented Groups." *Sociometry* 20:175–204.

Guetzkow, Harold, and Herbert A. Simon. 1955. "The Impact of Certain Communication Nets upon Organization and Performance in Task-Oriented Groups." *Management Science* 1:233–250.

Guither, Harold D. 1980. *The Food Lobbyists.* Lexington, MA: Lexington Books.

Guttman, Louis. 1968. "A General Nonmetric Technique for Finding the Smallest Coordinate Space for a Configuration of Points." *Psychometrika* 33:469.

Hadwiger, Don F. 1982. *The Politics of Agricultural Research.* Lincoln: University of Nebraska Press.

Hadwiger, Don F., and William P. Browne, eds. 1978. *The New Politics of Food.* Lexington, MA: Lexington Books.

Hall, Donald R. 1969. *Cooperative Lobbying—The Power of Pressure.* Tucson: University of Arizona Press.

Hall, Richard. 1987. "Participation and Purpose in Committee Decision Making." *American Political Science Review* 81:105–128.

Halliday, Terence C. 1987. *Beyond Monopoly: Lawyers, State Crises, and Professional Empowerment.* Chicago: University of Chicago Press.

Hansen, John Mark. 1987. "Choosing Sides: The Creation of an Agricultural Policy Network in Congress, 1919–1932." Pp. 183–229 in *Studies in American Political Development,* vol. 2, ed. Karen Orren and Stephen Skowronek. New Haven: Yale University Press.

Heclo, Hugh. 1977. *A Government of Strangers.* Washington, DC: The Brookings Institution.

————. 1978. "Issue Networks and the Executive Establishment." Pp. 87–124 in *The New American Political System,* ed. Anthony S. King. Washington, DC: American Enterprise Institute.

Heinz, John P. 1962. "The Political Impasse in Farm Support Legislation." *Yale Law Journal* 71:952–978.

————. 1983. "The Power of Lawyers." *Georgia Law Review* 17:891.

Heinz, John P., Robert W. Gettleman, and Morris A. Seeskin. 1969. "Legislative Politics and the Criminal Law." *Northwestern University Law Review* 64:277.

Heinz, John P., and Edward O. Laumann. 1982. *Chicago Lawyers: The Social Structure of the Bar.* New York and Chicago: Russell Sage Foundation and American Bar Foundation.

Herring, E. Pendleton. 1929. *Group Representation before Congress.* Baltimore: Johns Hopkins University Press.

Higley, John, and Michael G. Burton. 1989. "The Elite Variable in Democratic Transitions and Breakdowns." *American Sociological Review* 54:17–32.

Horsky, Charles A. 1952. *The Washington Lawyer: A Series of Lectures.* Boston: Little, Brown.

Humphries, Craig. 1990. "The Political Behavior of American Corporations." Unpublished Ph.D. diss., Washington University, St. Louis, MO.

Hunter, Floyd. 1953. *Community Power Structure: A Study of Decision Makers.* Chapel Hill: University of North Carolina Press.

Irons, Peter H. 1982. *The New Deal Lawyers.* Princeton: Princeton University Press.

Johnson, Terence. 1972. *Professions and Power.* London: Macmillan.

Jones, Charles O. 1979. "American Politics and the Organization of Energy Decision Making." *Annual Review of Energy* 4:99–121.

Jones, Charles O., and Randall Strahan. 1985. "The Effect of Energy Politics on Congressional and Executive Organizations in the 1970s." *Legislative Studies Quarterly* 10:151–180.

Kanter, Rosabeth Moss. 1977. *Men and Women of the Corporation.* New York: Basic Books.

Katzmann, Robert A. 1980. *Regulatory Bureaucracy: The Federal Trade Commission and Antitrust Policy.* Cambridge, MA: MIT Press.

Kernell, Samuel. 1986. *Going Public: New Strategies of Presidential Leadership.* Washington, DC: Congressional Quarterly Press.

Kingdon, John W. 1984. *Agendas, Alternatives, and Public Policies.* Boston: Little, Brown.

Knoke, David, and Franz U. Pappi. 1991. "Organizational Action Sets in the U.S. and German Labor Policy Domains." *American Sociological Review* 56:509–523.

Koford, Kenneth. 1989. "Dimensions in Congressional Voting." *American Political Science Review* 83:949.

Kolasa, B. D. 1971. "Lobbying in the Nonpartisan Environment: The Case of Nebraska." *Western Political Quarterly* 24:65.

Kruskal, Joseph B. 1964. "Multidimensional Scaling by Optimizing Goodness of Fit to a Nonmetric Hypothesis." *Psychometrika* 29:3.

Kruskal, Joseph B., and Myron Wish. 1978. *Multidimensional Scaling.* Beverly Hills: Sage Publications.

Landes, William, and Richard Posner. 1975. "The Independent Judiciary in an Interest-Group Perspective." *Journal of Law and Economics* 18:875.

Lane, R. E. 1966. "The Decline of Politics and Ideology in a Knowledgeable Society." *American Sociological Review* 31:649–662.

Lasswell, Harold D. 1936. *Politics: Who Gets What, When, How?* New York: World Publishing Co.

Latham, Earl. 1952. "The Group Basis of Politics: Notes for a Theory." *American Political Science Review* 46:376.

Laumann, Edward O. 1973. *Bonds of Pluralism: The Form and Substance of Urban Social Networks.* New York: Wiley.

Laumann, Edward O., and John P. Heinz, with Robert L. Nelson and Robert H. Salisbury. 1985. "Washington Lawyers: The Structure of Washington Representation." *Stanford Law Review* 37:465.

Laumann, Edward O., and David Knoke. 1987. *The Organizational State: Social Choice in National Policy Domains.* Madison: University of Wisconsin Press.

Laumann, Edward O., and Franz Pappi. 1976. *Networks of Collective Action.* New York: Academic Press.

Laumann, Edward O., Tony Tam, and John P. Heinz, with Robert L. Nelson and Robert H. Salisbury, 1992. "The Social Organization of the Washington Establishment." In *Research in Politics and Society,* vol. 4, *The Political Consequences of Social Networks,* ed. Gwen Moore and J. Allen Whitt. Greenwich, CT: Jai Press.

Leavitt, Harold J. 1951. "Some Effects of Certain Communication Patterns on Group Performance." *Journal of Abnormal and Social Psychology* 46:38–50.

Lehmbruch, Gerhard. 1984. "Concertation and the Structure of Corporatist Networks." Pp. 60–80 in *Order and Conflict in Contemporary Capitalism,* ed. John H. Goldthorpe. Oxford: Clarendon.

Lehmbruch, Gerhard, and Philippe Schmitter. 1982. *Patterns of Corporatist Policy-Making.* Beverly Hills: Sage Publications.

Lindblom, Charles E. 1977. *Politics and Markets.* New York: Basic Books.

———. 1983. "Comment on Manley." *American Political Science Review* 77:384–386.

Lingoes, James. 1973. *The Guttman-Lingoes Nonmetric Program Series.* Ann Arbor, MI: Mathesis.

Lipset, Seymour Martin, ed. 1986. *Unions in Transition: Entering the Second Century.* San Francisco: Institute for Contemporary Studies.

Lipset, Seymour Martin, and William Schneider. 1987. *The Confidence Gap: Business, Labor and the Public Mind.* Baltimore: Johns Hopkins University Press.

Lowi, Theodore J. 1964. "American Business, Public Policy, Case Studies and Political Theory." *World Politics* 16:677–715.

———. 1967. "The Public Philosophy: Interest Group Liberalism." *American Political Science Review* 61:12.

———. 1969. *The End of Liberalism: Ideology, Policy and the Crisis of Public Authority.* New York: Norton.

Lukes, Steven. 1974. *Power.* New York: New York University Press.

Lynn, Leonard H., and Timothy J. McKeown. 1988. *Organizing Business: Trade Associations in America and Japan.* Washington, DC: American Enterprise Institute.

MacKenzie, G. Calvin, ed. 1987. *The In and Outers: Presidential Appointees and Transient Government in Washington.* Baltimore: Johns Hopkins University Press.

March, James G., and Johan P. Olsen. 1976. *Ambiguity and Choice in Organizations.* Bergen, Norway: Universitetsforlaget.

Marmor, Theodore R. 1970. *The Politics of Medicare.* Chicago: Aldine.

———. 1983. *Political Analysis and American Medical Care Essays.* New York: Cambridge University Press.

Martin, Cathie Jo. 1989. "Business Influence and State Power: The Case of U.S. Corporate Tax Policy." *Politics and Society* 17:189–223.

Masters, Nicholas, Thomas H. Eliot, and Robert H. Salisbury. 1964. *State Politics and Public Schools.* New York: Knopf.

McConnell, Grant. 1966. *Private Power and American Democracy.* New York: Knopf.

McFarland, Andrew S. 1976. *Public Interest Lobbies: Decision Making on Energy.* Washington: American Enterprise Institute for Public Policy Research.

McFarland, David, and Daniel Brown. 1973. "Social Distance as a Metric: A Systematic Introduction to Smallest Space Analysis." Pp. 213–253 in *Bonds of Pluralism: The Form and Substance of Urban Social Networks,* ed. Edward O. Laumann. New York: Wiley.

Meidinger, Errol. 1985. "On Explaining the Development of 'Emissions Trading' in U.S. Air Pollution Regulation." *Law and Policy* 7:447–479.

Meier, Kenneth J. 1985. *Regulation: Politics, Bureaucracy and Economics.* New York: St. Martin's Press.

Merton, Robert K., David L. Sills, and Stephen M. Stigler. 1984. "The Kelvin Dictum and Social Science: An Excursion into the History of an Idea." *Journal of the History of the Behavioral Sciences* 20:319–331.

Meyer, John W., and Brian Rowan. 1977. "Institutionalized Organizations: Formal Structure as Myth and Ceremony." *American Journal of Sociology* 83:340–363.

Meyer, John W., and Richard Scott. 1983. *Organizational Environments: Ritual and Rationality.* Beverly Hills: Sage Publications.

Michels, Robert. [1915] 1959. *Political Parties: A Sociological Study of the Oligarchical Tendencies of Modern Democracy.* New York: Dover.

Milbrath, Lester. 1963. *The Washington Lobbyists.* Chicago: Rand McNally.

Miller, Arthur. [1949] 1957. *Death of a Salesman.* In *Collected Plays of Arthur Miller.* New York: Viking.

Mills, C. Wright. 1951. *White Collar: The American Middle Classes.* New York: Oxford University Press.

———. 1956. *The Power Elite.* New York: Oxford University Press.

Moe, Terry M. 1980. *The Organization of Interests.* Chicago: University of Chicago Press.

———. 1987. "Interests, Institutions, and Positive Theory: The Politics of the NLRB." Pp. 229–236 in *Studies in American Political Development,* vol. 2, ed. Karen Orren and Stephen Skowronek. New Haven: Yale University Press.

Moore, Gwen. 1979. "The Structure of a National Elite Network." *American Sociological Review* 44:673–691.

Mosca, Gaetano. 1939. *The Ruling Class.* New York: McGraw-Hill.

Nader, Ralph. 1970. "Law Schools and Law Firms." *Minnesota Law Review* 54:493.

Nader, Ralph, and Mark Green. 1973. *Corporate Power in America.* New York: Crowell.

———. *Verdicts on Lawyers.* 1976. New York: Crowell.

Nelson, Robert L. 1985. "Ideology, Practice, and Professional Autonomy: Social Values and Client Relationships in the Large Law Firm." *Stanford Law Review* 37:503.

———. 1988. *Partners with Power: The Social Organization of Large Law Firms.* Berkeley: University of California Press.

Nelson, Robert L., and John P. Heinz, with Edward O. Laumann and Robert H. Salisbury. 1987. "Private Representation in Washington: Surveying the

Structure of Influence." *American Bar Foundation Research Journal* 1987:141–200.

———. 1988. "Lawyers and the Structure of Influence in Washington." *Law and Society Review* 22:237–300.

Nivola, Pietro S. 1986. *The Politics of Energy Conservation.* Washington, DC: The Brookings Institution.

Nordlinger, Eric. 1981. *On the Autonomy of the Democratic State.* Cambridge, MA: Harvard University Press.

Olson, Mancur. 1965. *The Logic of Collective Action.* Cambridge, MA: Harvard University Press.

———. 1982. *The Rise and Decline of Nations: Economic Growth, Stagflation, and Social Rigidities.* New Haven: Yale University Press.

Oppenheimer, Bruce I. 1980. "Policy Effects of U.S. House Reform: Decentralization and the Capacity to Resolve Energy Issues." *Legislative Studies Quarterly* 5:5–30.

Ornstein, Norman J., Thomas E. Mann, and Michael J. Malbin. 1987. *Vital Statistics on Congress, 1987–88.* Washington, DC: Congressional Quarterly.

Parsons, Talcott. 1954. "A Sociologist Looks at the Legal Profession" *Essays in Sociological Theory,* ed. T. Parsons. New York: Free Press.

———. 1962. "The Law and Social Control." Pp. 65–78 in *Law and Sociology,* ed. William M. Evan. New York: Free Press.

Patterson, Samuel C. 1963. "The Role of the Lobbyist: The Case of Oklahoma." *Journal of Politics* 25:72–92.

———. 1978. "The Semi-Sovereign Congress." Pp. 164–166 in *The New American Political System,* ed. Anthony King. Washington, DC: American Enterprise Institute.

Peltzman, Sam. 1976. "Toward a More General Theory of Regulation." *Journal of Law and Economics* 19:211–240.

Peterson, Mark A. 1990. *Legislating Together: The White House and Capitol Hill from Eisenhower to Reagan.* Cambridge, MA: Harvard University Press.

Polsby, Nelson W. 1980. *Community Power and Political Theory.* 2d ed. New Haven: Yale University Press.

———. 1981. "The Washington Community." Pp. 7–31 in *The New Congress,* ed. Thomas E. Mann and Norman J. Ornstein. Washington, DC: American Enterprise Institute.

———. 1984. *Political Innovation in America: The Politics of Policy Initiation.* New Haven: Yale University Press.

Poole, Keith T., and Howard Rosenthal. 1991. "Patterns of Congressional Voting." *American Journal of Political Science* 35:228–278.

Posner, Richard. 1982. "Economics, Politics, and the Reading of Statutes and the Constitution." *University of Chicago Law Review* 49:263.

Poulantzas, Nicos. 1978. *State, Power, and Socialism.* London: New Left Books.

Powell, Michael. 1988. *From Patrician to Professional Elite: The Transformation of the New York City Bar Association.* New York: Russell Sage Foundation.

Priest, George L., and Benjamin Klein. 1984. "The Selection of Disputes for Litigation." *Journal of Legal Studies* 13:1–55.

Quirk, Paul J. 1981. *Industry Influence in Federal Regulatory Agencies.* Princeton: Princeton University Press.

Rogers, Joel. 1990. "Divide and Conquer: Further 'Reflections on the Distinctive Character of American Labor Laws.' " *Wisconsin Law Review* 1:1–147.

Rosenbaum, Walter A. 1987. *Energy, Politics, and Public Policy.* 2d ed. Washington, DC: Congressional Quarterly Press.

Rothenberg, Lawrence. 1992. "Do Interest Groups Make a Difference?" Chapter 8 in *From the Ground Up: Linking Citizens to Politics at Common Cause.* New York: Cambridge University Press.

Rueschemeyer, Dietrich. 1973. *Lawyers and Their Society: A Comparative Study of the Legal Profession in Germany and in the United States.* Cambridge, MA: Harvard University Press.

———. 1989. "Comparing Legal Professions: A State-Centered Approach." Pp. 289–321 in *Lawyers in Society: Comparative Theories,* ed. Richard Abel and Philip Lewis. Berkeley: University of California Press.

Salisbury, Robert H. 1968. "The Analysis of Public Policy: A Search for Theories and Roles." Pp. 151–175 in *Political Science and Public Policy,* ed. Austin Ranney. Chicago: Markham Publishing Co.

———. 1969. "An Exchange Theory of Interest Groups." *Midwest Journal of Political Science* 13:1–32.

———. 1979. "Why No Corporatism in America?" Pp. 219–236 in *Trends Toward Corporatist Intermediation,* ed. Philippe Schmitter and Gerhard Lehmbruch. Beverly Hills: Sage Publications.

———. 1984. "Interest Representation: The Dominance of Institutions." *American Political Science Review* 78:64–76.

———. 1990. "The Paradox of Interest Groups in Washington, DC: More Groups and Less Clout." Pp. 203–229 in *The New American Political System,* 2d version, ed. Anthony S. King. Washington, DC: American Enterprise Institute.

Salisbury, Robert H., John P. Heinz, Edward O. Laumann, and Robert L. Nelson. 1987. "Who Works with Whom? Interest Group Alliances and Opposition." *American Political Science Review* 81:1217–34.

Salisbury, Robert H., and Paul Johnson, with John P. Heinz, Edward O. Laumann, and Robert L. Nelson. 1989. "Who You Know versus What You Know: The Uses of Government Experience for Washington Lobbyists." *American Journal of Political Science* 33:175–195.

Salisbury, Robert H., and Kenneth A. Shepsle. 1981. "U.S. Congressmen as Enterprise." *Legislative Studies Quarterly* 6:559–576.

Schattschneider, Elmer Eric. 1935. *Politics, Pressure, and the Tariff.* New York: Prentice Hall.

———. 1960. *The Semi-Sovereign People.* New York: Holt, Rinehart and Winston.

Schiffman, Susan, M. Lance Reynolds, and Forrest Young. 1981. *Introduction to Multidimensional Scaling: Theory, Methods and Applications.* New York: Academic Press.

Schlozman, Kay L., and John T. Tierney. 1986. *Organized Interests and American Democracy.* New York: Harper and Row.

Schmitter, Philippe, and Gerhard Lehmbruch. 1979. *Trends toward Corporatist Intermediation*. Beverly Hills: Sage Publications.

Selznick, Phillip. 1949. *TVA and the Grass Roots*. Berkeley: University of California Press.

Shafer, Byron. 1988. *Bifurcated Politics*. Cambridge: Harvard University Press.

Shaw, Marvin E. 1954. "Some Effects of Unequal Distribution of Information upon Group Performance in Various Communication Nets." *Journal of Abnormal and Social Psychology* 49:547–553.

———. 1981. *Group Dynamics: The Psychology of Small Group Behavior*. 3d ed. New York: McGraw-Hill.

Shepsle, Kenneth. 1986. "Institutional Equilibrium and Equilibrium Institutions," Pp. 51–81 in *Political Science: The Science of Politics,* ed. Herbert F. Weisberg. New York: Agathon Press.

Sinclair, Barbara. 1977. "Party Realignment and the Transformation of the Political Agenda: The House of Representatives, 1925–38." *American Political Science Review* 71:940–953.

———. 1978. "The Policy Consequences of Party Realignment—Social Welfare Legislation in the House of Representatives, 1935–54." *American Journal of Political Science* 22:83–105.

Skocpol, Theda. 1985. "Bringing the State Back In: Strategies of Analysis in Current Research." Pp. 3–37 in *Bringing the State Back In,* ed. Peter Evans, Dietrich Rueschemeyer, and Theda Skocpol. New York: Cambridge University Press.

Skowronek, Stephen. 1982. *Building a New American State: The Expansion of National Administrative Capacities, 1877–1920*. Cambridge: Cambridge University Press.

Smith, Hedrick. 1988. *The Power Game: How Washington Works*. New York: Random House.

Smith, James Allen. 1991. *Brookings at Seventy-Five*. Washington, DC: The Brookings Institution.

Smith, Steven S. 1989. *Call to Order: Floor Politics in the House and Senate*. Washington, DC: The Brookings Institution.

Sorauf, Frank J. 1976. *The Wall of Separation*. Princeton: Princeton University Press.

———. 1988. *Money in American Elections*. Glenview, IL.: Scott, Foresman.

Starr, Paul. 1982. *The Transformation of American Medicine*. Cambridge: Harvard University Press.

Steiner, Gilbert Y., and Samuel K. Gove. 1960. *Legislative Politics in Illinois*. Urbana: University of Illinois Press.

Steinfels, Peter. 1971. "The Complexity of Acheson." *Commonweal* 95:102.

Stevens, Rosemary. 1971. *American Medicine and the Public Interest*. New Haven: Yale University Press.

Stigler, George. 1971. "The Theory of Economic Regulation." *Bell Journal of Economics* 2:3–21.

———. 1974. "Free Riders and Collective Action: An Appendix to Theories of Economic Regulation." *Bell Journal of Economics* 5:359–365.

Stinchcombe, Arthur L. 1975. "Social Structure and Politics." Pp. 557–622 in

Handbook of Political Science, vol. 3, ed. Nelson Polsby and Fred Greenstein. Reading, MA: Addison-Wesley.

———. 1989. "An Outsider's View of Network Analyses of Power." Pp. 111–133 in *Networks of Power, Organizational Actors at the National, Corporate and Community Levels,* ed. Robert Perrucci and Harry Potter. New York: Aldine.

Taylor, Paul. 1983. "Gladiators for Hire: Part II." *Washington Post,* August 1, p. A10.

Tilly, Charles. 1984. *Big Structures, Large Processes, Huge Comparisons.* New York: Russell Sage Foundation.

Tollison, Robert D., and Robert E. McCormick. 1981. *Politicians, Legislation, and the Economy.* Boston: Martinus Nijhoff.

Troy, Leo. 1986. "The Rise and Fall of American Trade Unions: The Labor Movement From FDR to RR." Pp. 75–109 in *Unions in Transition,* ed. Seymour Martin Lipset. San Francisco: Institute for Contemporary Studies.

Truman, David B. 1951. *The Government Process.* New York: Knopf.

Tullock, Gordon. 1965. *The Politics of Bureaucracy.* Washington, DC: Public Affairs Press.

Twain, Mark. 1897. *Following the Equator: A Journey Around the World.* Hartford, CT: American Publishing Co.

U.S. Bureau of the Census. 1991. *Statistical Abstract of the United States* (111th edition). Washington, DC: Government Printing Office.

U.S. Congress. Senate. Committee on Governmental Affairs. 1983. "Oversight of the 1946 Federal Regulation of Lobbying Act." Nov. 15, 16. 98th Congress, 1st session.

Useem, Michael. 1984. *The Inner Circle: Large Corporations and the Rise of Business Political Activity in the U.S. and U.K.* New York: Oxford University Press.

Uslaner, Eric. 1989. *Shale Barrel Politics: Energy and Legislative Leadership.* Stanford: Stanford University Press.

Vogel, David. 1989. *Fluctuating Fortunes: The Political Power of Business in America.* New York: Basic Books.

Walker, Jack L. 1983. "The Origins and Maintenance of Interest Groups in America." *American Political Science Review* 77:390–406.

Washington Representatives. 1981. Washington, DC: Columbia Books.

Weidenbaum, Murray. 1980. "The Changing Nature of Government Regulation of Business." *Journal of Post-Keynesian Economics* 2:345–357.

Western, Bruce. 1991. "A Comparative Study of Corporatist Development." *American Sociological Review* 56:283–294.

White, Harrison C., Scott A. Boorman, and Ronald L. Breiger. 1976. "Social Structure From Multiple Networks: I. Blockmodels of Roles and Positions." *American Journal of Sociology* 81:730–780.

Wiebe, R. H. 1967. *The Search for Order, 1877–1920.* New York: Hill and Wang.

Williamson, Oliver E. 1975. *Markets and Hierarchies.* New York: Free Press.

Wilson, Graham. 1979. *Unions in American National Politics.* London: Macmillan.

———. 1982. "Why Is There No Corporatism in the United States?" Pp. 219–236 in *Patterns of Corporatist Policy-Making,* ed. Gerhard Lehmbruch and Philippe Schmitter. Beverly Hills: Sage Publications.

———. 1985. *Business and Politics: A Comparative Introduction.* Chatham, NJ: Chatham House.

Wilson, James Q. 1973. *Political Organizations.* New York: Basic Books.

———. 1980. *The Politics of Regulation.* New York: Basic Books.

Wootton, Graham. 1970. *Interest-Groups.* Englewood Cliffs, NJ: Prentice Hall.

Yoffie, David. 1985. "Interest Groups v. Individual Action: An Analysis of Corporate Political Strategies." Working paper, Harvard Business School.

Zeigler, L. Harmon, and Michael Baer. 1969. *Lobbying: Interaction and Influence in American State Legislatures.* Belmont, CA: Wadsworth.

Zeigler, L. Harmon, and Hendrick Van Dalen. 1971. "Interest Groups in State Politics," Pp. 93–136 in *Politics in the American States,* ed. H. Jacob and K. Vines. Boston: Little, Brown.

Index